D1566076

De doctrina christiana
A Classic of Western Culture

Christianity and Judaism in Antiquity
Charles Kannengiesser, Series Editor
VOLUME 9

De doctrina christiana

A CLASSIC OF WESTERN CULTURE

Edited by

DUANE W. H. ARNOLD
and
PAMELA BRIGHT

UNIVERSITY OF NOTRE DAME PRESS
Notre Dame   London

Library of Congress Cataloging-in-Publication Data

De doctrina Christiana : a classic of Western culture / edited by
Duane W. H. Arnold and Pamela Bright.
    p.   cm. —(Christianity and Judaism in Antiquity; volume 9)
   Includes bibliographical references and index.
   ISBN 0-268-00874-4 (alk. paper)
   1. Augustine, Saint, Bishop of Hippo. De doctrina Christiana.
2. Bible—Criticism, interpretation, etc.—History—Early church,
ca. 30–600.   3. Theology—History—Early church, ca. 30–600.
I. Arnold, Duane W. H. II. Bright, Pamela, 1937– . III. Series:
Christianity and Judaism in Antiquity; volume 9.
BR65.A6552D63   1994
230'.14—dc20   94-15772
                                                  CIP

To
GERALD BONNER
a first gentleman
and a constant guide in Augustinian studies

This book has turned out to be longer than I desired and intended. It is not tiresome, however, for a reader or listener who finds it agreeable. If, by chance, there is someone who finds it tedious, but wishes to learn about it, they should read it in parts. On the other hand, a person who is reluctant to learn about what is in it should not complain about its length.

De doctrina christiana 4.31

Contents

Preface

Nineteen ninety-one marked the sixteenth centennial of Augustine's ordination as "minister of word and sacrament" *Confessiones* 11.2 in the coastal town of Hippo Regius in Roman Africa. This anniversary was the occasion for an international gathering of scholars of diverse fields of study: classicists, medievalists, theologians, philologists, rhetoricians, literary critics, philosophers, and specialists in hermeneutics entered into four days of lively exchange focused upon Augustine's *De doctrina christiana*, one of the most remarkable and influential books of late antiquity. The colloquy, under the title "*De doctrina Christiana*: A Classic of Western Culture," was organized by Charles Kannengiesser, Catherine F. Huisking Professor of Theology, and was jointly sponsored by the Department of Theology and the Medieval Institute of the University of Notre Dame. The key-note address was given by Professor Christoph Schäublin of the University of Berne.

The value of concentrating on a single Augustinian work was demonstrated by the enthusiasm of the participants during the colloquy. The multifaceted nature of *De doctrina christiana* provides an unusually rich opportunity for scholarly exchange, especially at the close of the second millennium as the various disciplines begin to assess the meaning of the western cultural heritage for a new pluri-disciplinary world. In this spirit the participants of the colloquy met toether from April 4 to April 7, 1991, under the distant, but still vital, guiding spirit of the bishop of Hippo.

Augustine began to write *De doctrina christiana* around 396, at the time of his episcopal ordination. The treatise was abruptly interrupted at paragraph 35 of book 3. Thirty years later, in 427, as Augustine was writing the *Retractions*, a review of his literary career, he rounded up the elaborate analysis of biblical hermeneutics in completing book 3. With the addition of book 4, in which he discusses how the understanding of the Scriptures is effectively communicated, the double purpose of this magisterial work was achieved. "There are two things necessary to the treatment of the Scriptures: a way of discovering those things which have to be understood, and a way of teaching what we have learned" (*DDC* 1).

The compositional history of *De doctrina christiana*, with its thirty-year hiatus, offers an unusual perspective for analyzing key issues of Augustine's thought over the long years of his active ministry. Even before he became assistant bishop in 396, as early as the first month of his ordination to the priesthood in 391, he begged his bishop, Valerian, to leave him time to study undisturbed by other pastoral works. Augustine felt that he had much to learn from Scripture and that he was not as yet qualified to come forward as a Christian teacher. From the chronology of his sermons we know that he was allowed, at the most, only two short years of study before he preached his first sermon, which was later widely read. From the time of that first sermon, clearly there was no going back. Yet Augustine, it seems, even in his early years of ministry and preaching, had already set out for himself a guide by which he would interpret Scripture. He also had a model for presenting what he had found within the sacred text which he would eventually explain, in lesser or greater detail, in *De doctrina christiana*.

The sources of Augustine's approach in *De doctrina christiana* are debated and interpreted by a wide variety of scholars within the pages of this present work. At its core, however, Augustine's purpose in this particular treatise was to provide magisterial guidance for those who wished to devote themselves to an intense study of Scripture. Furthermore, it is clear from what he writes in the treatise that he expected his advice to be faithfully followed by those who were already attentive to his teaching, both in North Africa and in the Latin-speaking world beyond.

De doctrina christiana is not a lengthy treatise. Nevertheless, it is filled with material that has shaped the Christian consciousness for close to sixteen hundred years. The first, and indeed many of the greatest, educators of the Middle Ages considered this single work to be unsurpassed. One need only think of Anselm, John of Salisbury, Abelard, Hugh of St. Victor, or Aquinas to find oneself among the greatest disciples of Augustine and, in particular, among those who valued and passed on to future generations the teaching that was contained within *De doctrina christiana*.

This volume presents material from the colloquy that pertains to *De doctrina christiana* itself in its composition and content, as well as in its immediate reception by Augustine's contemporaries. Two essays on the reception of Augustine's treatise in our own times, together with a bibli -

ography, conclude the volume. A second volume, *Reading and Wisdom: The* 'De doctrina christiana *of Augustine in the Middle Ages*, edited by Edward D. English and also published by Notre Dame Press, presents the colloquy papers concerning the medieval and Renaissance studies of *De doctrina christiana* as a classic of western culture.

August 28, 1993
Feast of St. Augustine

Acknowledgments

In the preparation of a volume of such scope and complexity, the editors have been assisted by many friends and colleagues. First among these is, of course, Professor Charles Kannengiesser, the convenor of the conference and the primary motivating force behind the publication of the present work. Others have lent their expertise which accompanies the final preparation of such a diverse text. We offer a special word of appreciation to Ms. Constance Shibley, department secretary in Theological Studies at Concordia University, for the retyping of the whole volume, to Dr. Paul Laverdure and his associates in Montreal for proofreading and computer assistance, and to Anne MacDonald, research assistant, for her diligence in preparing the index. We have been supported in our efforts not only by our publisher, James Langford of the University of Notre Dame Press, but also by our professional colleagues at the Department of Theological Studies, Concordia University, Montreal, and those of St. Chad's College, University of Durham. As a final acknowledgment, the editors thank Jeannette Morgenroth of the Press. Her astute judgment and uncompromising professionalism have enabled a finality to this work.

Contributors

DUANE W. H. ARNOLD, Saint Chad's College, University of Durham, Durham, England.

LEWIS AYRES, Merton College, Oxford University, Oxford, England.

WILLIAM S. BABCOCK, Department of Religious Studies, Southern Methodist University, Dallas, Texas.

PAMELA BRIGHT, Department of Theological Studies, Concordia University, Montreal, Canada.

J. PATOUT BURNS, Classics Department, Washington University, Saint Louis, Missouri.

JOHN C. CAVADINI, Department of Theology, University of Notre Dame, Notre Dame, Indiana.

DAVID DAWSON, Haverford College, Haverford, Pennsylvania.

CHARLES KANNENGIESSER, University of Notre Dame, Notre Dame, Indiana.

TAKESHI KATO, Rikkyo University, Tokyo, Japan.

R. A. MARKUS, University of Nottingham, Nottingham, England.

CYRIL O'REGAN, Department of Religious Studies, Yale University, New Haven, Connecticut.

ADOLF PRIMMER, Institute for Classical Philology, University of Vienna, Vienna, Austria.

CHRISTOPH SCHÄUBLIN, Institute for Classical Philology and Ancient Philosophy, University of Bern, Bern, Switzerland.

KENNETH B. STEINHAUSER, Department of Theological Studies, Saint Louis Universtiy, Saint Louis, Missouri.

LEO SWEENEY, Department of Philosophy, Loyola University of Chicago, Chicago, Illinois.

ROLAND J. TESKE, Department of Philosophy, Marquette University, Milwaukee, Wisconsin.

FREDERICK VAN FLETEREN, Department of Philosophy, La Salle University, Philadelphia, Pennsylvania.

Historia

Whatever that science which is called history may teach us about the sequence of past events is a most important aid to us. Through it we are assisted in understanding the Sacred Writings.

De doctrina christiana 2.28

The Interrupted *De doctrina christiana*

CHARLES KANNENGIESSER

I

The forty-two year old Augustine had a number of strong personal reasons for deciding to write a treatise *On Christian Instruction*. Three bear directly upon my topic.

1. The first and most vital reason for conceiving the project, *De doctrina christiana*, was undoubtedly his need to establish himself as a reputable expositor of Scripture. From his earliest steps toward acceptance of the Church's teaching eleven years earlier, the reading of the Bible had represented for Augustine a real challenge.[1] Overcoming his initial aversion to biblical language, Augustine found in the Christian Church an inspiring model of the biblical interpreter, Ambrose of Milan.[2] In the old Milanese priest, Simplicianus, Augustine met a counselor who would propel him insistently to the reading of the Scriptures as he advanced toward his own ordination.[3] In Rome before his return to Africa in 388, Augustine had many opportunities to reflect on Scripture in the framework of Catholic teaching as reflected in a number of his responses to the Manichaean doctrine.[4] With the fervor of a convert and as a kind of polemical exercise, he produced an anti-Manichaean exegesis of his own, with particular emphasis on the first chapters of Genesis and certain Pauline passages.[5]

He studied Scripture intensively for a substantial part of the two and a half years spent in Thagaste from the fall of 388 through the spring of 391.[6] When obliged to accept clerical status in early 391, his first reaction was to ask his new superior, Bishop Valerius of Hippo, for a leave of absence in order to complete his private study of Sacred Scripture.[7]

Finally, during the two years he served in Hippo as Valerius's assistant

3

bishop, Augustine recognized even more acutely the central relevance of the Bible in this new pastoral role. In a letter to Jerome in 393 or 395,[8] he refers to his awareness of the heavy demands of the role to be a leading expositor of Scripture and to teach "all educated people in the churches of Roman Africa" (*omnis Africanarum ecclesiarum studiosa societas*).

As Valerius's replacement, probably in the summer or fall of 395, Augustine found opportunity, in the middle of the distracting duties of his new position, to anticipate the fascinating project of his *Confessions* by writing, under the title, *On Christian Instruction*,[9] a separate essay on how to interpret Scripture. This latter work would lay out guidelines for the scriptural focus of the *Confessions*. Both works would illustrate in a complementary way the bishop's total submission to revelation as communicated in the Old and New Testaments. Thus the very idea of *De doctrina christiana* was born out of Augustine's personal and long-term commitment to the reading of Scripture.

2. The second reason that leaps to mind when one seeks to determine the inner dynamic which motivated Augustine in the writing of *De doctrina christiana* is his professional background as a teacher of rhetoric. Already in the full decade following the leisurely days of Cassiciacum, the newly installed bishop of Hippo had produced an impressive number of works which announced him as an apologist of his new faith. He had plied his literary gifts in a number of popular genres new to him.[10] By 391 his literary success had earned him the congratulations of his boyhood teacher in Madura, the grammarian Maximus, who remarked on "that vigorous eloquence which has brought you to universal fame" (the Latin is stronger: *facundiae robore atque exploso, qua cunctis clarus es*).[11]

What was missing from the young bishop's self-awareness was a reassessment of rhetoric as such, considered in the light of his responsibilities as a preacher and as a minister. His own rhetorical culture needed to be transferred from its former status, private and secular, to a new episcopal status, public and ecclesiastical. The new persona of Augustine as church leader needed to reinvest the professional past of Augustine the rhetor. Thus a second motive was at work in the bishop's mind, nurturing the seminal project of *De doctrina christiana*.

3. A third reason, or rather, a third aspect of the bishop's rhetorical and pastoral motivation in 396 is related to the local situation in Hippo and in its ecclesiastical surroundings in the civil provinces of Numidia and Africa proconsularis. This aspect of Augustine's motivation cannot be appreciated apart from the fact of the interruption of the essay itself. For, at first sight, the local setting of the work seems less obvious than either the concentration on biblical hermeneutics or the vivid awareness of the skills of rhetoric throughout the text of *De doctrina christiana*.

Before engaging in any speculative reconstruction of the social and local context behind Augustine's idea of writing *De doctrina christiana*, a few clear-cut facts deserve a little more attention:

First is the striking fact—so often ignored—of the interval of three decades between the early writing up to the last third of book 3 of *De doctrina christiana* in 396–397 and the later writing, resulting in the rest of book 3 and the complete book 4 in 426.[12] That long interruption seems to have entailed an early edition of books 1 and 2. These two books could have circulated separately for some time.[13] Augustine himself quoted book 2 in *Contra Faustum* in 400 and in the *City of God* around 415–416.[14] The Leningrad codex, from the early fifth century, transmits these first two books with a subscription in the singular: *Liber de doctrina christiana*. Therefore, the thirty-year interruption did not mean the same thing for the first two books circulated by Augustine and his friends as it did for the third book, which remained a *liber inchoatus*.[15]

Some critics have suggested that the interruption was due to Augustine's becoming too involved in the *Confessions*, or because from 399 on he was distracted by the projected *De trinitate*. But the *Confessions* were begun only after the death of Ambrose of Milan on 4 April 397,[16] and the first two books of *De doctrina christiana* were already written at that date.[17] In other words, the interruption of the treatise had nothing to do with its first two books.

More specifically, these two books were contemporaneous with three other important literary initiatives of Augustine: *De agone christiano*, the essay *Contra epistulam Manichaei quam vocant fundamenti*, and *De diversis quaestionibus*, started as early as 395.[18] A parallel writing of different works at any given period was part of a familiar pattern for Augustine from the earliest stages of his career, and he would follow such a practice unremittingly throughout his years in office. Therefore, the argument for an interruption of *De doctrina christiana* by sheer distraction or by the pressure of interfering projects is difficult to maintain.

The question of the thirty-year interruption of *De doctrina christiana* is not lightly side-stepped. Why was it after the successful completion of the first two books and the clear development of the lines of argument about "ambiguous signs in the Scriptures" to a certain point in book 3, that the treatise was laid aside?

It is a puzzling question, given the self-confident and ambitious schema announced by the young bishop at the outset of the work. First, he states the great importance of the reading and interpreting of Scripture.[19] He emphasizes the urgent need for a sort of programmatic treatise such as the one he is undertaking.[20] Then, in the first book, he concentrates all the spiritual riches of his personal vision which embraces a fullness of theological and philosophical issues related to the study of Sacred Scripture.[21] Then again he starts book 2 by introducing the thematic development of book 2 and book 3.[22] In a brilliant survey he discusses methodically the many requirements imposed by any "discovery" (*inventio*) of the so-called "unknown or ambiguous signs" in Scripture. In doing so he not only follows the program outlined at the beginning of the first chapter of his essay, but he seems frankly to enjoy the facility of his writing. Then, abruptly, he stops.

When resuming the writing in 426, he is a more cautious author who begins by quoting himself. In the prologue he had announced a first exposition dedicated to "discovery" (*modus inveniendi*). Now, in book 4, he adds what concerns "teaching," "delivery" (*modus proferendi*), as he explains in the introduction:

> This work of ours entitled *On Christian Instruction* was at the beginning divided into two parts. For after the prologue in which I replied to those who would criticize it, I wrote: there are two things necessary to the treatment of the Scriptures: a way of discovering those things which are to be understood and a way of teaching what we have learned.

II

1. It is worth underscoring the reference to the prologue (prooemium) of *De doctrina christiana* at the beginning of book 4, for this is the only clue given to us by Augustine that might allow us to understand why he was unable to complete his work in 396–397 and why he eventually completed it in the midst of his *Retractationes*.[23]

The prooemium of *De doctrina christiana* has generated a few scholarly articles, but its deeper links with the global structure of the treatise have received scant attention. Even the strikingly polemical character of the prooemium seems to be downplayed as of little relevance for the whole work. I propose to offer a different opinion.

Let me note first that Augustine had never before composed a polemical prooemium of that sort. Fighting against his former fellow Manichaeans, he always bluntly denounced their beliefs in the body of his anti-Manichaean writings. A cautious prologue would have been completely inappropriate. In his more youthful *Contra academicos*, Augustine was still too close to former friends for engaging in writing that would be overly aggressive.

Here in the prooemium of *De doctrina christiana*, the author is eager to prevent misunderstandings.[24] He regrets, in advance, to have to address a certain category of people who would fail to gain any durable advantage from his teaching. In addition to those who are basically unschooled,[25] and those who lack the needed expertise for applying rhetorical pre-cepts,[26] Augustine denounced a "third category of critics" (*tertium genus reprehensorum*)[27] who are of much more serious concern for him.

These unnamed opponents would simply refuse his recommendations, his *praecepta*, because they are accustomed to follow their own herme-neutical tradition.[28] They claim to clarify the meaning of the darkest recesses in Scripture, without any Augustinian *praecepta*, thanks to a special assistance of the Holy Spirit.[29] They rejoice so much in God's gift that they "pretend to understand the sacred books and to preach them" (*se sanctos libros intelligere atque tractare gloriantur*), without taking any notice of the devices explained by Augustine in his treatise.[30] It is no sur-prise if the "pride" (*superbia*) of those people deserves to be chastised.[31] They seem unaware that any language, including one's own mother tongue, requires a patient and methodical training.[32]

The anonymity of the prooemium's attacks betrays some embarrass-ment. Far from fighting here an "anti-paideia" current, deeply rooted in the past of the African church,[33] Augustine addresses contemporary fellow Christians who know very well what a consistent interpretation of Scrip-ture means (*qui diuinas scripturas re uera bene tractant*).[34] The paradoxical turn of the whole prooemium should not escape our atten-tion. In almost its entirety, the author protects himself against experienced interpreters of Scripture whom he refuses to call by name. Fighting against them, he nevertheless recognizes that "they are already equipped to expound the sacred books" (*facultatem exponendorum sanctorum lib-rorum se assecutos uident*).[35]

Even more intriguing is the fact that after the visionary synthesis of book 1, which laid the foundation for an Augustinian type of exegesis for centuries to come,[36] neither the second nor the third book of *De doctrina christiana*, as far as they were written in 396–397, includes a single word of reference to the unfriendly *tertium genus reprehensorum*. In fact, the whole writing on the treatise in 396–397 establishes all the grammatical and rhetorical precepts needed by the more humble categories of possible readers mentioned in the prooemium.

Only when the aging bishop resumes his writing of the treatise in 426, can the enigmatic opponents of that *tertium genus* at last be recognized. One name serves to identify all of them: "A certain Tyconius who wrote most triumphantly against the Donatists."[37]

2. The *Book of Rules*, probably published by Tyconius in Carthage shortly before Augustine returned from Europe in the fall of 388,[38] was indeed a stumbling block for Augustine, still infused with his allegiance to the Platonizing high culture which he had enjoyed so much in Milan. Au-relius, the bishop of Carthage, had given him a copy of that enigmatic

Liber regularis, as Tyconius himself called it,[39] and had asked the learned Augustine for his assistance in reading it.[40]

Understandably, the newcomer on the African scene failed to grasp the significance of Tyconius's enterprise. Some years later, in 396, precisely when he was deeply involved in the writing of the first two books of *De doctrina christiana,* Augustine was still lamenting his puzzlement over Tyconius's book and begging for help in his turn. In *Letter 41* he wrote to Aurelius: "On my part, I am not forgetting what you asked about the seven rules or keys of Tyconius, and, as I have written many times, I am waiting to hear what you think of it" (*Nam et ego quod iussisti non negligo et de Tyconii septem regulis uel clauibus sicut saepe iam scripsi cognoscere quid tibi uideatur expecto*).[41]

Augustine claims in this letter to be engaged in a writing ordered by Aurelius, but in doing so he still needs to clarify his thoughts about Tyconius's rules. The needed response of a sound biblical hermeneutic in a Catholic framing would fit the project of *De doctrina christiana.* I would argue that in Augustine's letter to Aurelius, we find a vital clue to the circumstances of the writing of *De doctrina christiana.*

The luminous first book of *De doctrina christiana* may well be Augustine's best response to African sectarianism in regard to biblical hermeneutics. Book 1 could easily circulate by itself. In books 2 and 3, the basics of secular rhetoric, as belonging to the general culture of the time, were set in the context of Christian spirituality and adjusted to the peculiarities of the biblical text. But when Augustine tried to explain certain "figurative expressions" in his *capitulum* 25 of book 3, he was no longer satisfied with his own distinctions.[42] The need to engage in a direct discussion of Tyconius's categories, which centered precisely on such *figuratae locutiones,* became imperative, and he was not yet prepared to do it. The best evidence of Augustine's perplexity is given to us by the very words he used in *Letter 41,* when asking Aurelius for advice (*de Tyconii septem regulis uel clauibus . . . quid tibi uideatur expecto*).[43]

In his initial reading of Tyconius's work Augustine had created for himself a morass of misunderstanding in establishing a synonymy between the *regulae* and the *claues,* the "rules" and the "keys," mentioned in the prologue of the *Liber regularis.*[44] This misunderstanding set the stage for his interpretation of Tyconius from that point on.

When Augustine interrupted his *Retractationes* to complete *De doctrina christiana* in 426,[45] he quoted Tyconius extensively,[46] but at the price of the same fatal misreading.[47] In Tyconius's understanding, the seven *regulae* were intrinsic features of the Sacred Book itself as authored by the Holy Spirit.[48] They were symbolically seven, like the seven seals of the Revelation of John, because of the revelatory nature of the Holy Book. The "keys" were Tyconius's own hermeneutical contribution. They were, as he said, "fabricated" by him, like "windows" in order to offer an access to the "rules."[49]

In conflating the two interpretive categories, the *regulae* and the *claues*, Augustine failed to understand correctly Tyconius's claim, namely, that "whatever is closed will be opened and whatever is dark will be illumined."[50] Tyconius was speaking of the "mystic rules,"[51] as he called them, and how they operate intrinsically in Scripture, when well perceived (*quarum si ratio accepta fuerit*); whereas Augustine thought Tyconius was boasting about his personal achievement as an interpreter.[52]

Only after thirty years could the author of *De doctrina christiana* feel free to integrate into his own work the *Liber regularum* that he continued to admire so much, despite his persistent misrepresentation. How Augustine twisted the Tyconian statements, in particular by imposing his own quotations of Scripture in summarizing Tyconius's rules, has been discussed by Pamela Bright.[53] My own purpose has been to focus more particularly on making some sense of the interrupted and resumed composition of *De doctrina christiana*.

Notes

1. *Confessiones* 3.5.9: *[illa scriptura] uisa est mihi indigna, quam Tullianae dignitati conpararem.*

2. *Confessiones* 6.1.1–4.6: *cum ea, quae ad litteram peruersitatem docere uidebantur, remoto mystico uelamento spiritaliter aperiret.*

3. A fruit of this encouragement was the work sent to Simplicianus just after Augustine had become a bishop (see n. 7).

4. Five essays, an "anti-Manichaean Pentateuch," as Paulinus of Nola (*Epistula* 25.2) called them, date from before Augustine's ordination: *De libero arbitrio*, started in Rome before summer 388, *De Genesi contra Manichaeos*, *De moribus ecclesiae catholicae*, *De moribus Manichaeorum*, and *De uera religione*, the latter written in Thagaste c. 390 and sent to Paulinus in 394. Shortly after his ordination, Augustine added four other essays: *De utilitate credendi*, *De duabus animabus*, *Disputatio contra Fortunatum*, and *Contra Adimantum*. In *De moribus ecclesiae catholicae*, written in Rome during the summer of 388, Augustine stated as a strict requirement for Catholics that "the explanation of the Scriptures should be sought for from those who are the professed teachers of the Scriptures" (1.1). He was speaking out of his recent experience.

5. *De moribus ecclesiae catholicae* presents a set of arguments based exclusively on the New Testament passages accepted by the Manichees, to which the author adds parallel texts from the Old Testament.

6. On Augustine's years as an *asceta laico e libro studioso*, see A. Pincherle, "Il decennio di preparazione di Sant'Agostino (386–396): Dal *De vera religione* al *Contra Adimantum*," *Ricerche Religiose* 3 (1931).

7. That study led to the immediate production of *De Genesi ad litteram imperfectus liber, De sermone Domini in monte, Expositio quarumdam propositionum ex epistula ad Romanos, Expositio epistolae ad Galatas,* and *Epistulae ad Romanos inchoata expositio.* Many of the questions dealt with in *De diuersis quaestionibus ad Simplicianum,* sent to Milan after April 397, had been discussed during the Bible sessions in Thagaste. On Thagaste, see George P. Lawless, O.S.A., "Augustine's First Monastery: Thagaste or Hippo?" *Aug (R)* 25 (1985): 64–78.

8. Letter 9 (*Epistula* 28).2 (Loeb Classical Library, trans. J. H. Baxter): "all the company of students in the African churches." Augustine was then begging the famous Jerome for some translations of Greek commentaries of Scripture, in particular by Origen.

9. The title, secured by Augustine himself (*Retractationes* 2.4.2), becomes problematic as soon as one translates it.

10. In addition to biblical exegesis, Augustine tried the homiletic genre, as in his earliest *Enarrationes in Psalmos*; the heavily didactic genre of propaganda-poetry, as in *Psalmus contra partem Donati*; the properly doctrinal genre as in *De fide et symbolo,* occasioned by the African synod of Hippo-Regius in 393.

11. *St. Augustine: Select Letters,* ed. J. H. Baxter, Loeb Classical Library (Cambridge, Mass., 1930), Letter 5 (*Epistula* 16), 18–19.

12. *Retractationes* 2.4.1: *libros de doctrina christiana, cum imperfectos comperissem, perficere malui quam eis sic relictis ad alia retractanda transire.*

13. Ms. Leningradensis Q.v.I.3, olim Corbeiensis, includes with *DDC* books 1 and 2, *De diuersis quaestionibus, Contra epistulam Manichaei, De agone christiano,* the first four works of Bishop Augustine. W. M. Green, "A Fourth Century Manuscript of St. Augustine?" *RBen* 69 (1959): 191–197.

14. *Contra Faustum* 22.91; *De ciuitate dei* 8.11. A separate edition of books 1–3, with book 3 completed, might be witnessed by Eugippius, who quotes only from these three books, and confesses that he acquired them through friends, in *Epistula ad uirginem* (*CSEL* 9:21).

15. Such "incomplete" essays were the contemporary *Commentary on Genesis* and the *Expositio inchoata* on Romans, interrupted three years earlier. Also *Contra epistulam Manichaei quam uocant fundamenti* was incomplete, according to what Augustine observes in *Retractationes* 2.2: he refuted only the "commencement" of the Manichaean *Epistula fundamenti,* and his additional comment is significant for *DDC* as well: "On the other parts of the epistle I have made notes as required, refuting the whole, and sufficient to recall the argument, had I ever had leisure to write against the whole." Augustine wrote the final part of *DDC* book 3 on the basis of notes he had kept since 396. See my complementary remarks in "The Local Setting and Motivation of *De doctrina christiana,*" *Collectanea Augustiniana* (1993).

16. ". . . vers la fin de 397 ou au commencement de 398" (P. de Labriolle, *Saint Augustin: Confessions,* vol. 2 [Paris, 1977], vi).

17. Josef Martin, "Abfassung, Veröffentlichung und Überlieferung von Augustins Schrift *De Doctrina Christiana,*" *Traditio* 18 (1962): 69–87, esp. 73, argues on the basis of *DDC* 2.40.61, *ut de uiuis taceam,* for a reference to Ambrose.

18. *De agone christiano* is dated from c. 395, *Contra epistulam Manichaei* from

c. 395–396, the *De diuersis quaestionibus* was in the making on Augustine's desk from 395 to 397.

19. "There are certain precepts for treating the Scriptures. . . . I have undertaken to explain these rules to those able and willing to learn, if God our Lord will not deny me, in writing, those things which he usually suggests to me in thought" (prologue, 1 [trans. D. W. Robertson, 3]).

20. ". . . precepts of the kind which I have undertaken to supply herewith" (prologue 3 [Robertson, 4]).

21. Rowan Williams, "Language, Reality, and Desire in Augustine's *De Doctrina*," *Journal of Literature and Theology* 3 (1989): 138–150. The author offers a penetrating analysis of book 1. He uses it as an interpretive basis for a comprehensive view of the whole work. He also shows how unfortunately the fact of the interrupted composition of *De Doctrina* remains ignored from such a viewpoint. For a more pedantic study of Augustine's thought in book 1, see G. Istace, "Le livre Ier du *De doctrina christiana* de saint Augustin," *Ephemerides Theologicae Lovanienses* 32 (1956): 289–330.

22. Augustine himself recognizes the thematic unity of book 2 and book 3 when he observes, at the start of book 3, "that the ambiguity of Scripture arises either from the words used literally or figuratively, both of which types we have discussed in the second book" (Robertson, 79).

23. Augustine did not rework or complete any other of his many writings, when engaged in the careful survey of the *Retractationes*. There would have been no interruption of *DDC*, but a banal "incomplete," had he not decided to write its final part in 426. How the author resumes his writing after three decades of interruption helps explain the very nature and cause of the interruption itself.

24. "But before I begin this task, it seems proper to answer those who will condemn these precepts, or who would condemn them if we did not placate them beforehand" (prologue 1 [Robertson, 3]).

25. "Some will condemn our work because they do not understand the precepts it contains" (prologue 2 [Robertson, 3]).

26. "Others, however, when they have understood our rules . . . but have been unable to clarify and explain what they wish. . . ." (prologue, 2); "those who have studied and learned these precepts and still do not understand the obscurity of the Holy Scriptures . . ." (prologue, 3 [Robertson, 3–4]).

27. Prologue, 2.

28. "These see, or think they see that they are already equipped to expound the sacred books" (prologue, 2 [Robertson, 3]).

29. " . . . without having read any of the observations which I have set out to make, so that they will declare that these regulations are necessary to no one, but that everything which may laudably be revealed about the obscurities of these books can be revealed with divine assistance" (prologue, 2 [Robertson, 3]).

30. " . . . they think these precepts superfluous" (prologue, 4 [Robertson, 4]).

31. "And let anyone teaching another communicate what he has received without pride or envy" (prologue, 5 [Robertson, 5]). Tyconius expressed the same thought in his own prooemium: "if the sense of these rules is accepted without envy as we have explained it" (Robertson, 105).

32. " . . . they should remember that they have learned at least the alphabet from men" (prologue, 4 [Robertson, 4]).

33. Eugene Kevane, "Paideia and Antipaideia: The Prooemium of St. Augustine's *De doctrina christiana,*" *AugStud* 1 (1970): 153–180.

34. " . . . who either treat the Sacred Scriptures well, or think they do so" (prologue, 2 [Robertson, 3]).

35. Prologue, 2.

36. From Cassiodorus's *De institutione diuinarum et secularium literarum* to Hugh of St. Victor's *Didascalicon* in the twelfth century, and Erasmus's *Enchiridion* in the sixteenth century.

37. *DDC* 30.42 (Robertson, 104).

38. All dates remain unsure in the case of Tyconius.

39. *Libellum regularem* prologue 2 (ed. William S. Babcock; *Tyconius: The Book of Rules,* Texts and Translations 31, ed. R. L. Wilken and W. R. Schoedel [Atlanta, Ga., 1989]).

40. See n. 48: "I am not forgetting what you asked about. . . ."

41. *Epistula* 41.2 (trans. W. Parsons, *St. Augustine's Letters,* vol. 1, FC 12 [Washington, 1951], 179).

42. In 396, just before quoting the image of "leaven" in Matthew 16:11 and Luke 13:20–21, Augustine had observed that "things are similar to other things in a great many ways." A much more adequate and theological distinction is introduced in 426, when Augustine resumes his writing. He wonders now if "wrath of God" refers only to "the ultimate penalty," or if it signifies "rather the grace of the Scriptures passing from the Jews to the Gentiles"; from formal rhetoric, the discussion of figurative locutions has shifted over to a problematic inspired by Tyconius's *Book of Rules.*

43. See n. 46.

44. Tyconius *Libellum regularem* prologue 3.95 (*CSEL* 80:105; F. C. Burkitt, ed., *The Book of Rules of Tyconius* [Cambridge, 1894, reprint 1967]): *Necessarium duxi ante omnia quae mihi uidentur libellum regularem scribere, et secretorum legis ueluti claues et luminaria fabricare. Sunt enim quaedam regulae mysticae.*

45. Augustine had reviewed about a third of the ninety-eight writings listed for his *Retractationes,* when he decided to complete *DDC.*

46. In *DDC* 30.42, the titles of Tyconius's seven rules are enumerated. In 30.43, the prologue of the *Book of Rules* is quoted literally. Then, from 31.44 through 37.56, by which Augustine closed book 3, one finds an extensive summary of Tyconius's whole work. Augustine recommends the latter as "elaborate and useful" in 30.42, and he adds: "I thought that this should be said so that this book, which is of great assistance in understanding the Scriptures, might be read by students" (Robertson, 105). This is a very rare, if not unique, occurrence in the Christian literature of the patristic era, where a strict guardian of ecclesiastical orthodoxy promotes the writing of a heretical or schismatic author, and more so specifically for the study of Holy Scripture.

47. He initiates his long comments on Tyconius in *DDC* 30.42, by stating: "A

certain Tyconius . . . wrote a book which he called *Of Rules*, since in it he explained seven *rules with which, as with keys* [emphasis mine] the obscurities of the Divine Scriptures might be opened" (Robertson, 104). Augustine expressed the same understanding of "rules" and "keys," as being equivalent, already in his letter to Aurelius, dated from 396 (see n. 48).

48. C. Kannengiesser and P. Bright, *A Conflict of Christian Hermeneutics in Roman Africa: Tyconius and Augustine: Protocol of th 58th Colloquy*, ed. Wilhelm Wuellner (Berkeley, 1989), 1–22, esp. 6–8, "Mystic Rules the Key-Notion of Tyconian Hermeneutic." Also Pamela Bright, *The Book of Rules of Tyconius: Its Purpose and Inner Logic* (Notre Dame, 1988), ch. 3, "The Logic of the Mystical Rules," 53–87.

49. *Secretorum legis ueluti claues et luminaria fabricare.*

50. *Clausa quaeque patefient et obscura dilucidabuntur.*

51. *Regulae mysticae.* The notion of "mystic rules" is proper to Tyconius, but he follows the well-defined usage of *regula* in Quintilian. See my forthcoming essay on "Quintilian's *regula* in Tyconius' *Book of Rules* and in Augustine's *De doctrina christiana*," to be published in *Illinois Classical Studies* 19 (1994), essays in honor of M. Marcovich, 1–14.

52. "However, not all the things which are so written that they are difficult to understand may be cleared up by means of these rules. . . . Nor would he [Tyconius] have given his reader and judge false hope by attributing too much to such an elaborate and useful work" (*DDC* 30.42–43 [Robertson, 104–105]).

53. P. Bright, "Tyconius and His Interpreters: A Study of the Epitomes of the *Book of Rules*," in Kannengiesser and Bright, *A Conflict of Christian Hermeneutics*, 23–39. The author's "brief analysis of the Tyconian text and its earliest summaries . . . demonstrates the radical changes introduced into the reading of the *Book of Rules* within fifty years of its composition" (37).

St. Augustine, Neoplatonism, and the Liberal Arts: The Background to *De doctrina christiana*

FREDERICK VAN FLETEREN

If *De civitate dei* can be called the charter of Christendom, and it has been,[1] then *De doctrina christiana* may be justly reckoned the charter of the Christian intellectual. In *De doctrina christiana* 2, Augustine writes:

> Nevertheless, if we can grasp something useful for understanding the Scriptures, we should not flee music because of the superstition of secular men; neither, if we learn something about zithers and organs which enables us to grasp the spiritual, should we turn toward the frivolities of their theater. Nor is it the case that, since they say that Mercury is their author, ought we not to learn letters; neither, since they dedicate temples to justice and virtue and prefer to worship in stones what ought to be done in the heart, should we flee justice and virtue. Indeed whoever is a good and true Christian should understand that, wherever he finds truth, it belongs to his own Lord. In confessing and recognizing it, he will also cast off the superstitious images of Holy Writ.[2]

Of course Augustine was not the first Christian to use the ancient learning of the Greeks and the Romans to aid him in the interpretation of the Scriptures. Nor is he the first Father to realize the importance of secular learning to the *catholica*. Augustine recognized that he was in a long line of Christian thinkers who put secular learning at the service of the *ecclesia*. Indeed, he gives us a partial list of his precursors at the end of *De doctrina christiana* 2.[3] But Augustine is the first one to outline an extensive program of the liberal arts to help the Christian reach an *intellectus fidei*; and he was also the first one in fact to achieve a Christian synthesis with secular letters in the Latin West. *De doctrina christiana* 1 sets the stage for such a program by sketching a Christian anthropology and a theology of the incarnation; book 2 contains a philosophy of signs; in

14

book 3, we find the great principles of the Augustinian hermeneutic; and in *De doctrina christiana* 4, the elderly bishop of Hippo writes a kind of Christian *De oratore*. But it is the program of the liberal arts which is the cardinal theme of the work and which represents its central importance for the history of Christian thought.

The justification for his scheme comes near the end of *De doctrina christiana* 2:

> Moreover if they who are called philosophers, especially the Platonists, perhaps say anything true and reconcilable to our faith, not only are these [truths] not to be feared, but they are to be appropriated into our use from them just as from unjust possessors. For just as the Egyptians used to have not only idols and heavy burdens which the people of Israel detested and fled, but also vessels and ornaments made from gold and silver, and clothing, which the people going out from Egypt took secretly for themselves, putting them as it were to a better use, not on their own authority, but on God's, with the Egyptians unwittingly providing those things which they were not using well (Ex. 3:12 and 12:33), thus all the teachings of the Gentiles have not only idols and supersitious images and heavy burdens of useless labor, which each one of us going out from Gentile society under the leadership of Christ ought to abominate and avoid, but also liberal disciplines more suitable for the use of truth; they also contain several very useful moral precepts; and some truths concerning the adoration of the one God are found in them. When the Christian separates himself in spirit from an unhappy alliance with them, the Christian ought to take away from them, for the just use of preaching the Gospel, just as gold and silver of theirs, those truths which they did not create, but which they dug out from certain, as it were, metals of divine providence, which is infused everywhere, and which the [Gentiles] perversely and harmfully abuse in their allegiance to daemons. Also it would be allowable for the [Christians] to receive and possess the [Egyptian] clothing, that is, those things of human creation, nevertheless suitable for human society, which must be possessed in this life, but which should be converted into Christian use.[4]

The gold, silver, and clothing which the Israelites had taken from the Egyptians in their flight from Egypt had long been used by Christian writers as an image to justify their use of secular learning.[5] We find the same figure used, in a somewhat abbreviated form in *Confessions* 7. In *De doctrina christiana*, Augustine distinguishes between truths of divine creation, signified by gold and silver, and truths of human institution, symbolized by clothing. The Christian is justified in placing both kinds of truths at the service of the Gospel. I cannot help but think that Augustine has Porphyry in mind when he speaks of those who traffic with daemons. The passage deals with the Platonists, and Porphyry is the one Platonist whom, more than all the others, Augustine accuses of trafficking with daemons.[6]

Augustine's passage to the construction of this program of the liberal arts was long and arduous, associated as it was to his own life's journey. He had received as fine an education in Madaura and Carthage as his father's modest means and the decline of the Roman Empire would allow. The inspiration of Cicero's *Hortensius* to the young man's pursuit of a life of wisdom indicates, among many other things, that he took his education seriously. Further, though it was devoted to the *verbum* and not the *res*, his career as the equivalent of university professor in Thagaste, Carthage, Rome, and Milan witnesses his commitment to the life of letters. Yet it was his reading of the *libri platonicorum* in the late spring or early summer of 386 in Milan which decisively influenced his views of the liberal arts with which he was already well acquainted.

The intellectual conversion which Augustine experienced at that time formed his categories of thinking; moreover, it influenced his life's project for the next several years. And the decisive event during that conversion was the direct, but fleeting, *intuitus* of the divine upon reading the Neoplatonists. Elsewhere I have discussed the mystical nature of these events.[7] Here I should like to emphasize once more the lasting effects that these experiences had in Augustine's life. He was convinced that a permanent vision of the divine was available to people in this life and that the reason why he had not sustained this *intuitus* was the lack of intellectual, and to some lesser extent, moral purity. And this set him in search of a path to attain this purification. The itinerary was to be an extensive program of study of the liberal arts, a project outlined in *De ordine* 2 but never completed.

The sources for these experiences have been widely discussed. To my mind and to many others, it is certain that Plotinus's *Ennead of Beauty* (*Enneads* 1.6) inspired Augustine, prepared as he was by the preaching of Ambrose, on these occasions. The sources for the program of purification through the liberal arts have, however, remained a much more controversial question. The training of the mind to see Good or Beauty is a common theme in ancient philosophy since the time of Plato, if not indeed Pythagoras. Undoubtedly both Varro's no longer extant volumes on the liberal arts and Cicero's *Hortensius* were influential on Augustine's views. Seneca also mentions use of the liberal arts.[8] Augustine was certainly aware of the reference to the use of the liberal arts for the purpose of purification in the *Ennead on Beauty* and could have been aware that Plotinus mentions the liberal arts in other places in the *Enneads* as well.[9] His reading of the various philosophical encyclopedias and his extensive knowledge of Roman literature must be borne in mind as we consider the question of sources.[10] However, I believe the primary inspirational source for *katharsis* through the liberal arts was, in all likelihood, the now lost *De regressu animae* of Porphyry.

The reasons for considering Porphyry to be the dominant source are both internal and external to Augustine's works. The premier justification for this program of intellectual purification occurs in *Soliloquia* 1.13.23 ff.:

It is certainly fitting that lovers of wisdom be such [as was described above]. She whose union is truly chaste and without contamination seeks such lovers. But we do not come to her by one road. Indeed, each one understands that unique and truest good according to his own health and strength. There is a certain ineffable and unknowable light of minds. That common light may teach us, insofar as it can, how that good exists. There are some eyes so healthy and vigorous that they turn themselves to the sun itself without any trembling as quickly as possible. For these, the light itself is in a certain way health; they do not need a teacher, but perhaps only an admonition. For them, it is sufficient to believe, hope, and love. Others are struck by the brightness itself which they strongly desire to see, and, once it is not seen, they often return to the darkness with delight. To these it is dangerous to wish to show what they still cannot see, as much as to such as can already be rightly called healthy. They must first be trained and their love must be postponed and nourished. First they ought to be shown certain objects which are not illuminated through themselves, but can be seen through the light, such as clothing and walls and anything of these kinds; next those things which shine not yet through themselves but nevertheless more beautifully through that light, such as gold, silver, and similar things, though it is not to so shine that it injures the eyes. Then perhaps that earthly fire is to be pointed out in due measure, next the stars, then the moon, next the light of dawn and the brightness of the white heaven. In these people, whether more quickly or more slowly, whether through the entire order or with some parts disdained, each one becoming accustomed according to his own health will see the sun without trembling and with great desire. The best teachers do something such to those who are very desirous of wisdom, who nevertheless already see, but not sharply. It is the duty of good training to arrive at wisdom by a certain order, but without order arrival at happiness is scarcely to be believed. . . . [*Soliloquia* 1.14.24:] There is one thing which I can command; I know nothing more. All sensible things must be absolutely avoided, and we must be exceedingly careful, while we activate this body, lest our wings be impeded by the glue of sensible things; it is necessary us to be whole and complete, so that we turn to that light from this darkness. This light does not yet deign to show itself to those enclosed in the cave unless they will be such that with that darkness broken and unbound they can ascend into the free air. Thus, when you will be such that absolutely no earthly thing delights you, believe me, at the same moment, at the same point of time, you will see what you desire.[11]

This passage is directed to the few who can attain understanding rather than to the many who cannot. At this time, Augustine was attempting to achieve some kind of synthesis between the *sapientia* of Cicero, the *nous* of Plotinus and Porphyry, and the *verbum* of St. John's prologue. According to this passage, there are those who can see the light immediately and others in need of an *exercitatio animae*. Such training the liberal arts can provide, varied according to the needs of the individual. Those who undergo such a program successfully will eventually see the light and attain a happiness scarcely to be believed. There can be no doubt that Augustine has in mind a terminal vision of God to be sustained in this life. It is in this spirit that Augustine in the *Retractationes* corrects his views, in his commentary on the *De ordine*, concerning what the liberal arts can deliver.[12]

In the succeeding passage of the *Soliloquia*, Augustine summarizes the entire program of intellectual and moral purification with the phrase *penitus esse ista sensibilia fugienda*. This phrase could describe the goal of human existence in the Platonic tradition in general, but it is most reminiscent of the phrase *omne corpus fugiendum* which Augustine ascribes to Porphyry, and only to Porphyry, throughout his corpus. In the *Retractationes* Augustine corrects this phrase explicitly in light of its Porphyrian sound.[13]

The reasons for thinking that this program of intellectual purification through the liberal arts is primarily Porphyrian in origin are many and need to be emphasized for a proper appreciation of Augustine's own change of mind in the *De doctrina christiana*. The remote origin of this image is, of course, Plato's allegory of the cave in *Republic* 7, a passage with which Augustine may have been familiar, albeit perhaps not directly, for some period of time. Nevertheless, a more proximate origin for the modifications and abridgments should be sought. What Varro's justification for his program of the liberal arts was, aside from an ascent from the corporeal to the incorporeal, from the visible to the invisible, we unfortunately do not know.[14] The nature of this image suggests a Neoplatonic source. A Porphyrian origin for the image of bird-lime hindering the flight of the soul has been suggested by Courcelle.[15]

Augustine connects the idea of purification more with Porphyry than with any other author. In the *Praeparatio evangelica*, Eusebius associates the doctrine of preparation for philosophy by means of the liberal arts with Porphyry's *Philosophy from Oracles*, a work mentioned by title at the beginning of the *Contra academicos*. In the *Vita Pythagorae*, Porphyry indicates that, if an individual is not instructed gradually in good discipline, a too-rapid conversion to the light will cause him to renounce the search for contemplation.[16] (In this regard it is instructive to note that in the *De ordine* Augustine ascribes the program of purification through the liberal arts to Pythagoras.)[17] Further, it was Porphyry who was viewed at that time, and indeed in our own, as the most learned of all the Platonists. Finally, the connection of the program of the liberal arts with the theme of the end and the means, so associated by Augustine with the Platonists from the time of his intellectual conversion and specifically with Porphyry's *De regressu animae* in *De ciuitate dei* 10, indicated a Porphyrian origin. For all these reasons, I conclude that the program of the liberal arts in the *De ordine* and the *Soliloquia* is Porphyrian in genesis.

The program of the liberal arts remained a project for Augustine during his early years. The undertaking, of course, was an enormous one. The *De musica* is the only completed work from this enterprise whose purpose it was to rise from things corporeal to things incorporeal. Further, it is the only example of such an extant work on music in the Latin West. The remainder of the scheme exists either in note form or not at all. Since it was Augustine's purpose during this period that he himself reach the vision of God in this life, the early works on the soul should be understood in conjunction with this project on the liberal arts. A Porphyrian or Plotinian ascent of the mind to God starts in material things but soon enters the interior person. The works on the soul, the *De immortalitate animae* and the *De quantitate animae*, should be studied as Augustine's attempts to reach a degree of self-knowledge, in understanding the true nature of the interior person as spiritual and immortal. Further, I suspect that the early community in Thagaste, perhaps more in its initial stages, was interested in this philosophical program of the liberal arts at least as much as in the nascent monastic life.

I have outlined elsewhere the texts which show that during the period 386–394 Augustine gradually left behind his early aspirations for the liberal arts. The reasons are many.[18] The fundamental reason, of course, is the impossibility of such a venture. He had asked of the liberal arts what they could not deliver. The ontological gulf between God and the human being, between the infinite and the finite, cannot be bridged by the liberal arts. No doubt, the enormity of the project had something to do with its not being completed. His ordination to the priesthood and the subsequent pastoral duties involved may also have left him little time for these intellectual endeavors. Nevertheless, the final nail was driven into the coffin of this project when, in 394, Augustine studied Paul's Epistles to the Romans and the Galatians for the first time in detail. There he found ample evidence that in Paul's view final salvation could come about only through the grace of God and in the next life. No longer could he ask the liberal arts to train his mind to see God.

Augustine must then have asked himself this question: If the liberal arts cannot provide this vision of God, do they have some other role in the life of the Christian? And his resounding affirmative answer to this question lies in *De doctrina christiana*. If the above analysis is correct, then *De doctrina christiana* should be interpreted as a kind of Christian answer to Porphyry and his followers. Augustine remained convinced, even until his dying days, that Neoplatonism was of all philosophies the closest to Christianity. And the greatest of the Platonists was Porphyry. Augustine thought that the Christian should use secular learning to come to an understanding of, and to interpret, the message found in the Old and New Testaments. The philosophical cum theological argument for such a position is found in *De doctrina christiana* 1. This book constitutes therefore Augustine's attempt to reinterpret Neoplatonic, and especially Porphyrian thought, in terms which the Christian could accept.

At least six passages from *De doctrina christiana* 1 are best explicated, at least in part, against a Neoplatonic, and perhaps Porphyrian, background:

1. The *uti-frui* distinction (*DDC* 1.3.3–4.4). Augustine begins the *De doctrina christiana* with a distinction among things (*res*) into those things which are to be enjoyed (*quibus fruendum est*), those which are to be used (*quibus utendum*), and those that are to be both used and enjoyed (*quae fruuntur et utuntur*). For several decades, the *uti-frui* distinction has been thought to take its origin in Greek metaphysics. For my part, I would see the distinction as another variation on the theme of the end of salvation and the means to that end, a theme found in Augustine from the very beginning of his writings, connected explicitly with his reading of the *libri platonicorum* in *Confessiones* 7, and associated explicitly with the name of Porphyry in *De civitate dei* 10.29 ff. Here Augustine adopts and adapts a Porphyrian matrix. For many decades, indeed for most of the Christian millennia, the debate has raged over the suitability of Athens to Jerusalem on this point. It would be arrogant to attempt to decide the suitability of the Greek *eros* world to the Bible on this point. Let it suffice for me to say that I am sympathetic to the attempt.

2. God as triune (*DDC* 1.5.5). The goal of human life, that which is to be enjoyed, is the triune God. In a certain sense, this is a correction of Neoplatonism since both Plotinus and Porphyry taught union with the One. Nevertheless, from his earliest contact with the Platonists, Augustine thought that the relationship between the Father and the Son was not unlike the relationship between the One and the *nous*. Olivier du Roy has analyzed the progress which Augustine made in his attempt to reach an *intellectus fidei* of the triune Godhead and has further emphasized the importance of this search for an understanding of the Trinity through

philosophical means for theology in the West.[19] In this passage, Augustine presents us with a doctrinal account, according to Christian belief, of the nature of the triune God. He offers us an understanding of the Trinity in terms of *unitas, aequalitas*, and *concordia*, to my knowledge a triad found explicitly only in this passage of Augustine's writings. This passage, then, offers an explicit correction of Neoplatonism on the nature of the highest being, the union with whom constitutes the goal of human existence.

3. The ineffability of God (*DDC* 1.6.6). Though Augustine was searching throughout his early works for a way of complete knowledge of God, from his earliest writings on he had an appreciation for apophatic theology. This tendency remained with him through his final work on the subject, the *De trinitate*. We know God more by not knowing him. When we speak of person and substance in God, we do so only that we might say something instead of nothing. The attempt to reach God by a direct *intuitus*, while realizing his complete ineffability, is certainly standard Neoplatonism and may well be a doctrine which Augustine assimilated from Porphyry, as has been suggested by others.

4. The necessity of purification for the human mind to see God (*DDC* 1.10.10).

> Wherefore, since that truth is to be enjoyed which lives unchangeably and in that truth the triune God, author and creator of the universe, gives counsel by means of those things which he created, the mind must be purified so that it can see that light and be united to it, once it is perceived. We contend that this purification is, as it were, a certain walking and sea voyage to the fatherland. We are not moved by place to him who is present everywhere, but by good desire and good morals.[20]

We have noted the association of the purification theme in Augustine with Porphyry. Here the former explicitly employs the Neoplatonic, and probably Porphyrian, theme of purification of the soul to see God immediately before bringing to Porphyrian thought a fundamental change of purification through the incarnation. The purification of the mind, the ultimate union with the light, the image of a land and sea voyage to the fatherland, and the specific invoking of omnipresence all seem to point, at least in part, to a Porphyrian background. However, the purification is to take place in a very un-Porphyrian way: God becoming man. I am fully aware that this theme, and this passage in particular, owes some debt to *Enneads* 1.6. Such a reference should not however be used to deny the apparently Porphyrian nature of the purification. Even as Augustine begins to see the ascent of the mind to God more in terms of Isaiah 11:2 and Matthew 5:3–10 than in terms of Neoplatonism, purification still remains necessary.

5. The purification of souls through the incarnation (*DDC* 1.11.11–21.19). Porphyry, beyond all others, was the great anti-Christian of his time. He made explicit what was implicit in the Platonic tradition: the incarnation, God becoming man, was impossible since any fall into the material world involves a degeneration in being. It is against this background that Augustine theologizes about the incarnation as the way of purification for humankind.

> Although [Wisdom] itself is therefore the Fatherland, he also made himself the way to the Fatherland for us. . . . And since [Wisdom] is present everywhere to the healthy and pure interior eye, he also deigned to appear to the fleshy eyes of those who have an infirm and unclean eye.[21]

One of the ironies of Augustine's thought is that he understood the role of God incarnate in terms of the philosophy of a pagan who explicitly denied its possibility.

6. Christ's role as the way to salvation (*DDC* 1.34.38). Since his reading of the *libri platonicorum*, Augustine had been looking for a way of salvation. Part of his conversion was to accept Christ as that way of salvation. In *De civitate dei* 10, Augustine explicitly associates the theme of the universal way of salvation with Porphyry's *De regressu animae*. In the *De doctrina christiana*, Augustine clearly develops this theme:

> Even though the Truth itself and the Word through whom all things were made was made flesh so that he might live among us, nevertheless see how the Apostle said: "And if we had known Christ according to the flesh, already we did not know him" (2 Cor. 5:16). Indeed he who willed to offer himself not only as a possession to those arriving, but also as a way to those coming to the beginning of his ways willed to take on flesh. Whence also is this passage: "The Lord created me in the beginning of his ways" (Prv. 8:22), so that they who wish to come might begin there. Thus although the Apostle still walked *in via* and followed God to the victory of a higher calling, nevertheless forgetting those things which are behind and extended to those things which are ahead (Phil. 3:12–14), [Paul] had passed the beginning of the ways; that is, he was not in need of that by which the road is nevertheless begun and led to all who desire to arrive at truth and to remain in eternal life. For [Christ] spoke thus: "I am the way and the truth and the life" (Jn. 14:6); that is, one comes through me, one arrives to me, one remains in me. For when one arrives to him, one also arrives to the Father; since he to whom he is equal is recognized through an equal, with the Holy Spirit conquering and also gluing us, by whom we can remain in the highest and unchangeable good. From which we understand how nothing ought to hold us *in via*, when not even the Lord himself, insofar as he deigned to be our way, wished to hold us, but to pass beyond; lest through infirmity we

cling to things temporal, even if taken up and done by him for our salvation; rather with ease we should easily run through them so that we might merit to traverse and make progress toward him who freed our nature from temporal things and placed it at the Father's right hand.[22]

In this passage, Augustine makes clear that Christ is the way as well as the term of salvation. From the very beginning of his works, Augustine has understood the incarnation as the means to our salvation. Human beings must pass through things temporal, even the incarnation and the deeds connected with it, to things eternal. This theme is articulated in *De trinitate* 13, where Augustine, to the consternation of some contemporary commentators, places the deeds and sayings of Christ as objects of *scientia*, not *sapientia*. Augustine explicates the theme of Christ as the means and term of salvation against the Neoplatonic, and perhaps Porphyrian, background of the way of salvation.

Such then is the journey which led Augustine to his final position concerning the liberal arts. He started as a modified Porphyrian; he ended with a program of his own. Secular learning is to be used by the Christian for the interpretation of the Scriptures. At first glance such an approach may seem to be, at least to us moderns, too narrow in scope. However, we should do well to remember that Christianity is preeminently a religion of the Word and of the Book. It was much more so for Augustine than even for our own century, when we have experienced a renewal in Scripture studies. For Augustine, the tools of secular learning, whether their objects be natural or conventional, must be placed at the service of the pursuit of truth and salvation. Truth, wherever it is, belongs to the Lord. But in so doing, if he is to be true to his calling, the Christian scholar, using the Holy Writ as the criterion, must discard the many idols found in secular learning. Twentieth-century daemons are certainly not Porphyrian; they are, however, nonetheless real. And to the relearning of this lesson a collection such as this has much to contribute.

Notes

1. J. J. O'Meara, *The Charter of Christendom* (Villanova, 1961).

2. *DDC* 2.18.28 (*PL* 34:40).

3. *DDC* 2.11.61.

4. *DDC* 2.11.60 (*PL* 34:63).

5. See Ragnar Holte, *Béatitude et Sagesse* (Paris, 1962), 121 ff.

6. See, for example, *De civitate dei* 10.23 ff.

7. See "St. Augustine and Mysticism," *Collectanea Augustiniana* 11, ed. F. Van Fleteren and P. Pulsiano (New York, 1992).

8. Seneca *Epistula* 21.22.

9. Plotinus *Enneads* 1.3.1 and 3.8.2.

10. See *Confessiones* 5.3.3.

11. *Soliloquia* 1.13.23 ff. (*PL* 32:881–882: *[Ratio] prorsus tales esse amatores sapientiae decet.*

12. *Retractationes* 1.3.2.

13. *Retractationes* 1.4.3.

14. See Claudianus Mammertus *De statu animae* 2.8 (*CSEL* 11:128).

15. P. Courcelle, "La colle et la clou de l'âme dans la tradition néo-platonicienne et chrétienne (*Phédon* 82e; 83d)," *Revue Belge de Philologie et d'Histoire* 36 (1958): 72–95.

16. Porphyry *Vita Pythagorae* 46.

17. *De ordine* 2.20.53.

18. F. Van Fleteren, "St. Augustine and the Possibility of the Vision of God in this Life," *Studies in Medieval Culture*, 11:9–17.

19. Olivier du Roy, *L'intelligence de la foi en la Trinité selon saint Augustin* (Paris, 1966).

20. DDC 1.10.10 (*PL* 34:23): *Quapropter. . . .*

21. DDC 1.11–12.11 (*PL* 34:23): *Cum ergo ipsa sit patria, viam se quoque nobis fecit ad patriam.*

22. DDC 1.34.38 (*PL* 34:33–34): *Vide quemadmodum cum ipsa Veritas, et Verbum per quod facta.*

Biblical Ambiguity in African Exegesis

PAMELA BRIGHT

Augustine's deliberate and soul-searching shift from "merchant of words" to "minister of the Word" is nowhere more evident than in the composition of *De doctrina christiana*. This *tour de force* begun in the early years of his episcopacy pauses in mid-thought on the question of ambiguity in Scripture.

In book 3, *capitulum 25*, Augustine warns that a thing may not always have the same signification in Scripture. Something condemned in one context may be praised in another. He cites Matthew 16:6–11, Christ's warning against the "leaven of the Pharisees," which he contrasts with the positive signification of the leaven hidden in the measure of flour, a symbol of the hiddenness of the Kingdom. Thirty years later, Augustine completes this citation from Matthew 13:33 and then begins an elaborate reflection upon things which have either "contrary" or "diversified" significations according to the context of the scriptural passage: *Huius igitur uarietatis obseruatio duas habet formas; sic enim atque aliud res quaeque significant, ut aut contraria aut tantummodo diuersa significant.*[1]

At first sight, this is an innocuous break in the text, easily attributable to the press of duties experienced by the bishop in the first decade of his office; but, to anyone familiar with the peculiarities of the exegetical tradition of the African church, the question of the contrariness of the signification of biblical terms is anything but marginal. Contrariness of signification, that is, that a single referent can be blameworthy in one context and praiseworthy in another, is the exegetical basis of an ecclesiology developed by certain African writers before the time of Augustine.

For these African theologians, duality of reference, or contrariness, is not so much a question of the fluidity of language as a principle of exegesis. The contrariness of the signification of the city of Jerusalem—praised in one context and blamed in another—is a revelation of the nature of the Church, itself at once a field of wheat and tares, a community of saints and sinners. This ecclesiology, traceable from the mid-third century, obviously challenged the rigorist ecclesiology of the Novatians in the third century and the Donatists in the fourth. Its most sophisticated formulation can be found in the writings of Tyconius, the formidable Donatist exegete whose *Book of Rules* was to be summarized and commented on by Augustine in the seven *capitula* that conclude book 3, the book in which the thirty-year pause in composition of *De doctrina christiana* occurred.[2]

This peculiarly African integration of exegesis and ecclesiology both attracted and repelled Augustine. On the one hand, he was obviously in sympathy with an ecclesiology that viewed the Church as the locus of repentance and forgiveness rather than as a "holy remnant." On the other hand, he was alienated by an exegetical system that ignored (or seemed to ignore) so many of the tools of interpretation which Augustine himself had sharpened over the course of his own rhetorical training and which he now sought to make available for the interpretation of the biblical text.

I will argue that the question of the ambiguity of Scripture marked a significant point of contact between a developed exegetical system in the African church and the thought of Augustine. The encounter was to produce no facile synthesis. While Augustine's eschatology and ecclesiology were to be marked by this encounter with the earlier tradition, the basic principles of African exegesis he both misunderstood and repudiated.[3]

I will analyze this point of contact, or rather, this point of divergence, by examining the development of the theme of ambiguity in *De doctrina christiana* and then the theme of contrariness, or duality of signification, in two writings of two earlier authors, the *Book of Rules* of Tyconius and an anonymous sermon of a third century African bishop writing against Novatian.

1. Ambiguity in *De doctrina christiana*

The discussion of ambiguity in Scripture properly begins in book 3 of *De doctrina christiana*. In the introduction of book 3 Augustine describes the argument of book 2 as a preparation for the study of ambiguity in Scripture: "Thus instructed he may turn his attention to the investigation and solution of the ambiguities of scripture." (*ueniat ita instructus ad ambigua scripturarum discutienda atque soluenda*).[4]

First, it is noteworthy that Augustine would describe the whole spectrum of knowledge outlined with such masterly finesse as *preparatory* to the study of ambiguity in Scripture. Second, it is interesting to note that he introduces the discussion of ambiguous signs in the same defensive and argumentative tone as that of the prooemium. With a rhetorical (or real) opponent in view Augustine once again anticipates the rejection of his instructions, this time on how to investigate and solve the ambiguities of scripture. "It may be that he will deride as puerile these ways which we wish to point out, either because of the greatness of his acumen or the brilliance of his illumination." This recalls the proud refusal of the "third objectors" in the prooemium: "Moreover, those who exult in divine assistance and who glory in being able to understand and to treat the sacred books without the precepts of the kind which I have undertaken to supply herewith."[5]

This introduction to book 3, beginning with a quick summary of book 2, indicates that the question of ambiguity is not just one of many issues to be treated in the course of such a project but is a topic that has been carefully planned for at the outset of the treatise. Although the examination of ambiguity of the language of Scripture is found in book 3, allusions to this problem are woven into the text of book 2 and book 3 and are punctuated by stinging attacks on those who would refuse the author's precepts for the interpretation of Scripture—until the interruption of the treatise in *capitulum* 25. After thirty years the bishop picks up his pen again and with a magisterial flourish completes his investigation into the fluidity of significations of certain words by urging a careful distinction between two kinds of ambiguity in figurative language, that which is contrary and that which is simply multivalent. Augustine celebrates the multivalency of language: "For what could God have more generously and abundantly provided in the divine writings than that the same words might be understood in various ways which other no less divine witnesses approve?"[6]

The first mention of ambiguity in *De doctrina christiana* occurs early in book 2 as Augustine begins his treatment of conventional signs: "But many and varied obscurities and ambiguities deceive those who read, casually understanding one thing instead of another."[7] Augustine suggests that the difficulty is a check to pride and at the same time is one of the delights of reading. "Thus the Holy Spirit has magnificently and wholesomely modulated the Holy Scriptures so that the more open places present themselves to hunger and the more obscure places may deter a disdainful attitude."[8] Conscious of the ever-present tendency to pride, Augustine outlines the seven gifts needed for the reading of Scripture: fear of the Lord, piety, knowledge, fortitude, counsel, purity of heart, and wisdom.[9] He focuses on the third charism, knowledge, and then explains that there are two causes of lack of understanding: unknown signs and ambiguous signs. The long development of the knowledge needed to deal with unknown signs concludes:

> Therefore when the reader has been prepared by this instruction so that he is not impeded by unknown signs, with a meek and humble heart . . . let him next turn to the examination and consideration of ambiguous signs in the Scriptures, concerning which I will essay to set forth in the third book what the Lord has granted to me.[10]

We note that the "thorough investigation" of ambiguity has been carefully placed within the structure of the argument of book 2 and book 3. Forewarned by constant admonitions against pride, the student of the sacred texts begins prepared and advances to the point where scriptural ambiguity may be investigated. Now in book 3, Augustine reminds his reader that the obscurities of figurative language need extraordinary attention and persistence. To underline the difficulty, Augustine devotes a long discussion[11] to distinguishing between the literal and figurative levels of the texts, a salutary reminder from his own days as a Manichee. "There is a miserable servitude of the spirit in this habit of taking signs for things so that one is not able to raise the eye of the mind above things that are corporal and created and drink in eternal light."[12]

Having cleared the ground, Augustine begins the long-awaited discussion of the ambiguity of figurative language by claiming that figurative language itself depends on the recognition of similarity: "But since things are similar to others in a great many ways, we must not think it to be prescribed that what a thing signifies by similitude in one place must always be signified by that thing."[13] Augustine introduces the double (and contrary) signification of the leaven from the Gospels of Luke and Matthew and then pauses for thirty years, leaving his text poised over the abyss of the ever-shifting referent of figurative language—a vertiginous prospect for unskilled interpreters of Scripture.

Three decades later, the bishop refocuses, explaining that while some texts could refer to contrary things, others may be diverse in their signification: "The things signified are contrary, that is, when one thing is used as similitude in a good sense and in another place in an evil sense, like leaven in the above example."[14] However, Augustine quickly points out that signification may be simply diverse. Water signifies people in Revelation, whereas in John's gospel, water refers to the Holy Spirit. Augustine concludes the section with the observation that diversity of meaning is governed by the context: "In the same way other things signify not one thing but more, and not only two diverse things, but sometimes many different things in accordance with the meaning of the passages in which they are found."[15]

In the light of this general principle, the careful distinction between *contrary* and *diverse* signification seems forced. However, if we follow Augustine's own recommendation to heed the context, the importance of the question of the contrariness of signification in the frame of his argument becomes more evident. The contrariness of certain biblical *figurae* is an essential feature in the hermeneutical system of the Donatist exegete, Tyconius, whose *Book of Rules* is summarized and commented upon by Augustine in concluding his treatment of figurative language in book 3.[16]

2. Ambiguity in Earlier African Exegesis

The summary and commentary on the *Book of Rules* in book 3 of *De doctrina christiana* is introduced in a tone that is both deferential and polemical. Augustine recommends the *Book of Rules* to his readers as an "elaborate and useful" work (*tam elaborato atque utili operi*),[17] an extraordinary instance of a schismatic's work being promoted by a church leader. For the purposes of the present inquiry, it may be even more significant that this exegetical system is based on a remarkable set of contrary references. In each of the seven mystical rules of Tyconius, the referent shifts between two contraries or dualities. For example, in rule 1 the referent shifts between Christ and his body, the Church, and Tyconius insists upon the importance of distinguishing between this double referent by careful attention to the context, while in rule 2 the distinction lies between what Tyconius calls the "left and right" of the church.

In insisting upon the importance of noting puzzling contrary references where "Jacob" is more praised, and condemned sometimes, within the same context of a prophetic text, Tyconius claims that in the very structure of the text of Scripture, the Holy Spirit has revealed the bipartite nature of the Church:

> Far more necessary is the rule concerning the bipartite character of the Lord's body; and so we must examine it all the more carefully, keeping it before our eyes through all the Scriptures. For just as the transition from head to body and back again, as indicated above, is only seen by reason, so also reason alone sees the transition and return from one part of the body to the other, from the right-hand part to the left, or from the left to the right, as was clear in the previous section.[18]

For Tyconius, the bipartite nature of the Church is revealed by the Holy Spirit in the prophetic literature as Jerusalem is first praised and then threatened in passages in close proximity. In the text of Isaiah, Jerusalem is promised that its "tents" will not be moved, and then a few lines further it is compared to a ship facing destruction.[19] For a Donatist to insist upon the presence of unholy members in the Church was for Augustine an absurdity: "A certain Tyconius who wrote most triumphantly against the Donatists, although he himself was a Donatist, and hence is found to have an absurd mentality, where he did not wish to abandon them altogether."[20] But Tyconius's stance and his hermeneutics begin to look less idiosyncratic if one takes into account the twists and turns of a long and elaborate exegetical tradition in the African church.

To look more carefully at the exegetical practice of the African church, as it was racked with dissension and outright schism from the third to the fifth century on the very question of the holiness of the membership of the Church, we return to the treatise of an anonymous bishop, a contemporary of Cyprian, in the aftermath of the persecution of Decius, and then of Gallus and Volusianus in the mid-third century. The bishop is agonizing over the question of whether to admit the lapsed back into the community:

> While I was meditating and impatiently tossing in my mind what I ought to do concerning those pitiable brethren who, wounded not of their own will, but by the outset of a raging devil, having lived until now, that is, through a long course of time in their endurance of their punishment; lo, there appeared another enemy . . . the heretic Novatian, who not only, as it is signified in the gospel, passed by the prostrate wounded man, as did the priest or Levite, but by an ingenious and novel cruelty would rather slay the wounded man by taking away the hope of salvation by denying the mercy of his Father, by rejecting the repentance of his brother.[21]

In attacking Novatian for rending the Church in schism, the bishop emphasizes the unity of the Church, "the one and only church in that ark" fashioned by Noah before the flood.[22] Linking the doctrine of the unity of the Church and the question of the reception of the lapsed, the bishop notes that in the ark "which alone was saved, and those that were in it," there were both "clean and unclean animals."[23]

The idea of the clean and unclean animals in the ark prompts Novatian himself to argue for the importance of the allegorical interpretation of Scripture,[24] whereas the African bishop immediately thinks in terms of the theology of the Church. But the African bishop has hermeneutical issues in mind as well as ecclesiological arguments. He introduces an unusual typological feature in his exegesis of the Genesis text: a typology of contrary significations. First, the releasing of the two birds, the raven and the dove, typifies the presence of good and evil members in the Church. Both leave the ark, but only the dove returns. The bishop carefully notes that this return has two aspects: the dove wishes to return, and Noah receives it back into the ark.[25] For the bishop the typology is clear: "Moreover, the dove which could not find rest for its feet bore a likeness to the lapsed."[26]

Being aware that the dove has positive connotations in African exegesis, the bishop adds:

Lest we seem to have made the comparison inconsiderately of the dove bearing the image of the lapsed, the prophet rebukes the city (Jerusalem) as a dove, that is, the character of the lapsed: The dove harkens not to the voice; that is, the illustrious and redeemed city receives not teaching and trusts not in the Lord.[27]

The bishop has carefully introduced the notion of a double typology:

The dove signifies to us of itself a double type (*dico illam id est columbam duplicem nobis per semetipsam significare figuram*). The first and chief [type] is the Spirit and by its mouth the sacrament of baptism which is provided for the whole human race, and by its heavenly plan it is celebrated in the Church only.[28]

The second type is that of the dove, sent out of the ark. The dove is the image of the lapsed, but it returns to the ark and then on its second return it bears an olive branch, the symbol of victory. For the bishop it is a clear symbol of those who lapsed under Decius and returned to the church in repentance and, so strengthened, remained firm in the second outbreak under Gallus and Volusianus.

Like Cyprian, this anonymous bishop, in focusing on questions concerning the holiness of the membership of the Church, offers no systematic innovation in African hermeneutics. He follows the traditional emphasis on typology.[29] It was the genius of Tyconius to systematize this unusual feature of typology by which a single referent had both positive and negative signification. The importance of the issue of this double nature of the biblical typology cannot be overestimated when one considers the ecclesial nature of African exegesis, that is, that Scripture speaks directly to the here-and-now of the Church in words of warning or encouragement. It was on double typology that Tyconius, the fourth-century African exegete, founded his hermeneutics of a bipartite typology of Scripture addressed to a bipartite Church community.

This reflection on Augustine's treatment of ambiguity in *De doctrina christiana* has been limited to historical and contextual questions rather than to an exploration of Augustine's rich intuitions about the multivalency of language.[30] The focus has been on the structuring of the discussion of ambiguity within the frame of the whole treatise. The importance that Augustine gives to this topic reflects his awareness that this is a key notion in the native African tradition. The question of scriptural ambiguity was the point of intersection between the earlier exegetical tradition and the thought of Augustine, whose powerful entrance into active ministry in the African church was to send shock waves through the older tradition. The significance of that impact has yet to be fully assessed.

Notes

1. *DDC* 3.25.36.

2. *DDC* 3.30–37.

3. See *A Conflict of Christian Hermeneutics in Roman Africa: Tyconius and Augustine: Protocol of Fifty-Eighth Colloquy*, ed. C. Kannengiesser and P. Bright (Berkeley, 1989): C. Kannengiesser, "A Conflict of Christian Hermeneutics in Roman Africa: Tyconius and Augustine," 1–22; P. Bright, "Tyconius and His Interpreters: A Study of the Epitomes of the *Book of Rules*," 23–39; Response by H. Chadwick, 49–55.

4. *DDC* 3.1.1 (*On Christian Doctrine*, trans. D. W. Robertson, Jr. [New York, 1958], 78).

5. *DDC* prologue (Robertson, 4).

6. *DDC* 3.27.38 (Robertson, 102).

7. *DDC* 2.6.7 (Robertson, 37).

8. *DDC* 2.6.8 (Robertson, 38).

9. *DDC* 2.7.9–11 (Robertson, 38–40).

10. *DDC* 2.8.12–42.63 (Robertson, 78).

11. *DDC* 3.5.9–24.34.

12. *DDC* 3.5.9 (Robertson, 84).

13. *DDC* 3.25.35 (Robertson, 100).

14. *DDC* 3.25.37.

15. *DDC* 3.25.37 (Robertson, 101).

16. *DDC* 3.30.42–37.55.

17. *DDC* 3.30.43.

18. *Tyconius: The Book of Rules*, trans. William Babcock, (Atlanta, Ga., 1989), 15.

19. *Tyconius: The Book of Rules*, trans. Babcock, 19.

20. *DDC* 3.30.42 (Robertson, 104).

21. *The Writings of Cyprian*, vol. 2, *A Treatise against Novatian*, trans. R. E. Wallis, Ante-Nicene Christian Library 13 (Edinburgh, 1884), 430. This treatise was published by Erasmus in 1520 among the works of Cyprian.

22. *A Treatise against Novatian*, trans. R. E. Wallis, 432.

23. *A Treatise against Novatian*, trans. R. E. Wallis, 432.

24. Novatian, *On the Jewish Feasts*, trans. R. E. Wallis, *The Writings of Cyprian*, vol. 2, Ante-Nicene Library 13: 384–386.

25. *A Treatise against Novatian*, trans. R. E. Wallis, 433.

26. *A Treatise against Novatian*, trans. R. E. Wallis, 434.

27. *A Treatise against Novatian*, trans. R. E. Wallis, 434.

28. *A Treatise against Novatian*, trans. R. E. Wallis, 433; *CSEL* 3:3, ed. G. Hartel (Vienna, 1871), 55:20–22.

29. See Michael Fahey, *Cyprian and the Bible: A Study in Third-Century Exegesis* (Tübingen, 1971).

30. See Rowan Williams, "Language, Reality, and Desire in Augustine's *De Doctrina*," *Journal of Literature and Theology* (July 1989): 138–150.

Codex Leningradensis Q.v.I.3: Some Unresolved Problems

KENNETH B. STEINHAUSER

1.1 Current state of the research

In a brief but important article entitled "A Fourth Century Manuscript of Saint Augustine?" published in 1959, William M. Green could hardly restrain his enthusiasm upon having been confronted with the oldest known manuscript of any work of Augustine.[1] In preparing a critical edition of *De doctrina christiana*,[2] Green had had opportunity to study Codex Leningradensis Q.v.I.3 in some detail. He came to two conclusions:

First, the manuscript was written sometime before 426. Green had observed that the last two books of *De doctrina christiana* were omitted from the manuscript. In 426 while writing the *Retractationes* Augustine noticed that he had neglected to complete *De doctrina christiana*; he informed his readers that he was interrupting the *Retractationes* to finish the work at that time. The Leningrad Codex is unique in that it is the incomplete edition of *De doctrina christiana*. Green concluded that the codex must have been written before the completion of *De doctrina christiana* in 426 since it contains the earlier incomplete version. It would have been illogical to produce a manuscript containing the earlier edition if the complete edition had already been available. Thus, the Leningrad Codex is the only known manuscript of Augustine's works to have been written during his lifetime.

Second, Green asserted that the manuscript had been produced in Hippo. This conclusion is based on the fact that a chronological catalogue as well as copies of the writings of Augustine must have been present at Hippo, where Augustine lived and worked. Since the Leningrad Codex contains four works of Augustine in the order in which they were written, the codex was probably compiled at Hippo where this information would have been readily available.

Green left one important question open, noting that "we have no indication at whose order it [the manuscript] was prepared."[3]

Almost a decade later, in 1968, Almut Mutzenbecher published a detailed study of the Leningrad Codex.[4] Her study, which is very useful, included a complete bibliography, three photographs of folios, and a physical description of the manuscript, its contents, paleography, abbreviations, orthography, decoration, corrections, and marginalia. She also traced the history of the manuscript from its possible origin in Africa, through northern Italy and France, from Corbie to its present resting place in Leningrad, formerly and again Saint Petersburg. I will occasionally refer to the details of her description to the extent that they may be necessary for my purposes here.

She took exception to Green's conclusion that the codex had been produced in Hippo. Certainly Augustine would have sent *De diuersis questionibus ad Simplicianum* immediately after its completion and would not have waited to append *Contra epistulam Manichaei quam uocant fundamenti*, *De agone christiano*, and the first two books of *De doctrina christiana* to the codex. Since paleographical investigation brings one no further, Mutzenbecher turned her attention to the text of the manuscript and, using three textual samples, demonstrated that the text is too deficient to have been written directly from Augustine's library in Hippo. She does concede, however, that the codex may have been produced at Carthage.

1.2 Present Hypothesis

At present I wish to advance a hypothesis which attempts to reconcile these opposing views concerning the place of production while at the same time addressing the still open question posed by Green: Who commissioned the codex? In my opinion, the Leningrad Codex or its immediate prototype had been commissioned by Augustine himself to be sent to his longtime friend, Simplicianus, bishop of Milan. The simplest way to justify this hypothesis is to construct a probable chronology of events surrounding the production of the manuscript.

2.1 *Interrogata Simpliciani*

Within several months after the death of Ambrose on April 4, 397, Simplicianus was appointed bishop of Milan. The exact date of his appointment is unknown and will probably never be known. The newly consecrated bishop Simplicianus wrote to the then presbyter Augustine asking him various questions concerning the letter of Paul to the Romans and the books of Kings. The fact that at the time Simplicianus was a bishop and Augustine a priest is consistent with the testimony of the usually reliable Gennadius of Marseilles.[5] For Augustine this type of request was not at all unusual. His correspondence is filled with similar petitions.

For example, *Letter 54* and *Letter 55* constitute a response to a certain Januarius on liturgical issues. Augustine seemed somewhat irritated with Januarius's request:

> I should prefer to know beforehand what answer you would give to the questions you have asked me; in that way I could answer much more briefly by approving or correcting your answers, as it would be very easy for me to agree with you or set you right.[6]

In other words, the busy Augustine wanted Januarius to do some of the intellectual work involved rather than simply expect him to provide all the answers.

We find a similar reaction to the questions of Deogratias, a priest of Carthage. In *Letter 102* Augustine wrote: "When you choose to refer to me the questions propounded to you, I imagine you are not actuated by sloth but by an excessive affection for me, which makes you want to hear me explain things which you know yourself."[7]

However, in his response to Simplicianus in *Letter 37* Augustine is extremely solicitous:

> But, whence comes this good fortune for my literary labor—and I have truly toiled over the writing of some of my books—that my works should be read by your Worthiness, except that the Lord to whom my heart is subject has wished to comfort my troubles and free me from fear?[8]

Augustine writes to Simplicianus of the "points of controversy which you have been so kind as to bid me solve."[9] Augustine was frequently prevailed upon to deal with theological and exegetical questions. Yet he is much more enthused about writing to Simplicianus than to others to whom he frequently shows irritation and even anger bordering on contempt. He is obviously delighted to write to Simplicianus in detail, and Augustine himself states that he labored arduously over the task.

Augustine's positive reaction to Simplicianus's request may have been due two factors. First, Simplicianus was an old friend. Augustine mentions him with fondness in his *Confessions*.[10] Furthermore, by urging Augustine to read the Neoplatonist philosophers Simplicianus had facilitated his conversion. Second, although the work of Simplicianus is lost, one suspects that his questions were erudite and detailed. Sophisticated questions which showed some thought in their formulation would have challenged Augustine who would welcome the opportunity of dealing with genuine intellectual problems. This contrasts with the questions of Januarius and Deogratias which appear to have been superficial and annoying to Augustine.

Gennadius mentions a pedagogical work of Simplicianus, written in the form of a letter, in which the bishop instructs by asking questions. Indeed, this may very well have been the writing to which Augustine was responding, especially since the comments of Gennadius are reminiscent of the title contained in the Leningrad Codex: *et multas ad eius personam scripturarum questiones absduit eius epistola propositionum in qua interrogando disciturus docet doctorem.*[11] Perhaps for this reason the first treatise in the Leningrad Codex is entitled *Ad interrogata Simpliciani* rather than the traditional *De diuersis questionibus ad Simplicianum.* From Augustine's own perspective he was dealing with some diverse questions. However, from the bishop of Milan's perspective, Augustine would have been answering Simplicianus's work entitled *Interrogata.* In any event, the *Interrogata Simpliciani* is lost.

2.2. De diuersis questionibus ad Simplicianum

Augustine was ordained bishop of Hippo shortly before August 28, 397, when his signature, for the first time as bishop, appears on the transcript of a provincial council at Carthage.[12] According to his own testimony the first work written after his episcopal consecration was the *De diuersis questionibus ad Simplicianum,* which the Leningrad Codex identifies as *Ad interrogata Simpliciani.*[13] In other words, although the *Interrogata Simpliciani* was sent to Augustine before his episcopal consecration, he wrote his response after having been ordained bishop.

2.3 The Lost "Letter Full of Good Joys" of Simplicianus to Augustine

Meanwhile, Simplicianus wrote a letter to Augustine congratulating him on his episcopal ordination and wishing him well. This letter is lost, but the existence of such a letter may be ascertained through a careful reading of Augustine's *Letter 37.* First and foremost, in spite of being joined in the Leningrad Codex, the *Epistola ad Simplicianum (Letter 37)* and *De diuersis questionibus ad Simplicianum* are separate literary pieces and must be analyzed as such. For example, *Letter 37* is redundant with the introduction and conclusion of *De diuersis questionibus.* Augustine is usually quite content to include personal greetings and remarks within the treatise he is writing when that treatise is directed to an individual. There are numerous examples of this practice among his works. Even his masterpiece, *The City of God*, begins with a personal greeting to Marcellinus.[14] Such personal comments are also to be found at the beginning of *De diuersis questionibus* and at its end, where Augustine excuses himself as being too long-winded and begs the prayers of Simplicianus for his errors.[15] Furthermore, in *Letter 37*, but not in *De diuersis questionibus*, Augustine asks Simplicianus to correct any errors he may find.[16] Since Simplicianus had posed complex and specific exegetical questions, it makes little sense for Augustine to respond to these questions in detail and then subsequently to ask Simplicianus to correct the answers to those very questions which Simplicianus, by his own admission, had been unable to answer.

Second, Augustine begins *Letter 37* by mentioning the congratulations or greetings of Simplicianus in the context of his own episcopal ordination:

> I have received the letter sent by the kindness of your Holiness, a letter full
> of good joys, because you are mindful of me, and love me, as you are wont,
> and because it is a personal satisfaction to you that the Lord has deigned in
> His mercy to confer on me something of His gifts, through no merits of my
> own.[17]

Taken in isolation the reference to "gifts" may be considered ambiguous. Mutzenbecher prefers to interpret the "gifts" as Augustine's literary talents.[18] Josef Martin, however, sees the passage referring to Augustine's elevation to the episcopacy.[19]

Much more significant than the "gifts" is the initial phrase of the letter, which is abundantly clear in Latin: *Plenas bonorum gaudiorum litteras, quod sis memor mei meque, ut soles, diligas . . . accepi.*[20] With explicit references to joy, love, and remembrance, Augustine is obviously responding to a profoundly personal greeting which he had recently received from Simplicianus. Perhaps one may need to recall that *litterae* is a plural form with a singular meaning—Augustine is referring to a single letter. Simplicianus's "letter full of good joys" must have been extremely important to Augustine, since the placing of the phrase at the very beginning makes it the dominant topic of Augustine's *Letter 37*. This would presuppose that Simplicianus had sent Augustine some sort of congratulations or best wishes—namely, "a letter full of good joys"—on the occasion of his episcopal ordination. The congratulations could not have been contained in the *Interrogata Simpliciani,* a theological treatise to which Augustine responded substantively in *De diuersis questionibus*. In addition, the work known to Gennadius, which enjoyed a wider and prior circulation, could not have contained such a personal greeting. Gennadius also maintains that Augustine and Simplicianus carried on an extended correspondence, which would account for the phrase *ut soles*. In summation, *Letter 37* implies the existence of a lost letter of personal congratulations from the bishop Simplicianus to the newly appointed bishop Augustine.

2.4 The Other Treatises of the Leningrad Codex

During the winter of 397 Augustine also wrote *Contra epistulam Manichaei quam uocant fundamenti*, *De agone christiano*, and *De doctrina christiana* up to the word *fermentaretur* in the third book.[21] His failure to send his response to the *Interrogata Simpliciani* immediately could hardly be considered an unreasonable or unnecessary delay since the Mediterranean Sea would have been closed to shipping for about six months of the year anyway. Even if Augustine had finished his *De diuersis questionibus ad Simplicianum* as early as September of 397, he would have been unable to send it until the following April, that is, in the spring of 398. In addition, the logistics of sending the codex overseas was by no means simple. Some individual would have had to have been entrusted to carry the manuscript personally to Simplicianus.

To illustrate the possibility of delay and ensuing confusion, one need only recall the correspondence of Augustine and Jerome, when Augustine's letter to Jerome was delayed en route in Rome. By the time the letter reached Jerome, its contents had leaked out and Jerome was angered with Augustine for having written nasty things about him behind his back. The letter in question was reported to be circulating at Rome and in Italy, and the only one to whom it did not come was the one to whom it was addressed.[22] Augustine insisted that he had written directly to Jerome and through no fault of his own the letter had been intercepted in Rome and made public. The animosity between Augustine and Jerome over that incident lasted many years. The incident demonstrates that, even after the commencement of shipping in the spring of 398, several months could easily have been needed for the codex to have arrived in the hands of Simplicianus.

This leads to an important question. Why did Augustine interrupt his *De doctrina christiana*? The reason for the interruption is disclosed indirectly in *Letter 38*, which is, according to the Augustinian corpus, chronologically the very next letter after *Letter 37* to Simplicianus. In *Letter 38* Augustine complains to the presbyter Profuturus of being temporarily disabled by ill health: "In spirit, as far as it pleases the Lord and he deigns to give me strength, I am well; but, in body, I am in bed, for I can neither walk nor stand nor sit because of the pain and swelling of hemorrhoids and chafing."[23] Rather than delay further, Augustine sent the manuscript with *De doctrina Christiana* incomplete.

Green maintains that Augustine would not have published an incomplete work.[24] That depends upon what one means by *incomplete*. Augustine certainly would not have published an unedited or uncorrected work, as occurred with *De trinitate*, which was published without Augustine's permission prior to final editing.[25] That incident so angered Augustine that he was tempted to abandon the project altogether. However, he did occasionally publish an "unfinished" work. For example, the *City of God* appeared in installments.[26] This is clearly the plan which he laid down in advance and the rationale behind the summaries of the previous installment at the beginning of each new installment. After discovering *De Genesi ad litteram imperfectus liber* in his library while writing his *Retractationes*, Augustine allowed that work to be published as is.[27] In other words, the publication of an unfinished work is not inconsistent with Augustine's customary practice. However, it is also clear that Augustine seldom, if ever, began writing without a plan. He hardly would have begun a work without knowing how that work would end. I would maintain that in 397 Augustine intended to write *De doctrina christiana* in four books. Because of ill health he simply failed to complete the task at that time.

2.5. Augustine's *Letter 37*

Finally, Augustine wrote *Letter 37*, which was prefixed to the collected four works. Actually, *Letter 37* is the key to understanding the Leningrad Codex and its composition. Augustine wrote the letter for two reasons. First, *Letter 37* was a response to the lost letter of Simplicianus, in which Simplicianus had congratulated Augustine on the occasion of his episcopal ordination. Second, *Letter 37* was an introduction not to *De diuersis questionibus* alone but to all four works contained in the codex. In other words, *Letter 37* was specifically intended to accompany the Leningrad Codex or its prototype on its journey to Simplicianus. In the letter, Augustine referred to a twofold literary activity—both those writings which Simplicianus wished him to undertake and those writings which might some day fall into the hands of Simplicianus. *Letter 37* only makes sense as an introduction to the entire codex because, as I demonstrated above, *Letter 37* is redundant with the introduction to *De diuersis questionibus*. However, *Letter 37* is not redundant with the entire codex because it alludes to three other items: first, those additional works of Augustine which Simplicianus did not request and should feel free to correct; second, the "gift" of Augustine's episcopal ordination; and, finally, the lost "letter full of good joys" sent by Simplicianus to Augustine. In summation, *Letter* 37, the last piece completed, was placed first in the codex not as an introduction to *De diuersis questionibus* but as an introduction to the entire codex and a greeting to Simplicianus.

3.1 The Production of the Leningrad Codex

Augustine then forwarded the material to Carthage, where an elegant manuscript was prepared at his command, which was subsequently sent to Simplicianus. Indeed, occasional red border decoration led Mutzenbecher to describe the Leningrad Codex as "pretentious."[28] There is sufficient evidence to maintain, as I do, that Augustine lived and wrote in Hippo but had his works copied in Carthage, which was more significant culturally, with both a university and a major scriptorium. In fact, in *Letter* 24 of the Augustinian collection, Paulinus of Nola mentions having sent a codex of Eusebius's *Ecclesiastical History* to Carthage for copying.[29] Of all the cities of Africa, why did Paulinus have the codex copied in Carthage? Obviously there must have been a workshop there. On the basis of paleographical evidence Bernhard Bischoff asserts that an elaborate Christian book trade was carried on at Carthage.[30]

Augustine certainly retained archival copies of his own works for reference at Hippo; he could not have written his *Retractationes* without having all his previous works at hand. Possidius states that Augustine's works were extensively and systematically circulated among the Christians of North Africa.[31] I maintain that manuscript production took place at Carthage and distribution went out from Carthage, a conveniently located port city and commercial hub. The recopying of the Leningrad Codex at Carthage would account for the textual errors which are so troublesome to Mutzenbecher. In fact, Martin, in preparing his edition of *De doctrina christiana,* posits the existence of a lost archetype to the Leningrad Codex.[32]

There remains a consensus of scholarly opinion which places the Leningrad Codex in Africa, at either Hippo or Carthage, and dates it early in the fifth century. If the Leningrad Codex did not emanate out of Augustine's residence at Hippo, it was certainly a very early copy of its exemplar.

3.2 The Program of the Leningrad Codex

The title page reads *Aurelii Augustini ad interrogata Simpliciani* in two lines covering two columns while the original titles and colophons of the remainder of the manuscript are limited to one column.[33] In other words, the entire manuscript is identified as being sent to Simplicianus. The indication of a title was an expected convention, since Augustine states in *Letter 40* that he was confused by the absence of a title from a work of Jerome, probably *De uiris illustribus.*[34] *Letter 37* does not contain its address in the Leningrad Codex.[35] This is not without reason since the letter was intended as a preface to the entire codex. Indeed, the letter itself was an address.

Green suggested that perhaps the Leningrad Codex represents the *Gesammelte Werke* of Augustine, containing all the works he had written, as bishop, to that time.[36] I would prefer to consider the Leningrad Codex a *Festschrift*—that is, a gift from Augustine, bishop of Hippo, to Simplicianus, bishop of Milan, on the occasion of Augustine's own episcopal ordination.

Furthermore, the earliest marginalia and secondary corrections may be traced to northern Italy, placing the first historical witness to the manuscript in the region to which it would have been sent. Paulinus of Nola mentions a similar gift in *Letter 24* where Paulinus thanks Alypius for sending his five books of Augustine.[37] Paulinus responded to this gift in turn by giving Alypius the copy of Eusebius's *Ecclesiastical History* which according to his direction had been copied at Carthage. In *Letter 25* Paulinus tells Augustine that the gift of his five books was beneficial "not only for our own instruction but for the profit of the church in many cities."[38]

In conclusion, the conceptual program of the Leningrad Codex emerges out of the reconstructed chronology of events surrounding its production. A codex, as a collection of several works, may have a purpose which goes beyond, or even differs from, the stated purpose of each work contained in that codex. In other words, the various treatises, their titles, their contents, and their order are all significant factors which need to be taken into consideration in evaluating an entire codex. The plan or arrangement of the Leningrad Codex indicates that it was a presentational volume, a gift prepared for the elderly bishop Simplicianus at the request of his younger protégé Augustine. Only when one interprets *Letter 37* in relationship to the entire codex which it introduces does that letter make sense. *Letter 37* refers to items extraneous to *De diuersis questionibus*— Augustine's episcopal ordination and other writings of Augustine. The works in the Leningrad Codex, with the exception of *Letter 37* which was prefixed to the beginning of the manuscript, appear in the order in which Augustine wrote them according to his own testimony in the *Retractationes.*[39] However, the works in that same order also constitute a very suitable gift to his long-time friend, mentor, and confidant Simplicianus. First, Augustine answered Simplicianus's questions on Romans and Kings in *De diuersis questionibus*, as Simplicianus himself had requested. Then, Augustine responded to the Manichaean catechism, the so-called *Fundamentum*.[40] Simplicianus would certainly have known of Augustine's Manichaean years. In fact, Simplicianus had helped Augustine overcome Manichaeism by introducing him to the writings of the Platonists or, more accurately, the Neoplatonists. Next, *De agone Christiano* and *De doctrina christiana* were two handbooks—the one for simple folk and the other for scholars. Simplicianus could have used *Christian Combat* in his pastoral ministry as bishop of Milan. With the first two books of *Christian Instruction* Augustine was giving Simplicianus a manual which would enable him to solve his exegetical problems on his own in the future. The Leningrad Codex itself has an organization, a message, and a coherence which identifies it as a presentational manuscript—a gift from Augustine to Simplicianus, *Aureli Augustini ad interrogata Simpliciani*.

Notes

1. William M. Green, "A Fourth-Century Manuscript of Saint Augustine?" *RBen* 69 (1959): 191–197.

2. *DDC* (ed. Green, *CSEL* 80).

3. Green, 197.

4. Almut Mutzenbecher, "Codex Leningrad Q.v.I.3 (Corbie): Ein Beitrag zu seiner Beschreibung," *SE* 18 (1967–68): 406–50; for an updated bibliography, see David Ganz, *Corbie in the Carolingian Renaissance*, Beihefte der Francia 20 (Sigmaringen, 1990): 155.

5. Gennadius *De uiris inlustribus* 36.171 (ed. Carl Albrecht Bernoulli, *Sammlung ausgewählter Quellenschriftung zur Kirchen- und Dogmengeschichte* [hereafter *SQ*] 11: 74).

6. *Epistula* 54. 1.1 (ed. A. Goldbacher, *CSEL* 34, 2:158–159; trans. W. Parsons, FC 12:252).

7. *Epistula* 102.1 (*CSEL* 34, 2:544; FC 18:148).

8. *Epistula* 37.2 (*CSEL* 34, 2:63; FC 12:168). *Epistula* 37 is also available in the edition of Almut Mutzenbecher, CC 44:3–4.

9. *Epistula* 37.3 (*CSEL* 34, 2:64; FC 12:168).

10. *Confessiones* 8.1–2 (ed. L. Verheijen, CC 27:113–16).

11. *De uiris inlustribus* 36.171 (ed. Bernoulli, *SQ* 11:74).

12. *Breuiarium Hipponense*, sessio diei 28.aug.397 (ed. C. Munier, CC 149:49).

13. *Retractationes* 2.1(27) (ed. A. Mutzenbecher, CC 57:89).

14. *De ciuitate dei* 1.prefatio (ed. B. Dombart and A. Kalb, CC 47:1).

15. *De diuersis questionibus ad Simplicianum* 1.prefatio (ed. A. Mutzenbecher, CC 44:7) and 2.conclusio (CC 44:90–91).

16. *Epistula* 37.3 (*CSEL* 34, 2:64).

17. *Epistula* 37.1 (*CSEL* 34, 2:63; FC 12:168).

18. Mutzenbecher, *CC* 44:xxxii, n. 6.

19. Josef Martin, "Abfassung, Veröffentlichung und Überlieferung von Augustins Schrift *De doctrina christiana*," *Traditio* 18 (1962): 77.

20. *Epistula* 37.1 (*CSEL* 34, 2:63).

21. *Retractationes* 2.4 (30) (*CC* 57:92).

22. *Epistula* 72.1.1 (*CSEL* 34, 2:256; FC 12:329).

23. *Epistula* 38.1 (*CSEL* 34, 2:64; FC 12:169).

24. Green, 193–194.

25. *Retractationes* 2.15(41) (*CC* 57:101).

26. *De ciuitate dei* 5.26 (*CC* 47:163).

27. *Retractationes* 1.18(17) (*CC* 57:54).

28. Mutzenbecher, "Codex Leningrad Q.v.I.3 (Corbie)," 412, uses the word *anspruchsvoll*.

29. *Epistula* 24. 3 (*CSEL* 34, 1:75).

30. Bernhard Bischoff, *Latin Palaeography: Antiquity and the Middle Ages* (New York, 1990), 184.

31. *Vita sancti Augustini* 7 (ed. Michele Pellegrino, 60–63).

32. Martin, 85.

33. Mutzenbecher, "Codex Leningrad Q.v.I.3 (Corbie)," 410–411.

34. *Epistula* 40.2.2 (*CSEL* 34, 2:71).

35. Mutzenbecher, *CC* 44:3: *Inscriptio deest in C.*

36. Green, 195.

37. *Epistula* 24.2 (*CSEL* 34, 1:74).

38. *Epistula* 25.l (*CSEL* 34, 1:78; FC 12:71).

39. *Retractationes* 2.1–4 (27–30) (*CC* 57:89–93).

40. For further information on the lost Manichaean catechism, see Erich Feldmann, *Die "Epistula Fundamenti" der nordafrikanischen Manichäer: Versuch einer Rekonstruktion* (Altenberge, 1987).

Litterae

Since, after words have reverberated upon the air, they pass away and last no longer than the sound they make, signs of words have been provided by means of letters.

De doctrina christiana 2.4

De doctrina christiana:
A Classic of Western Culture?

CHRISTOPH SCHÄUBLIN

Anyone who ventures to follow the development of Augustine's thought step by step through the four books of De doctrina christiana should, in the end, be in a position to give a fairly clear explanation to himself and others of the content, structure, and aims of the work. If he cannot, it is not the author's fault. For Augustine is evidently genuinely anxious to help his readers; in particular, he takes the opportunity, whenever he reaches the end of a passage of argument, to summarize what he has said and to give a preview of what is to come. Yet if we consider the lack of unanimity in recent research, it must be said that he has had little thanks for his efforts. He has actually been accused of incompetence in the arrangement of his material, because modern techniques of analysis failed to produce a satisfactory result. Furthermore, scholars have not been sure what the De doctrina christiana is really about; consequently, neither have they been able to decide on its intended audience.[1] Already Cassiodorus, who seems to have been the first writer to be clearly influenced by the work, seems no longer to have interpreted it entirely as Augustine intended,[2] and certain tendencies in the more recent history of thought have made their own contribution to the general disagreement. Surprisingly, it is only lately that scholars have managed to trace the course of Augustine's argument precisely and have thus discovered that from the outset it develops, with as much consistency as one could wish, a set plan.[3] As the next stage, it should now be possible to bridge the gap between the attempts made so far to understand the work.

Without more ado, then: De doctrina christiana is not a hermeneutical or rhetorical handbook for the preacher;[4] but neither does it contain the vision of a "culture chrétienne"[5] or the blueprint for a universal Christian "paideia."[6] The truth, if indeed it can be found, does not so much fall somewhere between these two propositions as lie hidden behind them. Their main significance for us is that—though they treat partial truths as the whole answer—we see in them the most recent examples of *De doctrina christiana*'s extraordinarily fruitful history of influence, which has continued for many centuries.[7]

What then, is Augustine talking about? He proposes to give "some instructions on the treatment of the Scriptures" (*praecepta quaedam tractandarum scripturarum* [DDC prologue 1]). This methodical "treatment" (*tractatio*)[8] is carried out in two stages: one first discovers (*invenire*) what must be understood by the text; and then one puts it into appropriate words, to show (*proferre*) what has been understood (*DDC* 1.1). Clearly Augustine alludes here to the well known system of rhetorical *partes* (*inventio, dispositio, elocutio, memoria, pronuntiatio* or *actio*),[9] but in fact he restricts his discussion to two: *inventio* and *elocutio*. *Elocutio* is discussed in book 4; the problems arising from it will not be dealt with here.[10] *Inventio* is at the forefront of the discussion for three-quarters of the work. Augustine attributes to it a new role, in that he expects it to contribute, not just to a successful style of argument, but to the correct understanding of Holy Scripture. In fact, it fulfills a hermeneutical function—and itself divides again into two *partes*.

In order to take the teaching of the Bible to heart, we must, on the one hand, understand the *res*—that is, know what the text is about—and, on the other, be aware of the problems that arise from the fact that the *res* are communicated by *verba* (or, as Augustine says [DDC 1.2], through *signa*); that is, by means of language and in written form. This distinction also has its roots in rhetorical teaching, one of the principles of which is that every utterance consists precisely of *res* and *verba*.[11] *Res* and *verba* are, respectively, the objects of *inventio* and *elocutio*.[12] Thus Augustine makes the same rhetorical schema on which he bases the work as a whole the basis for that part of it which he dedicated to *inventio*. Now as the object of *inventio* is the understanding of Holy Scripture, the terms *res* and *verba* acquire a different meaning. The *res* are not those ideas on which the "Christian orator" will speak at the end of his *tractatio scripturarum*, but are primarily the very *res* which the biblical authors are concerned to communicate. Equally, Augustine's reader should apply the rules of *elocutio* not for the purpose of manipulating words himself but in order to understand the implications of how the biblical authors harnessed the potential of language. For once this is understood, we ought to be able to make the step from Biblical *verba* to divine *res*. Basically, Augustine is simply developing a critical technique that was typical of both Christian and pagan textual analysis in the imperial period. Beginning with the assumption that every author works according to the codified principles of rhetoric, those same principles were adopted in reverse, so to speak, for the task of interpretation.

Now, of the three books which are taken up by the subject of *inventio*—that is, what the message of the Holy Scriptures is and how we gain access to it—the first book is dedicated to the *res*. Here Augustine sets himself the task of grasping and bringing to light the heart of the Bible's message. He finds this, the *summa* (*DDC* 1.39), in the *gemina caritas* (1.40) of love of God and love of neighbor and in finding it reveals at the same time the touchstone for all interpretation of the Scriptures. If an interpreter infers from any passage a meaning that goes against this double commandment to love, then he has not understood correctly. On the other hand, if this commandment does emerge from his interpretation, then no harm is done, even if he has not in fact hit upon the actual intention (*sententia*) of the biblical author.[13]

Clearly the difficulties of interpretation arise essentially from the demand for an interpretation that does justice to the author's *sententia* as well as—most importantly—helping to bring out the full force of the commandment to love. The main problem, apart from those relating to the transmission of the text, is that the Bible represents and gives expression to its message by means of *verba*, or *signa*. That is why Augustine concentrates on these in books 2 and 3. Yet not all the problems treated in these books belong to the domain of *elocutio*; indeed, Augustine's discussion raises many questions which are really the province of the *grammaticus*, the ancient philologist. This is especially the case where Augustine deals with words in their "true" sense (as *propria signa*). For he makes a further subdivision, a double one this time (*DDC* 2.5). A text resists comprehension either because it contains "unknown signs" (*ignota signa*), in other words those relating to areas of specialist knowledge; or because it is riddled with "ambiguous signs" (*ambigua signa*). Both types of *signa* can also appear sometimes in a literal, sometimes in a metaphorical sense (as *propria* or *translata*). This gives Augustine the pattern for his argument: in book 2 he will apply himself to *ignota* signa, in book 3 to *ambigua signa*, and in both books he deals with *propria signa* first and *translata signa* second.

Book 2 has given rise to more misunderstanding than the others, chiefly because many interpreters failed to recognize its position in the overall structure of the work. At first, though, there is no reason at all to doubt Augustine's intentions. Developing his argument according to the most rigorous logic, he asks what kinds of knowledge—that is, what disciplines—are needed for the interpretation of the *ignota signa* of the Bible. *Ignota signa propria* (i.e., unknown signs in their literal sense) arise from the fact that Latin speakers read the Scriptures in translation; indeed, in the case of the Old Testament, the Latin translators were themselves working with a translation—the Septuagint. What really unsettles the reader is that from time to time isolated words, such as interjections, are not translated; or that often the translations, in their "infinite variety" (*DDC* 2.16), differ markedly from one another. In either case it helps to know the languages—Greek and Hebrew—from which the translations were made.

With regard to the *ignota signa translata*, on the other hand, Augustine finds himself compelled to embark on a somewhat lengthier discussion. It is conceivable that in some cases these too may be understood if one has a good grasp of the languages (2.23); but more often the problem arises from the interpreter's ignorance of certain facts of history and nature, which were adopted into the figurative language of the biblical authors and thus acquired a special significance (2.24). Anyone who wishes to grasp the precise import of such passages must first understand the fact or phenomenon which forms the basis of the figure, by consulting the relevant science—be it zoology, petrology, botany, numerology, or music (2.24–28).

This brings Augustine to the topic of the sciences in general—the pagan sciences, that is. He regards the issue as so important that he proposes to conduct a thorough investigation (*DDC* 2.29).[14] The following discussion with which he fulfills this promise simply has been misunderstood;[15] it is, in fact, positively misleading. For on the one hand it is inseparably connected to the previous section on the figurative use of *ignota signa,* and several explicit references should do away with any doubt that Augustine does indeed look on it as part of a unified plan.[16] Thus, he evidently still intends to explain *ignota,* "the unknown," with reference to various specialist branches of knowledge. Yet, on the other hand, he now abruptly shifts his viewpoint and devotes himself no longer primarily to the *ignota signa* as they occur in the Scriptures; rather, he turns to describing in more general terms a fully developed system of sciences and to assessing the potential contribution of each individual discipline to the interpretation of the Bible (2.29–57).

With this end in view, he distinguishes and categorizes individual fields of knowledge according to a variety of criteria and arranges them in a complex hierarchy. The objects of knowledge either depend on "conventions" or they are simply "given" (the distinction made here is based on the ancient Greek one between νόμος and φύσις; although in most cases Augustine says not "given by Nature" but "instituted by God.")[17] "Conventions" may be agreed upon between men and demons (the "sciences" devoted to these "superstitious conventions" are magic, astrology, and all forms of divination [*DDC* 2.30–37]) or between men and men. These purely human "conventions" are either "superfluous" (all the arts) or "essential" (in other words, social conventions, most importantly writing and speech [2.38–40]). On the other hand, the "divine institutions" are divided into those concerning physical sensation and those which concern the intellect (2.41). The objects of knowledge through the senses are further subdivided, since they are not all apprehended in the same way. Some are "shown" or "notated," such as history and geography (2.42–45), others "demonstrated by proof," such as astronomy (2.46). The third class are handed on in the form of "practical experience," such as the work of craftsmen (2.47). The areas of knowledge which exercise the intellect are separate again; these are governed by the laws of logical thought and effective argument (dialectic and rhetoric) and those of numerical proportion (2.48–56). After a brief summary, Augustine finally allows himself, almost by way of an appendix, a reference to philosophy, and in particular to the Platonists (2.59–63). For, he says, we should not be afraid even of this, but make use of it, insofar as its subject matter and doctrines are true and compatible with our faith.

Looking back over this bare outline of a "system of sciences" we can be sure of two things. First, when the question of the sciences comes up and Augustine says that he wants to submit it to closer scrutiny (*DDC* 2.29), we have no grounds for assuming that he is moving on to a completely different topic. For if we try to define the place of this section in the overall plan of the work, we find that its only possible relevance is to the complex of arguments surrounding the *ignota signa* (in their figurative sense), and Augustine himself repeatedly characterized book 2 as being concerned exclusively with *ignota signa*.[18] And second, however, Augustine's exposition here touches on *ignota signa* only at certain points. Certainly history, geography, and astronomy may help to unlock their mysteries, but the question remains how far these sciences have to do with *signa translata,* and whether they are not more relevant to the understanding of *signa propria*. Dialectic and rhetoric, meanwhile, elude such a classification by their very nature. The fact is, as has been pointed out, that Augustine is here no longer primarily governed by the needs of the biblical interpreter but is allowing himself to follow a course dictated by a preexisting scheme. For the sake of a comprehensive treatment of this scheme, he goes so far as to include in his discussion such "sciences" as magic and astrology (2.30–37), which ought to be utterly shunned by a Christian. Moreover, his efforts to be thorough result in a second mention of the science of numbers (2.56), with which he has already dealt (2.25). Thus it becomes obvious that the "system of sciences" is a self-contained, extraneous element which does not precisely fit the context. If we consider the structure of the whole work, the intended function of this discussion within it is clear. However, because of the prearrangement of this foreign material, that function is fulfilled only in a limited sense, and not explicitly enough, so that it is easy to understand why modern scholars have found the passage confusing.[19]

Finding one's way through book 3 is much easier. It is dedicated to the study of *ambigua signa,* again starting with a brief reference to *propria signa,* after which the major part of the book is concerned with the *translata signa.* When an author speaks literally, rather than figuratively (*DDC* 3.2–8), ambiguity may arise for two reasons. Sometimes it is not clear how the words should be grouped together, because punctuation is uncertain. Elsewhere, the problem is a question of pronunciation: does *praedico* come from *praedicere* or *praedicare?* Generally it is for the grammarian to solve such problems, which come under the heading of *lectio* (ἀνάγνωσις).[20] To explain them is a preliminary exercise which unlocks the first barrier to understanding.

Anyone who succeeds in the next task—that of procuring for himself a sure means of dealing with *ambigua signa* in their figurative sense—will then hold the key, as it were, to the inner sanctum (*DDC* 3.9 ff.). Apart from the exegetes of Antioch,[21] there was widespread agreement within the church that the text of the Bible contained several different levels of meaning. Therefore Augustine's first, fundamental question concerns a threefold distinction: When can the interpreter pronounce himself satisfied with the "true" or "literal" meaning of the words? When must he attribute to them a figurative sense (*figurata locutio*)? And when must he consider both possibilities—that is, when does a passage, which makes sense if given its literal meaning, simultaneously function as a metaphor for something else? Augustine seems not to consider the possibility that the text operates at a number of different levels throughout.

His answer turns out to be remarkably sophisticated (3.14–34). He makes the general point that we undoubtedly have a *figurata locutio* on our hands if the statement, taken literally, conflicts either with "right conduct" (*morum honestas*) or with "true belief" (*fidei veritas*). However, "right conduct" is relative and is determined by contemporary attitudes and by "common practice" (*consuetudo*). Thus, for example, the polygamy practiced by the Old Testament patriarchs should not be condemned; more important is that the central tenets of the Scriptures should be observed, and displayed, in all the affairs of life. These tenets are the affirmation of love (*caritas*) and faith (*catholica fides*) on the one hand, and the suppression of base desires (*cupiditas*) on the other.

The very thoroughness alone with which Augustine develops his preliminary thoughts on method is worthy of close study. His concluding remarks are sketchy by comparison. Here Augustine briefly identifies the criteria for interpreting *figurae* ("similarity" or "affinity") and gives advice on how to proceed if a single correct interpretation does not suggest itself at once (*DDC* 3.34–39). Likewise he elaborates, but briefly, on the practice of the biblical authors, by expanding on the individual types of figure, or trope, which they use (3.40–41). He mentions *allegoria*, *aenigma*, *parabola*—all of which appear in the Bible—then *catachresis*, *ironia*, and *antiphrasis*—and then breaks off. He does not, after all, want to give a grammar lesson; that kind of knowledge can be obtained outside the Church.[22]

Still, we have now had explained to us what we must look for in the Scriptures (the *res* defined in book 1) and how to ensure that we grasp their message, even in those passages where it is obscured by accidents of transmission or by their literary style, whether through *ignota* (book 2) or through *ambigua signa* (book 3). Clearly these general observations lay the foundation for the real work on the text. However, by themselves they are not nearly substantial enough, and in specific instances they could hardly help to solve the riddles contained in the text. Augustine himself is clearly aware that the future exegete needs further instructions. He does not give these himself; but, rather, he refers to the seven rules of Tyconius the Donatist as a model and concludes book 3 with a discursive commentary on these principles (*DDC* 3.42–56). The work as a whole is then rounded off with a discussion in book 4 of the *modus proferendi*, that is, *elocutio*.

If my attempted analysis of the text is more or less correct, despite its brevity, then, as was pointed out at the beginning, Augustine, in composing *De doctrina christiana*, cannot have had in mind either a novel conception of a "culture chrétienne" (entirely subordinated to religion, that is) or a Christian "paideia" (a doctrine of education and moral development). For, whatever we understand by *culture* and *education,* those things which are considered to contribute something to them cannot in themselves be valueless. Yet Augustine would prefer simply to eliminate the arts and sciences altogether. He affords them a grudging tolerance only because, here and there, some special knowledge is needed in order to interpret the biblical "signs." *De doctrina christiana* is composed from a narrowly utilitarian, extremely reductivist viewpoint.[23] All that counts is the Bible and its message. If the interpreter had on hand to consult some handy works of reference, for example, the *Chronica* of Eusebius, concise encyclopedias, and suchlike, he would not have to devote so much time to subjects which basically do not get him anywhere (*DDC* 2.58–59).[24] For *artes liberales* in themselves bring him not a step nearer to divine truth; in that respect, Augustine's evaluation of them has changed radically since book 2 of the *De ordine* (composed before his baptism). For there he had conceded that they had a function of their own, if only in the early stages of preparation, in furthering one's progress towards the highest knowledge.[25] The comprehensive "system of sciences" developed in book 2 of *De doctrina christiana*—an extraneous element, as we have seen—should not be allowed to obscure this change in attitude. If Augustine makes any concession, then he does so only for philosophy, which is actually what is least needed by anyone who seeks to explain the Bible. Therefore it is no accident that Augustine (*DDC* 2.60) justifies his acknowledgment of philosophy with a simile that goes back ultimately to Origen:[26] one should avail oneself of philosophy in the same way as the fleeing Israelites availed themselves of the treasures of their former Egyptian masters.

The view that *De doctrina christiana* serves the practical needs of clerics also cannot seriously be sustained. Augustine both demands too much and offers too little for that. He gives too little instruction, in that he limits himself throughout to explaining the theoretical basis for the work of interpretation without ever going on to discuss the practice. For instance, he expressly refuses to speak on the use and interpretation of tropes, on the grounds that this can be learnt from grammarians.[27] Thus, anyone who consults *De doctrina christiana* must already have significant practical experience of exegesis. Nor is he supplied with any factual knowledge; he is merely told which disciplines he must master, if he has not already done so. Even with regard to the rules of Tyconius, Augustine stresses that he is merely citing them by way of example; in identifying them, he does not claim to be offering a comprehensive account.[28]

His demands go too far, on the other hand, in that they are unrealistically elaborate if regarded as preparation for the Sunday sermon; one can hardly imagine any priest actually fulfilling them. He himself may have approached his ideal, but how many others were of his caliber? As for his strictures on linguistic ability, his own Greek was limited, and he went through life without mastering Hebrew. Thus, not even the author himself was in a position to put fully into practice the concept outlined in the *De doctrina christiana;* still more must the claims he made for it have exceeded the power of his fellow Christians to fulfill, even if they belonged to the intellectual elite—with one possible exception: the trilinguist Jerome.

Now it is precisely Jerome who emphasises time and again that the Latin-speaking Christians of his day still had no serious work of "biblical scholarship" (*scripturarum ars*); his commentaries, in which he drew on earlier research, mainly that of Greek exegetes, were written chiefly in order to fill this gap. He felt that it was unacceptable for people to attempt an interpretation of the Bible who had never learned the systematic technique which alone ensures adequate understanding.[29]

In the same vein, though less polemically, Augustine in his preface to *De doctrina christiana* dismisses potential critics who believe that they do not need his *praecepta*.[30] In view of this we might say that Augustine, completing Jerome's efforts, as it were, on a theoretical level, embraces in *De doctrina christiana* the question of how such a science should ideally be presented and carried out. Presumably what Jerome calls *scripturarum ars* is precisely what Augustine means by *doctrina christiana*.[31] The title of the work, in fact, promises a "program," yet one directed, not towards a Christian culture or education, but entirely and specifically towards the study of the Bible.

Augustine envisages that study's aims as being, first, to pave the way to the understanding of divine truth, through the interpretation of biblical *signa*, and, second, to express appropriately in words what has been understood. Naturally it would be desirable that anyone who wishes to comment on the message of the Bible, whatever their motives, should adopt all of Augustine's recommendations. However, a single individual must not be expected to undertake a job that he cannot complete. It appears that Augustine, in formulating his "program," is at the same time creating, in modern terms, a research project requiring many coworkers to carry it out. These would each contribute to the whole according to their ability. Augustine expects his readers to be familiar with the general principles of interpretation, so that he can essentially confine his observations to what is specifically relevant for the Bible. Ideally, the end result of the project would be to make available a comprehensive and thorough commentary on the Bible, which took account of all the requirements of Augustine's program. *Inventio*, at least, would then have achieved its object, although there are rather different requirements for *elocutio*, discussed in book 4. In particular, clarification would be needed as to whom exactly Augustine envisages as "teacher of the church."[32]

We probably must abandon the popular notion that *De doctrina christiana*, looking ahead of its time, embodies a kind of Magna Carta of Christian education that links old and new, *Antike* and *Christentum*. Nevertheless, the work continues to merit a high degree of interest, also and especially from the point of view of the classical scholar. The condition of the manuscript tradition alone is remarkable, for the Codex Leningradensis Q.v.I.3 comes closer to the first written version of *De doctrina christiana* in the hand of an ancient author than does any other manuscript. It contains books 1 and 2 and is perhaps a first edition of those parts of the work completed that far; it could have been written under the eye of Augustine.[33] In this connection we should recall that the young bishop, according to the *Retractationes* (2.4), did not at first get farther than about the middle of book 3 (*DDC* 3.35), and that the work begun in 395 was not completed until a good thirty years later. The question arises whether, and to what extent, this intermission had an effect on the completion of the original plan; and in particular whether the section now occupied by the rules of Tyconius was originally intended for some expression of Augustine's own thought. Furthermore, the philologist is repeatedly made aware of how little progress has been made towards a satisfactory edition of such an important text.[34] Good as the textual tradition is, it is not free of corruption; for example, in *De doctrina christiana* 2.47 we probably cannot but remove the word *God* itself from the text.[35] But what is most important is that *De doctrina christiana* appears to be more or less unique; for books 1–3, at least, in their attempt to organize the methodological principles of textual interpretation into a comprehensive system, ancient literature can supply no parallel.

It is typical of Augustine's program that he strives to confine the use of pagan sciences to the narrowest possible bounds. However, this aim by no means prevents him from making constant use of pagan examples, and indeed these make not the least contribution to the distinctive liveliness of the text. A modern commentary which focused on such issues could bring to light many striking and very characteristic examples. Certainly, references to things pagan are often prompted simply by the subject matter, as in the fields of grammar and rhetoric: for example, when Augustine gives a rather skillful explanation of what an *interiectio* is;[36] or when he distinguishes between an *interrogatio* and a *percontatio*;[37] or when he observes that tropes are common to everyday speech also, and are used even by people who would not know how to identify the different kinds.[38] Elsewhere, it may have pleased him to show off his learning a little; at least, he could have illustrated the proposition that human conventions are not absolutes without the reference to Roman fashion, which only makes sense if the reader recalls a particular passage in Cicero's second Catilinarian.[39] More important than such incidental *lumina* are certain pagan modes of thought that essentially determine Augustine's own thought and his development of it. We cannot fail to observe how this affects the construction of the whole work. As we saw, this is organized—twice over—according to the rhetorical divisions known as *inventio* and *elocutio*. Likewise, we observed that the fundamental distinction of branches of knowledge into those concerned, respectively, with "conventions" and with things "given" by God or Nature, derives ultimately from the ancient Greek antithesis between νόμος and φύσις. Many other such examples could be cited.

This very antithesis between νόμος and φύσις affects Augustine's argument in a variety of ways. In particular it helps to explain his basically anti-Classical attitude to language (which surely is at least partly responsible for the vivid directness of his style). No doubt personal experience also played a part in this, in that as an African he could not agree with the Italians over the correct pronunciation of Latin; or in that contemporary critics apparently took it into their heads to accuse even Cicero himself of barbarisms and solecisms.[40] Augustine's reactions to this have far-reaching effects, notably with regard to the Latin Bible. He is undisturbed by solecisms such as *inter hominibus* or barbarisms such as *ignoscére* or *floriet*, so long as the meaning is clear (*DDC* 2.19 f.). He even suggests, for the word "bone," the bold substitution of *ossum* for *os*, to avoid confusion with the Latin word for "mouth" (3.7). Anyone who, on the other hand, insists on correct diction (*integritas locutionis*) shows nothing but vanity, for he is unmasked as one to whom the form (*signa*) matters more than the content (*res*). The "correct diction" he swears by is shown in the end to be merely the "preservation of conventions not one's own" (*alienae consuetudinis conservatio*)—of the "usage of the ancients" (*consuetudo veterum*). These ancients had spoken "with no little authority," and thus their language had been elevated as if to the status of law (2.19). Augustine's radical approach becomes even clearer when one considers what pains Jerome takes in his translations to preserve the *euphonia* of idiomatic, i.e., traditional, Latin.[41] Yet this abrupt break with tradition, and with a classicism that idolizes its ancient models, especially Cicero, is made possible precisely because Augustine applies an ancient concept more consistently than anyone before him: namely, that language is not given by nature; its rules are laid down by men, as a social convention (see also 2.37; 40), which may change from one age to the next.[42] However, Augustine's eyes and ears have been unmistakably opened to the claims of contemporary *consuetudo*, as against rules established by means of analogy, or learned authorities of the past, by Cicero himself and Quintilian as well as by grammarians of his own time,[43] though admittedly these authors would never have acknowledged an apparent mistake as correct on the sole grounds that it was widely used.[44]

Now the relative status of convention or *consuetudo* is also extremely important for the work of interpretation. As we already observed, in book 3 Augustine devotes himself at length to the central question of where in the Bible one has to reckon with a figurative or allegorical use of language (*DDC* 3.9–34)—namely, when the literal sense of the text clashes with the dictates of "right conduct" (*morum honestas*) or "true faith" (*fidei veritas* [3.14]). In *honestum* Augustine is introducing a term which the pagan grammarians used in a quite similar sense.[45] Yet what is most remarkable is the care with which Augustine seeks to define the sense of *honestum*: he recognizes that "right conduct," like speech, is subject to convention.

However, men are inclined to judge others' deeds according to the *consuetudo* of their own society (3.15), when they ought instead to be considering whether the action they are judging is right according to the moral outlook of quite another time and place (3.19). What counts is not the action in itself, but the moral attitude which it expresses (3.20 f.). Again Augustine's arguments are remarkably progressive—and in an area in which his relativism could get him into far greater trouble than in that of language.

In fact he seems well aware of this, for in the end he qualifies his argument—and, at the same time, implicitly reveals the source from which his views are derived (*DDC* 3.22). The range of *consuetudines* is fundamentally unlimited, and this has led "certain people" (*quidam*)—who were neither "sunk in the slumber of stupidity" nor "roused to the light of wisdom"—to the view that there is no "absolute right"; rather, every race regards only its own *consuetudo* as "right." Augustine must, of course, contradict this view: the Golden Rule, for example, admits of no alteration or adjustment. But who are the *quidam* who want to rob even the term *iustitia* of its absolute force? Without doubt Augustine refers to the speech of L. Furius Philus in Cicero's *De re publica* 3.9–32. In it Philus recalls the argument with which the Academic Carneades, on the occasion of the famous embassy of philosophers (156–5 B.C.E.), questioned the status of *iustitia* and deeply unsettled his Roman audience (especially as he had defended *iustitia* on the previous day). A considerable part of this speech amasses evidence to show that *mores, consuetudines,* and even *ius* and *iustitia* are different among different races and do not always stay the same even among the same races. In other words, right is no more anchored in nature than are any of the other factors that govern life in society. That *consuetudines* are contextually differentiated is supported by a mass of examples (*De re publica* 3.14–17).

That Augustine knew this remarkable speech is a priori probable and is clearly evident from *De civitate dei* 2.21.[46] However, his use of it in *De doctrina christiana* strikes one as most peculiar. Regarding the relative status of moral *consuetudines* Augustine follows Carneades entirely. In other words, faced with the fundamental question of whether a biblical narrative is to be interpreted literally or figuratively, one of the main criteria he employs originates in the Academic-Skeptic school. His only reservation is that the Academics took their relativism to extremes, in applying it even to values which are indisputably absolute.

That Augustine did not originally learn his techniques of interpretation—at least with regard to the biblical *signa*—in the Church, needs no special proof and is repeatedly made obvious. In particular, we should not underestimate his debt to his rhetorical schooling; it is evident already in the dedication of book 3 to *ambigua signa*. For the rhetorical doctrine of *status*, or more precisely the doctrine of *status legales*, which instructs the orator in the use of written evidence (laws or wills), is based on the theory that the very *ambiguum* of a text is one of the four elements from which arise the controversy of interpretation.[47] Apart from the *ignota* of book 2, Augustine seems to include in the term *ambiguum* any aspect of the text which requires explanation. It is worth pointing out that the solution of any given *ambiguum* should contain no *controversia* (*DDC* 3.39), which recalls the key notion of the *status legales*. Indeed, even some of the individual rules he cites are clearly borrowed, as, for example, when he advises the reader to explain an *ambiguitas* by reference to what precedes and follows—its immediate context. He probably owes this formulation directly to Cicero's treatment of *ambiguum* in his *De inventione*.[48]

But why did the authors of the Bible not set out to express themselves in such a way that their texts required no interpretation at all (*DDC* 2.7 f.)? By incidentally posing this question, Augustine implicitly assumes that their meaning could have been expressed absolutely unambiguously and that the innumerable difficulties—*obscuritates*, *ambiguitates*—were part and parcel of the literary style of the work. Indeed, the Bible reads for long stretches as a work of literature, even of poetry. Augustine reminds us, by way of example, of a verse from the Song of Songs (Song 4:2): "Thy teeth are like a flock of sheep that are even shorn, which came up from the washing; whereof every one bears twins, and none is barren among them." Certainly anyone who is compelled painstakingly to elicit from this verse its true, i.e., allegorical message for the Church (as Augustine does) is checked in any tendency to pride or arrogance. It must have been primarily for pedagogical ends, then, that these authors incorporated their *obscuritates* into the text.[49] A similar hypothesis is used by Neoplatonic interpreters of Aristotle, in the introductions to their commentaries on the *Categories*, to explain why the philosopher from time to time deliberately worked "obscurity" (*asapheia*) into his writings.[50] However, this is only one explanation, and Augustine also offers a more positive one: a simple style, unadorned with a metaphor, "pleases less" (*minus delectat*). The Bible—as poetry—is thus also to be judged by poetic criteria, for since ancient times critics have regarded "pleasure," next to "instruction," as one of the key functions of poetry.[51] When Augustine then goes on (*DDC* 2.8) to say that the teaching of the Bible strikes him "more sweetly" (*suavius*) with its clothing of figures than without; that he absorbs its instruction "more gladly" (*libentius*); that it seems "more pleasant" (*gratius*) to him—then we cannot help but be reminded of Lucretius's well known simile, in which he promises to promote Epicurus's teachings in verses full of the charm of the Muses, just as we administer a bitter draught to children by smearing the rim of the cup with sweet honey.[52] Once again Augustine tries to explain an important issue of "biblical scholarship" by means of ideas derived from his pagan education.

What, finally, is the aim of the interpreter? First of all it is essential that his interpretation accord with the *res* of the Bible as outlined in book 1, that is the dual commandment to love. If he succeeds, that is already an important achievement, even if he should mistake the author's own intention (*sententia*)—provided, at least, that there is no evil motive at work (in other words, that he is not deliberately lying). Still, just to be mistaken is dangerous and should be avoided (*DDC* 1.40 f.). For this reason one will make every effort to grasp also the *voluntas* or the *sententia* of the author, while always remaining aware that sometimes there may be several possible interpretations which are in sympathy with the divine truth. This may arise, either because the author actually has in mind a supplementary truth besides his own true *sententia*, or although he himself has not noticed this other truth. Given this complicated situation, though, the interpreter is in no little danger again (3.38 f.).

Augustine here further develops ideas that he first set out systematically in *De utilitate credendi* 10–13, namely, in the dispute with the Manichaeans over the correct interpretation of the Old Testament (10–13). In this former work he had a notion of three forms of error and two of correct procedure; these originated in the mutual relation of three key concepts: objective truth; the author's *sententia*; and the interpreter's understanding of both of these. Although enumerating and considering five possible relations, Augustine was concerned ultimately to ensure that the ecclesiastical exegesis of the Old Testament should never fall short of divine truth; but hypothetically at least, he allowed for the possibility that there might be discrepancies between the *sententia* of the Old Testament authors and the truth.

Now, in *De doctrina christiana*, Augustine limits the options for the sake of "biblical scholarship." A contradiction between objective truth and the *sententia* of a biblical author is no longer thinkable. The instructions to the interpreter are stricter than before: he must look for the *sententia* of the author, even when he thinks that he has hit upon an objective truth. However, the hermeneutical system outlined in the *De utilitate credendi* seems to have developed out of Neoplatonic debates on method concerning ἀλήθεια (truth) and διάνοια (intention) as expounded in the introductions to the commentaries on Aristotle's *Categories*.[53] If this is correct, Augustine is still, in the *De doctrina christiana* too, following in the wake of the Neoplatonists (as we saw, the pedagogical explanation of biblical *obscuritates* can be traced back to them too). Indeed, through the concentration on two possibilities—"truth alone," immediately and necessarily to be followed by "truth and *sententia*"—he comes perhaps still nearer to his sources of inspiration, with one important exception: he would never, like the Neoplatonists dealing with Aristotle, reach the point of being compelled to prefer truth to the author's intention since without exception all biblical authors are telling nothing but the truth.

A close reading has shown us that Bishop Augustine in the *De doctrina christiana* is in no way attempting to preserve—for its own sake—the pagan educational system, not even within narrow limits. At least there is little to suggest that this formed any part of his program for the work. Nonetheless, with *De doctrina christiana* he did produce one of the "classics of Western culture": more or less by accident, perhaps, since the work seems to have had a reception rather different from what he intended[54] (but "classics" usually are made during the process of reception rather than having been born as such!); and half unconsciously because—here as elsewhere—he could conceive and formulate most of his new ideas only within the framework of the old categories with which he had grown up. He passed on the knowledge, judgments, and conceptual framework of ancient culture to the following centuries, not by recommending them, but because he adopted them as a matter of course and used them freely— often implicitly, and even in cases where he believed that he ought to distance himself from them.

Notes

1. A good survey of the history of research, and the various tendencies to be observed in it, is given by G. A. Press, "The Subject and Structure of Augustine's *De doctrina christiana*," *AugStud* 11 (1980): 99–124.

2. Cf. I. Opelt, "Materialien zur Nachwirkung von Augustins Schrift *De doctrina christiana*," *JbAC* 17 (1974): 66–67.

3. It is especially G. A. Press to whom we owe this insight: see "Subject and Structure," 112–118; also idem, "The Content and Argument of Augustine's *De doctrina christiana*," *Aug (L)* 31 (1981): 165–182.

4. The literature relevant for this type of interpretation is listed by Press, "Subject and Structure," 100, n. 6.

5. This is the influential formula coined by H.-I. Marrou, *Saint Augustine et la fin de la culture antique*, 4th ed. (Paris, 1958), 331 ff.

6. Cf. E. Kevane, "Augustine's *De doctrina christiana*: A Treatise on Christian Education," *RecAug* 4 (1966): 97–133; idem, "Paideia and Antipaideia: The Prooemium of St. Augustine's *De doctrina christiana*," *AugStud* 1 (1970): 153–180.

7. Cf. Opelt, "Materialien zur Nachwirkung," 64–73. A comparable influence has been exerted by Saint Basil's short (and far less ambitious) Λόγος πρὸς τοὺς

νέους ὅπως ἂν ἐξ Ἑλληνικῶν ὠφελοῖντο λόγων.The most recent annotated editions are: N.G. Wilson, ed., *Saint Basil on Greek Literature* (London, 1975); M. Naldini, ed., *Basilio di Cesarea, Discorso ai giovani*, a cura di M. Naldini (Firenze, 1984). For the history of influence, cf. L. Schucan, *Das Nachleben von Basilius Magnus "ad adolescentes": Ein Beitrag zur Geschichte des christlichen Humanismus* (Genève, 1973).

8. For this term, cf. Press, "Subject and Structure," 107–118.

9. Cf., e.g., Quintilian *Institutio oratoria* 3.3.1: *omnis autem orandi ratio, ut plurimi maximique auctores tradiderunt, quinque partibus constat, inventione, dispositione, elocutione, memoria, pronuntiatione sive actione (utroque enim modo dicitur)*.

10. Cf. the contribution by A. Primmer in this volume, "The function of the *genera dicendi* in *De doctrina christiana* 4."

11. Cf. Quintilian's instructive wording (*Institutio oratoria* 3.5.1): *omnis autem oratio constat aut ex iis quae significantur aut ex iis quae significant, id est rebus et verbis*.

12. Cf. Quintilian *Institutio oratoria* 8 prooemium 6: *orationem porro omnem constare rebus et verbis; in rebus intuendam inventionem, in verbis elocutionem.* Cf. also 3.3.7.

13. DDC 1.40: *quisquis igitur scripturas divinas vel quamlibet earum partem intellexisse sibi videtur, ita ut eo intellectu non aedificet istam geminam caritatem dei et proximi, nondum intellexit. quisquis vero talem inde sententiam duxerit, ut huic aedificandae caritati sit utilis, nec tamen hoc dixerit, quod ille quem legit eo loco sensisse probabitur, non perniciose fallitur nec omnino mentitur.*

14. DDC 2.29: *sed ut totum istum locum—nam est maxime necessarius—diligentius explicemus: duo sunt genera doctrinarum.*

15. A highly characteristic judgment on the passage in question is given, e.g., by L. M. J. Verheijen, "Le *De doctrina christiana* de saint Augustin," *Aug (L)* 24 (1974): 10–20. He sees it as a "digression" comprising a "charte fondamentale pour une culture chrétienne," which is only loosely connected with the main body of the work, a "manuel d'herméneutique et d'expression chrétienne."

16. DDC 2.59: *et ideo magis ad ambigua solvenda et explicanda . . . legentes adiuvat* [sc. *ratio disputandi*] *quam ad incognita signa cognoscenda, de quibus nunc agimus.* DDC 2.63: *hac igitur instructione praeditum cum signa incognita lectorem non impedierint* (conclusion and summary of book 2).

17. E.g., right at the beginning of this part of the argument (*DDC* 2.29): *duo sunt genera doctrinarum, quae in gentilibus etiam moribus exercentur: unum earum rerum quas instituerunt homines, alterum earum quas animadverterunt iam peractas aut divinitus institutas.* All the same, the original antithesis can sometimes be seen gleaming through, as at *DDC* 2.38: *illa enim signa quae saltando faciunt histriones, si natura, non instituto et consensione hominum valerent;* and *DDC* 2.40: *adumbrata enim quaedam et naturalibus utcumque similia hominum instituta sunt.*

18. Cf. the passages cited in n. 16. Also, he expresses himself just as clearly in *DDC* 3.1, where he connects books 2 and 3: *homo timens deum . . . , ne amet certamina pietate mansuetus, praemunitus etiam scientia linguarum, ne in verbis*

lucutionibusque ignotis haereat, praemunitus etiam cognitione quarundam rerum
necessariarum, ne vim naturamve earum quae propter similitudinem, adhibentur
ignoret, adiuvante etiam codicum veritate . . . , veniat ita instructus ad ambigua
scripturarum discutienda atque solvenda.

19. Of course it is a different question where that "system of sciences" comes
from. Did Augustine encounter it somewhere, more or less ready made? Or did he
develop it himself, e.g., in the context of his once projected, yet never finished
work on the *artes liberales?* Cf. *Retractationes* 1.6 (1.5.6); and, on it, H. Hagendahl, *Augustine and the Latin Classics,* Studia Graeca et Latina Gothoburgensia
20 (Göteborg 1967), 592–593.

20. Cf. B. Neuschäfer, *Origenes als Philologe,* Schweiz. Beiträge zur Alter-
tumswissenschaft 18 (Basel, 1987), 1, 35.

21. Cf. C. Schäublin, *Untersuchungen zu Herkunft und Methode der Anti-*
ochenischen Exegese, Theophaneia 23 (Köln/Bonn, 1974).

22. *DDC* 3.40: *sciant autem litterati modis omnibus locutionis, quos gram-*
matici graeco nomine tropos vocant, auctores nostros usos fuisse multiplicius atque
copiosius, quam possunt existimare vel credere qui nesciunt eos et in aliis ista
didicerunt. quos tamen tropos qui noverunt, agnoscunt in litteris sanctis eorumque
scientia ad eas intellegendas aliquantum adiuvantur. sed his eos ignaris tradere non
decet, ne artem grammaticam docere videamur. extra sane ut discantur admoneo.

23. Cf. Hagendahl, *Augustine and the Latin Classics,* 558–569.

24. *DDC* 2.58: "The general rule is: 'the less the better'"(*in omnibus tenen-*
dum est: "ne quid nimis" [Terence *Andria* 61]). Cf. *DDC* 2.59: *sicut autem*
quidam de verbis omnibus et nominibus hebraeis et syris et aegyptiis . . . , quae in
eis [sc. *scripturis sanctis]* *sine interpretatione sunt posita, fecerunt, ut ea separa-*
tim interpretarentur; et quod Eusebius fecit de temporum historia propter
divinorum librorum quaestiones, quae usum eius flagitant: quod ergo hi fecerunt
de his rebus, ut non sit necesse christiano in multis propter pauca laborare, sic
video posse fieri. . . , ut quoscumque terrarum locos quaeve animalia vel herbas
atque arbores sive lapides vel metalla incognita speciesque quaslibet scriptura
commemorat, ea generatium digerens sola [uniuscuiusque rei notione] exposita
littera mandet. potest etiam de numeris fieri. The text, as given here, was restored
by H. Fuchs, "Enzyklopädie," *RACh* 5 (1962): 513; Fuchs also discusses the content of the passage and places it in its context.

25. Cf. *De ordine* 2.35 ff. For the difference of estimation of the *artes liberales*
in *De ordine* and *De doctrina christiana,* cf. H. Fuchs, "Die frühe christliche
Kirche und die antike Bildung," in *Das frühe Christentum im römischen Staat,* ed.
R. Klein (Darmstadt, 1971), 43–46.

26. Cf. Neuschäfer, *Origenes,* 2; 414, n. 137.

27. Cf. n. 22.

28. *DDC* 3.42: *quae quidem considerata, sicut ab illo* [sc. *Tyconio]* *aperiuntur,*
non parum adiuvant ad penetranda quae tecta sunt divinorum eloquiorum; nec
tamen omnia quae ita scripta sunt, ut non facile intellegantur, possunt his regu-
lis inveniri, sed aliis modis pluribus, quos hoc numero septenario usque adeo non
est iste complexus, ut idem ipse multa exponat obscura, in quibus harum regu-
larum adhibet nullam.

29. Cf. Jerome *Epistula* 53.6.2–7.1: *agricolae, caementarii, fabri, metallorum lignorumque caesores, lanarii quoque et fullones et ceteri, qui variam supellectilem et vilia opuscula fabricantur, absque doctore non possunt esse quod cupiunt.* *"quod medicorum est, / promittunt medici, tractant fabrilia fabri."* [Horace *Epistula* 2.1.115 f.]. *sola scripturarum ars est, quam sibi omnes passim vindicent.* *"scribimus indocti doctique poemata passim."* [Horace *Epistula* 2.1.117]. *hanc garrula anus, hanc delirus senex, hanc soloecista verbosus, hanc universi praesumunt lacerant docent, antequam discant.* Similarly *Epistula* 119.11.3 f.: *etenim si dialecticam scire voluero aut philosophorum dogmata et (ut ad nostram redeam scientiam) scripturarum, nequaquam simplices ecclesiae viros interrogare debeo . . . , sed eos, qui artem didicere ab artifice et in lege domini meditantur die ac nocte.* The *artifices* that Jerome has learned his *ars* from are in the main the Greek exegetes, from whose writings he makes excerpts, translates, and incorporates material in his own commentaries.

30. On the preface of *DDC*, cf., most recently, C. Kannengiesser, in C. Kannengiesser and P. Bright, *A Conflict of Christian Hermeneutics in Roman Africa: Tyconius and Augustine, Protocol of the Fifty-Eighth Colloquy* (Berkeley, 1989), 2 f., 75 f.

31. G. A. Press, "*Doctrina* in Augustine's *De doctrina christiana*," *Philosophy and Rhetoric* 17 (1984): 98–120 rightly observes that the *doctrina* announced in the title of the work is basically identical with the *tractatio scripturarum* that Augustine touches on in the introduction. Still, in the end he would like to attribute a far broader, probably too broad a sense to the term (again tending, all the same, towards "culture," "education"—because, as he says, this is the very function that "rhetoric," which is after all the subject in question, fulfilled for the ancients). It is also worth mentioning that by the time Augustine wrote *DDC* he had already contacted Jerome as well as being familiar with his writings (including *Epistula* 53? cf. n. 29). *Epistula* 28.2.2 (written in 392) asks for translations of Greek commentaries (the wording is revealing: *ut interpretandis eorum libris, qui graece scripturas nostras tractaverunt, curam atque operam inpendere non graveris*) of such works, that is, as Jerome used to derive his *ars* from.

32. *DDC* 4.6: *debet igitur divinarum scripturarum tractator et doctor, defensor rectae fidei ac debellator erroris, et bona docere et mala dedocere.*

33. Cf. W. M. Green, "A Fourth-Century Manuscript of St. Augustine?" *RBen* 69 (1959): 191–197; E. A. Lowe, *Codices Latini antiquiores* 11 (Oxford, 1966), nr. 1613.

34. Even the two critical editions most widely used today are far from reflecting the problematical state of the text: the one is by J. Martin (CC 32 [1962]), the other by W. M. Green (*CSEL* 80 [1963]). Cf. C. Schäublin, "Zum Text von Augustin, *De doctrina Christiana*," *Wiener Studien* N.F. 8 (1974): 173–181.

35. *DDC* 2.47: *artium etiam ceterarum, quibus aliquid fabricatur, vel quod remaneat post fabricationem artificis ab illo effectum—sicut domus et scamnum et vas aliquod atque alia huiuscemodi—vel quae ministerium quoddam exhibent operanti [deo]—sicut saltationum et cursionum et luctaminum—: harum ergo cunctarum artium et praeteritis experimenta faciunt etiam futura conici.* The entire context is dedicated exclusively and without ambiguity to the *operatio* of

the "artist" and the way it works, but not at all to that of God.

36. *DDC* 2.16: *et hoc maxime interiectionibus accidit, quae verba motum animi significant potius quam sententiae conceptae ullam particulam.* Cf. C. Iulius Romanus in Charisius *Ars grammatica* 2.16 (ed. Barwick, 311): *interiectio est pars orationis motum animi significans.*

37. *DDC* 3.6: *inter percontationem autem et interrogationem hoc veteres interesse dixerunt, quod ad percontationem multa responderi possunt, ad interrogationem vero aut "non" aut "etiam."* Cf. Donatus on Terence *Andria* 800: *interrogatio est, cui necessario respondetur aut etiam aut non, percontatio, cui nihil horum.* Eugraphius on Terence *Eunuchus* 293.

38. *DDC* 3.40: *quamuis paene omnes hi tropi, qui liberali dicuntur arte cognosci, etiam in eorum reperiantur loquellis qui nullos grammaticos audierunt et eo, quo vulgus utitur, sermone contenti sunt.* Cf. Quintilian *Institutio oratoria* 8.6.4: *incipiamus igitur ab eo* [sc. *tropo*], *qui cum frequentissimus est tum longe pulcherrimus, translatione dico . . . quae quidem . . . ita est ab ipsa nobis concessa natura, ut indocti quoque ac non sentientes ea frequenter utantur.*

39. *DDC* 3.20: *talares et manicatas tunicas habere apud romanos veteres flagitium erat, nunc autem honesto loco natis, cum tunicati sunt, non eas habere flagitium est.* Cf. Cicero *In Catilinam oratio* 2.22: *postremum autem genus est non solum numero verum etiam genere ipso atque vita quod proprium Catilinae est, de eius dilectu, immo vero de complexu eius ac sinu; quos pexo capillo, nitidos, aut imberbis aut bene barbatos videtis, manicatis et talaribus tunicis, velis amictos non togis.* That such tunics were considered indecent in earlier times is also attested by Aulus Gellius (*Noctes Atticae* 6.12).

40. Cf. *De ordine* 2.45: *si enim dicam te facile ad eum sermonem perventuram, qui locutionis et linguae vitio careat, profecto mentiar. me enim ipsum, cui magna necessitas fuit ista perdiscere, adhunc in multis verborum sonis Itali exagitant et a me vicissim, quod ad ipsum sonum attinet, reprehenduntur . . . soloecismos autem quos dicimus fortasse quisque doctus diligenter attendens in oratione mea reperiet; non enim defuit, qui mihi nonnulla huis modi vitia ipsum Ciceronem fecisse peritissime persuasisset. barbarismorum autem genus nostris temporibus tale conpertum est, ut et ipsa eius oratio barbara videatur, qua Roma servata est.*

41. Cf. Jerome *Epistula* 106.3.2; 23; 26; 29.2; 55.1; 59; 60.1. By *euphonia* Jerome understand "idiomatic correctness." He probably owes this notion to his teacher, Donatus; cf. the latter's *Ars maior* 2.10 (ed. Holtz, 627, 10 ff.): *sed scire debemus multa quidem veteres aliter declinasse . . . verum euphoniam in dictionibus plus interdum valere quam analogiam vel regulam praeceptorum.* So Donatus, too, is prepared to dissociate himself from the "ancients" at times. However, neither he nor Jerome ever conceded as much to the *consuetudo* of their own time as Augustine did: their fundamental attitude is more "classicistic." Cf. also nn. 43 and 44.

42. According to the ancient discussion about *Latinitas*, which is reflected in the works of several grammarians and can, hypothetically at least, be traced back to Varro (one of Augustine's favorites!), there are mainly four criteria constituting "correct diction": *natura, ratio, consuetudo, auctoritas*; cf. D. Fehling, "Varro und die grammatische Lehre von der Analogie und der Flexion," *Glotta* 35

(1956): 214–270. Augustine picks out one of them (*consuetudo*) and gives it special weight in order to undermine the very concept of *integritas locutionis* (= *Latinitas*).

43. Cf. Cicero *Orator* 159: *in verbis iunctis quam scite "insipientem" non "insapientem"* . . . *ex quo quidam "pertisum" etiam volunt, quod eadem consuetudo non probavit.* . . . *quin ego ipse, cum scirem ita maiores locutos ut nusquam nisi in vocali aspiratione uterentur, loquebar sic ut "pulcros, Cetegos, triumpos, Cartaginem" dicerem; aliquando* . . . *convicio aurium cum extorta mihi veritas esset, usum loquendi populo concessi, scientiam mihi reservavi.* Quintilian *Institutio oratoria* 1.6.43: *superest igitur consuetudo: nam fuerit paene ridiculum malle sermonem, quo locuti sint homines, quam quo loquantur. et sane quid est aliud vetus sermo quam vetus loquendi consuetudo?* Donatus, too, occasionally points out language changes that can be explained by changes of *consuetudo* (*Ars maior* 2.7 [Holtz, 623, 6]; 2.10 [Holtz, 627, 5 f.]) *horum multa cernimus consuetudine conmutata.* Euphonia, the "idiomatic sound," seems to be determined chiefly by *consuetudo*; the only point at issue, then, is how much may be conceded to it. Cf. also n. 41.

44. Cf. Quintilian *Institutio oratoria* 6.1.44 f.: *igitur ut velli et comam in gradus frangere et in balneis perpotare, quamlibet haec invaserint civitatem, non erit consuetudo, quia nihil horum caret reprensione* . . . , *sic in loquendo, non si quid vitiose multis insederit, pro regula sermonis accipiendum erit. nam ut transeam, quem ad modum vulto imperiti loquantur, tota saepe theatra et omnem circi turbam exclamasse barbare scimus. ergo consuetudinem sermonis vocabo consensum eruditorum, sicut vivendi consensum bonorum.* Unlike Cicero, Quintilian, Donatus, and Jerome, Augustine did not want to leave it to the "educated" (*eruditi*) alone to decide what was to be considered as *consuetudo*.

45. Cf. Servius Danielis *On Vergil's Aeneid* 4.170 (ed. Harvardiana [Oxford, 1965], 309): *alii* . . . *accipiunt facti qualitate aut respectu honestatis,* τῶι πρέποντι. Servius *On Vergil's Aeneid* 4.318: (ed. Harvardiana, 356): *tegit rem inhonestam.*

46. The passage in *DDC* is to be added, then, to E. Heck's collection in *Die Bezeugung von Ciceros Schrift De re publica*, Spudasmata 4 (Hildesheim, 1966), 111–153.

47. For the *status legales* (νομικαί στάσεις) in general, cf. H. Lausberg, *Handbuch der literarischen Rhetorik*, 2nd ed. (München, 1973), 109–123 (198–223). They are treated at length by Cicero in *De inventione* 2.116–154.

48. *DDC* 3.2: *quodsi ambae vel etiam omnes, si plures fuerint partes ambiguitatis, secundum fidem sonuerint, textus ipse sermonis a praecedentibus et consequentibus partibus, quae ambiguitatem illam in medio posuerunt, restat consulendus, ut videamus, cuinam sententiae de pluribus quae se ostendunt ferat suffragium eamque sibi contexi patiatur.* Cf. Cicero, *De inventione* 2.117: *deinde ex superiore et ex inferiore scriptura docendum id quod quaeratur fieri perspicuum.* For Augustine's knowledge of *De inventione*, cf. Hagendahl, *Augustine and the Latin Classics*, 157–159. Possibly, it is from such rules of interpretation of the *status legales* that the fundamental principle—of great consequence also for Christian exegesis—emerged that "each author is his own best interpreter" (best

known in the form of Porphyry's maxim, *Homēron ex Homērou saphēnizein*). Cf. C. Schäublin, "Homerum ex Homero," *Museum Helveticum* 34 (1977): 221–227; Neuschäfer, *Origenes*, 276 ff.

49. *DDC* 2.7: *quod totum provisum esse divinitus non dubito ad edomandam labore superbiam et intellectum a fastidio revocandum, cui facile investigata plerumque vilescunt.*

50. Cf. Ammonios, *Commentaria in Aritotelem Graeca* 18.1 (ed. Busse, H 7, 7 ff.: οὕτω καὶ ὁ Ἀριστοτέλης προκαλύμματι τῆς αὑτοῦ φιλοσοφίας κέχρηται τῆι ἀσαφείαι, ἵνα οι μὲν σπουδαῖοι δι'αὐτὸ τοῦτο ἔτι μᾶλλον τὰς ἑαυτῶν συντείνωσι ψυχάς, οἱ δὲ κατερραιθυμημένοι τε καὶ χαῦνοι τοῖς τοιούτοις προσιόντες λόγοις ὑπὸ τῆς ἀσαφείας διώκωνται. Similar explanations are offered in the other commentaries. The question διὰ τί τὴν ἀσάφειαν ἐπετήδευσεν ὁ Ἀριστοτέλης constitutes one of the "set problems" (the eighth in Ammonios) of the ten-part introduction to the philosophy of Aristotle which formed the beginning of the Neoplationists' "classes" on Aristotle, i.e., the "lecture course on the *Categories*." For this ten-part system, cf. C. Schäublin, "Augustin, *De utilitate credendi*, über das Verhältnis des Interpreten zum Text," *VigChr* 43 (1989): 61–63.

51. The idea became famous in the form it was given by Horace, *Ars poetica* 333 f.: *aut prodesse volunt aut delectare poetae / aut simul et iucunda et idonea dicere vitae.*

52. Lucretius *De rerum natura* 1.936–943: *sed veluti pueris absinthia taetra medentes / cum dare conantur, prius oras pocula circum / contingunt mellis dulci flavoque liquore, / ut puerorum aetas inprovida ludificetur / labrorum tenus, interea perpotet amarum / absinthi laticem deceptaque non capiatur, / sed potius tali pacto recreata valescat: / sic ego nunc.*

53. Cf. Schäublin, "Augustin, *De utilitate credendi*," 53–68.

54. Cf. Opelt, "Materialien zur Nachwirkung," 64–73.

The Function of the *genera dicendi* in *De doctrina christiana* 4

ADOLF PRIMMER

I would like to begin with a preliminary remark: The coherence and continuity between books 1–3 and book 4 of Augustine's *De doctrina christiana* is not to be discussed here but will be presupposed. Let me just refer to the studies by Steffen (1964) and Press (1980).[1]

My subject is a seemingly unimportant one, the *genera dicendi* in book 4, but I hope it will lead us somehow to the essentials of *De doctrina* 4. For when I talk about the *genera dicendi*, the three styles, I must automatically deal with Cicero's *Orator* and Augustine's response to it. As you know, in his *Orator*, Cicero linked the three styles, the *genera tenue*, *medium*, and *grande*, to two other three-stage categories: on the one hand, to the psychagogical *officia*, the duties of the speaker towards the listeners (*docere*, *delectare*, *flectere*); on the other hand, to the *res*, the topics of a speech, which are *parvae*, *modicae*, or *magnae*, i.e., graded according to importance or emotional appeal.[2] And Augustine devoted more than half of *De doctrina* 4—about thirty of altogether fifty pages—to a discussion of Cicero's pairing of the *officia* and *genera*. Now a comparison between Cicero's and Augustine's doctrines of style is certainly worthwhile. Augustine wrote *De doctrina* 4 after thirty-five years of preaching, basing his thoughts on the best *modus proferendi* in Christian homilies, on his wealth of practical experience in church; Cicero wrote his *Orator*, i.e., his book on the best oratorical style, after thirty-five years of practice in the senate and on the forum.

Naturally the dialogue of such experienced masters of speech has been treated and commented upon frequently, but, even in recent decades, research has come to no agreement about how to evaluate Augustine's borrowings from Cicero. To give some illustrations: Hagendahl (1967)[3] stressed the fact—which is at most partly true—that Augustine showed no originality when he adopted the framework of Cicero's rhetorical system. McNew (1957),[4] on the other hand, maintained that Augustine altered the meaning of traditional concepts such as *docere* and *flectere* to the extent that, in reality, he created a new Christian rhetoric. Should we keep a middle course between these two extremes and go along with Mohrmann's (1958) and Kennedy's (1980) judgment[5] that although Augustine christianized rhetoric, he still overemphasized the theory of the three styles? I quote Kennedy: "The weakness of Augustine's treatise is that it encouraged the identification of rhetoric with style and gave still greater authority to the categorization of styles and figures which was already an obsession of classical rhetoric."[6]

To counter the reproach that Augustine did not emancipate himself enough from Cicero, one's first reaction would be to say, defensively, that in his time Augustine had no alternatives to the three categories of style. But a closer examination of the text, an analysis of its overall structure and an appreciation of its inner dynamism in argumentation, will show how Augustine's baptizing of Cicero's rhetoric represents a step forward. We will see that, in the end, Augustine transcended the categorizations of classical rhetoric.

Let me outline some reasons for my positive assessment of *De doctrina* 4:

First, there is a pastoral aspect. When Augustine developed his ideas, he used to start on the level of his audience. Now the tripartite stylistic scheme had dominated rhetorical theory on style in the handbooks since the Auctor *ad Herennium* (who wrote in Cicero's youth); so Augustine chose to use it, even if his own aims were different.

Second, there is Augustine's sense and feeling for the functioning and the theory of language. Cicero accentuated the three duties of *docere, delectare, flectere* more than his predecessors, and Augustine saw this as an opportunity to improve the inadequate traditional linguistic model of *res* and *signa*. As we know today, the persons involved in the communicative situation are the third factor in how language works apart from *res* and *signa*. Augustine's focus on the duties of instructing, pleasing, and moving anticipates the differentiation of illocutionary acts in modern linguistics.

And third, there is an artistic and aesthetic issue. Both Cicero and Augustine are stylists with an extraordinary ability and predilection for creating sound effects and sentence parallelisms in the tradition of Isocrates, so they risk forfeiting the orator's credibility or the preacher's earnestness and dignity. Hence Augustine understood, better than anybody else, Cicero's defense of his style, i.e., comprehended the structure of the *Orator* as a closing argument, counsel's final oration on behalf of the defendant, and this knowledge enabled him to exploit this structure as a counterpart to his own treatise, thus demonstrating both his distance from Cicero and his personal solution to the problem of the Isocrateic pleasing style.

These pastoral, linguistic, and aesthetic points are important aspects in the following discussion.

I will try to outline the structure of the *Orator* (see Table 1, below, the scheme of Cicero's *Orator*). The work is a closing argument, an oration with the psychogogical form of argumentation typical of a counsel's speech. Unfortunately I cannot base my statements on any recognized findings, as, for example, Yon (1958) and Kytzler (1975)[7] deny the existence of a consistent overall structure in the *Orator*; Bringmann (1971)[8] comes closest to my own interpretation.

Table 1
Cicero's *Orator*

Line Numbers	Section	Function / Subject
1–32	(Preface)	
1–2	0.	INTRODUCTION: The "ideal" orator and the best style
3–19	0.1	The question is a philosophical one
18		M. Antonius, *Disertos se vidisse multos, eloquentem neminem*
20–32	0.2	The best "Attic" orator commands three styles. Praise of Demosthenes
33–112	Part 1	ANALYSIS: In search of the best orator/style
33–35	1.0	Preface to part 1
36–42	1.1	Wanted: the best style, not for *epideixis*, but for speech *in foro*
43–60	1.2	Wanted: the most important of the five fundamental *officia*: *elocutio*
61–74	1.3	Wanted: the best *genus dicendi*: The three styles
61–88	1.3.0	Not the philosophical, sophistic, historical, poetic styles
69–74	1.3.1	The *genus dicendi*, depending on the three *officia* (*docere, deletare, flectere*)

Line Numbers	Section	Function/Topic
75–99	1.3.2	Nature and description of the three styles
75–90	1.3.2.1	*Genus summissum*
76		Nature
77–90		Description
		No rhythm!
91–96	1.3.2.2	*Genus temperatum*
91		Nature
92–96		Description
		Rhythm
97–99	1.3.2.3	*Genus grande*
97		Nature
98–99		Dangerous if employed exclusively
		Description
100–112	1.4	Pseudo-peroration: Variation of *genera*, depending on *res*
		M. Antonius; Cicero; Demosthenes
113–236	Part 2	SYNTHESIS: Description of the ideal orator
113–133	2.1	The *orator doctus* (*ornatus rerum*)
113–119	2.1.1	He knows philosophy, law, history, etc.
120–133	2.1.2	He knows rhetoric, above and beyond school rhetoric (*staseis*, topic, *auxesis*, *ethos*, and *pathos*)
134–233	2.2	The ideal style
134–139	2.2.1	*Ornatus verborum* (*lumina*, *figurae*, . . .)
140–233	2.2.2	*Compositio verborum* (*numerus*, *clausulae*)
234–236	2.3	Peroration: Applause for the artist
		Demosthenes; Cicero
237–238	(Epilogue)	

As you know, Cicero's oratorical style was attacked by the so-called Atticists when he wrote the *Orator*. So he had to defend his passionate and Isocrateic *genus dicendi copiosum et ornatum*, particularly his sentence structure in regular periods with rhythmic closings (to quote his own words, he defends his *levis et structa et terminata oratio*,[9] or, in one word, his *numerus*).[10] It is not easy to defend prose rhythm, so he sometimes arranges his arguments in a structure that is cleverly ambiguous.

One of the two main structural principles is apparent uniformity; he creates this impression by directing an abundance of seemingly parallel elements in permanent crescendo towards the final apotheosis of *numerus*. Among other things, crescendo and abundance result from the change in aspects between parts 1 and 2 (cf. the scheme in Table 1). First, Cicero inquires into the criteria for the best orator: by contrasting his style with epideictic (1.1), by examining the five *officia—inventio, dispositio*, and so on (1.2)—and by discussing the three psychagogical *officia* (1.3). This analytical first part is then followed by a synthetical second part, in which Cicero initially gives a survey of the qualities and skills possessed by the *orator dictus* (2.1) and concludes (in 2.2) with the orator's artistry in constructing periods and rhythms.

The same principle of crescendo is observed in 1.3 and 1.4, i.e., in the sections on the three styles and their blending. Crescendo results from the tripartite pattern recurring three times and ascending in the *officia* from sober instruction (*docere*) to passionate emotional appeal (*movere, flectere*), in the *genera dicendi* from the low (*summissum*) to the grand (*grande, vehemens*), and in the *res* from trivial matters (*parvae*), to matters of magnitude (*magnae*).

However, Cicero the counsel entangles himself in certain difficulties when he describes the three *genera dicendi* in relation to the three *officia*. The crux is *numerus*. For prose rhythm, i.e., *clausulae*, is most frequently used not in the grand style, as the principle of crescendo would suggest, but in the middle style, with its aim of pleasing. In his own speeches, Cicero is more economical with *clausulae* in the low and grand styles.[11]

It should be of interest to us that in *De doctrina* 4 Augustine expresses agreement with Cicero's practice but not his theory. I quote a few sentences from Augustine's description of the three styles. The low style remains without ornaments (one of which would be prose rhythm), *non ornamenta verborum, sed rerum documenta desiderat*.[12] It is only when describing the middle style that Augustine talks of *hunc elocutionis ornatum qui numerosis fit clausulis*.[13] The frequency of *clausulae* may decrease from middle to grand style, because in the latter *ornatus* is only used facultatively: *non tam verborum ornatibus comptum est*.[14] Thus Augustine corrects Cicero's crescendo as regards rhythm although he does so very politely and discreetly, out of respect for his old mentor in rhetoric and philosophy.

But how does Cicero extricate himself from his difficulties? The simple answer is to say: in section 1.3 of his *Orator* he avoids describing the compromising details of the middle and grand styles,[15] and in 1.4 he introduces the concept of a "mixed" style so as to be able to speak about prose rhythm without making a difference between the three styles in part 2.

Let me give you some evidence from the text. In *Orator* 77 he states the description of the low style with the summons, "let's free him from the chains of periods and *clausulae" primum eum* [sc. *summissi generis oratorem] tamquam e vinculis numerorum eximamus*); and on these *numeri oratorii . . . observandi . . . alio in genere orationis* he makes the apparently casual remark, "we will deal with rhythm soon" (*de quibus mox agemus*). The reader expects the word *soon* to refer to the next sub-section on the middle style, but in *Orator* 92–96 Cicero speaks about other means of *ornatus*, not about rhythm. And in the following subsec-tion on the grand style (*Orator* 97–99), he avoids the issue of *ornatus* altogether. Furthermore, when he introduces the concept of the mixed style in 1.4, he cleverly exploits the opportunity to depart from the in-convenient link[16] between the aim of pleasing (*delectare*) and the middle style with its rhythmical periods. This middle style is now related to the *res modicae*, matters of medium value, because nobody would associate this expression with prose rhythm—which would probably have been the case with the duty of *delectare*.

So far, we have seen how Cicero uses his structural principle of ap-parent uniformity. There is a complementary second principle: apparent duality. His aim is, of course, to discuss and celebrate in part 2 the ef-fects of *numerus* without having to delve into the differentiated use of prose rhythm in the individual styles. Therefore he wants to stress the concept of the mixed style so that he can talk about prose rhythm in general. The means he uses to inculcate this concept into his audience's minds is this very strategy of duality. Hence he concludes part 1 with a striking peroration.[17] And how does he create the impression of a perora-tion? He resorts to two important concepts used in the introduction. There he exemplified the motif of the ideal orator (0.1) by quoting his teacher M. Antonius (*Orator:*[18] *in eo libro quem unum reliquit disertos ait se vidisse multos, eloquentem omnino neminem*); and he exemplified his polemical rejection of too rigid an Atticism by praising Demosthenes (0.2), who, mastering all three styles, came closest to the ideal orator. Now, in the pseudo-peroration in 1.4, M. Antonius and Demosthenes re-appear on stage: Antonius in its first sentences (*Orator* 100: "Now we've found the ideal orator . . . ," *tenemus igitur Brute quem quaerimus, . . . inventus profecto est ille eloquens quem numquam vidit Antonius*);[18] De-mosthenes at the end (in *Orator* 110 f.); and, to heighten the effect, Cicero himself between them (in 102–109), parading examples of his own abundance of various oratorical styles. And just as he excels with his mixed style in 1.4, he will reappear (together with Demosthenes) in the true peroration in 2.3, this time excelling with his prose rhythm.

I would like to make two final remarks on Cicero's *Orator.*

First, it is not surprising that the structure of the work has caused difficulties: Cicero's strategic game with two competing principles of structure—dualism on the one hand and uniformity and crescendo on the other—is not easy to grasp. We have been able to analyze it because we have recognized Cicero's problem with the description of the Isocrateic middle style.

Second, for a comparison with Augustine we should bear in mind what Cicero says in the two perorations (where, if not there?) as his most personal concern. Despite all his success as a politician and counsel he was proudest of his achievement as an artist of speech. He filled, as he says, the famished Roman ears with variation in style.[19] And, in his eyes, the great orator has to carry his audience away like a star actor: he must provoke not only agreement but also admiration and applause; it would be shameful if the audience preferred to watch or listen to anything else.[20]

Let us turn to Saint Augustine. First, I must repeat my similar initial remark on Cicero: there is no consensus on the structure of De doctrina 4. Scattered remarks made by Steffen (1964)[21] are the most useful; but Kennedy (1980)[22] and Alici (1989)[23] still present rather arbitrary analyses of structure. As far as I know, nobody has noticed, for instance, the bipartite organization Augustine adopted from Cicero,[24] although Augustine emphasized the originality of his own doctrine exactly by such contrasting intertextual relations (see Table 2, below, the scheme of Augustine's De doctrina christiana 4).[25]

Table 2
Augustine's De doctrina christiana 4

(Capitulum)	Paragraph	Section	Function / Subject
(1.1)	1–2	(Transition)	
(1.2)	3–13	0.	INTRODUCTION: Against overestimation and underestimation of rhetoric
(4.5)		Part 1	Duties and aims of preacher/preaching (officia)
	14–24	1.1	Priority of (biblical) sapientia over (human) eloquentia
(6.9)	25–60	1.2	Excursus: Biblical eloquentia—only partially imitable
(8.22)		1.3	Eloquentia subordinated to the listener
	61–73	1.3.1	Plane dicere docere
(12.27)	74–86	1.3.2	The three officia
(15.32)	87–95	1.4	Pseudo-peroration: pray for God's grace

(*Capitulum*)	Paragraph	Section	Function / Subject
(*17.34)		Part 2	Style of preacher/preaching (*genera dicendi*)
		2.1	The three styles (subordinated to *officia*)
	96–106	2.1.1	*Genera* not dependent on *res*
(20.39)	107–133	2.1.2	Examples of the three styles
(22.51)		2.2	Against mechanical application of the styles
	134–144	2.2.1	Necessity of mixing the *genera* (*genus temperatum* subordinated)
(26.56)	145–150	2.2.2	Necessity of mixing the *officia* (regardless of *genera*)
(27.59)	151–159	2.2.3	Exemplary life and truth—more effective than *genus grande*
(29.62)	160–165	2.3	Peroration: pray for God's grace
(31.64)	166	(Epilogue)	

Let us start by tracing the main lines of Augustine's argumentation, i.e., by observing how he adheres to the *Orator* in terms of structure in order to emphasize the contrast between the orator and the preacher in terms of content (cf. Tables 1 and 2). In Cicero's work everything progressed in the crescendo of apparent unity toward the climax of *copiose et ornate dicere*. When we look at Augustine's structure, we encounter the opposite: decrescendo and real coherence and unity of argumentation. Unlike in Cicero, part 1 does not even reach the topics of *genera dicendi* but ends with the pastoral interpretation of *officia*, especially *docere* and *movere*. The decrescendo movement starts on the level of divine wisdom: in 1.1 and 1.2 Augustine subordinates *eloquentia* to the *sapientia* of God and God's word in the Bible—the preacher and the *ornatus* of language are servants of divine truth. Section 1.3 demonstrates the same servitude toward the listeners of the word. The preacher must fulfill the duty of instructing the congregation and of trying to move them to do as they should; the goal of pleasing comes last.

At this point, Augustine's contrasting imitation of Cicero becomes particularly clear. It is with a view to the success of the speaker in court that Cicero words his well-known formula, *probare necessitatis est, delectare suavitatis, flectere victoriae:*[26] speaking in a clear, probable manner is no more than a prerequisite, speaking pleasantly entertains the listener, but appealing emotionally to the audience ensures the speaker's victory. Au-

gustine transforms this passage—which he quotes in *De doctrina* 4.74—
at the very beginning of the pseudo-peroration (in 87),[27] with the focus
not on the preacher but on God's wisdom and the listener's salvation. The
preacher speaks about just, holy, and moral things (this is Augustine's reference to *sapientia*), so he strives to help the listener receive the sermon
with understanding (*intellegenter,* the listener's response to *docere*), with
pleasure (*libenter,* in analogy to *delectare*), and in obedience (*oboedienter*, instead of *flectere*). Perhaps here it is worth mentioning that
Hagendahl, concentrating on Cicero, noted Augustine's quotation of
Cicero's passage in *De doctrina* 74,[28] but not its transformation in 87.

In the second part of the *Orator* Cicero had saved the subject of style
and *numerus* for the finale; Augustine continues his decrescendo line of
servitude. In part 1 the *officia* had to serve God and the audience. Now
(in 2.1) the three styles are, for their part, subordinated to the *officia*, and
in 2.2, Augustine even warns against overestimating the styles and applying them mechanically. For Cicero, the mixed style was the best;
Augustine discusses the blending of *officia*, regardless of style, as more important. And whereas Cicero had subordinated the *orator doctus* and his
philosophy to the finale with the *numerus*, Augustine in 2.2 reverses the
sequence and importance in two aspects, one already discussed and one
new: (1) service to the audience and, above all, to God's truth (*veritas*) is
more important than style, as Augustine stresses in his last variation on
Cicero's passage on the *officia* (*De doctrina* 4.157: *sive summisse sive
temperate sive graditer dicat, id agit verbis, ut veritas pateat* [cf. *docere*],
veritas placeat [cf. *delectare*], *veritas moveat*); and (2) the example of a
good life is also more effective in preaching than the grand style (*De doctrina* 4.151: *habet autem, ut oboedienter audiamur, quantacumque
granditate dictionis maius pondus vita dicentis*).

I hope you can see from this short outline of Augustine's main line of
argumentation how, on the one hand, his decrescendo technique places
emphasis on the subordinate function of style in humble Christian preaching and, on the other, how he achieves and enhances this effect by
creating a counterpart to Cicero's triumphant Orator.

This intertextual and interstructural relationship becomes even more
visible in the same technique of pseudo-peroration. From the aspect of
content, of course, Augustine needed the first peroration even less than
Cicero did; he just uses it to underline that *officia*, not style, have to be
the main concern of the preacher. Like Cicero, Augustine repeats in it
elements from the introduction. There he had defended the relative value
of rhetoric against its underestimation by posing the question as to who
might be so strict a fundamentalist as to disregard the psychagogical and
pastoral potential of rhetoric in the defense of truth (*De doctrina* 4.4:

quis ita desipiat ut hoc sapiat?); and he had warned against the overestimation of rhetoric and its prescriptions by assuring that the emulation of good Christian writers is sufficient to become a good preacher (*DDC* 4.9–11. In compliance with this, in section 2.1.2 about the styles, he offers, not rules for the three styles, but examples of them, taken from St. Paul, Cyprian, and Ambrose). Now these two introductory warnings are repeated in the pseudo-peroration and considered in greater depth.

First, the preacher should not overestimate himself, because not he, but God's grace, causes the listener's conversion. Hence the motto "First pray, then preach" (*sit orator ante quam dictor*).[29] For "who knows either what is better for us to say on a special occasion, or what is best for others to hear from us, if it be not he who sees the hearts of all?"[30] The preacher must rely on God's help, in *cuius manu sunt et nos et sermones nostri* (a quotation from Wis. 7:16). By the way, this will be the very sentence with which Augustine will also conclude the true peroration in *De doctrina* 4.165.

Second, in paragraphs 90–95 Augustine again goes into the reservations held by the fundamentalists against rational teaching in faith. Following the first Epistle to the Corinthians, they asserted, *non esse hominibus praecipiendum quid vel quemadmodum doceant, si doctores sanctus efficit spiritus.*[31] To placate them and to justify his instructing of preachers, Augustine presents a twofold testimony from St. Paul: first he quotes from the pastoral epistles, in which Paul summons his disciples Titus and Timothy to teach; then he quotes 1 Cor., warning against possible presumption and pride on the part of teachers (1 Cor. 3:7: *neque qui plantat est aliquid neque qui rigat, sed Deus qui incrementum dat*). It is presumably no coincidence that Augustine once more bases the concluding motifs of part 2 on the same group of Pauline epistles. To underline the precedence of the preacher's *vita* over his *verba*, he quotes, for instance, 1 Tim. 4:12 "Be thou an example of the faithful in word, in conversation, in charity, in faith, in chastity"; and to underscore the subordination of *verba* to the central message of Christianity, he cites 1 Cor. 1:17: *non in sapientia verbi, ne evacuetur crux Christi.*[32]

I hope that this quick outline of the main argumentation and structure of *De doctrina* 4 has given you an indication of Augustine's (sometimes doubted) stylistic and literary artistry, which he employed to put the subject of *eloquentia* into the unifying framework of evangelization. The few passages quoted were intended to show you how Augustine's *docere* also has the quality of an appeal; his quotations from authorities and his well-worded, motto-like doctrinal sentences, of course, only attain their full effect in their context.

Before we continue, one short remark: If *De doctrina* 4 is really as well structured as has been said, is it not strange that Augustine gives the preacher instructions on *inventio* (books 1–3) and *elocutio* (book 4) but not on *dispositio*? Of course the reason can again only be the homily's twin dependence on both the biblical text that the particular sermon explains and the current situation of the particular congregation, to which the preacher should respond, not with a prepared sermon, but in a spontaneous way with the help of God.

Let us now turn to observing in detail what Augustine says about the function of the *genera dicendi* in the main subsections of *De doctrina* 4. We will come to a better understanding of both his originality and his instrumentalizing of Cicero when we pursue the various adaptations of a specific technique of argumentation on three levels, which he often employs for pastoral and didactic purposes. In *De doctrina* 4, the lowest level is that of the general reader, so to speak: in late antiquity everybody was familiar with the rhetoric of manuals and everybody tended to equate rhetoric and style. We expect Cicero, as the *orator ductus* and as an artist, to be on a higher level and to be quoted as an authority to the lower level. Biblical and Christian wisdom is predestinated to form the top level.

In part 1 this three-level argumentation appears in its regular form. At the beginning of 1.1 Augustine meets the—largely justified—expectations that a listener on the lowest level would have of a preacher.[33] For instance, he should persuade the congregation by various ellocutionary acts—and by speaking *acute* (keenly, i.e., by *docere*), *ornate* (i.e., to *delectare*), and *vehementer* (passionately). Thus, from the very beginning, the preacher is expected to have a command of the three styles—but not in the eyes of St. Augustine. For instead of preferring the master of the three styles, who can speak *ornate*, *acute*, and *vehementer*, to a preacher who can only speak *obtunse* (obtusely), *deformiter* (in an ugly manner), and *frigide* (coldly), Augustine surprises us by recommending the man who speaks wisely, *sapienter*, rather than *eloquenter*. This relativizing of *eloquentia* is then[34] corroborated by an authoritative quotation from Cicero *quasi philosophus* (*De invent. rhet.* 1.1: *eloquentia* without *sapientia* could be ruinous in politics). From this Ciceronian level Augustine ascends to the biblical level, from profane *sapientia* to God's *vera* (!) *sapientia*,[35] and quotes from the Book of Wisdom: "The multitude of the wise (i.e., not of the eloquent) is the welfare of the whole world." This sentence, Wisdom 6:26, is the first literal quotation from the Bible in *De doctrina* 4, corresponding to the last one, Wisdom 7:16, in paragraph 165.

After an excursus on biblical style in 1.2,[36] we meet our pastoral three level argumentation again in 1.3. Once more Augustine starts on the lowest level, using a schema taken from the rhetoric handbooks. These manuals used to list four "qualities of style" (*virtutes dicendi*): *Latine dicere*, correct Latin; *plane dicere*, speaking clearly; *ornate*, with Isocrateic embellishment; and *congruenter*, adequately. Indeed, Augustine starts off by discussing the style of preaching according to the categories of *virtutes dicendi*. Their merits are judged in terms of their benefit to the listener: *Latine* and *ornate dicere* are least valuable. Then Augustine moves up to the second level by making use of the close relation between *plane dicere* and *docere*, and *ornate dicere* and *delectare*, thus arriving at Cicero's three *officia* (and reserving the fourth virtue, *congruenter dicere*, for later discussion in part 2). Augustine requires Cicero's passage, *docere necessitatis est, delectare suavitatis, flectere victoriae* (*De doctrina* 4.74), in order to prove that there are priorities among the three *officia*. Obviously the priorities are different for the counsel and politician, on the one hand, and for the Christian preacher, on the other. The preacher must, above all, instruct his flock; speaking with embellishment is insignificant and must be justified before God. At this point the authoritative biblical quotations characteristic of the third level recur (first in paragraph 81,[37] then, as already stated, in the first peroration).

Once again, the three-level argumentation forms the basis of 2.1, but we shall see that the relationship between Augustine and Cicero now becomes more complex. The concept of *congruenter* or *apte et convenienter dicere*, the fourth *virtus dicendi*, is no longer treated on the level of handbooks. Rather, Augustine immediately turns to the issue of the function or adequacy of the styles. He discusses the question on the Ciceronian level, and it turns out that Cicero's transition from the relation between duties and styles to that between styles and topics, *res*, poses problems for the Christian. On the forum, Cicero can distinguish between trivial and important subjects; but in church everything is important, as everything is concerned with salvation.[38] This is why Augustine rejects the relation styles/topics and differentiates the styles and their characteristic means solely according to their illocutionary impact on the listener. So his examples of *genus summissum* are only there to illustrate how a preacher can argue (*docere*): with biblical quotations, with the anticipation of objections, in the form of questions and answers—there is not one word about figures of sound or sentence parallels. In the *genus grande*, too, the essential element is the emotional impact of the text. Here I refer to Augustine's discussion of Galatians 4:10–20 in *De doctrina*, paragraphs 122–124. Augustine prefaces his quotation from Paul with the remark that the passage could only have been written in the grand style, although there is no embellishment in it, and he concludes by asking the question: "Do we have here examples of antithesis, of climax, or the resonance of parallel sentences? No, but nevertheless Paul's deep emotion does not cool off."[39] Please note the clear contradiction to Cicero, who allocates such verbal embellishments to the grand style. (I wonder why later readers of *De doctrina* 4 have been led astray to construe from this text an overestimation of figurative language.)

We found our three-level scheme in 2.1 for the last time; in 2.2, Augustine will not carry on Cicero's doctrines but dissociate himself discreetly from his master. So we see that our judgment on the relationship between Augustine and Cicero must be a differentiated one. On the positive side was Cicero's stimulus to reach a better comprehension of the concept of adequacy in style, *congruenter dicere*. But adequacy for what? That was an open question. Augustine exploits the relation between *officia* and *genera dicendi* employed in Cicero's *Orator* to point out the roles played by speaker and listener in the communicative process. Aristotelian tradition had stressed only the two aspects of *res* and *signa*, object and designation, in its linguistic model; now Augustine adds the element of *personae*, the persons involved in communication. In our concrete case the preacher has to serve the listener, and his style depends on the relevant duties.

Here we can look back at section 1.2, the excursus on biblical style, whose main tenor tends to be misunderstood. Mohrmann,[40] for instance, seems to be of the opinion that Augustine recommends the preacher to emulate the figures of style found in the Bible. This would sanction among other things the means of Isocrateic *ornatus*, since they are at times used by St. Paul. But there is the rule of adequacy: the authors of the Bible speak with such superhuman authority that their style is not applicable to human communication without further ado. "Eloquence does not deserve the name, if it be not in accord with the person who speaks. . . . With such eloquence have our authors spoken, no other is fitting to them, nor is theirs to others; for it perfectly accords with them."[41] So in 1.2 the question remains open as to whether and how Isocrateic *ornatus* can be used by preachers.

The negative side of our judgment about Cicero's usefulness for Augustine is connected with this open question. For Cicero's solution must necessarily be insufficient in Augustine's eyes. As we have seen, Augustine is quite aware of the fact that Cicero's justification of *ornatus* in the grand style is the product of oratorical deception. This is why, in section 2.2, Augustine abandons his three-level argumentation; Cicero could not have been an authority here. So this time Augustine does not ally himself with Cicero against the handbooks but with the handbooks and rhetoric in general against too mechanical an application of the theory of the three styles: "No one should suppose that it is against the rules of rhetoric (*contra disciplinam*) to mix these three styles."[42] The theory of the mixed style was a climax in the *Orator*)—and now Augustine nearly calls it a rhetorical cliché (as in fact it was).

In paragraph 139 and following there is a perceptible pinprick against Cicero. According to Cicero, the grand style can be recognized by the acclaim it provokes; and, with his well-known anecdote about his sermon in Caesarea Mauretaniae, Augustine adduces proof that the characteristic effect of the grand style is not acclaim but tears. Acclaim is the effect of the Isocrateic middle style; and in paragraph 143 and following Augustine says this about it: "In the low style, the preacher persuades the congregation that what he says is true; in the grand style, he persuades them to do what they know they should do; in the middle style he persuades them that he is expressing himself in a beautiful and embellished manner—but what is the point of this for Christians? That's for people who pride themselves on their language and who show off in Isocrateic panegyrics."[43] Besides, on hearing this, we see the point in Augustine's concluding his second peroration with the words, *qui gloriatur, in illo glorietur in cuius manu sunt et nos et sermones nostri.* [44]

In paragraph 144 Augustine, concluding *DDC* 2.2.1 about the mixing of styles, repeats once more that Christians may use the *genus medium*, but only in a subordinate function, in the service of *docere* and *flectere.*[45] There is general consensus today on the fact that in his practice as a preacher, Augustine really did subordinate elegance of style to pastoral responsibility. But this service in humility is not a slavish one. For after long categorizing and dividing of the psychagogical duties and the corresponding styles, in 2.2.2 Augustine surprises us by drawing a conclusion which may be unexpected but is nevertheless correct. Since he is aware that the pleasing style, if used in humility, can always be combined with *docere* and *flectere*, in paragraph 145 he infers that the preacher may mix the duties or *officia* as he sees fit, irrespective of the separate styles:

> *illa itaque*[46] *tria, . . . eum . . . id agere debere ut intellegenter, ut libenter, ut oboedienter audiatur, non sic accipienda sunt tamquam singula illis tribus dicendi generibus ita tribuantur, ut ad summissum intellegenter, ad temperatum libenter, ad grande pertineat oboedienter audiri, sed sic potius ut haec tria semper intendat et quantum potest agat, etiam cum in illorum singolo quoque versatur.*

Every psychagogical duty is to be fulfilled at any time by any style—even by the Isocrateic, if we (to repeat the condition from 144) *temperati generis ornatu non iactanter, sed prudenter utamur.*

There is another prerequisite for this free manner of preaching: besides Christian humility, Augustine's oratorical gift and psychological versatility are wanted to fulfill the preacher's duty to respond simultaneously to all the needs of his flock. Of course he does not speak openly about this personal presupposition, but in reality it is here that Augustine takes his concept of adequacy to its very consequence. Hence his style gains the flexibility and freedom we admire. In preparing an edition of his *Enarrationes in psalmos*, again and again I come across passages where the coherence of the text depends, for example, on reading an apparently objective statement as an appeal. A German proverb says, *Der Ton macht die Musik*, and Augustine's flexibility in tones, his pastoral sensibility in responding to his audience, grants him the freedom to use his stylistic abilities as a humble servant of God and his flock. This obedient "freedom of the children of God" renders Augustine's Isocrateic artistry possible. I think Augustine's justification of Isocrateism is more honest than Cicero's.

I would like to conclude with a text taken from this section of *De doctrina christiana* to give you an example of how Augustine blends *docere*, while talking about it, with *delectare*, i.e., with *genus temperatum* and its *numerus*:[47]

Plerumque autem dictio ípsa sùmmíssa,	*P1*
dum solvit difficíllimàs quaéstiónes	*V3*
et inopinata manifestatióne dèmónstrat,	*P1*
dum sententias acutissimas de nescio quibus	
quasi cavernis unde non seperabatur	
éruit et òsténdit,	*V*
dum adversarii convíncit èrrórem	*P1*
et docet falsum esse, quod ab illo dici	
videbátur invìctum,	*P1*
maxime quando adest eius quoddam décus nòn áppetítum	*V3*
sed quodámmodò náturále	*V3*
et nonulla non iactanticula,	
sed quasi necessaria	
atque ut ita dicam ipsis rébus èxórta	*P1*
numerósitàs claúsulárum,	*V3*
tantas adclamationes excitat,	
ut vix intelligatur ésse sùmmíssa.	*P1*

This text demonstrates how Augustine talks in Isocrateic manner not to boast of his abilities but to show how natural the free blending of styles can be.[48] As regards his literary performance in *De doctrina* 4 in general, I think we may apply to Professor Augustine what he himself said about a well-structured passage in Paul:

quanta sapientia ista sint dicta
vigilantes vident,
quanto vero etiam eloquentiae cucurrerint flumine,
et qui stertit advertit.[49]

Notes

1. C. Steffen, *Augustinus' Schrift 'De doctrina Christiana': Untersuchungen zum Aufbau, zum Begriffsgehalt und zur Bedeutung der Beredsamkeit,* Dissertation (Kiel, 1964): G. A. Press, "The Subject and Structure of Augustine's *De doctrina Christiana*," *AugStud* 11 (1980): 99–124.

2. The following scheme may be useful:

OFFICIA	GENERA DICENDI	RES
probare, docere	*tenue, summissum*	*parva*
delectare	*temperatum, medium*	*modica*
flectere, movere	*grave, grande*	*magna*

3. H. Hagendahl, *Augustine and the Latin Classics,* Studia Graeca et Latina Gothoburgensia 20, 1(Göteborg 1967). *DDC* 4 is treated on pages 558–568.

4. L. D. McNew, "The Relation of Cicero's Rhetoric to Augustine," *Research Studies of the State College of Washington* 25 (1957): 5–13.

5. C. Mohrmann, "St. Augustine and the *eloquentia*. *Etudes sur le latin des chrétiens,* vol. 1 (Roma, 1958), 351–370, see particularly p. 360 f.

6. G. A. Kennedy, *Classical Rhetoric and Its Christian and Secular Tradition from Ancient to Modern Times* (London, 1980), material on Augustine on pp. 149–160; the quotation in my text is from p. 158.

7. A. Yon, "Sur la composition de l'*Orator* de Cicéron," *Bulletin Association G. Budé* (1958): 470 ff.; B. Kytzler, *M. T. Cicero, Orator, lateinisch und deutsch* (München, 1975) p. 227 ff.

8. K. Bringmann, "Untersuchungen zum späten Cicero," *Hypomnemata* 29 (1871), discussion of *Orator* pp. 41–59.

9. Typically connected with the "grand style," e.g., Cicero *Orator* 20: *grandiloqui . . . fuerunt cum ampla et sententiarum gravitate et maiestate verborum, vehementes varii, copiosi graves, ad permovendos et convertendos animos instructi et parati; quod ipsum . . . oratione . . . consequebantur . . . levi et structa et terminata.* Cf. *Rhetorica ad Herennium* 4.8.11: *gravis est (oratio) quae constat ex verborum gravium levi et ornata constructione.*

10. On Cicero's concept of *numerus,* in which are contained both parallel periods and rhythmic *clausulae,* see A. Primmer, "Cicero *numerosus:* Studien zum antiken Prosarhythmus," *Sitzungsberichte der österreichischen Akademie der Wissenschaften (phil.-hist. Kl.)* 257 (1968), ch. 2.

11. Cf. Primmer, 226.

12. *DDC* 4.127 (for quotations I use the paragraphs of Green's *CSEL* edition, for correspondence to chapter numbers, see the schematic disposition): *Ambrosius summisso . . . dicendi genere utitur, quoniam res suscepta non ornamenta verborum aut ad flectendos animos commotionis affectum, sed rerum documenta desiderat.*

13. *DDC* 4.115 (in discussing passages from Romans written by St. Paul in *genus temperatum*): *sane hunc elocutionis ornatum, qui numerosis fit clausulis, deesse fatendum est auctoribus nostris.*

14. *DDC* 4.118: *grande autem dicendi genus hoc maxime distat ab isto genere temperato, quod non tam verborum ornatibus comptum est quam violentum animi affectibus.*

15. In *Orator* 1.3.2.1 (*genus summissum*), Cicero speaks about its nature, and in its description there are remarks about prose rhythm; in 1.3.2.2 (*genus temporatum*) not one word about rhythm; and in 1.3.2.3 (*genus grande*) no description at all. As far as I know, these gaps and their implications have not yet been noticed.

16. In *Orator* 1.3.1, the link between *delectare* and the middle style was welcome: there Cicero needed the three *officia* to lay a 'new' foundation for the three styles.

17. Cf. Bringmann, 48 f.; Kytzler, 231. Bringmann recognizes the bipartition, but ends part one too late, at *Orator* 120. Kytzler, on the other hand, notes the repetitions of motives, but not their significance for the pseudo-peroration.

18. Note how both sense ("Now we've found . . . ") and tone, with the repeated praising double cretics (*Brúte quèm quaérimùs* and *vídit Antóniùs*) bring about the impression of *peroratio*.

19. *Orator* 106: *ieiunas . . . huius multiplicis et aequabiliter in omnia genera fusae orationis aures civitatis accepimus easque nos primi . . . ad huius generis dicendi audiendi incredibilia studia convertimus.* Cf. his praise of the παθητικόν in *Orator* 128 f.: *magno semper usi impetu saepe adversarios de statu omni deisimus.* He could not be answered by Hortensius in the case against Verres, his speech silenced Catilina in the senate . . . : in his memory he fancies he exerted oratorical effects which, in reality, partly had different causes.

20. *Orator* 236: *Eloquens vero, qui non approbationes solum, sed admirationes clamores plauses si liceat movere debet, omnibus oportet ita rebus excellat, ut ei turpe sit quidquam aut spectari aut audiri libentius.*

21. See n. 1.

22. See n. 5.

23. L. Alici, *S. Agostino d'Ippona, La dottrina christiana*, introduction, translation, and notes (Milano, 1989).

24. Cf. the schematic outline. One additional remark: the borderline between ch. 16.33 (= paragraph 95) and chapter 17.34 (= paragraph 95) divides book 4 into exactly equal parts of 26 pages (Green).

25. These relations can be demonstrated here only by implicit proof: I refer mainly to the decrescendo argumentation instead of crescendo; the transformation of Cicero's rules concerning *officia* and *genera dicendi* discussed in the same sequence as in *Orator*; the bipartite structure and God's—not Cicero's or Augustine's—principal position in the perorations: see also n. 36.

26. *Orator* 69: *probare* [DDC 4.74 has *docere*] *necessitatis est, delectare suavitatis, flectere victoriae . . . sed quot officia oratoris, tot sunt genera dicendi: subtile in probando, modicum in delectando, vehemens in flectendo.*

27. DDC 4.87: *Agit itaque noster iste eloquens, cum iusta et sancta et bona dicit . . . ut intellegenter, ut libenter, ut oboedienter audiatur.*

28. Hagendahl, 526 f.

29. DDC 4.87: *haec* [sc. *ut intellegenter, libenter, oboedienter audiatur*] *se posse . . . pietate magis orationum quam oratorum facultate non dubitet, ut orando pro se ac pro illis, quos est allocuturus, sit orator ante quam dictor.*

30. DDC 4.88: *cum enim . . . multa sint quae dicantur et multi modi quibus di-*

cantur . . . quis novit quid ad praesens tempus vel nobis dicere vel per nos expediat audiri, nisi qui corda omnium videt? Et quis facit ut quod oportet et quem ad modum oportet dicatur a nobis, nisi in cuius manu sunt et nos et sermones nostri? For translations I usually quote or use T. Sullivan, *S. Aureli Augustini Hipponensis episcopi De doctrina christiana . . . liber quartus: A Commentary with a Revised Text, Introduction, and Translation,* Patristic Studies 23 (Washington, 1930).

31. *DDC* 4.90: *quid* refers to books 1–3; *quemadmodum,* to book 4.

32. *DDC* 4.155.

33. I refer to *DDC* 4.16 f.: *Haec . . . cuncta . . . omnes fere homines in his quae loquendo agunt facere* non quiescunt. [4.17] *Sed cum alii faciant obtunse, deformiter, frigide, alii acute, ornate, vehementer, illum ad hoc opus unde agimus iam oportet accedere, qui potest disputare vel dicere sapienter, etiamsi non potest eloquenter, ut prosit audientibus, etiam si minus, quam prodesset si et eloquenter posset dicere.*

34. In *DDC* 4.18.

35. *DDC* 4.18: *veram, hoc est supernam quae a patre hominum descendit* [cf. James 1:17] *sapientiam;* the next quotation is from *DDC* 4.23.

36. This excursus about a style which, although important for the preacher, must not be imitated, may be compared, in position and content, to Cicero *Orator* 37 ff., about the epideictic style: *non quo neglegenda sit [37] . . . non alienum fuit de oratoris quasi incunabulis dicere* [42].

37. Jer. 5:30 f.; note *sacerdotes plausum dederunt manibus et plebs mea dilexit sic.*

38. On this topic, see E. Auerbach, *Literatursprache und Publikum in der lateinischen Spätantike und im Mittelalter* (Bonn, 1958). For authoritative biblical quotations, see *DDC* 4.99 ff., for instance (Lk.16:10) *qui in minimo fidelis est, et in magno fidelis est.*

39. *DDC* 4.124: *numquid his aut contraria contrariis verba sunt reddita aut aliqua gradatione sibi subnexa sunt aut caesa et membra circuitusve sonuerunt? Et tamen non ideo tepuit affectus, quo eloquium fervere sentimus.*

40. Mohrmann, 365, 369.

41. *DDC* 4.26: *sicut . . . nec iam dicenda est eloquentia si personae non congruat eloquentis, ita est quaedam quae viros summa auctoritate dignissimos planeque divinos decet. Hac illi locuti sunt, nec ipsos decet alia nec alios ipsa: ipsis enim congruit.* Cf. *DDC* 4.60: *Quapropter et eloquentes quidem, non solum sapientes canonicos nostros auctores doctoresque fateamur tali eloquentia qualis personis eius modi congruebat.*

42. *DDC* 4.134: *nec quisquam praeter disciplinam esse existimet ista miscere; immo quantum congrue*[!] *fieri potest, omnibus generibus dictio varianda est.* We should remember that Augustine introduced *apte et convenienter = congrue dicere* as an anonymous concept on handbook level (*DDC* 4.96); cf., in contrast, *DDC* 4.74: *dixit ergo quidam eloquens* [i.e., Cicero], *et verum dixit*[!], *ita dicere debere eloquentem ut doceat, ut delectet, ut flectat.*

43. *DDC* 4.143 f.: *persuadet autem in summisso genere vera esse quae dicit, persuadet in grandi ut agantur quae agenda esse iam sciuntur nec aguntur, persuadet in genere temperato pulchre ornateque se dicere. Quo fine nobis quid opus*

est? [144:] *Appetant eum, qui lingua gloriantur et se in panegyricis talibusque dictionibus iactant. ubi nec docendus nec ad aliquid agendum movendus, sed tantummodo est delectandus auditor.*

44. Here Augustine combines 1 Cor. 1:31 (the *floria*-motif) and Wis. 7:16.

45. DDC 2.2.1, paragraph 144: *ita fit ut etiam temperati generis ornatu non iactanter* [like Cicero], *sed prudenter utamur, non eius fine contenti quo tantummodo delectatur auditor eos.*

46. *Itaque* (DDC 2.2.1, paragraph 145) refers to paragraph 144, quoted n. 45.

47. DDC 4.146: the signs for the *clausulae* are those adopted in A. Primmer, "Rhythmus und Textprobleme in IVL. *Aug. op. imperf.* 1–3," *Wiener Studien* 88(1975): 186 ff.: P1 is $\stackrel{\smile}{-}\smile\stackrel{\smile}{-}\stackrel{\smile}{-}$. V3 is $\stackrel{\smile}{-}\smile\stackrel{\smile}{-}\smile\stackrel{\smile}{-}\stackrel{\smile}{-}$.

48. We must beware of reading the three *dum*-clauses as a premeditated static scheme. Augustine proceeds gradually, i.e., dynamically. The instructing style is first "defined" (*solvit difficillimas quaestiones*), then qualified as surprising and illuminating both in plain language (*inopinata manifestatione demonstrat*) and in metaphors (*de nescio quibus quasi cavernis . . . eruit*), then its effect is praised (*convincit . . . invictum*); in the end, *decus non appetitum, quodammodo naturale,* and *numerositas clausularum* (three times V3) supervene—the result is: *adclamationes.*

49. DDC 4.35.

Sonus et Verbum:
De doctrina christiana 1.13.12

TAKESHI KATO

The present paper[1] attempts to treat the relationship between the sound and the meaning of words in Augustine's writing. Drago Pintaric[2] concisely pointed out, in his *Sprache und Trinität* (1983), a fundamental change in Augustine's attitude on this problem. Initially, Augustine had separated the sound of words and their meaning, but later he thought it better to combine them.

I would like to shed some light on the problem of voice by analyzing the following specific texts in detail. In chronological order, these are:

1. *De fide et symbolo* 3.3–4 (393)
2. *De doctrina christiana* 1.13.12 (c. 396)
3. *De doctrina christiana* 2.2.3 (c. 396)
4. *De doctrina christiana* prologue (397)

De fide et symbolo reveals Augustine's earliest comment on our question. Although it contains only brief references to the relationship between sound and meaning, *De doctrina christiana* represents a crucial turning point in Augustine's thought.

After examining these four texts, I would like to consider the criticism raised by Wittgenstein in his later period over Augustine's philosophy of language, with the hope of illuminating some aspect of the problem concerning the possibility of true communication between human beings. My interest in this final question provided the original motivation for this research. I hope to build upon work already done on this problem.

I. Analysis

1. *DE FIDE ET SYMBOLO* 3.3–4

A plenary Council of the African Church was held at Hippo in October 393. At this meeting Augustine, recently ordained presbyter, made an exposition on the doctrine of the Creed that contains some important reflections on the significance of words.[3] Augustine tried to compare human words which are changeable and the Word of God which is unchangeable:

> We must not think that the Word is like our words which proceed from our mouths and are passed on by vibrations in the air and abide no longer than the sound of them remains. The Word abides unchangeable. [4]

What Augustine noted here is merely the unchangeableness of the Word of God. The transcendental character of the Logos of God is dominant. So Augustine cites, "Remaining in herself, she renews all things" (Wis. 7:27).

Then Augustine indicates some resemblance and difference between our human expressions and the manifestation of the Father through the Word, Christ. Why is there resemblance? We let hearers know something by means of signs (*per signa huiusmodi*). Likewise, the Father makes his will known to us through his Word, as revealed to us by the Son of God. Where is the difference, then? We make (*facimus*) verbal sounds but do not beget them. On the contrary, God, who is, begets (*genuit*) the Word. That is exactly the reason why our communication is imperfect and we cannot understand fully other people's thinking: "But we cannot produce anything exactly like our minds, and so the mind of the speaker cannot make itself known with complete (*penitus*) inwardness. *Hence also there is room for lying.*"[5]

If this is so, what is the possibility of true communication? Or, is true communication impossible after all? This is a question of great importance for which I can get a hint from Augustine's reference to the process of speech.

2. *DE DOCTRINA CHRISTIANA* 1.13.12

De doctrina christiana 1.13.12, probably written three years after *De fide et symbolo*, takes some remarkable steps toward the unification of sound and meaning. Augustine explains the mystery of incarnation by comparison with the speech of human beings.

> How did He come except that *"The Word was made flesh, and dwelt among us"*? It is as when we speak. In order that what we are thinking may reach the mind of the listener through the fleshly ears, that which we have in mind is expressed in words and is called speech. But our thought is not

transformed into sounds; it remains entire in itself and assumes the form of word by means of which it may reach the ears without suffering any deterioration in itself. In the same way the Word of God was made flesh without change that He might dwell among us.[6]

It is a matter of common knowledge that Augustine's theory of speech is based upon the Stoic dyadic distinction between the "concept signified" (*semainomenon*) and the "object." However, he added some important modifications to this concept. Markus remarked that for Augustine the relation of signifying is a "three-term relation."[7] Augustine's "stress was laid on the subject or the interpreter."[8] Furthermore, the sound and the meaning are more closely connected than in the *De fide et symbolo*. Augustine says that "the word which we carry in our mind . . . assumed the form of *sound*."[9]

It may safely be supposed that this expression, "assuming the form of" (*formam vocis . . . assumit*), was borrowed from Philippians 2:6–7, which shows clearly the unity of the two natures in Christ: "Who being *in the form of God*, thought it not robbery to be equal of God: But made himself of no reputation, and took upon him *the form of a servant*, and was made in the likeness of men."

This term "form" (*forma*) is almost interchangeable with the word "person" (*persona*). In *Sermo* 288.4 (401), Augustine says: "John bore the person of the voice with him in sacrament."[10]

According to R. Drobner, however, there is some difference between "form" (*forma*) and "person" (*persona*). He says, "Schon hier ist der Übergang der exegetischen Terminologie zu einer metaphysischen festzustellen."[11] Although his observation is correct, it is also true that here lies the assumption of a close relation between sound and meaning. By comparison with the looser connection found in the *De fide et symbolo*, we can say that Augustine's theory of language has undergone a crucial change.

3. DE DOCTRINA CHRISTIANA 2.2.3

Augustine takes up the doctrine of signs in book 2 of *De doctrina christiana*. In the early chapters he presents three definitions of signs:

1. Things are learned by signs.
2. Signs are natural or given.
3. What are "given signs"?

Conventional signs are those which living creatures show to one another for the purpose of conveying, in so far as they are able, *the motions of their spirits* (motus animi) or something which they have sensed or understood. Nor is there any other reason for signifying, or for giving signs, except for bringing forth and transferring to another mind w*hat is in our mind* [*id quod animo gerit*] in the person who makes the sign.[12]

Augustine explains the cycle of communication between sign-giver and sign-receiver (interpreter). His interest lies exclusively in the interpretation of Scripture.

Now I would like to bring up the question of the possibility of true communication again. Is it possible for us to decode signs sent by another person without our misunderstanding them? Augustine seems to be pessimistic, but at the same time optimistic, on this point.

According to Augustine, "dissension" arose and spread because of the pride of human beings (*DDC* 2.4.5).[13] In order to cure this disease of speech, the Holy Scripture was given to human beings by God (*DDC* 2.5.6). The interpretation of ambiguous signs in the Holy Scripture is necessary and it is helpful as a "spiritual exercise" (*exercitatio animi*) (*DDC* 2.7–9). After Adam's fall, the shortcut of intuition was closed to human beings, and for this reason we need to take a roundabout course. In effect, the true communication of Scripture is a medicine that allows us to recover true communication. What is the common point between the doctrine of incarnation in *De doctrina* 1.2.2–3 and the doctrine of communication later on, at 2.3.4? They are not connected, but I would like to search for the point in the prologue.

4. THE PROLOGUE OF *DE DOCTRINA CHRISTIANA*

Now we shall take up the prologue of *De doctrina christiana*, especially chapters 6 and 8. Augustine wanted to give certain precepts for treating the Scriptures to those who were working with them. However, some charismatic people[14] regarded such precepts as superfluous; indeed, these objectors insisted that they could understand the Scriptures without being taught any rules. In order to explain the necessity of being taught these rules, Augustine says:

> We should be aware of most proud and most dangerous temptations of this kind and think rather that the Apostle Paul himself (Acts 9:3 ff.), although prostrated and *taught* by the divine and heavenly voice, was nevertheless sent to a man that he might receive the sacraments and be joined to the church. And the centurion Cornelius (Acts 10:1 ff.), although an angel announced to him that his prayers had been heard and his alms recognized, was sent to Peter *for instruction*. He not only received sacraments from him but was also taught what should be believed, what should be hoped, and what should be loved. And all of these things in both instances might have been done by an angel, but the condition of man [*conditio humana*] would be lowered if God had not wished to have men supply His word to men

through men. . . . For charity itself, which holds men together in a knot of unity, would not have a means of infusing souls and almost mixing them together if men could teach nothing to men.[15]

In this paragraph two points are noted: the role of another person as a mediator is essential in the cycle of communication; and (2) as a matter of respect for the human condition and in order to foster charity and unity, communication is mediated to human beings by means of human beings.

According to C. P. Mayer,[16] such an ontological characteristic of the human being as mediator reflects Neoplatonism. But the evaluation of the role of the human being seems to me rather to be based on the incarnation of God. These passages remind me of the last lines of the opening page of the *Confessiones*: "You breathed it into me by the humanity of your Son, by the ministry of your preacher."[17]

Here the incarnation of God and the ministry of the preacher are mentioned in parallel. In the prologue of *De doctrina* Augustine abstractly explains the *double* structure of communication, i.e., between God and human beings, and, at the same time, among human beings. In the *Confessiones*, Augustine concretely depicts the instruction by the Truth through human beings.[18] As in the case of Cornelius and Paul, Augustine had been taught not only by Ambrose, preeminent preacher, but also by Simplician, the bishop; Pontician, the high official; and by Monica, the pious mother!

II. Wittgenstein's Arrow

Wittgenstein shot one of the keenest arrows of criticism into Augustine's theory of language. But did the arrow hit the target? I would like to examine his criticism further.

Let us begin with the passage in Augustine that Wittgenstein takes as his point of departure:

When they (my elders) named some object, and accordingly moved towards something, I saw this and grasped that the thing was called by the sound they uttered when they meant to point it out. (*Confessiones* 1.8.13, quoted in *Philosophical Investigations.*)[19]

Reading the above passage of Augustine, Wittgenstein drew, in the *Philosophical Investigations*, the conclusion that Augustine had a primitive idea. Wittgenstein summarized Augustine's theory as follows: "Every word has a meaning. This meaning is correlated with the word. It is the object for which the word stands."[20]

However, for Augustine, the word has meaning only in context. Augustine states in the last lines quoted by Wittgenstein: "Accordingly, I gradually gathered the meaning of words, occurring in their places in different sentences and frequently heard" (*Confessiones* 1.8.13). [21]

What is more important are the following remarks by Wittgenstein:

> And now, I think, we can say: Augustine describes the learning of human language . . . as if it [the child] could already *think*, only not yet speak. And "think" would here mean something like "talk to himself."[22]

Wittgenstein is criticizing Augustine's theory of language,[23] and, in this case, Wittgenstein is right. Here Augustine represents the closed cycle of communication in childhood, observing the first stage of a child's language acquisition.

But if Wittgenstein had had a chance to read *De doctrina christiana* as well as the *Confessions* what would he have said? In the prologue of *De doctrina* Augustine seems to describe a liberation from a closed cycle, a liberation made possible by the incarnation of God.

In closing, I would like to cite Ps. 35:6 and Ps. 17:3, quoted by Augustine himself in *Confessiones* 13.15.18: "For 'in heaven, Lord, is your mercy and your truth reaches the clouds' (Ps. 35:6). 'The clouds pass' (Ps. 17:13) but the heaven remains."[24] Here I suggest we can understand *truth* as "meaning" and *clouds* as "sound." However, Augustine is suggesting that meaning and sound are not completely separate but, rather, that meaning is incorporated with sound.

Notes

1. In Takeshi Kato, La voix chez Origène et saint Augustin, *Collectanea Augustiniana: Mélanges T. J. Van Bavel* (Louvain, 1991), 1:245–258, I compared Origen's *Commentary on Saint John* 6 (*PG* 14) with Augustine's *Sermo* 288.3–5 (*PL* 38). The present essay is a continuation of this article.

2. D. Pintaric, *Sprache und Trinität: Semantische Probleme in der Trinitätslehre des hl. Augustinus* (Salzburg-München, 1983), 94–99.

3. G. Madec, *La Patrie et la Voie: Le Christ dans la vie et la pensée de saint Augustin* (Paris, 1989), 199. O. du Roy, *L'Intelligence de la foi en la trinité selon saint Augustin: Genèse de sa theologie trinitaire jusqu'en 391* (Paris, 1966), 429.

4. *De fide et symbolo* 3.3 (*PL* 40:183 [trans. J. Burleigh]): *Quod tamen Verbum non sicut verba nostra debemus accipere, quae voce atque ore prolata verberato aere transeunt, nec ditius manent quam sonant. Manet illud Verbum incommutabiliter.*

5. *De fide et symbolo* 3.4 (*PL* 40:184): *quia tale aliquid proferre non possumus, et ideo non potest loquentis animus penitus innotescere; unde etiam mendaciis locus patet.*

6. *DDC* 1.13.12 (*PL* 34:24; trans. D.W. Robertson): *Quomodo venit, nisi quod "Verbum caro factum est, et habitavit in nobis?" Sicuti cum loquimur, ut id quod animo gerimus, in audientis animum per aures carneas illabatur, fit sonus*

"verbum quod corde gestamus," et locutio vocatur; nec tamen in eumdem sonum cogitatio nostra convertitur, sed apud se manens integra, "formam vocis" qua se insinuet auribus, sine aliqua labe suae mutationis assumit: ita Verbum Dei non commutatum, caro tamen factum est, ut habitaret in nobis.

7. R. A. Markus, *Saint Augustine on Signs* (New York, 1972), 74; B. D. Jackson, "The Theory of Signs in *De doctrina christiana*," *REAug* 15 (1969): 9–49.

8. Markus remarks, "Augustine's theory of the 'word' [in *De trinitate*], approaches language from the side of the speaker, unlike the sign-theories of the *De Magistro* and the *De Doctrina Christiana*. The latter are the theories of meaning for the spectator and the interpreter" (*Augustine on Signs*, 81). His remark is suitable for the *DDC* 2.1.1, but not perhaps for the present paragraph. Augustine's stress is laid upon the sign maker, not upon the interpreter.

9. *DDC* 1. 13.12 (*PL* 34:24; trans. Robertson): *id quod animo gerimus . . . formam vocis . . . assumit.*

10. *Sermo* 288.4 (*PL* 38, 1306): *Personam gerebat Joannes vocis in sacramento.*

11. H. R. Drobner, *Person-Exegese und Christologie bei Augustinus, zur Herkunft der Formel "UNA PERSONA"* (Leiden, 1986), p. 146.

12. *DDC* 2.2.3 (*PL* 34:37; trans. Robertson): *"Data" vero "signa" sunt, quae sibi quaeque viventia invicem dant ad demontrandos, quantum possunt, "motus animi" sui, vel sensa, aut intellecta quaelibet. Nec ulla causa est nobis significandi, id est signi dandi, nisi ad depromendum et trajiciendum in alterius animum id quod animo gerit is qui signum dat.* The following two elements are observed in the above definition: (1) For rendering of *signa data*, "given signs" are more accurate and preferable to "conventional signs." J. Engels, "La doctrine du signe chez saint Augustin," in F. L. Cross, ed. *SP* 6 (Berlin, 1962): 366–373, cited by Jackson, "Theory of Signs," 96 ff.; and (2) the phrase *motus animi* refers to "an attending what has been apprehended." It has the same meaning as the phrase *id quod animo gerit.* According to Jackson, ("Theory of Signs," 103), there are two ways of interpreting *motus animi.* First, it refers to emotion. Second, it refers to a certain reflection, which involves more than apprehension (*animos movent. . . , diverse: DDC* 2.24.37 [*PL* 34:54]). I prefer the second interpretation. For *id quod animo gerit* seems to me to signify "conception" (*cogitatio: De trinitate* 11.3.6), begotten from *scientia* (see Jackson, "Theory of Signs," 105).

13. Takeshi Kato, "The Roundabout Course of Interpretation in the *De doctrina christiana* (2.7–12)," *St. Paul's Review*, Art and Letters, Faculty of General Education, Rikkyo University, 44 (1985): 26–44 (in Japanese). See P. Ricoeur, *De l'interprétation: Essai sur Freud* (Paris, 1965), 45–63.

14. U. Duchrow, *Sprachverständnis u. biblisches Hören bei Augustin* (Tübingen, 1960), 206–213; P. Brunner, "Charismatische und methodische Schriftauslegung nach Augustinus Prolog zu *Doctrina Christiana*," in *Kerygma und Dogma*, 85; Takeshi Kato, *On the Christian Doctrine*, introduction, translation, and notes (Tokyo, 1988), 329–331; C. P. Mayer, "*Res per signa*: Der Grundgedanke des Prologs in Augustins Schrift *De doctrina christiana* und das Problem seiner Datierung," *REAug* 20 (1974). I support C. P. Mayer.

15. *DDC* prologue 6 (*PL* 34:18; trans. Robertson): *Caveamus talem tentationes superbissimas et periculosissimas, magisque cogitemus et ipsum apostolum Paulum, licet diuina et coelesti voce prostratum et instructum, ad hominem tamen missum esse, ut sacramenta perciperet, atque copularetur Ecclesiae, et centurionem Cornelium quamvis exauditas orationes eius eleemosynasque respectas ei angelus nuntiaverit, Petro tamen traditum imbuendum; per quem non solum sacramenta perciperet, sed etiam, quid credendum, quid sperandum, quid diligendum esset, audiret. Et poterant utique omnia per angelum fieri, sed abjecta esset humana conditio, si per homines hominibus Deus verbum suum ministrare nolle videretur . . . Deinde ipsa caritas, quae sibi invicem homines nodo unitatis adstringit, non haberet aditum refundendorum et quasi miscendorum sibimet animorum, si homines per homines nihil discerent.*

16. C. P. Mayer, "Grundgedanke des Prologs," 102, 112.

17. *Confessiones* 1.1.1 (*PL* 32:661): *. . . quam inspirasti mihi per humanitatem Filii tui, per ministerium praedicatoris tui.*

18. P. de Labriolle considers this *praedicator* to be Ambrose. P. Courcelle and A. Solignac regard this *praedicator* as Jesus Christ. I favor the first interpretation, because the term *ministerium* is exclusively applied to man, not to God, in the usage of Augustine.

19. *Confessiones* 1.8.13 (*PL* 32:66f.): *cum ipsi appellabant rem aliquam, et cum secundum eam vocem corpus ad aliquid movebant, videbam et tenebam hoc ab eis vocari rem illam, quod sonabant, cum eam velle ostendere.*

20. Ludwig Wittgenstein, *Philosophical Investigations*, trans. G.E.M. Anscombe, 3rd. ed. (Oxford, 1989), 1.1, p. 2e.

21. *Confessiones* 1.8.13 (*PL* 32:667; trans. H. Chadwick): *Ita verba in variis sententiis, locis suis posita, et crebro audita, quarum rerum signa essent, paulatim colligebam.* See D. E. Zoolalian, "Augustine and Wittgenstein: Some Remarks on the Necessity of a Private Language," *AugStud* 9 (1978): 28.

22. Wittgenstein, *Philosophical Investigations* 1.32: "Augustine, we might say, does describe a system of communication." This remark seems to be very significant.

23. Zolollian, "Augustine and Wittgenstein," 29: "Augustine only claims to be learning to 'speak' a language. He does not claim to be learning to 'speak' a language as if he had none and was acquiring his first."

24. *Confessiones* 13.15.18 (*PL* 32:853; trans. Chadwick): *In coelo enim, Domine, misericordia tua, et veritas tua usque ad nubes. Transeunt nubes, coelum autem manet.*

Sensus

But now, when I come to the treatment of signs, one should not consider in them what they are, but rather direct his attention to the fact that they are signs, namely, that they signify something. A sign is a thing which, apart from the impression that it presents to the senses, causes of itself some other thing to enter our thoughts.

De doctrina christiana 2.1

Signs, Communication, and Communities in Augustine's *De doctrina christiana*

R. A. MARKUS

Hier ist des Säglichen Zeit, hier ist Heimat.

Rilke

The explosion of semiotics during the second half of our century has not left the study of ancient Christian literature untouched; and no work has been more directly exposed to the blast than *De doctrina christiana*.[1] Indeed, it might even be held to have contributed to the force of the explosion; for Augustine's discussion of signs has been described as the first to merit the name of *semiotics,* its originality consisting in its success in rounding off the achievements of classical antiquity in a new synthesis.[2] Augustine is widely said to be the first to have integrated the theory of language—"fifteen centuries before De Saussure"[3]—into that of the sign. Of this very large subject my paper will be concerned with only one corner: the sign as a means of communication and the way that the notions of sign and communication opened a way for Augustine to speak of communities.

Community in some sense is a necessary condition of any communication—a community of understanding, whether it be of gesture, words, or other significant acts. Augustine was clearly conscious of this in defining and classifying *signa*. I begin with a summary of these definitions and the classification.

Signs

In *De doctrina christiana* Augustine defines signs twice over: First, signs are "things which are used to signify something" (*res . . . quae ad significandum aliquid adhibentur* [DDC 1.2.2]): the relationship is between the sign thing, its user, and that which he uses it to signify. Similarly in the second, slightly more elaborate, definition Augustine gives a little later: "A sign is a thing which causes us to think of something in addition to the impression it makes upon the senses" (*res praeter speciem quam ingerit sensibus aliud alquid ex se faciens in cogitationem uenire* [DDC 2.1.1]). Here the relationship is between the sign thing, its perceiver (for the present purpose this is the chief difference from the first definition, which refers to the sign user), and that further thing which it brings to its perceiver's mind, the signified.

Of the three terms in Augustine's two definitions, two are constant: the sign and the signified. The third term differs, according to the different points of view from which the two definitions are given: the first from the point of view of the sign giver (or user); the second from that of the sign receiver (or perceiver). The reason why his more elaborate definition is given from the point of view of the sign receiver rather than from that of the sign giver becomes clear from the classification of signs which immediately follows the second definition: for not all signs are *given*, though all—because a thing is a sign insofar as it stands for something to somebody; to be a sign, a thing must necessarily be experienced by some subject—are received.

We must now look at this division of *signa* into the two great classes distinguished by Augustine: (1) *signa naturalia*, "natural signs," which Augustine defines as those which "from themselves make known something other than themselves without any wish or desire on anybody's part of signifying; as, for instance, smoke signifies fire" (*quae sine uoluntate atque ullo appetitu significandi praeter se aliquid aliud ex se cognosci faciunt* [DDC 2.1.2]); and (2) *signa data*, given signs, those which "living beings give to one another in order to indicate, as far as they can, their feelings, their perceptions or their thoughts" (*quae sibi quaeque uiuentia inuicem dant ad demonstrandos, quantum possunt, motus animi sui, uel sensa aut intellecta quaelibet* [DDC 2.2.3, a little freely translated]).

The first class, "natural signs," thus comprises those which stand for something in virtue of their link—by causal dependence, logical implication, being a syndrome—with that which they signify. The second class, "given signs," consists of those which signify in virtue of their givers' intention. The sign, to be a sign, in all cases has a relation to two other terms: the signified and the giver or perceiver; which of the two classes it falls into will, however, be determined by whether it depends on the giver or on the signified. Both the definitions given in *De doctrina christiana* are, in other words, triadic, though this triadic relation presupposes a (dyadic) relation of dependence between the sign and either the signified or the giver/perceiver.[4]

Intentional, "given," signs result from acts of communication. As Augustine observes, the only reason for signifying, that is, for giving signs (*significandi, id est signi dandi*), is to bring forth (*ad depromendum*) what is going on in the mind of the sign-giver and to communicate it (*ad traiciendum*) to another's mind (*DDC* 2.2.3). We need not go into the philosophical problems of what it is that is being communicated in such acts of communication;[5] what is important for our discussion is Augustine's view on how the sign receives its meaning. He appears to resolve the ancient debate about whether signs have their significance by nature or by convention by distinguishing among "given signs" some, such as, apparently, signs made by animals to warn of danger and the like, which signify by nature, from others, such as letters of the various alphabets and words (spoken or written), which signify by convention.[6]

Most (though not necessarily all) "given signs," Augustine evidently thought, have their meanings conferred on them by convention.[7] Convention, however, is a notion with a more complex sense than Augustine's statements sometimes suggest. This is clearest when we examine what he has to say about those signs through which human beings communicate with demons in magical and other "superstitious" practices. All these rest on "pacts about certain meanings agreed with demons by contract" (*pacta quaedam significationum cum daemonibus placita atque foederata* [*DDC* 2.20.30]). The idea of such an agreement is at first sight puzzling. But Augustine insists on it repeatedly, in language of almost legal precision.[8] He leaves us in no doubt that he thought of the agreed symbolic system as the bond of association: "these arts of idle and noxious superstition [are] constituted by a certain association through faithless and deceitful friendship" (*pacta infidelis et dolosae amicitiae* [*DDC* 2.23.36]); "they [omens, auguries etc.] are valid only to the extent that they have been established by presumptuous minds as a common language agreed with demons" (*tantum ualent, quantum praesumptione animorum quasi communi quadam lingua cum daemonibus foederata sunt* [*DDC* 2.24.37]). Like words,

> all these meanings are understood according to the conventions of the society, and, as these conventions differ, are understood differently; nor are they agreed upon among men because they already had a meaning, but they receive their meaning from the agreement.
>
> (*hae omnes significationes pro suae cuiusque societatis consensione animos mouent et, quia diuersa consensio est, diuerse*

mouent, nec ideo consenserunt in eas homines, quia iam uale-
bant ad significationem, sed ideo ualent quia consenserunt in
eas). (DDC 2.24.37)

But, of course, magicians and soothsayers do not make an agreement with demons and then go on to use the conventions agreed on. It must be the intention to enter such an association that lies at the roots of the conventions which hold it together. It is as if a person entered the "contract" with the demons in the very movement of his will towards the demons with whom he associates himself. In this, these signs are like all "given," intentional, signs: they are "the kind of thing which starts a motion towards what it signifies and, mediately, towards whomever employs it as a sign."[9]

Communication

Communication is a necessary condition for community; but direct communication between human minds, a transparency of mutual understanding, is not possible in the fallen human condition.[10] Language arises from the conflict of this impossibility with the natural human need for community: "there could be no solid association between men unless they could communicate (*nisi colloquerentur*), and unless they could thus share, as it were, their minds and their thoughts" (*sibi mentes suas et cogitationes quasi refunderent*). For this reason, "that which is rational in us . . . and is drawn into association by a kind of natural bond with those with whom it shares its rationality . . . has imposed words, that is to say, certain meaningful sounds, upon things."[11] Language bridges the gulf that has opened up between fallen human beings; but words are fragile vehicles of meaning, they slip, slide, and will not stay still, and every attempt to communicate is a wholly new start, for, as Augustine wrote, "understanding flashes like lightning through the mind, but speech is slow and sluggish, and hopelessly inadequate" (*locutio tarda et longa est, longeque dissimilis*).[12]

For Augustine semantic activity—understanding and communicating through language—was the index of the human need for transcendence in the most general terms: for union with other minds in the very act of understanding a shared world. Take the occurrence in conversation of a word whose meaning is unknown: What is the nature of the frustration it causes, what is the object of the urge to clear up its meaning? Augustine's answer is most fully given in a richly dense chapter of the *De trinitate*. Here he argues that, assuming the unknown word to be a sign, i.e., to have meaning, we will have the urge to discover that meaning, to free ourselves from confinement within a wall of opaque signs. "Knowing it to be a sign and not a mere brute noise, he will wish to know it perfectly" and thus to know its meaning (*De trinitate* 10.1.2). The driving force is what Augustine calls *love*, the term which includes what we should call urges, desires, passions, setting a value upon things. The distinction he makes at the beginning of *De doctrina christiana* (1.3.3) between two modes of loving, *frui* and *uti*, "enjoying" and "using," or loving (desiring, setting a value on) something either for itself or for the sake of something else,[13] is crucial to the theory of signs and meaning to which the second book is devoted. For, as Rowan Williams has shown in an impressive study,[14] "it is the means whereby Augustine links what he has to say about language with what he has to say about beings who 'mean' and about the fundamentally desirous nature of those beings—a link which is undoubtedly the most original and interesting feature of the treatise." To "enjoy" something that is less than the ultimate, infinite satisfaction, that is to say, to allow the will to rest in its possession; or to wish to "enjoy" it, that is to say, to limit desire to its attainment, without pointing to a further horizon, is a perversion of the natural and rational order of willing. To allow desire to cease in this way is premature closure of the Christian life, a denial of the restlessness in the depth of the human heart.

This is Augustine's way of affirming the necessity of keeping our horizons perpetually open, of seeking meaning in things experienced as signs, and to be inclined to suspect that what is not so experienced ought to be. We thwart this drive of our nature only at the cost of blocking off the process of learning and growth that living in the midst of this realm of limited and unstable things ought always to remain. A tendency to discover things to be signs is central to Augustine's understanding of what it is to be human, and doubly so to his idea of being Christian. It is hardly surprising to find that this understanding is also the foundation of his view on the meanings of scriptural symbols, of the Old Testament,[15] and of the created world as a whole.[16] These, however, are large themes I cannot go into here. I keep here to the most fundamental point, the understanding of signs itself. What is it that makes us want to understand meaning? What is it that we are engaged in when we try to penetrate the obscurity of an unknown sign, to refuse to be confined within opacity?

Augustine's answer as it is worked out in chapter 10 of the *De trinitate*—the fullest he gives anywhere, so far as I know, and deeply Platonic in its inspiration—is formulated in terms of *love*. What is it that is loved in the search for meaning launched by the frustration of hearing a word not understood? Nothing can be loved that is not known, so the object of desire cannot be the unknown object referred to; nor, evidently, is it the opaque sign itself; nor the known fact that it has a meaning. So what is the object of the desire that urges one to seek understanding? What else is it but the knowledge and the awareness in the principles of things (*in rationibus rerum*) of the beauty of the knowledge (*pulchritudo doctrinae*) which reveals the meaning of all signs, and of the value of that skill (*peritia*) by which human beings communicate with one another in their societies? Only thus can human groups avoid being worse, through inability to share their thoughts by communicating, than any kind of solitariness.

This beauty and this usefulness, Augustine concludes, is what the soul loves in seeking meanings: the search for meaning is the quest for transcendence—transcendence of the self imprisoned among opaque signs, isolated from the linguistic community no less than from the realm of meanings. Escape from this isolation is what "he who seeks the meaning of unknown significant sounds seeks to realise within himself." He will have to limit his studies to what he has hope of achieving; in principle, however, the whole world of meanings challenges him to pursue, "burning with fervent longing" (*ferventius amore inardescit*), an understanding in which opacity will disclose its meaning.

> He who seeks [the meaning of an unknown word] is in the grip of a quest for discovery (*in studio discendi*) and would seem to love something unknown; but in reality this is not the case. For his soul is touched by that idea (*species*) which he knows and is aware of, in which the value of an association of minds communicating in the hearing and the uttering of understood words is made apparent (*in qua elucet decus consociandorum animorum uocibus notis audiendis atque reddendis*); this is what kindles the ardor of one seeking to understand what he does not know, aware though he is of a known form (*notam formam*) to which it refers, which is the object of his love. . . . For nearly all rational souls are prone to see the beauty of this skill, by which the objects thought among men are known through the enunciation of meaningful sounds. (*De trinitate* 10.1.2)[17]

So in learning the meaning of signs we discover a shared world and are simultaneously integrated into our linguistic community. Integration in the linguistic community is discovery of meaning, and, conversely, the search for meaning heals ruptures in the linguistic community. These are the two sides of the liberation from captivity to the sign. To seek meaning is to enact transcendence.

Augustine expounds this most fully in *De trinitate*, in the context of his investigation of the love which impels the human soul to recognize itself as the image of the triune God. The same conception is succinctly expounded in *De doctrina christiana* (especially 2.8.12–9.13). Here, although his objectives are more limited, the recognition that "language in its fluidity and displacements is inseparably interwoven with the restlessness or openness of desire that is what is fundamentally human"[18] underlies, and gives unity to, the whole discussion of *De doctrina christiana*.

Communities

Augustine knew perfectly well how hard we find it to learn foreign languages; and in the chapter of *De trinitate* we have just been considering, he recognizes the natural desire to expand our linguistic equipment to infinity but makes generous concession to our need to restrict it to the sphere within which we have some hope of attaining our objective. In fact, our many separate languages will always restrict us to moving within a limited variety of linguistic communities and will therefore limit the boundaries of attainable meaning for us in a variety of ways. If in *De trinitate* Augustine is more interested in the furthest reach of the potential for transcendence, in *De doctrina christiana* he is more concerned to explore limited human communities. Book 2 of *De doctrina* is nothing less—though it may be rather more—than an account of how communities are constituted by how they understand the symbolic systems (i.e., all that Augustine includes under his category of *signa data*) in use within them.

A particular human group is defined by the boundaries of the system of signs in use among its members. This is the consequence of Augustine's theory of signs. Signs must mean something to somebody; the somebodies who agree on their meaning will constitute a (linguistic) community.

The triadic relation of signification is the key to Augustine's entire hermeneutic theory. A sign is a "thing" standing within the signifying relation between a subject, the sign thing itself, and the signified object. The latter in its turn can be, or become, a sign when drawn into a further relationship of signification. Thus many signs may have meanings on two levels. Transferred (or "figurative," as they are generally described) signs are, in Augustine's definition, quite simply signs whose signifieds are placed into a second relationship of signification: they occur when "the things signified by their proper literal names (*propriis uerbis*) are in their turn used to signify something else" (*DDC* 2.10.15).[19] Augustine gives the example of the word *ox*, used literally to signify the beast normally designated by the word; in its figurative sense it will signify the evangelist to those familiar with the scriptural discourse within which the beast itself can stand for the evangelist.[20] Hence the importance which Augustine attaches (*DDC* 2.16.24) to the exegete being at home within the relevant secular discourses: How can he appreciate the scriptural symbolism of the serpent if he does not know what snakes really are like? This possibility of meaning on two levels gives rise to a language constituting linguistic communities on two levels. We might say that someone who understands the word *ox* belongs to a primary linguistic community (e.g., of English speakers), someone who understands what its signified (the ox) can mean in a further (e.g., scriptural) context belongs, further, to a secondary linguistic community.

What distinguishes the Christian from the Jewish community is such an openness to the New Testament context within which the things spoken of in the Old Testament receive a further meaning. Lack of it is the "servitude" of the Jewish people, the closure of their biblical discourse short of the new realm of meaning it would enter in the light of the incarnation (*DDC* 3.5.9–6.10); and it is from this servitude to the sign that "Christian freedom has liberated those it found in subjection to useful signs . . . by raising them, through interpreting the signs to which they were subject, to the things of which those signs were the signs" (*DDC* 3.8.12). Captivity to the sign is inability, or refusal, to pierce its opacity; not knowing, or not seeking, the range of potential further meaning it can have in a larger discourse (*DDC* 3.9.13).

The Jews who refused to understand the Old Testament as interpreted in the New thus remained captive to the closed world of its "useful" signs. As so often in Augustine's thought, this patristic commonplace becomes part of a deeply thought-out general view with much wider bearings. The theory of signs and meaning in terms of which it is worked out also provides his means for defining other communities within the overall human community. *De doctrina christiana* is the work in which he first undertook the task, to which he returned on a grand scale in *The City of God*, of defining the identity of the Christian community within the context of the institutions—the *culture,* as we might not inappropriately say—of the secular world in which it is set.

De doctrina christiana can be read as exploring the place of a Christian subculture within the literary culture shared among the educated Roman public. Augustine is here at grips with questions about "the function of effects of specialised forms of language in the life of the religious community, of how this affects the way in which a community is perceived from the outside, and, not least, of how it is possible for individuals to be bilingual and bicultural—like Augustine—in this respect."[21] Augustine expounds his notion of a community constituted by its symbolic systems in what he has to say about the *instituta* of human beings. Human *instituta* are one of the two sectors into which he divides knowledge: it is either of things instituted by human beings themselves, or of the things they have discovered and observed in what has been instituted by God (*DDC* 2.19.29): *nature* and *culture,* as we might roughly label them. It is *culture* we must explore here; as Augustine's discussion indicates, it includes such things as languages, arts, sciences, and disciplines, as well as customs and rites carried out within a society. This human "culture" Augustine divides into two sorts: that which is superstitious, and that which is not.

The idolatrous, magical, divinatory, or astrological practices Augustine groups together under the heading "superstitious" are enumerated in five paragraphs (*DDC* 2.20.30–22.34). The class comprises practices (*quicquid institutum est ab hominibus*) that pertain to the making and worshiping of idols, or to the worship of creatures, or parts of creatures, as divine, or to consultation and "pacts about certain meanings agreed with demons by contract" (*DDC* 2.20.30).

In these superstitious practices the demons, Augustine tells us, are parties to the agreement which established the conventions. The very language that constitutes this community is inherently demonic. But words can belong to more than one language. There is a hint, for instance, that some practices can be ambiguous: hanging certain objects on one's body, for instance, or taking certain foods or drinks, might be either sinister acts of superstition or sensible medication (*DDC* 2.20.30; cf. 29.45). Augustine seems to treat such signs as capable of belonging to two different languages: either to one resting on demonic convention, or to another resting on human convention. This element of polysemy takes us into the second branch of his division of human *instituta*.

This is the class of human institutions which are not superstitious, "that is to say, instituted not with demons, but [only] among men themselves" (*DDC* 2.22.38). Augustine further subdivides these into a class containing those *instituta* which are "useful and necessary" (*commoda et necessaria*), and a class of those which are "superfluous and extravagant" (*superflua et luxuriosa* [*DDC* 2.22.38]). In *De doctrina christiana* Augustine is interested in the part of the secular culture that is "useful and necessary" to a Christian, and therefore he does not go to any trouble to specify what, apart from fictitious fables and falsehoods, he would include among the "superfluous and extravagant," though he allows us to guess that he would, at any rate, include the pleasures of the theater and the like.[22] We should note a significant difference between how Augustine deals with such institutions and how they are treated in a tradition of patristic rhetoric well established since Tertullian, for whom they were nothing short of demonic: "every monument [of the circus] is a temple."[23] "By this shall they know a man for a Christian," Tertullian wrote, "that he has repudiated the shows."[24] For Augustine, a frequenter of the shows would, at worst, have counted as a depraved pleasure-seeker, not an idolater. But the institutions he is interested in here are the useful and necessary: those, like the conventions of dress, weights and measures, and the innumerable kinds of symbolism (*innumerabilia genera significa-tionum*), which are useful and necessary to the smooth functioning of human societies (*sine quibus humana societas aut non omnino aut minus commode geritur* [DDC 2.25.39]). Such institutions and symbols helped to secure the cohesion of civil society and were to be valued on that account. Christians should be encouraged to pursue secular disciplines, "soberly and critically," that is to say, under no illusion that they are capable of bringing salvation; they must avoid those which imply association with the demonic realm and should abstain from those that are superfluous and luxurious; but they must not neglect "those institutions which are of value to human beings living together in groups (*quae ad societatem conuiuentium ualent*) in the pursuit of the needs of this life" (*DDC* 2.39.58; cf. 25.40).

Here is that vivid sense of the importance of appreciating and fostering secular institutions catering for the cohesion of a mixed society which Augustine will explore far more fully in the *City of God*. There it is formulated in terms of the intermediate goods which are to be valued by members of both the earthly and the heavenly cities.[25] In *De doctrina christiana* Augustine is more concerned with the possibilities of a shared culture. The terms in which he explores the relationships of groups sharing a culture, or of subcultures within a society, are those of a hermeneutic of symbolic systems. In the *De doctrina christiana* Augustine has devised a sophisticated and powerful conceptual scheme for discussing the whole realm of human culture and activity which he had once summed up as *magna haec et omnino humana* (*De quant. an.* 33.72): "these great, and wholly human, achievements."[26]

Notes

1. See the bibliography at the end of this volume for references by author's name (and date where applicable). References to works not listed there are given in full in the notes below (and second and subsequent citations given by author's surname and short title of work).

2. See T. Todorov, *Théories du symbole* (Paris, 1977), 55–56; 179; and n. 3, below.

3. U. Eco, *Semiotics and the Philosophy of Language* (London, 1984), 33; cf. Simone (1972: 9–10, 29–30), and S. A. Handelman, *The Slayers of Moses: The Emergence of Rabbinic Interpretation in Modern Literary Theory* (Albany, 1982), 107–120. I concluded this in my study, "St. Augustine on Signs" (1957). My argument (and that of subsequent writers who have accepted it) on Augustine's originality needs to be qualified in the light of Jackson (1969) and Duchrow (1965: 50–51).

4. Markus (1957: 73–74), endorsed by Jackson (1969: 96). See also Jordan (1980: 184). Similarly, G. Bouchard, "La conception augustinienne du signe selon

Tzvetan Todorov," *RechAug* 15 (1980): 343–344, on *De dialectica*. This is obscured in much modern semiotic writing, e.g., Eco (*Semiotics*), though he mentions Peirce's three-term definition (p. 14) and writes (p. 46) that "a Sign is not only something which stands for something else; it is also something that can and must be interpreted," in fact generally speaks of the sign in terms of a relation between two terms. I avoid the terminology of "signifier" and "signified," and use Augustine's "sign" and "signified." Kirwan (1989: 38) argues (unconvincingly) that Augustine's definition fails to take into account undetected signs.

5. The best discussions are Jackson (1969: 107–111) and G. P. O'Daly, *Augustine's Philosophy of Mind* (London, 1987), 175–178. See also Kirwan (1989: 39–40).

6. *DDC* 2.24.37. See Jackson (1969: 97–98) for details. For a discussion of the historical significance of this view of language, see J. Milbank, "Theology without Substance: Christianity, Signs, Origins," *Literature and Theology* 2 (1988): 1–17 and 13–52.

7. In my paper (1957: 74–76), I called "given" signs "conventional." Jackson (1969: 97), rightly remarks that this is going beyond what Augustine is asserting in these chapters. Similarly J. Engels "La doctrine du signe chez saint Augustin," *Studia Patristica* 6 [1962], 366–73), who argues that they are to be described as "intentional." I have adopted this terminology.

8. *DDC* 2.20.30; 22.34; 23.36; 24.37; 25.38; 39.58.

9. Jordan (1980: 186).

10. *De Genesi contra Manichaeos* 2.4.5; it will be restored in the risen body: *patebunt etiam cogitationes nostrae inuicem nobis* (*De ciuitate dei* 22.29.6). Cf. C. P. Mayer, *Die Zeichen in der geistigen Entwicklung und in der Theologie des jungen Augustinus*, Cassiciacum 24, 1 (Würzburg, 1969). Cf. also Beierwaltes (1971:185) on word as communication, with references in n. 17; Louth (1989:156–157); and, especially, Duchrow (1961).

11. *De ordine* 2.12.35. Cf. Kuypers (1934: 60) on man's social nature as based on semantic activity.

12. *De catechizandis rudibus* 2.3.

13. The classic discussion of this is Lorenz (1952/3); see also the important study by O'Donovan (1982: 361–397).

14. Williams (1989). The quotation is from p. 139. I owe much to this paper, especially in this section.

15. See especially Jordan (1980: 189–191).

16. On this, see especially C. P. Mayer, "Significationshermeneutik im Dienst der Daseinsauslegung—Die Funktion der Verweisung in den *Confessiones* X–XIII," *Aug (L)* 24 (1974); his other studies listed in the bibliography give a fine account of the uses to which Augustine put his theory of signs.

17. See the commentary on this passage by O'Daly, *Augustine's Philosophy of Mind,* 209. Cf. Duchrow (1965: 119–120), commenting on this chapter of the *De trinitate* and comparing its more positive perspective (made possible by the stress on the role of love) with that of *Confessiones* 1.7–13.

18. Williams (1989: 148), and the fine study of Jordan (1980), especially 194–196, on the "dialectical" character of signs.

19. This is, of course, the position widely adopted by modern theories of metaphor, e.g., in P. Ricoeur, *The Rule of Metaphor: Multi-disciplinary Studies of the Creation of Meaning in Language* (London, 1978) quoting (p. 188) P. Henle, "Metaphor," in *Language, Thought, and Culture*, ed. P. Henle (Ann Arbor, 1958): "the word is 'an immediate sign of its literal sense and a mediate sign of its figurative sense'" (quoted from p. 175). Cf. P. Ricoeur, *Time and Narrative* (Chicago, 1984), x–xi, for a good summary of Ricoeur's views. On scriptural hermeneutics and allegory, see his *Essays on Biblical Interpretation*, ed. L. S. Mudge (London, 1981), 51–53: "Scripture appears here [in medieval *lectio divina*] as an inexhaustible treasure which stimulates thought about everything, which conceals a total interpretation of the world. . . . Hermeneutics is the very deciphering of life in the mirror of the text."

20. The same distinction is made in *DDC* 1.2.2: on scriptural *res* which are "things in such a manner that they are also signs of other things."

21. Williams (1989: 138).

22. I have argued in *The End of Ancient Christianity* (Cambridge, 1990), 110–123, that Augustine would not have included among the "superfluous and extravagant" some of the *spectacula*, such as the circus races, before April 399; information recently come to light may suggest that Augustine did not abandon his earlier views until as late as 407–408. On the recently discovered sermons, see F. Dolbeau, "Sermons inédits de S. Augustin dans un manuscrit de Mayence (Stadtbibliothek I 9)," *REAug* 36 (1990): 355–359.

23. *Tertullian De spectaculis* 8.3. On this subject, see my *The End of Ancient Christianity*, 101–102, 120–121.

24. *De repudio spectaculorum—De spectaculis* 24.3.

25. See my *Saeculum: History and Society in the Theology of Saint Augustine*, 2nd ed. (Cambridge, 1988), 45–71.

26. I wish to thank Gerard O'Daly for most helpful comments.

Criteria for Figurative Interpretation in St. Augustine

ROLAND J. TESKE

I. The Different Criteria

When making a translation of *De Genesi contra Manichaeos*, I had to deal with Augustine's exegetical principles as they were embodied in his first written attempt at scriptural interpretation.[1] Augustine wrote this work in 388 or 389, soon after his conversion and his return to Africa from Italy, but prior to his ordination.[2] His principal audiences were the Manichees, especially those whom he himself had led into that sect, such as Honoratus and Romanianus, and the uneducated "little ones" of the *Catholica* who were easy prey for the Manichaean objections to the Old Testament.[3] Especially in the second book, the work presents a highly figurative interpretation of the Genesis narrative—so much so that Agaësse and Solignac suggest that in this earliest commentary on Genesis Augustine regarded the paradise story as a parable without historical basis or as allegory in the modern sense which denies or excludes, rather than presupposes, a literal and historical sense.[4] Nonetheless, the reasons that Augustine gives for providing a figurative interpretation of the text in this work always center around the impossibility of taking the text in its proper sense and, at the same time, avoiding blasphemy, impiety, or absurdity in speaking about God. That is, his stated reasons for having recourse to a figurative interpretation of the text were those which Jean Pépin pointed out in his article, "A propos de l'histoire de l'exégèse allégorique: L'absurdité, signe de l'allégorie."[5]

Pépin found that among Christians of the first centuries, such as Origen and Augustine, "the principal indication that a biblical text had been written with an allegorical intent and ought to be understood as such is the absurdity of the text as long as one sticks to the literal sense."[6]

He maintains that this absurdity criterion is the same among pagan authors in their interpretation of classical literature.

Given the reasonableness of this criterion, which is the one Augustine claims to use in *De Genesi contra Manichaeos*, I was quite startled to find that Augustine stated in the later *De doctrina christiana* another criterion for figurative interpretation that clearly goes far beyond this early, more limited one. There he writes: "You should know that whatever in the word of God cannot in the proper sense be referred to the goodness of morals or the truth of the faith is figurative."[7]

Henri-Irénée Marrou refers to this rule as Augustine's fundamental law of spiritual interpretation: "We find the theory formulated in the *De doctrina christiana*: it is summed up in a fundamental law: everything in Scripture that does not directly refer to faith and morals must be regarded as figurative."[8] Marrou asks his readers to weigh the import of this fundamental law and points out that "Saint Augustine does not merely say that we must take as figurative everything in Scripture which is *contrary* to faith and morals, but also everything that is not directly related to them."[9]

Obviously, this law maximizes the amount of Scripture that has a figurative sense, for a vast amount of Scripture does not in its proper or literal sense deal directly with matters of faith or of moral conduct. One need only think of Augustine's treatment of the miraculous catch of fish in John 21, where he finds a figurative meaning in the number of disciples engaged in the fishing expedition, in the 153 fishes that were caught, in the lowering of the nets on the right side of the boat, in the fact that Jesus was standing on the shore, in the fact that the nets did not break, etc.[10] That is, given Augustine's fundamental law of figurative interpretation, none of these things could have been mentioned pointlessly. Since in its proper sense such a passage does not present us with things we are to believe or with moral precepts, it must be taken as figurative of something else or of many other things.

That is, while the criterion for figurative interpretation that Augustine claimed to be using in *De Genesi contra Manichaeos* is that comparatively sober and limited one (allegorical interpretation is appropriate when literal interpretation would lead to absurdity) which I have, following Pépin's lead, suggested, the criterion stated fewer than ten years later in *De doctrina christiana* (whatever is not related directly to faith and morals is to be taken figuratively) is anything but sober and limited.[11] I began this paper convinced that there were in Augustine these two, quite different criteria for figurative interpretation, and the question I set out to answer was this: Why did Augustine move from the sober and reasonable absurdity criterion that Pépin pointed out to the maximizing criterion found in the *De doctrina christiana*? The conclusion I have come to is that my initial conviction was mistaken and my question misguided. The remainder of this paper will explain what had led me to my original hypothesis and why I now believe it to have been incorrect.[12]

II. The Case for the Absurdity Criterion

It is well known that Augustine found serious difficulties with the Scriptures that contributed to his leaving the faith of Monica and becoming a Manichee.[13] It is also well known that it was the preaching of Ambrose that led him to see, first, that the Catholic faith could be defended and, later, that the spiritual men of the *Catholica* did not believe the "infantile nonsense" that he had thought they did.[14] Hence, it is reasonable to suppose that Augustine's account of Ambrose's influence will throw light upon the criterion for figurative interpretation that played a decisive role in his own return to the faith of the Catholic Church and that he used in his first venture at scriptural interpretation, *De Genesi contra Manichaeos*.

In the *Confessions* Augustine reports two occasions on which Ambrose's preaching significantly influenced his understanding of the Scriptures. In the first passage, which marks an early contact with Ambrose, probably dating from late 384, Augustine tells us that he began to think that the Catholic faith could be defended against the attacks of the Manichees:

> especially after having often heard [Ambrose] resolve one or more of the enigmas from the Old Testament, where I was being killed, when I understood it according to the letter. When he had spiritually explained many passages from those books, I blamed that despair of mine, at least insofar as I believed that the Law and the Prophets could in no way stand up against those who hated and mocked them.[15]

As a result of this first influence of Ambrose, Augustine came to see that the Catholic way was undefeated, but not so undefeated that it had won the victory.[16]

Augustine later mentions the second influence of Ambrose's preaching, which probably dates from late in 385. At that point, he tells us, he was overjoyed to discover that the spiritual sons of God did not hold that humankind's being made to God's image and likeness entailed that God himself was confined to the shape of the human body. Even though Augustine himself still had no suspicion of what spiritual substance was, he rejoiced that he had so long been opposed, not to the Catholic faith, but to the figments of a carnal imagination.[17] Augustine tells us that Ambrose, in his sermons to the people, taught that

> "the letter kills, but that the spirit gives life," when he removed the mystical veil and uncovered the spiritual sense of those things which in their literal meaning seemed to contain a perverse doctrine. He did not say anything that offended me, though I still did not know whether what he said was true.[18]

Given the importance of Ambrose's spiritual interpretation of the Old Testament for Augustine's subsequent conversion, it is not surprising to find that in his first attempt at scriptural exegesis he has recourse to the criterion for figurative and spiritual interpretation that he had found most helpful in the sermons of the bishop of Milan.[19]

If we turn to *De Genesi contra Manichaeos*, we find that he explicitly appeals to the absurdity criterion. In *De Genesi contra Manichaeos* 2.1.1, Augustine announces that in Genesis 2 "the whole narrative unfolds not openly, but in figures, in order to exercise the minds of those seeking the truth and to call them away from carnal concerns to a spiritual concern."[20] Then, after having presented the account of the creation and sin in Genesis 2 and 3 and after having admonished the Manichees that they should rather seek to understand the secrets of the text than find fault with it, Augustine proposes to examine the whole account first as history and then as prophecy, that is, first as narrating the facts and then as foretelling the future. Then he says:

> Of course, if anyone wanted to take everything that was said according to the letter, that is, to understand it exactly as the letter sounds, and could avoid blasphemies and explain everything in harmony with the Catholic faith, we should not only envy him but regard him as a leading and highly praiseworthy interpreter. But if there is no way in which we can understand what has been written in a manner that is pious and worthy of God without believing that these things have been set before us in figures and enigmas, we have the apostolic authority by which so many enigmas from the books of the Old Testament are solved.[21]

That is, Augustine admits that he himself cannot interpret the text of Genesis 2 and 3 "exactly as the letter sounds," but that he would welcome the interpretation of someone else who could do so. The grounds for resorting to figurative interpretation lie in his inability to "avoid blasphemies and explain everything in harmony with the Catholic faith." He cannot understand the text "in a manner that is pious and worthy of God" unless he believes that Genesis presents us with events "in figures and enigmas." That is, the only reason for believing that the text contains figures and enigmas is that such a belief provides the only escape (*exitus*) from understanding the text in a manner that is blasphemous, lacking in piety, and unworthy of God.

Much later, in *De Genesi ad litteram*, Augustine reports that, when he came to deal in his first commentary on Genesis with the narrative of chapters 2 and 3,

> it did not then occur to me how I could interpret everything in the proper sense, and I thought that everything could not, or was hardly able, or was able only with difficulty to be so interpreted. Hence, in order to avoid delay, I explained as briefly and as clearly as possible the figurative meaning of those things for which I could not find a literal interpretation.[22]

That is, Augustine reports that he had recourse to a figurative interpretation of the text only because of his inability or great difficulty in interpreting everything in the text in its proper sense. But he went on to tell us that in the later work he "thought that it could be shown even by him that these things [i.e., the creation narrative in Genesis 2 and 3] were written in a proper, not in an allegorical mode of expression."[23]

The criterion for a figurative interpretation of a scriptural text that, according to the *Confessions*, Augustine learned from Ambrose's preaching and that played a decisive role in his conversion was the limited and sober absurdity criterion. In *De Genesi contra Manichaeos* Augustine explicitly tells us that he used this criterion in his first venture at an interpretation of the opening chapters of Genesis. Furthermore, in retrospect he tells us in *De Genesi ad litteram* that he had recourse to figurative interpretation in *De Genesi contra Manichaeos* only because he could not then interpret the text in its proper sense. Hence, I said of Augustine's practice in *De Genesi contra Manichaeos* that "he almost always resorts to regarding the text as figurative only if he cannot take it literally without blasphemy or having it say something unworthy of God."[24]

There is, however, at least one passage in *De Genesi contra Manichaeos* where Augustine's theory of figurative interpretation goes beyond the absurdity criterion. In speaking of Eve's being made from Adam's rib, Augustine explicitly distinguishes between a proper and a figurative expression:

> For a proper expression is one thing; quite another is a figurative expression, such as we are dealing with here. Hence, even if in terms of history a visible woman was first made from the body of the man by the Lord God, she was certainly not made in this way without a reason, but to convey some secret.[25]

Augustine points out that there was plenty of mud available for God to make the woman as he had made the man and that he could have taken the rib from the man painlessly while he was awake.

Whether, then, these things were said figuratively, or whether they were also done figuratively, they were not said or done in this way to no point. Rather they are clearly mysteries and sacraments, whether they are to be interpreted and understood in the way our modest talent is trying or in some better way, though in accord with sound faith.[26]

In this one passage in *De Genesi contra Manichaeos* Augustine offers a criterion for figurative interpretation that goes beyond his more modest criterion, namely, that of the impossibility of taking the text in the proper sense without absurdity or impiety. Here he claims that the making of Eve could not have been done or described as it was to no point (*frustra*) and that the events reported are mysteries and sacraments. However, there is on the basis of this text no reason to suppose that all the events reported in Genesis are mysteries and sacraments or that all the events reported either teach matters of faith and morals or are figurative of something else.

It is important to see what Augustine means by the text being figurative. He speaks of "figures of speech" and "figures of things."[27] By "figures of speech" he means such devices as metonymy, amphiboly, and metaphor.[28] By "figures of things" he means something that either symbolizes or prefigures something else. Thus, the days of the Genesis narrative prefigure the six ages in the history of salvation and the six stages in the life of every person.[29] As a narrative of past events Genesis is history; as prefiguring what is to come it is prophecy. Augustine treats the text of Genesis in each book of *De Genesi contra Manichaeos* first as history and then as prophecy. But "figures of things" not merely prefigure what is to come; they also symbolize or are signs of other things, often of spiritual or incorporeal things.[30] Thus in Genesis 2 where we are told that everything unfolds in figures, Augustine understands by "the green of the field" an invisible creature such as the soul, and by the spring that watered the whole earth he understands the fountain of truth from which souls drank before the fall. So too by the tunics of skin he understands the mortal bodies the first couple received after their sin. Clearly in these cases the text contains figures that are enigmas or allegories.[31] When Augustine says of Genesis 2 and 3 that "the whole narrative unfolds in figures," he is primarily speaking of the text as history, for even Genesis 1 prefigures the future ages of each person and of human history. That is, he is stating that the whole narrative is expressed by words used not in their proper sense but in a transferred or figurative sense. And his reason for recourse to such a figurative sense lies, he claims, with the absurdity criterion.

III. The *De doctrina christiana* Criterion

The fundamental law for figurative interpretation from *De doctrina christiana* is precisely a criterion for distinguishing between terms being used in their proper sense and terms being used in a transferred or figurative sense. At the beginning of book 3 of *De doctrina christiana*, Augustine points out that the ambiguity of Scripture lies in words used either properly or metaphorically.[32] Earlier he distinguished proper and metaphorical signs:

> [Signs] are called proper when they are used to signify these things on account of which they are instituted, just as we say "ox" when we understand the animal that all who speak the Latin language call by this name along with us. They are metaphorical when the things themselves to which we refer by the proper terms are used to refer to something else, just as we say "ox" and by that one syllable understand the animal that is usually called by this name, but again by it we understand an evangelist to whom Scripture referred, as the Apostle has shown, "You shall not muzzle the ox that treads the grain."[33]

Augustine first deals with ambiguity in words used in their proper sense, pointing out that here ambiguity may arise from dividing a sentence incorrectly, from mispronouncing a word, or from the similarity of the forms for different Latin cases.[34] But ambiguities of terms used in their proper senses rarely present problems that cannot readily be solved.

Ambiguities in metaphorical terms, on the other hand, demand considerable care and hard work. One must, first of all, avoid taking a figurative expression literally. Augustine points out that the Apostle's words, "The letter kills, but the spirit gives life" (2 Cor. 3:6), are pertinent here:

> For when one takes what was said figuratively as if it were said in the proper sense, one thinks in carnal terms. . . . For one who follows the letter regards metaphorical terms as proper and does not refer that which is signified by the proper sense of the word to another signification.[35]

As examples of such carnal thinking, Augustine points to understanding sabbath as merely referring to one of the seven days of the week, or understanding sacrifice as only referring to the sacrifices of animals or of the fruits of the earth. Such understanding mistakes signs for things, and that is a "wretched slavery of the mind."[36]

Augustine also warns against a second danger, namely, of taking a proper expression as if it were figurative.[37] Obviously there is need of a way to discover whether an expression is proper or figurative. He then states the general criterion by which one can determine this: "And in general the method is that you should know that whatever in the word of God cannot in the proper sense be referred to the goodness of morals or to the truth of the faith is figurative."[38]

Augustine explains that goodness of conduct has to do with loving God and neighbor, while the truth of faith has to do with knowing God and neighbor. But, if that is the case, then any passage of Scripture that cannot in its proper sense be understood as either a matter of faith or of morals is to be understood as figurative. Here we have what I have referred to as Augustine's maximizing rule for figurative interpretation.

IV. The Different Criteria Reexamined

Up to this point I have indicated the two criteria that Augustine articulated for having recourse to a figurative interpretation of Scripture. In his earliest commentary on Genesis Augustine both articulates and employs the absurdity criterion. According to the *Confessions* it was this same criterion that Augustine learned from the preaching of Ambrose and found most helpful toward his own conversion. The second criterion, articulated in *De doctrina christiana* and used in much of Augustine's scriptural exegesis, goes far beyond the absurdity criterion and claims that whatever is not related to faith and morals is figurative. I mentioned earlier that I now regard my initial question, namely, why Augustine moved from the absurdity criterion to the maximizing criterion of *De doctrina christiana*, as mistaken. Let me sketch my reasons for changing my initial hypothesis.

When writing the introduction to the translation of *De Genesi contra Manichaeos*, I focused too much upon what Augustine said was the criterion for figurative interpretation rather than the interpretation that Augustine actually gave of the text. Years ago Henri de Lubac said that "il importe avant tout de voir Origène a l'oeuvre plutôt que de se tenir a quelque exposé méthodique abstrait,"[39] even though the abstract explanation was given by Origen himself. Similarly, it is of prime importance to observe Augustine at work rather than to take at face value his stated criterion for figurative interpretation. In focusing upon the criterion that Augustine stated in *De Genesi contra Manichaeos*, I overlooked the criterion that he actually used, which in fact goes far beyond the absurdity criterion. Hence, I do not now believe that Augustine moved from the absurdity criterion to the maximizing criterion of *De doctrina christiana*.

The criterion of *De doctrina christiana* does, nonetheless, represent an advance over that found in Augustine's earlier works, but it represents an advance not so much in practice as in the articulation of exegetical principles. The difference in the articulation of the criteria for recourse to figurative interpretation should not come as a surprise. For *De Genesi contra Manichaeos* is, after all, directed to the Manichees, and in justifying his use of figurative interpretation Augustine makes explicit appeal to the criterion that he found most helpful in his own conversion and that he might reasonably hope would be most of help to his readers, especially his Manichaean friends and "the little ones" of the *Catholica*. The criterion articulated in *De doctrina christiana*, on the other hand, was intended for believers who were ready, able, and eager to understand the hidden richness of the word of God. One should not after all attempt to teach the deeper and figurative meaning to those unwilling to learn.[40]

Furthermore, it may well be that the sharpness of the distinction I drew between the criteria should be blurred or that one would speak more correctly of a single criterion with two functions or emphases. For example, Marrou ties the criterion found in *De doctrina christiana* with another that Augustine states in *De Genesi ad litteram* 9.12.22.[41] Augustine there says that he undertook the exposition of Genesis with two goals in mind: first, "to show that what some superficial or unbelieving readers might think impossible or contrary to the authority of Holy Scripture . . . was neither impossible nor contrary to it"; second, to show "that what appears possible and has no semblance of contradictoriness, but could seem to certain people to be either superfluous or lacking sense, was not something produced in the natural or ordinary course of events. Thus . . . we might believe that it has a mystical meaning, since nothing can be found there that is lacking sense."[42] That is, though it was not Augustine's aim in *De Genesi ad litteram* to examine the hidden prophetic meaning (*prophetica aenigmata perscrutari*), he still would show that things that might seem superfluous or pointless were not simply natural events but ones that we should believe have a mystical or hidden meaning.[43] The sense of the passage will depend upon the force one gives to *superfluum* and *stultum*. For if one takes *stultum* as "foolish" or "fatuous," one comes close to the "absurdity" criterion for taking a text as figurative. Much the same thing occurs, if one takes *superfluum* in the sense of *otiosum* (cf. Mt. 12:36).[44] This passage from *De Genesi ad litteram* is, in any case, merely a generalization of the criterion we saw in *De Genesi contra Manichaeos* for interpreting the creation of Eve as figurative.

Marrou suggests two reasons for Augustine's having adopted what I have called his maximizing criterion for figurative interpretation. The first reason suggested is that Augustine took very literally the text from Timothy: "We have then to seek a hidden meaning for all those passages whose usefulness is not apparent in the literal sense" (*omnis scriptura divinitus inspirata utilis est.*)[45] Marrou points to the fundamental idea underlying this position: "Nothing in the Bible is useless, not even less useful; it is in its entirety inspired, and the inspiration is equally portioned out, and has everywhere the same density."[46]

Marrou's second reason for Augustine's having adopted the maximizing criterion is that his training in rhetoric taught him to study a text verse by verse and word by word rather than sentence by sentence. "The tendency is reinforced by the habit inherited from the profane grammarian that consists in reading the text verse by verse, in commenting on it word by word, in breaking it down into isolated fragments which are examined each separately in the utmost detail."[47] Similarly, Joseph Lienhard has said quite well, "The ancients' first unit of understanding was not the pericope, or the sentence, but the single word. The word as the starting point for understanding was an assumption of ancient education in poetics and rhetoric."[48] Coupled with Marrou's first reason, this second reason means that divine inspiration bears upon individual words and phrases rather than upon larger units of meaning.

Another reason for Augustine's having had recourse to the more ample criterion for figurative interpretation is tied to his conviction that Scripture contains only a few truths to be believed and a few moral precepts to be followed. After stating his fundamental law, he points out that "good moral conduct has to do with loving God and the neighbor, and the truth of the faith has to do with knowing God and the neighbor."[49] Furthermore, our hope lies in our consciousness of progressing in the knowledge and love of God.[50] The truths to be believed and the moral precepts to be followed are comparatively few in number. Scripture "merely states the Catholic faith in things past, present, and future . . . , but all of these serve to nourish and strengthen charity and to conquer and extinguish cupidity."[51] The whole of Christian morality is summed up in fostering charity and conquering its opposite, cupidity.[52] Then Augustine makes the startling claim: "One supported by faith, hope, and charity and firmly holding unto them has no need of the Scriptures save for teaching others."[53] And he appeals to the example of Christian hermits who have lived without the Scriptures.[54] Given Augustine's view that the essence of Scripture is contained in the Creed and the commandments to love God and neighbor, the vast majority of the Bible would be *superfluum* and *stultum* unless it contained hidden meanings, enigmata, and figures to be understood by those who would seek to understand the word of God at a more profound level. Hence, most of the Bible would be pointless and senseless if we were not to take it as figurative.

One final thought: In *De doctrina christiana* Augustine says that Scripture teaches us the historical events in which we must believe and that the purpose of this faith is to nourish and strengthen charity. Had I not earlier read *De Genesi contra Manichaeos* with almost exclusive attention to the absurdity criterion, I might have noticed that the cherubim and the flaming sword set to guard paradise were interpreted by Augustine as signifying that we can return to the tree of life only through the flaming sword, i.e., through tribulations, and through the cherubim, i.e., the fullness of knowledge, as he assures us the term means in Hebrew. But the fullness of knowledge is the fullness of the Law, that is, the full content of Scripture. And, as Augustine points out, Paul has assured us that the fullness of the Law is charity (Rom. 13:10). Hence, with a bit of Augustinian exegesis of Augustine, one might argue that the core of the *De doctrina christiana* criterion was already present in his earliest work on Genesis, where "the whole narrative unfolds, not openly, but in figures, to exercise the minds of those seeking the truth."[55]

Notes

1. Cf. *Saint Augustine On Genesis: Two Books on Genesis against the Manichees and On the Literal Interpretation of Genesis: An Unfinished Book*, trans. Roland J. Teske (Washington, D.C., 1991).

2. Cf. *De Genesi ad litteram* 8.2.5 (*BA* 49:14), and *Retractationes* 1.10.1 (*CC* 57:29).

3. Cf. *Saint Augustine on Genesis*, 6–15.

4. Cf. their introduction to *De Genesi ad litteram* in *BA* 48:33–34 and 38.

5. Jean Pépin, "A propos de l'histoire de l'exégèse allégorique: L'absurdité signe de l'allégorie," *Studia Patristica*, in *Texte und Untersuchungen* 63 (1955): 395–413.

6. "La réponse des chrétiens des premiers siècles est claire: le principal indice qu'un texte biblique a été écrit dans un dessein allégorique et doit être entendu comme tel, c'est son absurdité aussi longtemps que l'on s'en tient au sens littéral" (Pépin, 397).

7. *DDC* 3.10.14 (*CC* 32:86); cf. the following note for the Latin.

8. "Nous en trouvons la théorie formulée dans le *De doctrina christiana*: elle se résume en une loi fondamentale: tout ce qui dans l'Ecriture ne se rapporte pas directement à la foi et aux moeurs doit être tenu pour figuré, *quidquid in sermone divino neque ad morum honestatem, neque ad fidei veritatem proprie referri potest, figuratum est cognoscas*" (Henri-Irénée Marrou, *Saint Augustin et la fin de la culture antique* [Paris, 1938], 478).

9. "Saint Augustin ne dit pas seulement qu'il faut dans l'Ecriture prendre au figuré tout ce qui est *contre* la foi et les moeurs, mais bien tout ce qui ne s'y rapport pas directement" (Marrou, 479).

10. Cf. *In Ioannis euangelium* 122.5–9 (*CC* 36:670–675.

11. Though Augustine completed the third book and added the fourth at the time of his writing the *Retractationes*, he completed the third book up to the point at which he broke off writing, i.e., at *DDC* 3.25.35, 11.9–11, no earlier than the end of 397. Cf. the preface to *CC* 32:vii–xi.

12. Apart from Marrou, I have not found anyone else who has discussed these two criteria or who has dealt with the relations between them. In her *Saint Au-*

gustin exégète du quatrième évangile (Paris, 1930), M. Comeau, for example, simply passes over my concern. Madeleine Moreau, in her "Lecture du *De doctrina christiana*" in *Saint Augustin et la Bible*, ed. Anne-Marie la Bonnardière (Paris, 1986), 253–285, simply notes, "Il importe tout d'abord d'éviter absolument tant la confusion entre valeur métaphorique et valeur propre d'une expression que la confusion inverse. Le critère à appliquer relève de la foi et des moeurs: tout ce qui, dans le texte biblique, est, dans sa littéralité, étranger à la morale ou à la vérité de la foi requiert une interprétation figurée" (267). Marrou speaks of the twofold function of recourse to a mystical sense: "le recours au sens mystique a chez lui, comme première fonction, celle qu'il avait déjà chez Origène: c'est un moyen d'expliquer tous les passages choquants de l'Ancien Testament, anthropomorphisme divin, immoralité de certaines prescriptions ou de certains récits, contradictions entre l'ancienne et la nouvelle loi" (478). But then he points out that the fundamental law goes way beyond this function in terms of what I have called the maximizing criterion.

13. Cf. *Confessiones* 3.5.9 (*BA* 13:376); and 3.7.12–10.18 (*BA* 13:384–398).

14. *Confessiones* 6.4.5 (*BA* 13:526): *ecclesia unica . . . non saperat infantiles nugas.*

15. *Confessiones* 5.14.24 (*BA* 13:508–510): *maxime audito uno atque altero et saepius aenigmate soluto de scriptis ueteribus, ubi, cum ad litteram acciperem, occidebar. spiritaliter itaque plerisque illorum librorum locis expositis iam reprehenderam desperationem meam illam dumtaxat, qua credideram legem et prophetas destestantibus atque irridentibus resisti omnino non posse.*

16. *Confessiones* 5.14.24 (*BA* 13:510): *ita enim catholica non mihi uicta uidebatur, et nondum etiam uictrix appareret.*

17. In *De beata vita* 1.4 (*CC* 29:67), Augustine describes hearing Ambrose and Theodorus speak as though one should not think of a body when one thinks of God or the soul.

18. *Confessiones* 6.4.6 (*BA* 13:528): *"littera occidit, spiritus autem uiuificat,"* cum ea, quae ad litteram peruersitatem docere uidebantur, remoto mystico velamento spiritaliter aperiret, non dicens quod me offenderet, quamvis ea diceret, quae utrum uera essent adhuc ignorarem.*

19. I stress Augustine's recourse to the criterion for figurative interpretation he found most helpful, since Ambrose's use of figurative interpretation certainly tends to be far less restrained than Augustine's. That is, there is good reason to suppose that Augustine also derived from Ambrose's preaching the grounds for maximizing the figurative interpretation.

20. *De Genesi contra Manichaeos* 2.1.1 (*PL* 34:195): *Quae omnis narratio non aperte, sed figurate explicatur, ut exerceat mentes quaerentium veritatem, et spiritali negotio a negotiis carnalibus avocet.*

21. *De Genesi contra Manichaeos* 2.2.3 (*PL* 34:197).

22. *De Genesi ad litteram* 8.2.5 (*BA* 49:14:).

23. *De Genesi ad litteram* 9.2.5 (*BA* 49:16): *extimarem etiam per me posse secundum propriam, non secundum allegoricam locutionem haec scruota esse monstrari.* In the intervening years Augustine had attempted another literal interpretation of Genesis, namely, *De Genesi ad litteram liber imperfectus.* Of this

work he tells us, *in scripturis exponendis tirocinium meum sub tanta sarcinae mole succubuit, et nondum perfecto uno libro ab eo quem sustinere non poteram labore conquieui* (*Retractationes* 1.18 [CC 57:54]).

24. *Saint Augustine on Genesis*, 27, n. 54.

25. *De Genesi contra Manichaeos* 2.12.17 (*PL* 34:205).

26. *De Genesi contra Manichaeos* 2.12.17 (*PL* 34:205–206).

27. Cf. *De Genesi contra Manichaeos* 1.22.34 (*PL* 34:189), and 2.2.3 (*PL* 34:197).

28. Cf. *Augustine on Genesis*, 21–24.

29. Cf. *De Genesi contra Manichaeos* 1.23.35–25.43 (*PL* 34:190–194).

30. Cf. *De Genesi ad litteram* 8.1.4 (*BA* 49:14). Augustine speaks of what the text teaches *figurata significatione . . . sive ipsarum spiritalium naturarum vel affectionum sive rerum etiam futurarum.*

31. In *De Genesi ad litteram liber imperfectus* 2.5 (*CSEL* 28:461), Augustine says that to understand a text as allegory is to understand it as presenting something in figures. An enigma simply means a riddle or puzzle. In *De Genesi contra Manichaeos* Augustine seems to use "allegory" as synonymous with "enigma."

32. *DDC* 3.1.1 (*CC* 32:77): *sciat ambiguitatem scripturae aut in uerbis propriis aut in translatis.*

33. *DDC* 2.10.15 (*CC* 32:41).

34. As an example of the first, Augustine gives the Arian division of John 1:1: *In principio erat uerbum et uerbum erat apud deum et deus erat; uerbum hoc erat in principio apud deum* (*DDC* 3.2.3 [*CC* 32:78]). As an example of the second, he uses *os*, which can mean either "mouth" or "bone," depending upon whether the vowel is long or short. As an example of an ambiguity of the Latin case, he cites 1 Thes. 3:7, where *fratres* might be either accusative or vocative. Cf. *DDC* 3.3.7–4.8 (*CC* 32:81–82).

35. *DDC* 3.5.9 (*CC* 32:82–83): *Cum enim figurate dictum sic accipitur, tamquam proprie dictum sit, carnaliter sapitur. . . . Qui enim sequitur litteram, translata uerba sicut propria tenet neque illud, quod proprio uerbo significatur, refert ad aliam significationem.*

36. *DDC* 3.5.9 (*CC* 32:83): *miserabilis animi seruitus.*

37. *DDC* 3.10.14 (*CC* 32:86).

38. *DDC* 3.10.14 (*CC* 32:86): *Et iste omnino modus est, ut quidquid in sermone diuino neque ad morum honestatem neque ad fidei ueritatem proprie referri potest, figuratum esse cognoscas.*

39. H. de Lubac, *Histoire et esprit: l'intelligence de l'Ecriture d'après Origène*, Théologie 16 (Paris, 1950), 34.

40. For example, in the late work, *Contra adversarium legis et prophetarum* 1.16.31 (*CC* 49:59).

41. Marrou, 479.

42. *De Genesi ad litteram* 9.12.22 (*BA* 49:120–122).

43. Marrou also points to *Speculum*, praef. (*PL* 34:887–889). This position does not have the force of the criterion in *DDC* since it admits reports of human and divine actions as matters merely to be known and since it seems to limit figurative interpretations to the area of Old Testament commands and prohibitions.

44. In his *De trinitate* ch. 19, when arguing that the Father could only speak one Word, William of Auvergne argues that he who has forbidden that we speak an idle word would certainly not do so himself. So too, one might argue that God could hardly have uttered an idle word in Scripture.

45. "Or saint Paul nous dit (2 Tim. 3:16) que toute l'Ecriture est divinement inspirée et utile. . . . Il faut donc chercher un sens caché à tous les passages dont l'utilité n'apparaît pas au sens littéral" (Marrou, 479).

46. "Rien dans la Bible n'est inutile, ni même moins utile; elle est tout entière inspirée, et l'inspiration y est également répartie, a partout la même densité" (Marrou, 480).

47. "Tendance que renforce l'habitude, héritée du grammairien profane, qui consiste à lire le texte verset par verset, à le commenter mot par mot, à le décomposer en fragments isolés qu'on examine chacun séparément avec la plus stricte minutie" (Marrou, 480).

48. J. Lienhard, "'The Glue Itself Is Charity': Ps. 62:9 in Augustine's Thought," *Collectanea Augustiniana* 3, forthcoming.

49. DDC 3.10.14 (CC 32:86): *Morum honestas ad diligendum deum et proximum, fidei ueritas ad cognoscendum deum et proximum pertinet.*

50. DDC 3.10.14.

51. DDC 3.10.15 (CC 32:87): *Non autem adserit nisi catholicam fidem rebus praeteritis et futuris et praesentibus . . . sed omnia haec ad eandem caritatem nutriendam atque roborandam et cupiditatem uincendam atque exstinguendam ualent.*

52. DDC 3.10.15 (CC 32:87): *Non autem praecipit scriptura nisi caritatem nec culpat nisi cupiditatem et eo modo informat mores hominum.*

53. DDC 1.34.43 (CC 32:31): *Homo itaque fide et spe et caritate subnixus eaque inconcusse retinens non indiget scripturis nisi ad alios instruendos.*

54. DDC 1.39.43 (CC 32:31).

55. *De Genesi contra Manichaeos* 2.1.1 (PL 34:195).

Sign Theory, Allegorical Reading, and the Motions of the Soul in *De doctrina christiana*

DAVID DAWSON

Ancient Christian allegorical readings of Scripture have often been regarded as the means by which interpreters translated the unique images and stories of the Bible into the abstractions of classical metaphysics and ethics, but Augustine's recommendations concerning how to interpret Scripture suggest that nonliteral translation ought to move in the opposite direction.[1] Rather than dissolving scriptural language into nonscriptural categories, allegorical reading should enable the Bible to refashion personal experience and cultural ideals by reformulating them in a distinctively biblical idiom.[2] In *De doctrina christiana*, Augustine draws on a subtle theory of signs to offer his fullest and most detailed description of how such allegorical refashioning might proceed. I will examine three interrelated aspects of his proposal that appear both in *De doctrina christiana* and in several other treatises: the role of linguistic signs in the communication of the will; the failure of sign communication because of human sin; and the relation between Scripture's sign character, the incarnation of the Logos, and allegorical reading (in contrast to "mere" literalism and ideological projection). Augustine suggests that an allegorical reading of Scripture enables God to heal the soul because that particular mode of reading replicates and makes real for the reader the therapeutic self-humiliation of an incarnate deity. This divine self-humiliation, embodied in the literary character of the text and appropriated through its proper allegorical reading, provides an antidote to the *superbia* that otherwise disorders the motions of the reader's soul.

I

The reader of Scripture presupposed in *De doctrina christiana* is an embodied soul.[3] While in no sense a material entity, the soul can nevertheless be "moved," either by the vicissitudes of the body (such as pain or fatigue) or by its own "motions" (which we would call affections, passions, or emotions). In *De doctrina christiana*, Augustine concentrates attention on the motions that the soul generates by itself, thinking principally of the four passions familiar to classical thinkers: joy (*laetitia*), grief (*tristia*), desire (*cupiditas*), and fear (*metus, timor*). Such movements, though immaterial, are more than metaphorical: the immaterial soul mysteriously endures, as it is moved, through time.[4] Augustine can even draw on materialistic Stoic metaphors to imagine the character of these immaterial motions: "Our affections are motions of souls. Joy is the extending of the soul; sadness the contraction of the soul; desire the soul's going forward; fear the soul's flight" (*In Ioannis evangelium tractatus* 46.8).[5]

The soul's various motions are caused by the human will, which in its capacity to modify the soul in proper or improper ways is also called love.[6] Whether the soul's motions are proper depends not on their own intrinsic quality or character but on the kind of willing—the sort of love—that has generated them: "The good and bad alike desire, fear, and rejoice, but the former in a good way, the latter in a bad manner, according as their will is right or wrong" (*De civitate dei* 14.8).[7] Emotions are forms of volition that either move one toward God or back toward one's self. They are "our feet," writes Augustine, and "according to the affection which each individual has, according to the love which each has, he draws near to, or moves away from, God" (*Enarrationes in Psalmos* 94.2).[8] "We are," he declares in *De doctrina christiana*, "on a road which is not a road from place to place but a road of the affections" (*in via sumus . . . adfectuum* [DDC 1.17.16; cf. 1.36.41]). This interrelationship of emotions, will, and love of God informs nearly every page of *De doctrina christiana*. Throughout the treatise, Augustine repeatedly insists that the very meaning of Scripture is its capacity to move the soul in love toward God and one's neighbor.[9] If that movement of the will of the Scripture reader has not occurred, Scripture has either not been understood at all, or, if understood, has been deliberately resisted.

It seems that Augustine understood the meaning of Scripture (as love of God and neighbor) and the character of the reader of Scripture (as an embodied soul capable of self-movement or volition) to be, at their most fundamental level, nonlinguistic in character—psychological, rather than semantic, entities. But (for reasons to be explored in part II of this essay), human beings must nevertheless forge their desired relationships of love through linguistic signs. Consequently, in *De doctrina christiana*, Augustine relates the soul's emotions to the signs that give them expression. He characterizes signs both according to their own nature and to their place within the larger process of communication. By itself, a sign is "a thing which causes us to think of something beyond the impression the thing itself makes upon the senses" (*DDC* 2.1.1).[10] As such, any sign has three aspects: its own nature as a sensuous thing (*res*), whether spoken, written, or gestural; its referent, that is, some other thing (*res*) to which it gestures; and the thought, idea, or meaning (*significatio, dicibile*) that it engenders in the mind. Drawing on an ancient Stoic formulation, Augustine describes the sign in a way that Saussurian linguistics has made familiar to modern readers: a sign consists of signifier, referent, and signified meaning.

Augustine thinks of this complex sign within a larger rhetorical framework: he is interested in signs primarily as the means by which rational beings seek to communicate with one another.[11] A sign giver uses a sign to signify something to another rational being. This communicative context leads Augustine to highlight the centrality of the will in his discussion of signs. Because his ultimate concern is with the capacity of God to use scriptural signs to move readers to conversion, he is not content to limit the function of a sign to its meaning (that is, to the concept or idea that it transfers from one mind to another). He wishes to probe deeper—to the act of will that impels one person to speak or write to another. As book 4 of *De doctrina christiana* makes clear, Augustine thinks one should read Scripture for the same reason that one would attend to any other sort of rhetorical performance: not primarily to have one's mind filled with ideas, but to have one's will moved (*DDC* 4.25.55).[12] Consequently, Augustine defines the sign by pointing to the capacity of human speech to express a motion of the sign user's soul: when we hear the voice of a person, that voice is a sign leading us to "attend to the emotion of soul (*adfectio animi*) it expresses" (*DDC* 2.1.1).[13] That is, the speech of another impels us to respond first of all to the speaker's inner disposition. And it does seem to be the case that before we reflect on the content of another's remark, we generally respond to its tone, reacting to what we sense as its reflection of the speaker's own inner state or attitude toward us.

It is true that signs can sometimes signify emotions that occur unintentionally, as when the face of an angry or sad person automatically reveals the motion of her soul (*affectio animi* or *motus animi*) to others (*DDC* 2.1.2). However, Augustine is not primarily interested in such "natural" signs (*signa naturalia*) of the soul's motions, but in those "given" signs (*signa data*), by which persons intentionally signify these motions to others. Such signs, expressing emotions as forms of volition, are the means by which persons communicate and interact with one another. According to *De doctrina christiana*, persons signify for a single reason: "to bring forth and transfer to another soul what is going on in the soul of the person who makes the sign" (*ad depromendum et traiciendum in alterius animum id quod animo gerit qui signum dat* [DDC 2.2.3]).

The heart of the act of communication is expressed by the phrase *id quod animo gerit* ("what is going on in the soul"). Although it is tempting to interpret this phrase as referring to the thoughts (*cogitationes*) resulting from the mind's attention to its own internal images, doing so would obscure Augustine's more fundamental concern. He uses the general phrase *id quod animo gerit* rather than the more specific *cogitatio* because he wants to focus on the underlying movement of will that impels the mind to engage in thought as well as to feel in a certain way.

This act of will motivates all of the soul's more variously and subsequently qualified motions.[14] Hence, in *De magistro*, Augustine can write that "he who speaks gives forth by an articulate sound a sign of his will" (*suae voluntatis signum* [De magistro 1.2.45–47]), and in *De doctrina christiana* he declares that we use signs in order "to make [another person] a participant in our will" (*volumus per hoc signum voluntatis nostrae participem facere* [DDC 2.3.4]).[15] Perhaps even more revealingly, Augustine declares elsewhere that "there is no voice to reach the ears of God save the emotion of the soul" (*animi affectus* [De catechizandis rudibus 9.13.5]). The root of communication with both God and other persons lies, then, in the deepest motions of the soul, which are fundamentally acts of will (cf. *De vera religione* 14.28).

In *De trinitate* 15, Augustine offers what initially seems to be a somewhat different account of the various aspects of the sign and its role in communication. There he describes the movement of language from its origin in the deepest recesses of the self to its outermost expression. In this movement, language assumes four related forms: two denoting processes that are internal to the soul (inner word and inner meaning or thought) and two that are external (outer speech and written letters). Language begins with an act of knowing a sensuous or an intelligible thing (*res*) that produces a "content" with two dimensions, epistemological and semantic. These two dimensions are utterly isomorphic: the content of what the mind knows is identical with the content of what Augustine describes as an "inner" (*intus*) word. This inner word or *verbum* is, however, unlike anything we customarily regard as a word. It is prior to all signs by which it might subsequently be signified, and it is not part of Greek, Latin, or any other human language. Augustine refers to it as the word that we "carry in our mind" (*mente gerimus*) or "speak in our heart" (*in corde dicimus*). The inner *verbum* may then be expressed in signs, which are the "outer" (*foris*) bodily forms of speech (*locutio, vox,* or *dictio*) or gesture. In addition, images (*species*) of such signs may be attended to by the mind in silence, as, for example, when one's memory ruminates over poems or melodies one has once heard. This internal image seems to be the sensuous equivalent of the nonsensuous "meaning" (*dicibile*) that the sign conveys to the mind rather than to the ear or eye. Finally, vocal signs may themselves be represented by written signs (*litterae*), which are the means by which we signify to those who are not present.[16]

The phrases in *De trinitate* that denote the mysterious, presignificatory "internal" *verbum* represent the same act of emotional volition (*motus animi*) denoted by *De doctrina christiana*'s phrase *quod in animo gerit,* as well as echoing phrases in *De fide et symbolo.* Other synonymous phrases denote the point at which language mysteriously originates in the soul of the speaker: *id quod animo gerimus* (DDC 1.13.12); *id quod animo gerit* (DDC 2.2.3); *verbum quod corde gestamus* (DDC 1.13.12); *verbum est quod in corde dicimus* (*De trinitate* 15.10.19); *verbum quod mente gerimus* (*De trinitate* 15.10.19); *quidquid secretum in corde gerimus* (*De fide et symbolo* 3.3); and *id, quod intus est* (*De fide et symbolo* 3.4). *Gerimus* (*gero*) and *gestamus* (*gesto*) are synonyms meaning "to bear," "to carry," or "to manifest." *Animus* (mind) and *cor* (heart) also appear to be synonymous here, "heart" perhaps chosen to emphasize the emotional inflection of language at its inception. *Dicimus* is used only metaphorically since *De trinitate* makes it clear that even silent mental speech is a step removed from the mysterious internal word which is unlike any human language. In short, all of these expressions denote that most basic movement of the soul that gives birth to language. This movement, though it leads to the thinking of a concept or the having of an emotion, is at its origin a movement of will.

Although *De doctrina christiana* suggests only in passing that successful communication means making another person a "participant" in one's will, the idea receives more explicit development in some of Augustine's other works. In his sermon *De fide et symbolo,* preached before a gathering of bishops in 393, Augustine began to explore matters of language and communication that he would take up again only several years later in *De doctrina christiana.* In the sermon, Augustine describes the purpose of human communication this way:

> What else are we trying to do [when speaking to another] but to bring our mind (*animus*), as far as it can be done, into contact with the mind (*animus*) of him who listens to us, so that he may know and understand us? We remain in ourselves and take no step outside ourselves, yet nevertheless we put forth such a remarkable sign (*indicium*) by means of which there

may be knowledge of us in another; so that, if opportunity is afforded, "another mind," as it were, is put forth by [my] mind, through which it [my mind] signifies itself (*se indicet*). We do this, making the attempt with words, and with the mere sound of utterances, and with looks, and with bodily gestures—with so many devices—desiring to make known that which is within (*id, quod intus est*). (*De fide et symbolo* 3.4)

Augustine offers another description of human expression in *De catechizandis rudibus* as part of his effort to help the catechist avoid boredom while repeating simplistic lessons. He draws on the example of the compassionate love of family members for one another to illustrate the shared disposition of mind to which even the most basic catechetical instruction should aspire:

> Again, if it be distasteful to us to be repeating over and over things that are familiar and suitable for little children, let us suit ourselves to them with a brother's, a father's, and a mother's love, and when once we are linked to them thus in heart these things will seem new even to us. For so great is the power of a sympathetic disposition of mind (*tantum enim valet animi compatientis affectus*), that when people are affected by us as we speak and we by them as they learn, we dwell each in the other and thus both they, as it were, speak in us what they hear, while we, after a fashion, learn in them what we teach. (*De catechizandis rudibus* 12.17)

Together, then, these two passages help explicate more fully than does *De doctrina christiana* itself Augustine's understanding of the mysterious act by which human beings seek to express themselves to others through signs.

II

The preceding passages might give the impression that Augustine views the communicative process as unproblematic. And it is the case that the beginning of interpersonal communication—the expression of a sign that will convey the deepest essence of the speaker—resembles divine self-expression through the generation of the Logos. *De fide et symbolo* regards human verbal expression as an appropriate analogy for imagining the mysterious generation of the divine Logos:

> For as by our words, when we speak truly, our mind lets him who hears them know something, and by signs of that kind brings to the knowledge of another what we hold secretly in our heart (*quidquid secretum in corde gerimus*), so wisdom whom God the Father begat is most appropriately called his Word, because through him the Father who dwells in utmost secrecy (*secretissimus*) becomes known to worthy minds. (*De fide et symbolo* 3.3)

But unlike God, human beings are unable to replicate their essence perfectly by verbal expression. Although there is no gap between signifier
(Logos) and signified knowledge (the divine essence) in the generation of
the Logos, just such a gap exists for human beings:

> There is a vast difference between our minds and the words with which we
> try to show what is in our minds. We do not beget verbal sounds but make
> them; and in making them we make use of the body as material. Now there
> is a great difference between mind and body. When God begat the Word,
> the Begetter was "he who is." He did not make the Word out of nothing
> nor out of any ready-made material but from his eternal nature. This is
> what we, too, try to do when we speak the truth, though not when we lie,
> if we closely consider the purpose we have in mind in speaking. (*De fide et
> symbolo* 3.3–4).

Human efforts at communication—at making others participants in our
will—aim for the same degree of adequacy of sign to signifying will that
is found in the divine self-communication through the Logos. But in contrast to the divine Logos, our words are made, not begotten. Although
speakers strive to emulate God by producing their own speech, they in-
variably fail: "We cannot put forth anything just like [what is within], and
so the mind of the speaker cannot become known with complete inwardness" (*De fide et symbolo* 3.4).

Augustine recounts his own frustration with the limits of his natural
communicative powers in *De catechizandis rudibus*. His desire to speak
to the prospective catechumen begins when "intuition floods the mind, as
it were, with a sudden flash of light." But he can express this intuition
only by copying the content of memory images in the "slow, drawn-out,
and far different process" of speech (*De catechizandis rudibus* 2.3.3).
Much is lost in this copying because there remains a gap between "the
sound of our voice" and "that instantaneous flash of intellectual apprehension" since the sound "does not resemble even the memory impression" (*De catechizandis rudibus* 2.3.6). The difference contained in
the distinction between signifier and signified meaning, as a general feature of ancient sign theory, is intensified here, as it is replicated in a series
of gaps or differences within the signifying soul. Just as readers of all signs
attend to the distinction between signifier and signified meaning, so too
speakers produce signs that fail to convey their motivating intentions.
Thus the "making of others participants in our own will" through signs
would seem to be, in some deep sense, unattainable.[17]

So far, problems in communication seem to be generated by the difference between mind and body, a dualism in which God does not share.
There is as yet no suggestion that human difficulties in communication are

anything other than a necessary and entirely appropriate consequence of humanity's finite and embodied nature. But the problem is in reality more serious, for it is complicated and intensified by a deep perversion of the human will. Pride turned what presumably might have been a language isomorphic with meaning into a series of signs. Consequently, the path from creation to Babel is marked by a movement from communication that is unmediated and successful to that which is oblique and frustrated, epitomized in the diverse and often mutually unintelligible signs of the various human languages.

In his early treatise *De Genesi contra Manichaeos*, Augustine interprets the opening chapters of Genesis allegorically to argue that Adam's sin led to the very institution of signs as a means of communication between God and human beings. Augustine links Genesis' distinction between the internal spring watering the earth from within and the rain from clouds that came later (Gen. 2:5–6) to prelapsarian and postlapsarian modes of divine-human communication. Before the fall:

> God watered [the invisible creature, that is, the human soul] by an interior spring, speaking in its intellect, so that it might not receive outward words like rains from the clouds . . . but might be satiated by its own spring, that is, from the truth dwelling in its innermost part. (*De Genesi contra Manichaeos* 2.5)

But humanity "abandoned its innermost part through pride," and since then, God has tried to "make souls revive by his word" by watering them from the clouds, that is, from the Scriptures of the prophets and the apostles. Since the fall, divine teaching has had to come from human words, "just as rain comes from the clouds" (*De Genesi contra Manichaeos* 2.6). Unmediated knowledge, lost in the fall, is now only an eschatological hope. Only in the eschaton, thanks to Christ's incarnation, will "the entire face of our earth be watered by the internal spring of water welling up" (*De Genesi contra Manichaeos* 2.6). Until then, postlapsarian pride (*superbia*) has led God to communicate with human beings only through signs; it has also resulted in the bewildering diversity of human languages, signified by the Tower of Babel, which Augustine calls a "sign of pride" (*superbiae signum* [*DDC* 2.4.5; cf. *De civitate dei* 19.7]) and a "punishment for pride" (*DDC* 3.36.53).[18] Filled with self-concern, human beings continue to separate themselves from one another by means of their varied languages as they engage in mutual domination.[19]

In his account of the relation between language and human will, signs and motions of the soul, Augustine has combined ancient sign theory with an interpretation of Pauline anthropology. Without something like a theology of sin and fallenness, classical sign theory itself described only a neutral distinction between signifier and signified meaning. Such a neutral distinction might be based simply on a linguistic extrapolation from a doctrine of creation: signifiers could represent the created order, and signified meanings could be viewed as ideas in the mind of the creator God, the "forms" with which created objects (or language) bear some relation but are nevertheless distinct. But the notion of sin magnifies the lack of congruence between signifier and signified meaning by specifying the cause of the frustration of both the sign user, who cannot express intention in language, and the sign reader, who cannot infer intention from someone else's language. (The sign reader's frustration is intensified by Scripture's semantic obscurity, a divinely intended affront to human hermeneutical pride.)[20] We seem, then, to have arrived at a vicious circle: human beings have separated themselves from God and neighbor by self-seeking pride and consequently are forced to rely on signs, and yet, Augustine tells us, "in the knowledge of signs," it is "very difficult not to be proud" (*DDC* 2.13.20).[21] How, then, will one be able to read Scripture in a way which makes its signs an antidote, rather than a catalyst, for sin? Given the failure of signs in general, how will the reading of scriptural signs be able to heal the soul at all?

III

Augustine suggests in *De doctrina christiana* that God's rhetorical use of signs in Scripture successfully brings the divine will into a therapeutic relation with readers' human wills, enabling them to "participate in," and thus be redirected by, the divine will.[22] He argues that those who read

> Sacred Scripture, by which so many maladies of the human will (*morbi humanarum voluntatium*) are cured . . . desired to find in it nothing more than the thoughts and will (*voluntas*) of those who wrote it and through these the will of God (*per illas voluntatem dei*), according to which we believe those writers spoke. (*DDC* 2.5.6)[23]

If the divine will is incarnational, and if the literal text of Scripture is to convey the character of that will to its readers, it must be read in a way that enables the proud reader's soul to submit to the literal text as its "other" meaning. Just as the Logos "accommodates" itself in humility to fleshly embodiment, so, through allegorical reading,[24] is the proud soul of the reader to be "accommodated" to those textual signifiers that, as "the flesh of Christ made text," so to speak, function as the medicine of humility. Augustine begins to make this process clear in the middle of book 1 of *De doctrina christiana*, where he brings together human linguistic expression and divine incarnation. He draws once again on the phrase he had applied earlier (*DDC* 2.2.3) to the soul's motions as expressed by signs ("what is going on in the soul" [*id quod animo gerit*]). But now he uses the phrase in order to compare the soul's expression by signs of its inner motions to God's own self-revelation through the incarnation of the Logos:

> How did he come except that "the Word was made flesh, and dwelt among us"? It is as when we speak. In order that what is going on in our mind (*id quod animo gerimus*) may reach the mind of the listener through fleshly ears, the word that we bear in our heart (*verbum quod corde gestamus*) becomes sound (*sonus*) and is called speech (*locutio*). (*DDC* 1.13.12)[25]

After presenting the analogy, Augustine emphasizes the specific soteriological efficacy of the incarnation by highlighting its example of humility. As the character of the divine signifying intention or will, humility precisely counters pride, which is the character of the human signifying intention: "The medicine of Wisdom by taking on humanity is accommodated to our wounds. . . . Because man fell through pride, He applied humility as a cure" (*Quia ergo per superbiam homo lapsus est, humilitatem adhibuit ad sanandum* [*DDC* 1.14.13]).[26]

Augustine often uses the word "type" (*typus*) to signal that the cure of humility has been applied through the allegorical reading of Hebrew scripture—not, as some modern commentators would have it, in order to draw an invidious contrast between "typology" and "allegory," but as a way of pointing toward the degree to which an allegorical reading has enabled the reader's soul to submit to the text as the literary representation of the incarnate and crucified messiah.[27] For Augustine, the presence of interpreted "types" indicates the degree to which nonliteral meanings (the motions of the proud reader's soul) have capitulated to the literal text (which, in both its theme,[28] as well as its sublimely humble style,[29] replicated the incarnation).

According to Augustine, "types," which Jewish readers read but fail to interpret, and which Christian readers interpret in light of their christological fulfillment, produce a scale of the will's submission: Jewish readers only partially submit to the text, while Christian readers, when reading properly, submit completely. For Christian readers, "the covering [of Hebrew Scripture] has been removed which concealed useful truth," which "is what happens to those who earnestly and piously, *not proudly and wickedly*, seek the sense of the Scriptures" (*De utilitate credendi* 3.9; my emphasis). In contrast to both Jewish and Christian readers, pagan readers fail to submit at all:

> If only you [philosophers] had recognized the grace of God through Jesus Christ our Lord! If only you had been able to see his incarnation, in which

he took a human soul and body, as the supreme instance of grace! . . . But humility was the necessary condition for submission to this truth; and it is no easy task to persuade the proud necks of you philosophers to accept this yoke. (*De civitate dei* 10.29)

Such pagan readers illustrate the opposite of Augustine's own movement from initial criticism of Scripture's mere *humilitas* to defense of its humble sublimity via the allegorical reading taught him by Ambrose. For Augustine, the transformation of allegorical reading into, rather than away from, the text's representation of divine humility kept the allegorical defense of Scripture from becoming yet another opportunity for pagan literary pride.[30] He views allegorical interpretation as precisely the sort of sophisticated reading that will most appeal to the proud and yet simultaneously have the best chance of curing them with divine humility. This becomes clear in *De catechizandis rudibus*, where Augustine links the notion of divine incarnation as medicinal humility to a specifically nonliteral or allegorical reading of Scripture. He begins by making the allegorical reading of Hebrew Scripture depend on the proper orientation of the will: only those "who do not seek in pride" can understand Hebrew Scripture "spiritually," thus recognizing that "in the Old Testament the New is concealed, and in the New the Old is revealed." Only they "are made free by the bestowal of love" (*De catechizandis rudibus* 4.8.9). Augustine then continues by suggesting that proper allegorical reading, in which the bestowal of love provides freedom, necessarily embraces divine self-abasement in Christ as the antidote to unloving pride:

Since therefore nothing is more opposed to love than envy, and the mother of envy is pride, the same Lord Jesus Christ, God-Man, is at once a token of divine love towards us and an example among us of man's lowliness (*humilitas*), to the end that our swollen conceit, great as it is, may be healed by an even greater antidote. For the misery of man's pride is great, but the commiseration of God's humility is greater (*Magna est enim miseria superbus homo, sed maior misericordia humilis deus*). (*De catechizandis rudibus* 4.8.10)

De doctrina christiana echoes this point when it insists that although the pilgrim on the "road of the affections" had formerly found her path blocked "by the malice of . . . past sins," God's response was "to lay down himself" as a means of her return, "by being crucified" (*DDC* 1.17.16).[31] We have, it seems, a distinctively Augustinian version of the hermeneutical circle: allegorical reading is the medium by which the present reader of Scripture benefits from the past incarnation and crucifixion, even as the scripturally mediated incarnation and crucifixion makes proper allegorical reading of Scripture possible.

Augustine argues further that when allegorical reading as the appropriation of a divine rhetoric of incarnation fails, one becomes either a mere literalist or a nonliteral ideologue. Each of these forms of misreading Scripture results from relaxing the letter-spirit tension of allegorical reading. Exclusive focus on the letter alone (the "Jewish" mode of misreading) by refusing to turn from the sign to the thing signified is a "miserable servitude of the spirit" that leads to its "death" (DDC 3.5.9). On the other hand, exclusive focus on signs that point to useless or fictional things is worse. The pagans, says Augustine, read signs allegorically (for example, interpreting Neptune as the sea), but neither their allegorical signs (Neptune) nor their allegorical meanings (the sea) are divine. Consequently, although they, unlike the Jews, manage to "transfer . . . [their] affections from these signs to what they signify," they nevertheless succumb to "a servile and carnal burden and veil" (DDC 3.7.11).[32]

Augustine argues that pagan misreading, as "error" rather than "servitude" (DDC 3.9.13), is worse than Jewish because it offers no basis for correction. Jewish literalists were not incorrigible because the signs they read were themselves correct and "usefully instituted" (DDC 3.7.11), and a little additional interpretation (to which many Jews were close, and which some—the prophets and Jesus—attained) might have elevated their souls "to the things which the signs represented." Of course, whenever this happened, such readers ceased to be Jewish at all, and came to constitute "the Churches of the holy Israelites" (DDC 3.8.12). But pagan error is irredeemable because the signs themselves are "instituted for spiritually useless things" and can never be the basis for a correct interpretation (DDC 3.7.11). When pagans do try to interpret their false signs, they produce only anthropological projections, "simulated gods" (DDC 3.8.12).[33] The two modes of misreading are not, then, literalism and nonliteralism, but rather an uninterpreted ("mere") literalism and an ideology of nonliteral, anthropological projection.

Both forms of misreading result from misdirected will or cupidity, even among those who profess to take the Bible as authoritative. Cupidity leads readers to determine the degree of figurativeness in the text according to the extent to which the literal sense endorses personal and cultural norms and practices. If the text seems literally to endorse my desires, I can read it literally, and if it literally conflicts with my desires, I can read it allegorically.[34] But the one message of the divine rhetorician remains constant despite the hermeneutical evasions of readers: "Scripture teaches nothing but charity, nor condemns anything except cupidity, and in this way shapes human life" (DDC 3.10.15). It does so, I have suggested, by textually replicating the humility of the incarnation, which is then appropriated by an allegorical reading. As a result, one approaches a *visio dei* that begins, as Augustine observes, with that fear of God which leads to

> a recognition of his will, so that we may know what he commands that we desire and what he commands that we avoid. Of necessity this fear will lead us to thought of our mortality and of our future death and will affix all our proud motions (*superbiae motus*), as if they were fleshly members fastened with nails, to the wood of the cross. (*DDC* 2.7.9)

If Augustine's allegorical reading had sought to escape the constraints of the text (as allegorical readers of Scripture are typically charged with doing), we might expect to find him advocating some sort of correlative "ascent" Christology—an apotheosis of the man Jesus into the Word of God. Indeed, at one time he had embraced just such a view:

> I thought of Christ, my Lord, as no more than a man of extraordinary wisdom, whom none could equal. . . . And I thought he was superior to other men, not because he was Truth in person, but because in him human nature had reached the highest point of excellence and he had a more perfect share of divine wisdom. (*Confessiones* 7.19)

But this Christology Augustine came to reject. His increasing insistence on the limitations of Neoplatonic philosophy (for which allegorical escape from the literal text, no less than from the body, was a central hermeneutical goal) coincides with his rejection of an ascent or adoptionist Christology, in favor of a divine incarnation:

> For I was not humble enough to conceive of the humble Jesus Christ as my God, nor had I learned what lesson his human weakness was meant to teach. . . . He would cure them of the pride that swelled up in their hearts and would nurture love in its place, so that they should no longer stride ahead confident in themselves, but might realize their own weakness when at their feet they saw God himself, enfeebled by sharing the garment of our mortality. (*Confessiones* 7.19)

The hermeneutical correlate of this divine *kenosis* is an allegorical sensibility that consistently "abases" nonliteral meanings (in this case, the disordered motions of the proud reader's soul), so that they might be moved to "give up" their self-sufficiency and turn toward, and become reinterpreted by, divine grace in scriptural form. As a result, the reader's self-aggrandizing *superbia* is neutralized; the formerly disordered motions of her soul become ordered; she now rejoices, desires, sorrows, and fears appropriately.

Notes

1. Earlier versions of this essay were presented at the University of Notre Dame conference on *De doctrina christiana*, 4–7 April 1991, and the Eleventh International Conference on Patristic Studies, Oxford University, 19–24 August 1991. I wish to thank William Babcock, J. Patout Burns, Richard Luman, and R. A. Markus for their helpful comments.

2. By "distinctively biblical idiom," I do not mean that such a thing self-evidently exists and that Augustine simply noticed it. Instead, I use the phrase to refer to Augustine's own idiosyncratic construal of the "Bible's essential meaning," a construal that is deeply rooted in, and determined by, his own conceptions of the ongoing conflict between human pride and divine humility.

3. My discussion of Augustine's notion of the soul is based on Gerard O'Daly, *Augustine's Philosophy of Mind* (Berkeley and Los Angeles, 1987), ch. 2, "General Theory of the Soul," 7–79. Latin citations (except those from *De dialectica*) are taken from the *CSEL* and *CC* editions when available, otherwise from *PL*. For *De dialectica*, I have used the edition in *De Dialectica*, trans. B. Darrell Jackson, ed. Jan Pinborg, Synthese Historical Library: Texts and Studies in the History of Logic and Philosophy, ed. N. Kretzmann, G. Nuchelmans, and L. M. de Rijk, vol. 16 (Boston, 1975). Translations from *On Genesis against the Manichaeans* are my own. Other English translations, occasionally modified in light of the original Latin, are taken from the following: *Concerning the City of God against the Pagans*, trans. Henry Bettenson with an introduction by David Knowles (Baltimore, 1972); *Confessions*, trans. and introduction R. S. Pine-Coffin (Baltimore, 1961); *On Christian Doctrine*, trans. D. W. Robertson, Jr., Library of Liberal Arts (Indianapolis, 1958); *The Trinity*, in *Augustine: Later Works*, selected and trans. John Burnaby, Library of Christian Classics, Ichthus Edition (Philadelphia, 1955); *The Teacher*, *Of True Religion*, *The Usefulness of Belief*, and *Faith and the Creed*, in *Augustine: Earlier Writings*, selected and trans. with introductions by John H. S. Burleigh, Library of Christian Classics, Ichthus Edition (Philadelphia, 1953).

4. Cf. *De vera religione* 10.18.

5. Trans. in O'Daly, *Augustine's Philosophy of Mind*, 48.

6. See *DDC* 3.10.16 on charity and cupidity as the two fundamental directions of the soul's motions. For a discussion of the motion of sorrow in relation to the virtue of charity in light of literary patterns in the *Confessions*, see William Werpekowski, "Weeping at the Death of Dido: Sorrow, Virtue, and Augustine's Confessions," *Journal of Religious Ethics* 19, 1 (Spring, 1991): 175–191.

7. Trans. in O'Daly, *Augustine's Philosophy of Mind*, 50. See also *De civitate dei* 14.7 (trans. in O'Daly, 50): "The morally right will is therefore a good love, and the wrong will is an evil love. Love, then, longing to have what is loved, is desire; and having and enjoying it, is joy; and fleeing what is opposed to it, is fear; and feeling what is opposed to it when this has affected it, is grief. Now these emotions are evil if the love is evil, and good if it is good."

8. Trans. in O'Daly, *Augustine's Philosophy of Mind*, 48.

9. See *DDC* 1.35.39–36.41; 3.10.14; 3.12.18. Augustine makes it clear that his analysis of *signa data* applies to the use of signs given by God in Scripture "since they were presented to us by the men who wrote them" (*DDC* 2.2.3).

10. This is the more elaborate of the two basic definitions of a sign offered in *DDC*. Earlier in the treatise, Augustine simply says that signs are "things used to signify something" (*DDC* 1.2.2). In *DDC* 2.10.15, Augustine elaborates these definitions by distinguishing literal from figurative signs, adding an important point absent from the initial definitions: the figurative sign includes the literal sign (with its sign-referent relation) but goes further by making the referent itself a sign of something else. As a result, although there can be a literal sign that is not figurative, there can be no figurative sign that is not itself based on a prior literal sign. In this way, Augustine makes figurative language dependent on literal signification, with the knowledge of those things that are the referents of the literal signs as the crucial intermediary—a point made even clearer in his discussion of the failure of Jewish literalists, who do not interpret the thing signified as itself a sign (*DDC* 3.5.9).

11. R. A. Markus, "St.Augustine on Signs," in *Augustine: A Collection of Critical Essays*, ed. R. A. Markus (Garden City, N.Y., 1972), 61–91, especially 74 ff., emphasizes this aspect of Augustine's theory of signs. He argues that Augustine's concern for the subject or interpreter to whom the sign signifies marks an innovation, going beyond the classic Stoic distinctions. Markus understands the use of signs to involve three principal functions: the sign, the signified object, and the sign receiver (subject or interpreter). He then construes the two basic kinds of signs discussed in *DDC* (*signa naturalia* and *signa data*) as built out of two dyadic relations: a sign produced by its referent is a *signa naturalia* or "symptom," a sign intentionally signified to a subject or interpreter is a *signa data* or "symbol."

12. See also *DDC* 2.36.54; 4.4.6; 4.7.21; 4.12.27–13.29; 4.24.53. It is the "grand style" that is most "forceful with emotions of the spirit" (*animi affectus*)" (*DDC* 4.20.42).

13. Even small parts of speech express the soul's motions. For example, in the sentence, *Si nihil ex tanta superis placet urbe relinqui* (If it pleases the gods that nothing be left of so great a city), *si* (if) expresses the doubt "found in the mind" (*in animo*) (*De magistro* 2.3), and *nihil* expresses the state of mind (*affectio animi; mentis affectio*) of one who thinks that the object of his search does not exist (*De magistro* 2.3; 7.19). Cf. *Confessiones* 1.8, in Ludwig Wittgenstein, *Philosophical Investigations*, trans. G. E. M. Anscombe, 3rd ed. New York, c. 1953), 2e, where Wittgenstein comments on the passage in which Augustine describes learning a language for the first time. Augustine says that when people pointed out an object and named it,

> their intention was shown by their bodily movements, as it were the natural language of all peoples: the expression of the face, the play of the eyes, the movements of other parts of the body, and the tone of voice which expresses our state of mind [*affectio animi*] in seeking, having, rejecting, or avoiding something. Thus as I heard words re-

peatedly used in their proper places in various sentences, I gradually learnt to understand what objects they signified; and after I had trained my mouth to form these
signs, I used them to express my own desires.

Wittgenstein's construal of this passage is interesting precisely for the way it ig-
nores Augustine's emphasis on the motions of the soul that give rise to language,
or that motivate the subsequent use of language:

These words [of Augustine], it seems to me, give us a particular picture of the essence
of human language. It is this: the individual words in language name objects—sentences are combinations of such names.—In this picture of language we find the roots
of the following idea: Every word has a meaning. This meaning is correlated with the
word. It is the object for which the word stands."

14. B. Darrell Jackson, "The Theory of Signs in St. Augustine's *De doctrina
christiana*," in *Augustine: A Collection of Critical Essays*, 92–147, downplays the
significance of the will by emphasizing the intellectualist aspects of Augustine's understanding of signification (although he does mention the role of the will in
passing, e.g., 113, 114). He interprets the *id quo animo gerit* as *cogitatio*, of the
which the content is the *dicibile* (perhaps equivalent to the Stoic *lekton*). Cf. *De
dialectica* 5.50–52; 60–62: "But whatever is perceived of a word, not by the ears,
but by the mind, and is held fast within the mind itself, is called a 'meaning' (*dicibile*) . . . what I have called the 'meaning' is a word, yet it does not indicate a
word, but rather what is understood in a word and retained in the mind."

15. On the mutual participation of wills, cf. *DDC* prologue, 6: "For charity
itself, which holds men together in a knot of unity, would not have a means of *infusing souls and almost mixing them together* if men could teach nothing to men"
(my emphasis). Consider also Augustine on the negative example of his own difficulty in expressing his will verbally when he was an infant:

For when I tried to express my meaning by crying out and making various sounds
and movements, *so that my wishes should be obeyed*, I found that I could not convey
all that I meant or make myself understood by everyone whom I wished to understand me.

When Augustine later learns language, he says that he "began to express my
wishes" and "in this way made my *wants* known to my family and they made
theirs known to me, and I took a further step into the stormy life of human society" (*Confessiones* 1.8.13, my emphasis).

16. Cf. *DDC* 3.29.40: "For letters from which grammar takes its name . . . are
indeed signs of sounds made by the articulate voice with which we speak."

17. Perhaps this is why Augustine alludes in *DDC* to those instances in which
one language cannot be translated into another when the signs, such as *racha* and
hosanna, are especially rooted in motions of the soul. "For there are some words
in some languages which cannot be translated into other languages. And this is especially true of interjections which signify the motion of the spirit (*motus animi
significant*) rather than any part of a rational concept." (*DDC* 2.11.16).

18. Augustine thinks of the translation of Scripture into many languages as the
means by which the divine text originally "set forth in one language" might me-

diate salvation to post-Babel readers (see *DDC* 2.5.6; 3.26.53). Such a view gives additional nuance to Augustine's otherwise traditional praise of the Septuagint translation: "it is now said that this translation was so inspired by the Holy Spirit that *many men spoke as if with the mouth of one*"; "Latin translations of the Old Testament . . . are to be emended on the authority of the Greeks, and especially on the authority of those who, although there were seventy, are said to have *spoken as if with one voice*" (*DDC* 15.22, my emphasis).

19. See Ulrich Duchrow, "*Signum* und *superbia* beim jungen Augustin (386–390)," *REAug* 7, 4 (1961): 369–372. Although the human use of signs is not as adequate as divine self-signification through the Logos, it is not entirely defective. If the human use of signs failed completely, such failure might suggest that language itself was not merely distorted, but actually produced, by an evil fall—there would have been an original linguistic fall from sheer immediacy into language itself. Augustine does not hold this position. The tension that makes divine humility possible is the same tension that, on a human level, keeps human language from becoming altogether a result of original sin.

20. See *DDC* 2.6.7.

21. Augustine is referring in particular to those who are easily offended by grammatical and stylistic errors.

22. Cf. *De vera religione* 16.30.

23. Here Augustine draws a parallel between the wills of the human writers of Scripture and the will of God. See *DDC* 3.27.38, where Augustine draws distinctions between the intentions of the human writers of Scripture and the more fundamental intention of the single divine author who inspired those writers and who can ensure that their multiple and conflicting intentions do not obscure his fundamental meaning; see further *DDC* 2.9.14 and 3.1.1 on reading Scripture in order to "seek the will of God."

24. In *DDC*, Augustine seldom uses the term "allegory," preferring instead to speak more generally of "figurative" expressions. He regards *allegoria* in the narrow sense as one of the tropes (along with *aenigma* and *parabola*) of genuinely figurative language (cf. *DDC* 3.29.40), but he can also use the term "allegory" as a synonym for figural language in general. For example, he takes up the problem of scriptural passages that concern "bitterness or anger in the words or deeds of the person of God or of his saints," arguing that such expressions should be regarded as figurative only if they are not obviously intended for the "destruction of the reign of cupidity." He offers Gal. 5.24 ("And they that are Christ's, have crucified their flesh, with the vices and concupiscence") as an illustration of such a nonfigurative (and thus nonallegorical) expression, commenting that

> although certain figurative words are used here (*quaedam verba translata tractantur*) like "wrath of God" and "crucified," there are not so many that they obscure the sense or make an allegory or enigma (*allegoria vel aenigma*) of the kind which I call a figurative locution in the proper sense (*proprie figurata locutio*). But it is said to Jeremiah, "Lo, I have set thee this day over kingdoms, to root up, and to pull down, and to destroy." There is no doubt that this whole expression is figurative and is to be referred to that end [i.e., the destruction of cupidity] of which we have spoken. (*DDC* 2.11.17)

Just as Augustine can use the term "allegory" as a synonym for figurative language, so he also regards the nature of such language as an extension of his theory of signs. He notes that the rules of Tyconius, with one exception, "cause one thing to be understood from another, a situation proper to figures of speech" (*tropicae locutionis*). Indeed, "wherever one wishes to say one thing so that another is understood, even though the name of the particular trope employed is not found in the art of rhetoric, he uses a figurative expression (*tropica locutio*)" (*DDC* 3.37.56). These definitions of figurative language echo the definitions of signs offered in book 1; consequently, Augustine can conclude these remarks on figurative locutions (and on book 3 as a whole) by announcing that "enough has been said concerning signs" (*DDC* 3.37.56). Figurative speech and allegory are essentially the same in *DDC*, and they share the linguistic structure of the sign.

25. The same comparison of the incarnation of the Logos and the production of linguistic signs occurs in *De trinitate* 15.11.20.

26. Cf. *De catechizandis rudibus* 31; 33; 40. Augustine makes the same point in *De fide et symbolo* 4.6 following his analogy of the generation of signs and the incarnation. In *De Genesi contra Manichaeos*, we find Augustine pointing to the incarnation as the means by which the original immediate, nonsemantic communication between God and human beings might be recovered. Jesus himself hints at the recovery of the internal spring of divine illumination when he says that "it will become in him a spring of water welling up to eternal life" (Jn. 4:14). Augustine explains:

> For because of that cloudy weather [of sin], our Lord, worthy to assume our flesh, poured out a most abundant shower of the holy Gospel, even sending that which, if anyone should drink of its water, would return to that person his innermost spring, in order that he would not seek rain from outside [i.e., divine nourishment via language]. (*De Genesi contra Manichaeos* 2.6)

27. See *DDC* 2.41.62.

28. Cf. *DDC* 3.23.33: "There is hardly a page in the holy books in which it is not shown that God resists the proud but to the humble offers grace."

29. See *DDC* 2.42.63: "the wonderful nobility and remarkable humility of the Holy Scriptures." See also Erich Auerbach, "Sermo Humilis," in *Literary Language and Its Public in Late Latin Antiquity and in the Middle Ages*, trans. Ralph Manheim, Bollingen Series 74 (New York, 1965), 27–66. Augustine often stresses that the Logos must not suffer change in the incarnation. This insistence is related to the inner logic of the notion of humility. Divine humility requires that the Logos assume flesh "without deterioration" or "without change" because otherwise humility would immediately be lost once the incarnation had occurred; at that point, the tension that makes humility possible would be gone. The hermeneutical equivalent of such dissolving the mystery of "hypostatic union" is the relaxing of the tension that allegory preserves between the "spirit" and the "letter."

30. See *Confessiones* 3.5; 6.5; *DDC* 2.42.63.

31. For "in the Sign of the Cross," writes Augustine—and for him Scripture is a collection of clear and obscure signs of that single sign—"the whole action of the Christian is described" (*DDC* 2.41.62).

32. "Jews" and "pagans" should be understood first of all as heuristic fictions constructed by Augustine in order to contrast two hermeneutical alternatives that he opposes. The relation between such constructions, actual contemporary religious groups, and their hermeneutical practices is a different issue requiring further investigation.

33. Cf. *De vera religione* 55.108: "Let not religion consist in phantasms of our own imagining. Any kind of truth is better than any fiction we may choose to produce."

34. *DDC* 3.10.15: "It so happens that if Scripture commends something despised by the customs of the listeners, or condemns what those customs do not condemn, they take the scriptural locution as figurative if the authority of the word conquers their soul [or "if they accept it as an authority"—*si animum eorum iam verbi vinxit auctoritas*]. . . . Again, if the minds (*animi*) of men are subject to some erroneous opinion, they think that whatever Scripture says contrary to that opinion is figurative."

Doctrina

The entire treatment of the Scriptures is based upon two factors: the method of discovering what we are to understand and the method of teaching what has been understood.

De doctrina christiana 1.1

Caritas and Signification
in *De doctrina christiana* 1–3

WILLIAM S. BABCOCK

In *De doctrina christiana*, Augustine provides a guide of sorts to what he calls the *tractatio* of Scripture.[1] All *tractatio*, he tells us (*DDC* 1.1.1), rests on two things, a mode of discovering what is to be understood (*modus inveniendi quae intelligenda sunt*) and a mode of expressing what has been understood (*modus proferendi quae intellecta sunt*); and, in fact, the *De doctrina christiana* falls into just this pattern. The first three books deal with the *modus inveniendi*. The fourth and final book deals with the *modus proferendi*. What Augustine has in mind under this second heading is at least relatively clear. The fourth book can be described, more or less adequately, as a manual for those who face the task of setting forth the truth of Scripture in clear and persuasive speech. The first three books, however, are another matter. They plainly have to do with discovering the content or meaning of Scripture. But it is something of a problem to find an apt account of just how Augustine conceives and executes his project. Certain portions of the work tempt us into supposing that he is delineating a program in Christian education or that he is sifting the classical tradition in order to determine what can be retained in a specifically Christian culture. Such interpretations, however, seem to extend their reach far beyond their grasp, taking smaller components within the work as if they set the program for the whole; and they largely ignore the idiom in which Augustine himself casts his consideration of the *modus inveniendi* of what is to be understood in Scripture.[2]

That idiom is unmistakably the idiom of signification. "All doctrine," Augustine asserts, "has to do either with things or with signs; but things are learned through signs" (*DDC* 1.2.2). From the outset, then, Augustine makes it clear that he is going to speak about signs and about the things that they signify.[3] Anything else that he has to say will come into play, presumably, because it pertains to—and contributes to—his discussion of signs and things, not because it has an independent interest in its own right.[4] Certainly it is beyond dispute that the notions of *res* and *signum* determine the structure of the first three books of *De doctrina*, "things" being the topic of book 1 and "signs" the topic of books 2 and 3; and, so far as I can tell, there is no reason to suppose that Augustine breaks with this organizational scheme at any point along the way.

At this early stage of the discussion (i.e., in *DDC* 1.2.1), Augustine provides only preliminary definitions of *res* and *signum*. A thing, he says, is something that is not employed to signify anything (*quae non ad significandum aliquid adhibentur*), while signs are things that are employed to signify something (*res eas videlicet quae ad significandum aliquid adhibentur*). Since Augustine lists examples of things which are not employed to signify (e.g., *lignum*, *lapis*, *pecus*, etc.), it is possible to conclude that he means to distinguish two classes of things, some that are not used to signify, others that are. He immediately goes on, however, to cite instances in which just these things are indeed used to signify (at least, in Scripture); and it seems more probable that he is distinguishing two standings that things may have rather than two kinds or classes of things. Thus a thing will count as a sign, if it is used to signify; and it will count as a thing, if it is not.[5] It is important to add, of course, that there will be two cases in which a thing will have the standing of a thing, one when it is not a factor in signification at all, the other when it is the *terminus* of a given instance of signification (i.e., when it is the thing signified by a sign, but does not itself signify any further thing). Now it seems clear enough which of these two cases Augustine has in mind (even though he himself says nothing explicit on the point). Just because he so obviously casts his discussion in the idiom of signification, the presumption must be that his interest lies in things as the *termini* of signification, as the things signified by the words of the scriptural text. Thus the mode of discovering *quae intelligenda sunt* in Scripture, we can now say, will be the mode of discovering the things signified by the verbal signs of Scripture.

Augustine's actual procedure, however, poses something of an anomaly. Despite his own declaration that "things are learned through signs" (*DDC* 1.2.2), he starts not with signs but with things.[6] He starts, that is, by specifying what is signified in Scripture, the *quae intelligenda sunt*;[7] and only then does he turn to the signs that signify what he has already identified as Scripture's content or meaning. But the anomaly is also a clue to how Augustine conceives his project. It suggests that he is acutely aware, from the beginning, that signs can be construed wrongly; that they can be

given the wrong *terminus*; that they can be arranged in patterns of signification that point away from, rather than toward, what he considers the
true content, the true meaning, of Scripture.

His procedure provides the corrective. It stipulates in advance what the
terminus of the scriptural signs is and thus establishes the control in the
light of which we are to interpret those signs.[8] Augustine's is not, then, a
neutral or disinterested concern with signs and with signification. His
treatment of signs will be wholly designed to show that (and how) they
signify what he has already stipulated that they signify—and to ward off
the danger that they might be invested with some other meaning or given
some other signification. At the very heart of his concern, therefore, will
be the question of just how signs are invested with meaning, of how they
come to be associated with the things they are taken to signify. And in addressing this question, he will be taking up an issue that we, in our
current reckoning of the academic disciplines, would assign not only to
the philosophy of meaning, but also to the sociology of knowledge.[9]
Before we turn to Augustine's treatment of signs, however, we need at
least briefly to review his account of things.[10]

Augustine's discussion of things unfolds from his initial classification
of things into three categories: those that are to be enjoyed, those that are
to be used, and those that do the enjoying and the using (*DDC* 1.3.3). Enjoyment and use, of course, Augustine defines in terms of love (*DDC*
1.4.4). To enjoy a thing is, in the well-known Augustinian definition, to
cling to it with love for its own sake (*amore alicui rei inhaerere propter
seipsam*). To use a thing, in contrast, is to refer it to the attaining of what
is loved (*ad id quod amas obtinendum referre*). On the one hand, then,
there is an objective order of things ranked by value: some are to be enjoyed (these are the things that bring genuine fulfillment, *beatitudo*, to
those who love and attain them), some are to be used (these are the things
that do not themselves offer genuine fulfillment but can serve as aids to
the attainment of those that do).[11] On the other hand, there is a subjective
order of love according to which persons take some things as objects of
enjoyment and others as objects of use. The problem is, of course, that
these two orders can go desperately out of phase. Those who do the enjoying and the using can take as the object of their love a thing that is
properly to be used and thus is not properly to be loved for its own sake;
and, at the same time, they can use a thing that is properly to be enjoyed,
not loving it for its own sake but rather using—or, more properly, abus-
ing (1.4.4)—it in order to attain what they do love. Such a love is horribly
misdirected. Asking the impossible—that an object for use should supply
the fulfillment that only an object for enjoyment can, in fact, provide—is
self-deluding and therefore inevitably self-defeating.

The remedy will lie in a prescription for a properly ordered love; and Augustine finds just this prescription in Scripture's double command of love for God and neighbor.[12] God is the one "thing" that offers genuine fulfillment and is therefore the one "thing" that is to be loved for its own sake.[13] The neighbor, if not a "thing" to be enjoyed for its own sake, is nevertheless, like us, a "thing" that enjoys and uses and is therefore, like ourselves, to be loved *in Deum* or *propter Deum* because capable of enjoying God with us (*DDC* 1.22.20, 27.28, 29.30). Love for God and neighbor, then, is love set to rights, love brought into conformity with the objective order of things. It is a rightly ordered love, neither loving what ought not to be loved, nor failing to love what ought to be loved, nor loving anything in inappropriate degree (*DDC* 1.27.28). No longer self-deluding and therefore no longer self-defeating, it loves the triune God in whom alone *beatitudo* is to be found; and it loves those with whom this love for God can be held in common. Everything else it relegates to the realm of use.

Near the end of the first book of *De doctrina christiana* (*DDC* 1.35.39), Augustine remarks that the sum of all he has said in discussing things is this: that the fullness (*plenitudo*) and end (*finis*) of the Law—and of all the Divine Scripture—is love for the thing that is to be enjoyed (*rei qua fruendum est*) and for the thing that is capable of enjoying that thing with us (*rei quae nobiscum ea re frui potest*). (Translated into English, Augustine's language loses whatever elegance it may have had in the Latin original; but the point stands out sharply enough.) In effect, Augustine has used his discussion of things to stipulate what is signified in Scripture. Some may think that they have understood Scripture, he observes, but they have not yet understood if their views do not build up this *geminam caritatem* of God and neighbor (*DDC* 1.36.40). In contrast, those whose views do build up this double love will escape serious error even if they mistake what the biblical writers actually had in mind (*DDC* 1.36.40–41). Anyone who knows that love is the end of the Law, Augustine assures us, can approach the *tractatio* of Scripture with confidence (*DDC* 1.40.44). If we already know what the signs signify, there is no danger that we will ultimately associate them with the wrong things or give them the wrong *termini*.

In books 2 and 3, then, Augustine is not so much concerned to establish what the biblical signs signify—that he has already done—as he is to ward off the danger that they will be invested with the wrong signification in uncertain or ambiguous cases.[14] We need to start, however, with the theory of signs that he outlines in the opening sections of book 2, and specifically with his distinction between *signa naturalia* and *signa data*. A sign, Augustine states, is a thing that, beyond the impression (*speciem*) it makes on the senses, brings the thought of something else to mind (*DDC* 2.1.1). It does so, apparently, in virtue of some established pattern of association between the sign and the thing that it is taken to signify.[15]

Given this definition, the *signa naturalia* (*DDC* 2.1.2)—e.g., smoke as a sign of fire—are signs that make something else known without any will or desire to signify (*sine voluntate atque ullo appetitu significandi*). We learn the pattern of association between sign and thing by observing (*animadversione*) and taking note of (*notatione*) the things that we experience (*rerum expertum*); and that, perhaps, is the key point about *signa naturalia*.[16]

Signa data, on the other hand, are signs that living beings (*viventia*) give to each other in order to show, so far as possible, how their minds are working or what is in their minds (*DDC* 2.2.3). These signs obviously do involve the will to signify (since they would not be given if the sign giver did not will to do so); and, unlike the *signa naturalia*, they are explicitly intended for communication (since we have no reason for giving signs except to convey what is in our mind to the mind of someone else). In this context, however, Augustine says nothing to indicate how the association between sign and thing is established in *signa data*. That question must simply be left open. And in particular, I might add, it must not be foreclosed by adopting the customary translation, "conventional signs," for *signa data*.[17] It will become clear, I think, that Augustine actually envisages at least two ways in which given signs and things come to be associated. Convention, it will turn out, is only one of these, and the one most to be regarded with suspicion.

Among human beings, of course, words constitute by far the largest class of *signa data* (*DDC* 2.3.4); and words, specifically the written words and locutions of the scriptural text, are the particular object of Augustine's concern. Now verbal signs become an obstacle to understanding either when their meaning is unknown or when their meaning is ambiguous (*DDC* 2.10.15). Either way, however, the difficulty can appear at two levels. On Augustine's analysis, verbal signs may be either *signa propria* or *signa translata*. They count as *signa propria* when they are employed to signify the things for which they were instituted in the first place (as when we use the word *ox* to signify an ox); they count as *signa translata* when the things they signify are themselves employed to signify some further thing (as when we use the word *ox* to signify an ox and the ox to signify an evangelist). Verbal signs, then, can be unknown or ambiguous either in their usage as *signa propria* or in their usage as *signa translata*.

On the whole, however, I think it is fair to say that Augustine finds the difficulties posed by unknown or ambiguous *signa propria* to be relatively minor and the remedies more or less technical. So far as unknown *signa propria* are concerned, the main point is to learn the relevant biblical languages or, at least, to check alternate translations of the Scriptures into Latin (*DDC* 2.9.16–15.22); and, in cases of ambiguous *signa propria*, we are chiefly to ascertain the proper punctuation of a biblical locution or to determine which syllable carries the stress in a biblical word (*DDC* 3.2.2–4.8). Apparently, so long as words are being employed to signify only what they ordinarily signify (and no further signification is at issue), the obstacles to understanding can be dissolved simply by discovering what the words do ordinarily mean or how they fit into the locutions in which they appear or which words the words in question actually are. At this level, the more serious issues of signification do not arise.

Signa translata, however, are another matter. Augustine's discussions of unknown (book 2) and of ambiguous (book 3) *signa translata* are complex; and I cannot hope to trace them in full detail here. If I have understood Augustine correctly, however, the chief question at issue in both cases is precisely the question of how patterns of association between signs and things come to be established in human culture. I want to start, however, with another caution about translation. Just as it has become customary to render *signa data* as "conventional signs," so it has become more or less standard to render *signa translata* as "figurative signs." Augustine's own vocabulary invites this rendering, for he often uses *figurata* as a synonym for *translata* (e.g., *DDC* 2.16.24; 3.10.14). Yet "figurative signs" will prove misleading, if it suggests that associations between words and things, rather than associations between things and other things, are at the center of Augustine's attention. As I have already indicated, a verbal sign counts as a *signum translatum* for Augustine when the thing that it signifies itself signifies some further thing. But what occupies Augustine, what he finds problematic, is not the signification of the words but the signification of the things. How does one thing come to be reckoned the sign of another? How is a thing invested with significative meaning in this sense? That is the point at issue in Augustine's discussions of unknown and ambiguous *signa translata*.

Augustine's approach to unknown *signa translata* suggests that—outside the Christian context, at least—he envisages two possibilities.[18] Turning his attention from particular signs to the wider systems or patterns of signification in which individual signs inhere—the term Augustine employs is *doctrinae*—he asserts that two kinds of such systems obtain in pagan culture (*DDC* 2.19.29). On the one hand, there are patterns according to which some things are taken as signs of other things that have been established by human institution (*quas instituterunt homines*). On the other, there are patterns of signification that have simply been recognized—rather than instituted—by human beings as they take note of (*animadverterunt*) signifying relationships between things that are already in place (*iam peractas*) or that were instituted by God (*divinitus institutas*).

In the first case—Augustine is thinking especially of divination and astrology (2.20.30–24.37)—the scheme of signification is entirely a social construction, and the signs that it creates by investing things with meaning are finally to be discounted as merely imaginary signs (*imaginariis signis* [DDC 2.23.36]). But Augustine is acutely aware of the social basis and the social force of such humanly instituted patterns of signification. Taking material things—e.g., the entrails of birds, the stars—as signs of human destinies, they draw human beings into the cult of idols or into the worship of created things as if they were divine (*DDC* 2.2.30). The meanings that they ascribe to things rest, in Augustine's own image, on a kind of pact or treaty concluded not only among human beings themselves, but also between human beings and the demons who here, as always, support and reinforce the shared delusions that humanity imposes on itself (*DDC* 2.22.34, 23.35–24.37).

The pact joins humans and demons, then, in a common social order (*societas* [DDC 2.23.36]) and establishes, as it were, a common language for them to speak (*quasi communi quadam lingua cum daemonibus* [DDC 2.24.37]). Thus Augustine's account of such humanly instituted schemes of signification anticipates the themes of what we would now call the sociology of knowledge.[19] What he has described is, for all practical purposes, the social construction of a worldview that supplies the bonds that hold a society together and provides the system of significations according to which human beings understand, interpret, and negotiate their world.

Augustine is also acutely aware, however, that such humanly instituted systems of meaning cannot ultimately fulfill their social function. The societies that they create are always societies on the lip of dissolution. The social bonds that they apparently secure do not actually join person to person. At best, they merely disguise the private desires that separate human beings and set them in competition with each other. The significations that such systems of meaning contain are not, Augustine says, divinely and publicly constituted for the love of God and neighbor (*DDC* 2.23.36). Instead they dissipate and scatter "the hearts of the wretched through their private desires for temporal things" (*sed per privatas appetitiones rerum temporalium corda dissipant miserorum*). They derive ultimately from a demonic deception, an illusion perpetuated by the lying angels (*praevaricatoribus angelis*) and thus itself a lie (*DDC* 2.23.36). The demons so contrive matters that these patterns of signification affect different persons in different ways (*DDC* 2.24.37) that accord with their own thoughts and presumptions (*diversis diverse proveniet secundum cogitationes et praesumptiones suas*). Far from joining person to person in genuine sociality, then, such a worldview actually caters to their private desires, reinforces their separate presumptions, and thus tacitly undermines the very social order that it appears to secure.

Augustine does not contend that all humanly instituted systems of signs and signification are based on pacts concluded between human beings and the demons.[20] For the most part, however, he contends that they come to the same thing.[21] The only systems of this sort that escape his censure are those—e.g., systems of weights and measures, systems of coinage—that serve the most pedestrian and least theory-laden social purposes and that have an indisputable social utility (without them society could not function or, at least, could not function effectively [see *DDC* 2.25.38–26.40]).

The true alternatives to humanly instituted systems of signification, however, are to be found in those areas of learning which are, so to speak, recognized or noticed rather than instituted by human beings.[22] Here Augustine has in mind a variety of disciplines that range from natural history through logic and rhetoric to philosophy. In each case, however, he singles out the aspects of these disciplines which he does not believe to be the result of human contrivance or subject to human manipulation. In logic, for instance, he considers the forms of valid argument to have been discovered, not created by human beings (*DDC* 2.32.50); and similarly in rhetoric, he insists that we have discovered, not created, the effects that certain types of discourse will have upon the audience (*DDC* 2.36.54). In deciphering unknown *signa translata* in Scripture, then, we can draw on these patterns of signification just because (and just to the extent that!) they are not humanly instituted or socially constructed—just because, that is, they do not ascribe to things meanings that are not really there.

Without attempting to review Augustine's treatment of each of the disciplines he takes under consideration, I want to make two general points about his discussion taken as a whole. The first is simply to note that certain elements in Augustine's treatment suggest that he is at least tacitly assimilating these schemes of signification to *signa naturalia*. Like *signa naturalia*, they involve associations between signs and things that hold quite apart from any human intervention, either because they have already been established in the past or because they have been instituted by God (*aut transacta temporibus aut divinitus instituta* [*DDC* 2.27.41]). Thus Augustine can say, in this instance or in that, that they obtain by the force of nature (*vi naturae* [*DDC* 2.29.45]) or because they are embedded in the rational order of things (*in ratione rerum* [*DDC* 2.32.50]), not on the basis of human agreement or consent. They are, therefore, the very opposite of "conventional signs." In addition, they resemble *signa natu-*

ralia in the way that they are learned. We learn these schemes of signification by adverting to them, by taking note of them, by observing what is
there to be observed.[23] But Augustine nowhere invests these systems of
meaning with the social import that he ascribed to humanly instituted
patterns of signification. They do not rest on any pact or treaty. They do
not derive from agreement or consent. And apparently they do not constitute social bonds joining persons in a common social order. It is
tempting to conclude that it is just because they are so like *signa naturalia*
that they lack this social force. Such systems of signification, it appears,
do not constitute worldviews or bind societies into one.

Thus, if they represent true alternatives to humanly instituted schemes
of signification, that is not because they constitute full patterns of
meaning—complete cultures—in their own right. Although not themselves socially constructed, they function only as subsystems within yet
wider patterns of meaning that derive their central definition either from
pacts concluded between human beings and demons or from the love of
God and neighbor already stipulated as the core "thing" signified in
Christian Scripture.[24]

When we turn to Augustine's discussion of ambiguous *signa translata*
the dominant issue remains the same. The chief question that Augustine
has in mind is this: How are we to know which verbal signs in Scripture
are figurative (i.e., *signa translata*) and which are not? Or, putting the
matter in slightly different terms: How are we to know when the thing
signified by a verbal sign in Scripture itself signifies some further thing and
when it does not? Once again, then, we face the issue of how things come
to be reckoned as signs; and once again, Augustine will insist, the stakes
are high. On the one hand, there is the danger that we will take *signa
translata* as if they were *signa propria*, failing to discern the ultimate *terminus* of the verbal sign and thus cutting ourselves off from its ultimate
meaning (*DDC* 3.5.9). In such cases, we enslave ourselves to the immediate things signified by the verbal signs in their proper sense because we
do not refer those things to any further signification (*neque illud quod
proprio verbo significatur, refert ad aliam significationem*). To take signs
for things is, then, a miserable servitude of the soul (*miserabilis animae
servitus*): the mind's eye is unable to rise above the bodily creature in
order to take in the eternal light.[25]

On the other hand, there is the opposite danger that we will read *signa
propria* as if they were *signa translata*, investing them with a further
range of signification that they do not actually have as they occur in the
biblical text (*DDC* 3.10.14). What we need above all, then, is some means
of discerning (*modus inveniendae*) when scriptural locutions are to be
read in a proper, and when in a figurative, sense; and it comes as no sur-

prise that Augustine finds that means precisely in the double love of God and neighbor which he had already stipulated as the *terminus* of all biblical signification. He first states the rule in rather abstract form: "anything in Scripture which cannot be referred in its proper sense either to the integrity of morals or to the truth of faith (*neque ad morum honestatem, neque ad fidei veritatem*), you know to be figurative" (*DDC* 3.10.14). In the following sentence, however, he converts the abstract statement into the more vivid terminology of his earlier discussion of things: integrity of morals has to do with loving God and neighbor (*ad diligendum Deum et proximum*); the truth of faith has to do with knowing God and neighbor (*ad cognoscendum Deum et proximum*).[26] We might draw the conclusion in this way: it is precisely by knowing what Scripture signifies that we put ourselves in a position to discern how it signifies what it signifies, whether by proper or by figurative signs, and thus put ourselves in a position to resolve the ambiguity about whether to read scriptural locutions as *signa propria* or as *signa figurata* in any given case.

To stop at this point, however, would be to miss the force of the solution that Augustine proposed. In his discussion of ambiguous, as in his discussion of unknown, *signa translata*, Augustine's concern is at least as much to ward off the danger that scriptural signs will be invested with the wrong signification as it is to insure that they will be given the right signification. The danger that Augustine has in mind lies especially in the universal human inclination to judge according to the customs and standards that prevail in one's own time and place (*DDC* 3.10.15). With regard to questions of morality in particular, Augustine fears, we will assume that Scripture's words are to be taken in their proper sense when they conform to our own standards of moral judgment and that they are to be construed in a figurative sense when they do not. When Scripture commands something of which we disapprove, that is, or condemns something of which we approve, then we will presume that we are dealing with a figurative locution; and we will bring Scripture into conformity with our own culture either by investing the things signified by its verbal signs with a further signification that they do not really have or by stripping them of a further signification that they do. Plainly enough, here again, it is the social construction of meaning—in this instance of moral meaning—that lies at the heart of Augustine's concern.

To this socially constructed meaning, rooted in, and reinforced by, prevailing social custom, Augustine counterpoises the stark declaration (*DDC* 3.10.15) that Scripture prescribes nothing but *caritas* and condemns nothing but *cupiditas* and, in this way, forms human moral character (*informat mores hominum*). At issue, of course, is a good deal more than the mere assigning of apt signification to scriptural signs. By *caritas*, Augustine explains, he means the soul's movement toward the enjoyment of God for God's own sake and of self and neighbor for God's sake (*DDC* 3.10.16). *Cupiditas*, in contrast, is the soul's movement toward the enjoyment of self or neighbor or any bodily thing for reasons other than God (*non propter Deum*). The effects of cupidity are first vice (*flagitium*) and then crime (*facinus*), i.e., harm to self and others. For cupidity reduces the self to a kind of impoverished need (*ad quamdam egestatem*) in which it attacks others in order to remove impediments or to seek aids to the realization of its own misdirected desire.[27] It need hardly be said that *caritas* is the antithesis. It works benefit to self and others, what Augustine calls utility (*utilitas*) in the case of self and beneficence (*beneficentia*) in the case of others.[28]

Having set out this schematic antithesis of *caritas* and *cupiditas*, Augustine has put himself in a position to restate his rule for determining when the moral prescriptions of Scripture have a figurative sense and when they do not. If a locution—he can now say—is prescriptive either in forbidding vice or crime or in commanding utility or beneficence, it is not figurative (*DDC* 3.16.24). If, however, it appears to command vice or crime or to forbid utility or beneficence, then it is figurative. In effect, Augustine has yet again made it clear that, once we know what Scripture signifies, we can discern whether its locutions are figurative or not in any given case. But he has done more. He has also intimated once again that any socially constructed alternate scheme of signification must rest on a flawed social order. Any prevailing set of social customs that does not conform to *caritas* must express *cupiditas*. There is no other alternative. And just because *cupiditas* works harm to self and others, just because it reduces self to a state of need in which it can respond to others only as hindrances or as helps to the realization of its own imperious desires, it tacitly undermines any social order that it might appear to sustain. It sets person against person; it does not join them in a common bond. Finally at issue in the question of ambiguous, as in the question of unknown, *signa translata* are the bonds that hold societies together; and thus the right interpretation of Scripture, the proper identification of which locutions are figurative and which are not in the biblical text, will be the one that works for the destruction of the reign of cupidity (*ad cupiditatis regnum destruendum* [*DDC* 3.11.17]) and is directed toward the reign of *caritas* (*ad regnum caritatis* [*DDC* 3.15.23]).[29] For *caritas* does link person to person in a common love for God and join them in love for each other in *Deum* and *propter Deum* (see especially *DDC* 1.29.30). It supplies the bonds that *cupiditas* cannot.[30]

What, then are we to conclude? What would be an apt account of just how Augustine conceives and carries out the project that he undertakes in the first three books of De doctrina christiana, the project of delineating the *modus inveniendi quae intelligenda sunt* in Scripture? I have tried to suggest certain points. Augustine is concerned with signs and what they signify; or, more particularly, he is concerned with how things come to be taken as signs and how they come to be associated with the further things that they are taken to signify. He casts his work in the idiom of signification at the beginning, and, so far as I can tell, he nowhere abandons it. Despite his own declaration that "things are learned through signs" (*DDC* 1.2.2), however, he approaches the matter in reverse order, first stipulating what Scripture signifies in his discussion of things and only then taking up the signs by which it is signified. His aim, it turns out, is not so much to consider biblical signs in some general way as it is to show how, in uncertain and ambiguous cases, they signify what he has already determined that they signify—and, perhaps even more important, to ward off the danger that they will be invested with some other signification.

This last point is critical. It carries Augustine beyond the philosophy of meaning and into what we would call the sociology of knowledge. Augustine recognizes, in effect, that schemes of signification are socially constructed; and he recognizes that such schemes serve a social function, providing the shared system or pattern of meanings that enables human beings to understand and negotiate their world in common and that joins them in a common social order. It is striking that Augustine does not ascribe this function to schemes of signification that do not rest on human institution (but, like *signa naturalia*, are learned by taking note of what has already been established in some other way); and it is equally striking that he exposes the social weakness of schemes of signification that rest only on human institution. These schemes appear to sustain, but in fact undermine, the bonds of society. They cater, in the end, to private desire rather than inculcating a common love. They are rooted in a cupidity that draws persons into vice (*flagitium*) and then into crime (*facinus*) as it seeks to remove all impediments to the realization of its misdirected desire. The antithesis to such schemes is, of course, a pattern of significations that is rooted in *caritas*, the *caritas Dei et proximi* that—as Augustine has stipulated—is signified by the whole system of meanings that is given in and carried by Scripture. We cannot say, of course, that this pattern is humanly instituted (it is defined and given by God);[31] but we can construe it, in an inevitably somewhat equivocal sense, as a social construct. For it is realized on the human plane when human beings actually make this pattern of meanings their own by turning from one type of love to another, from *cupiditas to caritas*, and thus build a culture that genuinely does join person to person in a truly common social order.

By way of conclusion, then, let me suggest that the first three books of *De doctrina christiana* might well be located on the line that led Augustine from the early *De libero arbitrio* to the mature *De civitate Dei*. Precisely in its "treating" or "handling" of Scripture, it seems to represent a major step along the way from the classification of human beings either as lovers of eternal things or as lovers of temporal things (*De libero arbitrio* 1.15.31) to the famous dictum that "two loves have made two cities" (*De civitate Dei* 14.28). It seems to represent, that is, an attempt to delineate the system of significations that defines and sustains the culture of the social order created by *amor Dei usque ad contemptum sui* in contrast to the systems of signification that define and only appear to sustain the culture of social orders created by *amor sui usque ad contemptum Dei* (*De civitate Dei* 14.28).

Notes

1. To make any statement at all about the subject of *DDC* is unavoidably to plunge into deeply controverted issues. Here I follow the lead of Gerald A. Press, "The Subject and Structure of Augustine's *De doctrina christiana*," *AugStud* 11 (1980): 99–124, who himself takes his cues from Augustine's statements in *DDC* prologue 1 and 1.1.1. The term *tractatio* stems, as Press shows (107–112), from the Latin rhetorical tradition; but it carries no particularly precise or technical meaning. As suggested already by Gilbert Istace, "Le livre Ier du *De doctrina christiana* de saint Augustin," *Ephemerides Theologicae Lovanienses* 32 (1956): 289, n. 2, the best translation of *tractatio* in the *DDC* would probably be "treating," "handling," or some equally informal expression. Again following the lead of Istace (289–290, and 301, n. 26) and Press (especially 112–118), I would also want to insist that the subject of the *DDC* is precisely the treating of Scripture, not an account of Christian education or of Christian culture in general. Just because the work says so much about so many things, it is easy to overlook or to forget this point; and it is difficult to avoid "the feeling that there is simply too much going on"—as Oliver O'Donovan remarked in a different connection ("*Usus* and *Fruitio* in Augustine, *De doctrina christiana* I," *Journal of Theological Studies*, n.s. 32 [1982]: 383). Despite all that "goes on" in the *DDC*, however, its purpose is to address the treating of Scripture; and everything it contains is meant, in one way or another, to serve that purpose.

2. For an appraisal of such interpretations, with bibliography, see Press, "Subject and Structure," 99–107 (note also the comments of Istace, "Livre Ier," 301, n. 26). More recently, Rowan Williams has characterized the *DDC* as "Augustine's treatise on Christian education," in a sense that is far more sophisticated—and far more adequate—than is usual among those who take this view of the work; and

he most certainly does not ignore the idiom in which Augustine casts his discussion of the *modus inveniendi* (see Rowan Williams, "Language, Reality, and Desire in Augustine's *De doctrina*," *Journal of Literature and Theology* 3 [1989]: 138–150; the quoted phrase appears on 138). What Williams has in mind might be construed as an "education of desire"—I borrow the phrase from the title of Michel Despland's *The Education of Desire: Plato and the Philosophy of Religion* (Toronto, 1985)—which takes place through learning to see that the created world and all that it contains ultimately signify God and therefore are never themselves to be taken as "the end of desire" (140). The risk run by Williams's interpretation, for all of its merits, is that it will blur Augustine's own immediate and focal concern, the treating of Scripture itself, by diverting our attention too much from the reading of the text to the reading of the cosmos—and, one might add, from the social construction of meaning to a semiotics of the created order.

3. The now-classic studies of Augustine on signs and signification are R. A. Markus, "St. Augustine on Signs," *Phronesis* 2 (1957): 60–83; and B. Darrell Jackson, "The Theory of Signs in St. Augustine's *De doctrina christiana*," *REAug* 15 (1969): 9–49. Both are reprinted in *Augustine: A Collection of Critical Essays*, ed. R. A. Markus (Garden City, N.Y., 1972), 61–147.

4. As Williams remarks ("Language, Reality, and Desire," 138), "Augustine's account of interpretation in the *De doctrina* . . . is a set of variations on a single theme, the relation of *res* and *signum*, thing and sign, reality and representation."

5. It is important to make this point because it prepares the ground for what I take to be of central importance for Augustine, namely, the question of just how things come to function as signs, i.e., how they come to be associated with other things which they are taken to signify. If some things just do serve as signs and others just do not, then the question of how a thing might come to have the standing of a sign—which it also might not have—does not arise. On this view, there is no sense in which a thing might gain or lose the standing of a sign. It either is used to signify or it is not; and there is nothing more to be said.

6. Thus, as previously noted, he discusses things in the first book of *DDC* and signs in the second and third books.

7. The discussion of things in *DDC* 1 is one of the points at which it is easy to overlook or to forget that the entire treatise has to do with the *tractatio* of Scripture (see n. 1, above)—and that the first three books have to do with the *modus inveniendi quae intelligenda sunt*. If the context in which Augustine places his discussion of things is kept in mind, however, it is clear that these things are precisely the *quae intelligenda sunt* in Scripture.

8. On this point, see Press, "Subject and Structure," 113: "It is worth emphasizing the precise object of invention—those things which *are to be understood*. Augustine is not teaching rules for getting some meaning or other out of a text. He is teaching us how to read and interpret a certain group of texts . . . but of the many possible interpretations of those texts only one is to be understood—only one is correct—and it is how to discover this one that Augustine teaches in books 1–3." I would add only that it is in book 1—as Press himself recognizes—that Augustine sets out the essential ingredients in this one correct interpretation.

9. By the sociology of knowledge I mean the kind of enterprise represented by Peter L. Berger and Thomas Luckmann, *The Social Construction of Reality: A Treatise in the Sociology of Knowledge* (Garden City, N.Y., 1966) or, perhaps more remotely, by the approach to the interpretation of cultures sketched out in Clifford Geertz, *The Interpretation of Cultures* (New York, 1973), especially insofar as that approach involves "sorting out the structures of signification . . . and determining their social ground and import" (9).

10. Istace, "Livre Ier," provides a particularly clear, careful, and detailed analysis of *DDC* 1; and O'Donovan, "*Usus* and *Fruitio*," is unsurpassed on Augustine's use of the *usus-fruitio* distinction in this context as well as on the import of the distinction for Augustine's attempt to work out a satisfactory account of love for God and neighbor. In the summary account of things that follows, I have taken my bearings from these two works (although without simply reproducing either position).

11. As Augustine puts it, the things that are to be enjoyed *beatos nos faciunt*; by those that are to be used, on the other hand, *tendentes ad beatitudinem adiuvamur . . . ut ad illas quae nos beatos faciunt, pervenire, atque his inhaerere possimus* (*DDC* 1.3.3).

12. See *DDC* 1.22.2–35.39. From Augustine's complex discussion of love of God, love of neighbor, love of self, and love of body, I have abstracted the two elements of love of God and love of neighbor. These are the two that Augustine himself singles out in his summation in *DDC* 1.35.39 and that he makes the key to the interpretation of Scripture in 1.36.40. For discussion of the difficulties Augustine faces in trying to correlate love of neighbor with the claim that God alone is to be enjoyed (and thus loved) while all else is to be used (and thus not loved), see O'Donovan, "*Usus* and *Fruitio*," 383–390.

13. Augustine is well aware, of course, that God is not a thing in any ordinary sense (*DDC* 1.5.5).

14. Once again, it seems to me, Press has seen the matter rightly: "The substance of both Book 2 and Book 3, is therefore, not a theory of signs, but guidelines for avoiding or eliminating the problems in understanding the things through the signs. So Book 2 is actually, On the Remedies for Unknown Signs . . . Book 3 is On the Remedies for Ambiguous Signs . . ." ("Subject and Structure," 114).

15. Augustine does not state this point explicitly. All of his examples suggest as much, however; and the conclusion seems inescapable that one thing signifies some other thing—i.e., brings the thought of it to mind—in virtue of some established pattern of association between the one and the other.

16. In the case of *signa naturalia*, that is, the patterns of association between sign and thing signified are not socially constructed. They are simply given in the relations that obtain between one thing and another—and thus are not constructed, as when persons associate two things in such a way that they take the one as a sign of the other. Consequently *signa naturalia* are learned through observing or noticing what is there, rather than by being socialized into a system of signification.

17. See the discussion of the translation question in Jackson, "Theory of Signs," 13–15. Jackson distinguishes between the occurrence and the significance

(what I have called the signification) of *signa data* and observes that the translation "conventional signs" obscures the distinction. The Latin *signa data* refers to the occurrence of given signs—they occur when they are given—not to their signification. Jackson notes, however, that according to Augustine, *signa data* acquire their signification by agreement (*placitum*) and consent (*consensio*); and he intimates, at least, that *signa data* are appropriately construed as "conventional signs" with regard to their signification. But even here I have scruples. Augustine notes that the divinely given signs contained in Scripture belong to the class of *signa data* because they were made known to us by human beings, i.e., the scriptural writers (*DDC* 2.2.3); and I doubt that these signs acquired their signification by agreement or consent. Thus some *signa data* may not be "conventional" even with respect to their significance. Furthermore, "conventional" in this context tends to highlight the arbitrary character of the assignment of signification to signs rather that its social character (*placitum, consensio*) and thus—even without reference to *signa divinitus data*—may subtly obscure what Augustine appears to have in mind.

18. The discussion of unknown *signa translata* begins at *DDC* 2.16.23 and occupies the rest of book 2. It opens with the claim that such signs are to be investigated partly by means of a knowledge of languages and partly by means of a knowledge of things. Under the first of these headings, Augustine has in mind chiefly the interpretation of Hebrew names (2.16.23) and, under the second, chiefly a knowledge of the characteristics of things such as animals, stones, and plants (2.16.24), or numbers (2.16.25), or music (2.16.25). A knowledge of their characteristics will help us to understand how these things, when they are mentioned in Scripture, signify other things. Outside the Christian context, however, music is associated with the muses; and Augustine finds that he must separate knowledge of music itself from the wider cultural system or pattern of signification to which music belongs in the non-Christian culture of his era (2.17.27–18.28). This concern then leads him to shift the focus of his discussion—from the characteristics of things to the wider systems of signification that appear in Roman culture—and to set out a general distinction that will guide his appraisal of these patterns or systems. There are, he asserts, two kinds of doctrines that obtain in pagan culture (*duo sunt genera doctrinarum, quae in gentilibus etiam moribus exercentur*): one consists of those which human beings have instituted themselves; the other, of those which human beings take note of (*animadverterunt*) as already in place (*iam peractas*) or as divinely instituted (12.19.29). From this point on, the distinction between these two kinds of doctrines governs Augustine's discussion of unknown *signa translata* and converts it from a consideration of particular signs to a consideration of the systems of signification within which particular signs (in association, of course, with other signs) function. The discussion becomes, therefore, a discussion of the grounds of human culture (although still outside the Christian context) and, in the case of *doctrinae* instituted by human beings in particular, a discussion of the "social ground and import" of the "structures of signification" (Geertz, *Interpretation of Cultures,* 9) that obtain in human culture.

19. See n. 9, above.

20. The kind of doctrines instituted by human beings, Augustine says, is in part superstitious (*partim superstitiosum est*) and in part not (*DDC* 2.19.29). Only the superstitious doctrines are instituted with demons; the others are instituted by human beings alone (2.25.38).

21. See *DDC* 2.22.34: *Quare istae quoque opiniones quibusdam rerum signis humana praesumptione institutis, ad eadem illa quasi quaedam cum pacta et conventa referendae sunt.*

22. Augustine's discussion of these areas appears in *DDC* 2.27.41–42.63.

23. Thus the form of valid argument (*connexio*) is not instituted but observed and noted (*non instituta, sed animadversa est . . . et notata*) by human beings (*DDC* 2.32.50). Similarly the science of rhetoric is not instituted but discerned by human beings (*neque ab hominibus instituta, sed in ratione rerum comperta* [2.35.53]). And again the science of numbers is not instituted by human beings but, rather, traced out and discovered or discerned by them (*non . . . ab hominibus instituta, sed potius indagata atque inventa . . . neque ullo modo ab hominibus institutas, sed . . . compertas*) (2.38.56).

24. Because Augustine considers the disciplines he reviews in *DDC* 2.27.41–42.63—or, more accurately, the aspects of those disciplines that he singles out as divinely, rather than humanly, instituted—to be subsystems of signification rather than full systems and because he considers them to be discerned or discovered rather than socially constructed, and therefore not to be derived from human contrivance or subject to human manipulation in their patterns of signification, he can endow them with a limited, but positive, value that is independent of the wider patterns of meaning in which they appear and can treat them as capable of transfer, more or less intact, from one system of signification to another. Thus he concludes the second book of *DDC* (see 2.41.62–42.63) by urging that Christians, too, should learn and make use of the relevant aspects of these disciplines in interpreting Scripture—warning only that knowledge of these is not to "puff up" (1 Cor. 8:1) the Christian knower, since such "puffing up" is fatally opposed to the *caritas* that defines Christian culture.

25. It is important to note that Augustine treats the Jews in this context not as the prime case but rather as a special case of the servitude that comes from taking signs for things (see *DDC* 3.6.10). They represent an exception to the otherwise general rule because, prior to the incarnation, they pleased God through their servitude and because the signs that they took as things had been usefully (*utiliter*) instituted (3.7.11)—i.e., by God rather than by human beings (3.9.13). In contrast, the Gentiles were taking as things, signs that had been instituted as signs of useless things: and thus, even when they understood these things as signs, they referred (*referebant*) them to the worship of the creature (3.7.11). The difference, then, appears to be that the Jews were taking as things signs that had been divinely instituted and thus belonged to a system that signified rightly, while the Gentiles had taken—and continued to take—as things, signs that had been humanly contrived and thus belonged to a system that signified wrongly (the worship of the creature rather than of God). Thus the Gentiles, even when they took the signs as signs, were actually no better off than they were in taking the signs as things. Either way, they remained cut off from the eternal.

26. Augustine himself explicitly identifies these points with what he had discussed in DDC 1: *De quibus omnibus primo libro dictum est* (DDC 3.10.14).

27. Here Augustine is drawing on a theme that he had elaborated at least as early as *De libero arbitrio* 1.4.10: *mali* [i.e., those motivated by *cupiditas* for temporal things] *autem, ut his fruendis cum securitate incubent, removere impedimenta conantur et propterea facinorosam sceleratamque vitam . . . gerunt.* And he is deploying a doublet—*flagitium / facinus*—that he had already joined to this theme in *Expositio quarundam propositionum ex epistola ad Romanos* 6: *quoniam quisque perniciosam dulcedinem flagitiorum sequens, dum impedientes personas removere conatur, pergit in facinus.* More generally, on Augustine's early understanding of *cupiditas* and its social consequences, see my "*Cupiditas* and *Caritas*: The Early Augustine on Love and Human Fulfillment," in *The Ethics of St. Augustine*, ed. William S. Babcock (Atlanta, 1991), 39–66.

28. On this passage, see O'Donovan, "*Usus* and *Fruitio*," 392, and his earlier remarks on 387–390.

29. And precisely through the destruction of *cupiditas* is *caritas* enhanced: *Quanto autem magis regnum cupiditatis destruitur, tanto caritatis augetur* (DDC 3.10.16).

30. I have not carried my analysis beyond DDC 3.25.35, i.e., the point at which Augustine stopped writing in 397—or perhaps as early as 395 (see O'Donovan, "*Usus* and *Fruitio*, 395, for the suggestion that DDC 1 might be dated this early. I consider it likely that the date of the first book would hold also for the second and third.) I have stopped at this point partly for the sake of chronological coherence; i.e., my concern has been to explore the views Augustine held and expressed in the mid-390s, not thirty years later at a very different stage of his career. At the same time, however, I suspect that, when Augustine returned to the DDC in 427, he did not complete the work he had earlier begun. It is obviously true, of course, that Augustine did follow the broad plan he had already announced for the work, continuing his discussion of signs in the remainder of book 3 and taking up the *modus proferendi quae intellecta sunt* (see DDC 4.1.1) in book 4. The continuation of book 3 does not seem, however, to be tightly focused on ambiguous *signa translata*, the topic announced in 3.5.9 and presumably meant to govern—on the analogy of unknown *signa translata* in book 2—the rest of the book. Rather, despite Augustine's characterization of Tyconius's *regulae* in 3.37.56 as rules that function to make one thing understood through another thing, it seems to address the matter of ambiguities and obscurities in Scripture in a much looser and more general sense. Furthermore, the idiom of signification is itself much less dominant in the final portion of book 3 than it is in the first two books and the earlier sections of the third. It is present, to some degree, in 3.25.36–28.39 and in 3.37.56, but virtually absent from the long discussion of Tyconius that occupies 3.30.42–37.56. And it is even more striking that Augustine no longer seems to make *caritas Dei et proximi* the governing factor that is to control all interpretation of Scripture. Instead, when the question arises, he speaks of interpreting obscure passages in terms of those that are clear (see 3.27.38 and 28.39, this second passage seeming also to reflect Tyconius's appeal to reason to untangle certain scriptural obscurities, as in the *regula prima* of the

Liber regularum [*Tyconius: The Book of Rules*, trans. William S. Babcock (Atlanta, 1989), 2]). In fact, the whole dialectic of *cupiditas* and *caritas* that is so dominant in the discussion of ambiguous *signa translata* up to 3.24.35—and also a crucial element in the treatment of unknown *signa translata* in book 2—simply disappears from signs in the completion of book 3. I find, therefore, that I am unable to agree that the placement of Tyconius's rules at the end of book 3 represents a "compositional master stroke" on Augustine's part or that the rules stand as the "intended high point of the third book" (see Hermann-Josef Sieben, "Die *res* der Bibel: Eine Analyse von Augustinus, *De doctr. christ.* I–III," *REAug* 21 [1975]: 87). Augustine's discussion of the *regulae* seems to me, at least, to come more as a dissipation than as the culmination of the themes that predominate in book 3 up to 3.24.35 (as in books 1 and 2).

31. Nowhere does Augustine apply the imagery of pact or treaty or speak of consent or agreement in relation to the significations carried by scriptural *signa*—as he does in relation to humanly instituted systems of signification (e.g., *DDC* 2.22.34, 23.36, 24.37).

The Sweetness of the Word:
Salvation and Rhetoric in Augustine's
De doctrina christiana

JOHN C. CAVADINI

In book 2 of *De doctrina christiana*, Augustine discusses briefly the "precepts" of eloquence. He classifies eloquence with the sciences "not of human institution but rather discovered in the logic of things."[1] To us, the rules of rhetoric may seem to be anything but natural, but Augustine points out that if speech is to be persuasive, it must adapt itself to the contours of human understanding and motivation, and these are givens:

> It was not instituted by human beings that an expression of charity should win over a listener . . . or that the variety of discourse should keep listeners attentive without annoyance. . . . That which moves minds to long for or to avoid something is not invented but discovered.[2]

In a way, the study of rhetoric is the study of human motivation, or at least of the motivating of human beings.[3]

It is precisely as such that Augustine talks about the theory of "rhetorical art"[4] in book 4. The primary aim of the *Scripturarum tractator*[5] *et doctor* is not only to teach what he has learned but also to present it in such a way that it will "move minds."[6] "Healthful teaching"[7] is of no avail if it has no power to delight those to whom it is presented. It is not enough simply to speak the truth; in fact, if one's teaching is "wise" or "healthful" it is all the more crucial that it be eloquent.[8] Augustine is quick to point out that his remarks will not teach the precepts of eloquence themselves: he recommends that persons be trained in them at the appropriate time or else read eloquent literature and teach themselves thereby.[9] What we have in book 4 is less a theory of rhetoric *per se* than a theory of conversion. The art of rhetoric is useful not so much in its particular rules but precisely because it embodies a science of human motivation and therefore helps us to learn what will make the truth not only true but *moving*. The fact that it is true is not, normally, enough.[10]

In particular, if the truth is to be moving, it must be presented *suaviter*—sweetly—i.e., in such a way that it will delight the listener. Eloquence is the art of speaking sweetly:

> For one who speaks eloquently speaks sweetly; one who speaks wisely, speaks healthfully; . . . But what is better than a sweetness with the power of healing, or a power of healing that is sweet? The more eagerly the sweetness is desired, the more readily the power of healing (*salubritas*) avails.[11]

Scripture itself is characterized by such an eloquence;[12] the role of the Christian *tractator* and *doctor* is to make its sweetness, its power to move to conversion, available to others. Thus will Augustine, slightly later, present Ambrose—the "sweetness of his speaking" caught Augustine and made him finally appreciate the "delights" of God's "law."[13]

"Sweetness" of discourse can be cultivated improperly as an end in itself,[14] but "if the just rather than the wicked" are to be *willingly* heard (*libenter audiantur*), they must speak *suaviter*—"persuasively," i.e., "sweetly."[15] And although, when Augustine, in his interpretation of Ciceronian theory, associates the effect of "sweetness" more narrowly with the "moderate" style of speaking (as opposed to the simple and the grand styles),[16] nevertheless no speech can finally move anyone if it is not in some way "sweet," if it does not in some way "delight."[17] The effect of the grand style, used with adequate "sweetness," is dramatic. The orator is to expect, not applause, but tears. The audience shows the effect "rather through their groans, sometimes even through tears, and finally through a change of their way of life."[18] This sounds familiar—it is in fact an apt description of the state to which Augustine is reduced at his final conversion as he describes it in *Confessions* 8.

What has the student of the art of speaking finally learned? "If he wants to delight or to persuade the person to whom he speaks, he will not do it simply by speaking in any way at all; whether he does it depends upon the way in which he speaks."[19] This, presumably, applies to God as well. If conversion is a matter of persuasion, then if God is to convert anyone, God too must speak persuasively. In this way, book 4 of *De doctrina christiana*, precisely because it is not a treatise on rhetoric *per se* but on (in effect) the dynamics of conversion, provides a kind of commentary on, or key to, the interpretation of the rest of the work.[20] For when we hear that we are distant from God, Neoplatonic wanderers, as it were, from our homeland (*patria*), and when we hear that what this means is that we are "tangled up in perverse sweetness"[21] and that our way back to God will not be a "road from one place to another but a road of the feel-

ings,"[22] we cannot doubt that we have thus been aptly described as subjects ripe for the persuasive power of an eloquent speaking that will
disentangle us from perverse sweetness and will delight us with that
"sweetness which actually would make us happy."[23] When we hear that
our plight is that we "enjoy" things which we should not,[24] and that we
need to learn to place our "delight" in something which presently does
not delight us,[25] and that we are to learn to "refer" all our present delights
to that final goal,[26] who can fail to see that what we need is not simply to
be told the truth but to be told it in a way that will delight us? Who
cannot see that, just as the sweetness of the moderate style is to be used
not as a pleasure in itself but to refer us to the final end of conversion,[27]
so too we are in the position of needing to be persuaded to transfer willingly our affections' goal elsewhere? We are in need not simply of a
teacher but of a persuasive speaker, a delightful speaker.

And so (citing 1 Cor. 1:21 twice in the same chapter) "it pleased God,
by the foolishness of preaching, to save them that believe."[28] The Wisdom
of God comes to us not from place to place but by appearing in mortal
flesh.[29] She who is the goal has become the way, but this way consists of
"unblocking" our affections: like the rhetor, God's Word speaks not only
wisely (and indeed is Wisdom herself) but movingly, and in some sense,
sweetly: this is the "foolishness of preaching." The Word made flesh is
God's Wisdom made not simply visible but persuasive; it is God's eloquence:

> Indeed, the resurrection of our Lord from the dead (and his ascension into
> heaven), once believed, has supported our faith with a great hope. For it
> shows very clearly how freely it was that he laid down his life for us, since
> he had the power to take it up again. How great a trust with which the
> hope of believers consoled, as they consider that such a man suffered so
> greatly for people who were not yet believers! When he is awaited as the
> judge from heaven of the living and the dead, the thought strikes great fear
> into the indifferent, so that they are converted to diligence and prefer to
> long for him in doing good than to fear him in doing evil.[30]

From the perspective of book 4, we easily recognize here the effects of
grand eloquence. Jesus' laying down of his life as the revelation of God's
compassion "unblocks" our affections or feelings, disentangling them
from false and truncated enjoyments:

> Moreover, since we are on a road and it is not a road from one place to an-
> other but a road of the feelings, which was blocked by the bad will of our
> past sins as if by a thorny hedge, what more generous and compassionate
> thing could he do—he who willed to lay down himself as a means for our
> return—than to forgive all the sins of those converted, and to tear away the
> firmly fixed prohibitions against our return by being crucified for us?[31]

Christ's work is not finally to teach us something—knowledge is not enough—in fact, it "puffeth up" (1 Cor. 8:1).[32] Christ's accomplishment is to rework our affections, that is, to create in us a new character, described, again with 1 Corinthians (13:8, 13), as "faith, hope, and charity." One who achieves this character does not need the Scriptures except to teach[33] and, in fact, has become by this very fact, eloquent,[34] a mirror of God's eloquence. In book 1 of *De doctrina christiana* Augustine has presented an interpretation of 1 Corinthians by offering an analysis of God's work in Christ with a paradigm that is unmistakably rhetorical.[35]

This is a fundamental shift—or at least the articulation of a fundamental shift—in Augustine's understanding of the work of Christ and of salvation. We might think of his earlier paradigm as philosophical. As is well known, the language of "return to the fatherland" is Neoplatonic and is familiar from Augustine's earliest treatises. The language of referring our enjoyment of things to enjoyment of God is drawn from the vocabulary of the Neoplatonic ascent to contemplation. One ascends, through consideration of corporeal things, to contemplation of the incorporeal. But because we have become entrapped in things corporeal, because of the influence of the body,[36] our ascent is impeded. So much *De doctrina christiana* holds in common with such works as *De beata vita, Contra academicos, De ordine*, etc., and even *De libero arbitrio*.

But in the earlier works, what we need to complete this ascent is philosophy. In a well-known passage from the *Contra academicos* directed to his patron Romanianus, Augustine describes his conversion precisely as a conversion to "philosophy":

> . . . a soreness of the chest compelled me to give up the bombastic profession [i.e., rhetoric] and to flee to the bosom of philosophy. And now, in the leisure which we have always desired, it sustains and comforts me. . . . It teaches—and rightly so—that we ought to have no concern for anything that can be discerned by mortal eyes, or reached by any of the senses, but rather that all such things are to be disregarded. It promises to give a lucid demonstration of the most true and distinct God, and even now it deigns to furnish a glimpse of him, as it were, through transparent clouds.[37]

Augustine notes how he is presently attempting to convert Romanianus to philosophy (from Manichaeism),[38] hoping in the example of Romanianus's son Licentius and other young charges who are even now living with Augustine the philosophic life.[39] This life involves a program of study in the liberal arts, which exercise the mind to purify it of its carnal attachments and prepare it for the interior ascent and incorporeal vision.[40] The liberal arts are studied so that philosophy may take hold, and in this vein Augustine undertakes the writing of a kind of encyclopedia of the liberal arts, of which the *De musica* is the sole surviving artifact.[41]

In this scheme (overgeneralized here but adequate for our purposes), the function of Christ, the Word made flesh, is simply to admonish us to interiority, that is, to philosophy.[42] Because our minds are fixed on visible things, Wisdom herself becomes visible, but only to admonish us authoritatively to recognize our essential identity and destiny as spiritual, and to invite us to philosophy and to a study of the liberal arts that will prepare us for philosophy. If Christ gives us faith, hope, and love, it is faith, hope, and love that we will eventually come to sight, i.e., we will make the ascent, even if, because we are "little ones" who cannot understand philosophy, it is postponed to the afterlife.[43] What did the reading of the Apostle Paul reveal to Augustine as he relates it in the *Contra academicos?*—Philosophy.[44] But the Christ of these earlier works, from the point of view of *De doctrina christiana*, is naive—he is an orator who attempts merely to teach, thinking that knowledge and understanding of the truth alone will suffice, not understanding that teaching in and of itself cannot persuade; not understanding, finally, the well-springs of human motivation. He would certainly not qualify as a professional rhetor.

De doctrina christiana presents a cohesive rethinking of Augustine's earlier philosophical synthesis of Christian doctrine. What we have instead is what we might think of as a rhetorical synthesis. But by this I do not mean that the philosophical Christ of the earlier works has simply learned to be less naive—more suave, as it were, more streetwise—and to give admonitions to the inner life which are more rhetorically compelling. Augustine in fact seems already to have tried this in *De libero arbitrio*. In book 2 of that work Augustine had described our plight thus:

> O Wisdom, most sweet light of the purified mind! . . . Those who love what you make in place of you yourself are like people who, when they hear a wise and eloquent speaker, listen too eagerly to the sweetness of the voice and the arrangements of carefully placed syllables, and so lose the principle matter, the meaning of the speaker, of which the words are only signs.[45]

Here, Augustine draws on the vocabulary of rhetorical theory to help us understand our problem. But here what we need is to be somehow unlocked from our attachment to the signs of Wisdom, that is, her creatures, so that we can see their meaning—in other words what we need to be shown is that creation is merely like an eloquent speech.

And in book 3 of *De libero arbitrio*, Christ is presented, in perhaps one of the only really moving (if brief) passages in this most philosophical of works, as one who does not merely teach, but who acts in such a way that our attention is diverted from the sweetness of the speech. Augustine presents Christ as a model of humility: "While the devil showed himself a model of pride, the Lord should show himself, through whom we are promised eternal life, a model of humility." But then he modulates into something more:

> Thus the blood of Christ having been offered for us after unutterable (*ineffabile*) distress and pain, we ought to follow our savior with such charity, and be so enraptured by his brightness (*claritate*), that no lower object may detach us from so superior a sight (*a conspectu superiore*).[46]

Christ's "ineffable" Passion moves us better than the "speech" of lower things, but this only serves to remove us from the realm of speech, the realm of the finite and contingent, and to return us to the contemplation of the highest unchangeable Wisdom,[47] to the invisible things within, i.e., to the bosom of philosophy. And yet, in the hint that it is in the Passion which we see the splendor of eternal Wisdom, in the hint that it is the Passion which is the content of the *conspectus* to which we arrive, there is signaled a change, even if the final reference is ultimately philosophical.

In *De doctrina christiana* the balance is shifted, and the change consummated. Our plight is depicted in terms drawn from the vocabulary of the Neoplatonic ascent of the soul. But that language is refigured, recontextualized, as soon as the saving eloquence of God—Christ—is presented not only as the way of our ascent but as the goal as well. Interpreting John 14:6, "I am the Way and the Truth and the Life," Augustine notes that the Word made flesh means to say, "you are to come through me, to arrive at me, and to remain in me," because arriving at Christ, we arrive also at the Father (Jn. 14:10). Augustine glosses his own comment by saying that it is not Christ's intention, having become our way, to hold us on the way,[48] but this does not mean that we leave the humanity of Christ behind, as though it were separable from him. Rather, we simply do not absolutize it as though it were not a way, that is, as though it were not God's moving eloquence but simply just another "thing" to be attached to. It means seeing Christ's humanity as speech, but only *in* the speech do we see the meaning; we do not depart from the realm of speech, from the realm of the temporal. God's eloquence gives everything else a voice, invests the world of temporal things with significance, but only by keeping our attention fixed on God's eloquence can anything else speak. We "remain in Christ." We are "freed" from temporal things, that is, from clinging to them as though they were our end, but our attention does not leave the temporal realm; instead, it becomes, for the first time for us, a way: we can "use" it.

The content of that "use" is not, however, philosophical introspection. This use is our traveling of the "way of affections," but that way has been, and is, formed for us by the sweet eloquence of God, Christ. Christ becomes the content of our affections—he is our way of affections; we do not depart from his continuing formation of them in faith and in hope, and in the charity which they yield.[49] Our "use" of *res* is the very charity which the divine eloquence forms in us, the love of God and neighbor— but, in particular, the love of neighbor. For God's moving eloquence consists in God's having become our neighbor out of compassion,[50] and this moves us to love of, instead of "enjoyment" of, the neighbor. The refusal to rest in the neighbor, to "enjoy" him or her as though they were our personal ends, constitutes "enjoyment" of God and proper enjoyment of the neighbor: "The highest reward is that we enjoy [God] and that all of us who enjoy him may enjoy one another in him."[51]

This means that we cease to take part in the social project of constructing the neighbors as our personal ends, as subjects to be dominated.[52] It means that we do not escape the realm of the neighbor, the realm of the temporal, the historical, the contingent, to make an inward ascent to the enjoyment of the eternal. Our enjoyment of God is not the result of philosophy or inward ascents but an enjoyment whose content and substance are continual acts of charity performed toward whatever neighbor chance or circumstance sends us.[53] This is the *via* that God's eloquence forms in us. "Scripture teaches nothing but charity."[54]

We encounter in *De doctrina christiana* a significant advance over the paradigm presented in *De libero arbitrio*. In the *De libero arbitrio*, created things are in and of themselves speech, speech so beautiful that we become captivated by its sweetness. But in *De doctrina christiana*, the sweetness which captivates us and holds us to created things is much more sinister; it is not anything resident in the things themselves but a "perverse sweetness" that we invent and invest them with. It is an artificial sweetness, furthermore, which is culturally constructed. In book 2, in passages which sound (without actually being) almost Tertullianesque, we learn how permeable culture is to idolatry,[55] described as the construction of the universe as though it were a language which we invented,[56] the rendering of creation into a set of "imaginary signs," and then worshiping it as though it were the creator.[57] But what we are worshiping is a construct of our own sign systems. In effect we use culture, the realm of signs and signification, to construct ourselves as the creators and this is the perverse sweetness which "delights"[58] us—it is our own pride, and we are worshiping—ourselves. Even those arts and sciences which are not directly idolatrous are nevertheless infected because we use them in the service of pride—they "puff up."[59]

As for philosophy, it has a use, but its utility is exactly the same as any other useful thing. If it has a usefulness, that usefulness is constructed by Christ and not separable from him. It has no independent, useful value to which Christ admonishes us.[60] We may take the gold of the Egyptians,[61] but only through the Pasch which is the blood of Christ:

Thus one will feel that, although he has fled rich from Egypt, he cannot be saved unless he has observed the Pasch. "For Christ our pasch is sacrificed" (1 Cor. 5:7), and the sacrifice of Christ emphasizes for us nothing more than that which he said as if to those whom he saw laboring under pharaoh: "Come to me . . . for my yoke is sweet and my burden light" (Mt. 11:28–30). To whom is it thus light except to those . . . whom knowledge does not puff up but charity edifies (1 Cor. 8:1)?[62]

We do not leave our new way of affections, i.e., charity, the work of God's eloquence within us, when we engage in philosophy. Our attention does not leave the realm of eloquence, the temporal and the historical, where Christ's blood was poured out. By our clinging to faith in these, even philosophy can be referred to the love of God.

And, as for the liberal arts, Augustine notes,

> . . . It seems to me that studious and intelligent youths who fear God and seek the blessed life might be helpfully admonished that they should not pursue those studies (*doctrinas*) which are taught outside of the Church of Christ as though they might lead to the blessed life.[63]

This is a direct unsaying of the premise of *De musica* and the encyclopedia of which it was to be a part.[64]

We can think, in the last analysis, of *De doctrina christiana* as a revisioning of the projected encylopedia, as that project which in effect replaced the encyclopedia, rendering it obsolete.[65] For the earlier conception of an encyclopedia of the liberal arts was predicated upon a conception of our predicament as one of being trapped by the sweetness of created (and especially corporeal) things, and the belief that the best of culture—liberal arts and philosophy—had value because they could detach us from these sweetnesses. The view of *De doctrina christiana* is different. *De doctrina christiana* recognizes that there is no culturally unmediated sweetness inhering directly in things; that in fact we construct the sweetnesses which trap us in things, that these sweetnesses are really a delight in pride, and that these delights are *culturally* constructed. Into this situation, knowing well how to move us, the sweet Wisdom of God speaks persuasively with her blood, disentangling us from the web of sweetnesses that is our own construction, and forming our affections instead by her charity. Charity, as it were, deconstructs[66] those sweetnesses, dismantling them in the ultimate sign (*signum*), the sign of the cross.[67] There is no question of a philosophical escape from temporal things into the eternal. As long as we live, we never leave the realm of sign and signification, of eloquence and the word, to arrive at an inner world apart from them. In the sign of the cross is our breadth, length, and height.[68] But this means also that *De doctrina christiana* is not an attempt to establish a "Christian culture."[69] What finally renders any cultural artifact "useful" is the sign of the cross, "the foolishness of God . . . the foolishness of preaching" which disassembles the sweetnesses formed by perverse sign systems, and which turns everything else into a sign—in effect a sacrament—of God's Wisdom.[70] We never leave the temporal because in Christ the temporal becomes sacramentalized; it becomes our enjoyment of God.

Notes

1. *DDC* 2.35.53.3–4: *neque ab hominibus instituta sed in rerum ratione comperta* (spoken with immediate reference to dialectics but characterizing the whole class of sciences consideration of which began in 2.27). Rhetoric, the *praecepta uberioris disputationis, quae iam eloquentia nominatur* (*DDC* 2.36.54.1–2), is clearly in this class. All references to the *DDC* are to the edition of Martin, in *CC*, by book, chapter, section, and line(s).

2. *DDC* 2.36.54.5–13: *Nam neque hoc ab hominibus institutum est, ut caritatis expressio conciliet auditorem . . . aut varietas . . . sine fastidio teneat intentos; et . . . quae . . . ad expetendum fugiendumve animos movent, et inventae potius quod ita se habeant, quam ut ita se haberent institutae.* This view is recalled and implied in what Augustine has to say at 4.4.6.13–15: *Ibi obsecrationes et increpationes, concitationes et coercitiones, et quaecumque alia valent ad commovendos animos, sunt necessaria.*

3. Compare Cicero's view, as at *De oratore* 1.12.53, where the best orator will have thoroughly considered *naturas hominum, vimque omnem humanitatis, causasque eas quibus mentes aut incitantur, aut reflectuntur* (cf. 1.15.68–69). No speaker will be able to move anyone without having studied *rerum omnium naturam, mores hominum atque rationes* (1.51.219; cf. 1.51.223–52.224).

4. *DDC* 4.2.3.1–2 ff.: *Nam cum per artem rhetoricam et vera suadeantur et falsa.* Although written later, Augustine's comments here clearly echo those at 2.36.54. In both places Augustine stresses the value-neutral character of rhetoric as a natural art, and thus its usefulness for arguing truth as well as falsehood.

5. For a study of this word and its cognates (*tracto-tractatio*) in the *DDC* as a way of learning how to understand the aim and character of the work, see Gerald A. Press, "The Subject and Structure of Augustine's *De doctrina christiana*," *AugStud* 11 (1980): 99–124 (with an exhaustive survey of the literature). Press argues that "the *whole* work concerns the 'treatment' of scriptures and the whole work [not just book 4] therefore falls within the rhetorical tradition" (118), books 1–3 being concerned with discovery (*inventio*) of what is to be understood, and book 4 with the manner of setting forth (*modus proferendi*) what has been understood. The emphasis on *inventio* is a return to a conception of rhetoric characteristic of ancient theorists (here, Aristotle and then Cicero), but Augustine's insistence that what is invented is *quae intellegenda sunt*, i.e., "the proper meaning of a text or a group of texts" (120), and that (further) there is in fact a correct interpretation to be discovered, shifts the whole focus and concern of ancient

rhetoric: "The aim of this rhetoric, therefore, is to discover the truth in texts, the articles of the Christian faith, and to teach it to others. Thus rhetoric is reborn as an important social force" (121). Marrou, however, long ago pointed out the tendency of ancient culture to base itself upon the deep knowledge and explication of a privileged text. Of the *DDC* Marrou says, "Le double problème posé à l'intellectuel chrétien est celui-là même que grammairiens et rhéteurs s'étaient depuis tant de siècles attachés à résoudre" (H.-I. Marrou, *Saint Augustin et la fin de la culture antique*, 4th ed. [Paris, 1956], 403, cf. 409; Peter Brown, *Augustine of Hippo* [Berkeley, 1966], 263, echoes Marrou).

6. *DDC* 4.4.6.15: *ad commovendos animos,* echoing 2.36.54.11, *animos movent.*

7. E.g., at *DDC* 4.5.8.40 ff.: *Qui enim eloquenter dicunt, suaviter; qui sapienter, salubriter audiuntur. . . . Sicut autem saepe sumenda sunt et amara salubria, ita semper vitanda est perniciosa dulcedo. Sed salubri suavitate, vel suavi salubritate quid melius? Quanto enim magis illic appetitur suavitas, tanto facilius salubritas prodest.* The "health" metaphors are echoes of the discussion of God's economy of healing in book 1 (see e.g., 1.12; 1.14).

8. *Nam cum per artem rhetoricam et vera suadeantur et falsa, quis audeat dicere, adversus mendacium in defensoribus suis inermem debere consistere veritatem, ut videlicet illi, qui res falsas persuadere conantur, noverint auditorem vel benevolum, vel intentum, vel docilem prooemio facere; isti autem non noverint? . . . illi animos audientium in errorem moventes impellentesque dicendo terreant, contristent, exhilarent, exhortentur ardenter; isti pro veritate lenti frigidque dormitent?* (*DDC* 4.2.3.1–6, 10–13).

9. See *DDC* 4.1.2; 4.3.4. Brown (*Augustine*, 267–268) observes that Augustine did not envision the collapse of the pagan schools of rhetoric. For Marrou, Augustine's profoundest innovation was to separate "eloquence" from "rhetoric," thinking of the rules and culture of rhetoric as useful but not indispensable: "Il faut mesurer la hardiesse d'une telle affirmation. Poser cela, n'était rien moins que rompre avec une tradition huit fois séculaire, s'opposer à ce qui, pour les hommes de son temps, paraissait l'essential de la culture. Séparer l'éloquence de la rhétorique, concevoir toute une formation de l'orateur qui délibérément ignorera ces recettes, cet art sur lequel depuis des siècles tant d'attention a été concentrée, c'était là vraiment innover" (echoed in part by Brown, *Augustine*, 267, who, however, thinks that Augustine was apt to underestimate the degree of sophistication and training that had gone into the construction of his "simplicity" of style). *DDC* 4.1.2 may be usefully compared to the answer given by Augustine to Dioscorus in 410–411 (beginning and end of the letter), and also to *DDC* 2.28.42, which refers to history as useful even if learned *praeter Ecclesiam puerili eruditione* (cf. *DDC* 2.39.58, also envisaging a course of study outside of the Church, *doctrinas quae praeter Ecclesiam Christi exercentur,* which Augustine expects a student to have followed).

10. One could think of this as fundamental premise of the whole rhetorical project. It does not imply a very flattering view of human nature. The rhetorical paradigm for conversion, if it may be so called, is stated well by Cicero at *De oratore* 2.42.178–179: *Plura enim multo homines iudicant odio aut amore aut*

cupiditate aut iracundia aut dolore aut laetitia aut spe aut timore aut errore aut aliqua permotione mentis, quam veritate aut praescripto aut iuris norma aliqua aut iudicii formula aut legibus.

11. See n. 7, above.

12. *DDC* 4.6.9; 4.7.21; cf. *Confessiones* 3.5.9; 6.5.8 (ed. L. Verheijen, O.S.A., CC 27).

13. *Confessiones* 5.13.23.19 and 11.2.4.43–44 (cf. 3.19). Note that this is not the way Augustine presents the effect of Ambrose's preaching in his earlier works, where he is customarily presented only as teaching that God is incorporeal and as helping Augustine to see that the Scriptures are in agreement with such a doctrine (that is, from the point of view of rhetorical theory, that they are *merely* true): see *De beata vita* 1.4 (ed. W. M. Green, CC 29); *De utilitate credendi* 8.20. On the notion of the "congruous" ("effective" or "persuasive") vocation, the call to conversion which is effective because given in a way that is congruent to a person's place and character, see J. Patout Burns, *The Development of Augustine's Doctrine of Operative Grace* (Paris, 1980), especially 37–51.

14. *DDC* 4.14.30; cf. 4.28.61. These are clear echoes of a theme prevalent in book 2 as announced, e.g., at 2.13.20.29–33: *eo sunt infirmiores [homines], quo doctiores videri volunt, non rerum scientia, qua aedificamur, sed signorum qua non inflari omnino difficile est, cum et ipsa rerum scientia saepe cervicem erigat* (1 Cor. 8:1); also see 4.28.61.6–10, with further reliance upon 1 Cor.: *In ipso etiam sermone malit rebus placere quam verbis nec aestimet dici melius, nisi quod dicitur verius, nec doctor verbis serviat, sed verba doctori. Hoc est enim, quod ait Apostolus: "Non in sapientia verbi, ne evacuetur crux Christi"* (1 Cor. 1:17). Compare this passage with the exhortation in *De catechizandis rudibus* (ed. I. B. Bauer, CC 46) 9.13.8–11 (c. 400) to the rhetor who would be a Christian: *discant non contemnere quos congnoverint morum vitia quam verborum amplius devitare; et cordi casto linguam exercitatam nec conferre audeant quam etiam praeferre consueverant.*

15. *DDC* 4.14.30.18–19.

16. See *DDC* 4.17.34.

17. At *DDC* 4.26.56.4–16. Augustine explains that anyone using any one of the styles must nevertheless aim for the effects associated with each of the three. On the need for the grand style to be "sweet" as well, see 4.26.58.

18. *DDC* 4.24.53.4–5 (trans. D. W. Robertson, Jr., Library of Liberal Arts [Indianapolis, 1958]): *Grande autem genus plerumque pondere suo voces premit, sed lacrimas exprimit. . . . quid in eis [hominibus] fecerit sapientis granditas dictionis, non clamore potius quam gemitu, aliquando etiam lacrimis, postremo vitae mutatione monstrasse.* This effect is described as *conversion* in the example Augustine gives of the Mauretanians: *Moxque sermone finito ad agendas deo gratias corda atque ora converti* (lines 20–21).

19. *DDC* 4.12.27.11–13: *Quod si etiam delectare vult eum, cui dicit, aut flectere, non quocumque modo dixerit, faciet; sed interest, quomodo dicat, ut faciat.*

20. The fourth book and the final sections of the third were added by Augustine as he reexamined the work during the writing of the *Retractationes* (in 427;

see *Retractationes* 1.30.1). The fourth book thus clearly gives clues to how Augustine understood the work upon his rereading of it in 427, and in any interpretation of the work in its final form this must be decisive. However, Augustine's thinking on the nature and place of rhetoric does not develop significantly between the earlier books and the last, as the connections between book 4 and books 1 and 2 given above (especially in notes 2, 4, 6, 7, and 14) demonstrate. In a letter of 395 (*Epistula* 29, to Alypius), Augustine describes his own preaching in terms very similar to how he talks about preaching in general in *DDC* 4. In particular, his description of how he reduced the congregation to weeping is much like the similar description at *DDC* 4.24.53.

21. *DDC* 1.4.4.12–13: *perversa suavitate implicati alienaremur a patria, cuius suavitas faceret beatos.*

22. *DDC* 1.17.16.1–2: *nec via ista locorum est, sed affectuum.*

23. *DDC* 1.4.4.13.

24. *DDC* 1.3.3.7–8: We are those who *eis quibus utendum est frui voluerimus.* On the precise, and sometimes shifting, nuances attached to *uti* and *frui* in the *DDC*, see the excellent study by Oliver O'Donovan, "*Usus* and *Fruitio* in Augustine's *De doctrina christiana* I," *Journal of Theological Studies* n.s. (1982): 361–397.

25. To "enjoy" is to "use with delight" (*vicinissime dicitur frui, cum delectatione uti*, [*DDC* 1.33.37.21]); what we should enjoy is the Trinity (1.5.5); for us that means transferring our delight from the vehicles of the journey to the goal (1.4.4).

26. E.g., at *DDC* 1.22.21.37–42: *Quisquis ergo recte diligit proximum, hoc cum eo debet agere, ut etiam ipse toto corde, tota anima, tota mente diligat Deum. Sic enim eum diligens tamquam se ipsum, totam dilectionem sui et illius refert in illam dilectionem dei, quae nullum a se rivulum duci extra patitur, cuius derivatione minuatur.* Cf. 1.33.37.21–24: *Cum enim adest, quod diligitur, etiam delectationem secum necesse est gerat, per quam si transieris eamque ad illud ubi permanendum est, rettuleris; uteris ea, et abusive, non proprie, diceris frui.*

27. See *DDC* 4.26.57.

28. *DDC* 1.12.11.3–6; 12.14–15.

29. *DDC* 1.12.12.1–2.

30. *DDC* 1.15.14.1–9: *Iam vero credita domini a mortuis resurrectio et in caelum ascensio magna spe fulcit nostram fidem. Multum enim ostendit quam voluntarie pro nobis animam posuerit, qui eam sic habuit in potestate resumere. Quanta ergo se fiducia spes credentium consolatur considerans, quantus quanta pro nondum credentibus passus sit? Cum vero iudex vivorum atque mortuorum exspectatur e caelo, magnum timorem incutit neglegentibus, ut se ad diligentiam convertant eumque magis bene agendo desiderent, quam male agendo formident.*

31. *DDC* 1.17.16.1–7: *Porro quoniam in via sumus nec via ista locorum est sed affectuum, quam intercludebat quasi saepta quaedam spinosa praeteritorum malitia peccatorum, quid liberalius et misericordius facere potuit, qui se ipsum nobis, qua rediremus, substernere voluit, nisi ut omnia donaret peccata conversis, et graviter fixa interdicta reditus nostri pro nobis crucifixus evelleret?*

32. See, e.g., *DDC* 2.41.62.3–4; 42.63.15; 13.20.31–32; etc.

33. *DDC* 1.39.43.1–3: *Homo itaque fide et spe et charitate subnixus eaque inconcusse retinens non indiget Scripturis nisi ad alios instruendos.*

34. This character is itself an *instructio* (*DDC* 1.39.43.7); it is itself a *copia dicendi* (4.29.61.35; cf. 4.27.59.1–2: *Habet autem ut oboedienter audiamus, quantacumque granditate dictionis maius pondus vita dicentis).*

35. We may remember that Cicero says that the perfect orator would have to be God/a god (*Orator* 5.19, cf. *De oratore* 1.46.202). Also, note Augustine's description of the work of "the Son of God" at *Confessiones* 13.15.18.47–48: *Attendit per retia carnis et blanditus est et inflammavit, et currimus post odorem eius.* This sounds very much like the orator who has spoken in the right mixture of the moderate and grand styles, and Augustine in this passage has just finished speaking of Scripture's eloquence: *Non novi, domine, non novi alia tam casta eloquia, quae sic mihi persuaderent confessionem et lenirent cervicem meam iugo tuo et invitarent colere te gratis* (*Confessiones* 13.15.17.21–23).

36. In many of the early works there is evident a strong Platonic disgust with things bodily simply because they are bodily: one is converted *to* God *from* the "uncleanness of the body and its stains" (*De ordine* 1.8.23 [ed. W. M. Green, CC 29]—the context is Augustine's partial defense, against Monica, of Licentius's singing, in the latrine, Psalm 79:8, "O God of Hosts, convert us." In the *Soliloquies* (*CSEL* 89), Reason (at 1.14.24) demands that Augustine forsake things of the senses and the sticky lime of bodily things (cf. *Retractationes* 4.3.37–42 [ed. A. Mutzenbecher, CC 57]).

37. *Contra academicos* 1.1.3.71–73, 75–81 (ed. W. M. Green, CC 29; trans. Denis J. Kavanagh, FC 1): *me pectoris dolor ventosam professionem abicere et in philosophiae gremium confugere coegisset. Ipsa me nunc in otio, quod vehementer optavimus, nutrit ac fovet. . . . Ipsa enim docet et vere docet nihil omnino colendum esse totumque contemni oportere, quicquid mortalibus oculis cernitur, quicquid ullus sensus attingit. Ipsa verissimum et secretissimum deum perspicue se demonstraturam promittit et iam iamque quasi per lucidas nubes ostentare dignatur.* .

38. The whole of *De ordine* 1.1 is an extended exhortation to Romanianus, as is 2.1–2 (at 2.2.3.1 Augustine entreats Romanianus, *Ergo adgredere mecum philosophiam!*); cf. 1.9.25.51–52.

39. *Contra academicos* 1.1.4; 1.9.25.53–55. Note that it was a reading of Cicero's *Hortensius* that accomplished the conversion—this is apparently a part of Augustine's curriculum (1.1.4.97–98).

40. For the best account of this "Reductio Artium ad Philosophiam," see Marrou, *Saint Augustine* 277–327. Note that the paradigm for conversion here is different from the rhetorical paradigm given in *DDC* (and *De oratore*). The paradigm in the earlier works is more philosophical and Platonic, not only because the *terminus ad quem* of conversion is, by and large, the "port of philosophy" (*De beata vita* 1.1.1–2), but because it proceeds on the assumption that the truth, once glimpsed, in and of itself is enough to persuade. Education in the liberal arts provides the gradual strengthening necessary to bear the dazzling brilliance of the vision of truth. This is illustrated at *Soliloquia* 1.13.23, which concludes: *Nam ordine quodam ad eam [sapientiam] pervenire bonae disciplinae officium est,*

where *ordine*, in the extensive metaphor preceding, was compared to a process of introducing someone's eyes to the light of the sun in stages. At another point in the *Soliloquies*, training in the liberal arts is unmistakably conflated with a process of Platonic reminiscence: *Tales sunt qui bene disciplinis liberalibus eruditi; siquidem illas sine dubio in se ablivione obrutas eruunt discendo, et quodammodo refodiunt: nec tamen contenti sunt, nec se tenent donec totam faciem veritatis, cuius quidam in illis ortibus splendor iam subrutilat, latissime atque plenissime intueantur* (2.20.35; cf. *Retractationes* 4.4). In the earlier dialogues, one can take the figure of Licentius as an illustration of this paradigm of conversion. In the *Contra academicos*, Augustine tells Romanianus that Licentius is applying himself to philosophy, but that Augustine is restraining him so that he may first acquire strength from education (*ut discipulis necessariis prius excultus vigentior et firmior insurgat* [2.3.8]). In the *De ordine*, Augustine exults in the progress of his student, saying (1.6.16.20–22, 23–25): *ego me ipsum non caperem gaudio, quod videbam adulescentem, carissimi amici filium . . . cuius studiem vel in mediocres litteras desperaveram, quasi aspecta possesione sua toto impetu in mediam venire philosophiam.* Licentius himself, singing Psalm 79:8, "O God convert us . . . ," goes on to report, *alia, longe alia nescio quid mihi nunc luce resplendit. Pulchrior est philosophia, fateor, quam Thisbe, quam Pyramus, quam illa Venus et Cupido talesque omnimodi amores.—Et cum suspirio gratias Christo agebat* (1.8.21.4–8). He is pictured as unable to find words to express his experience, and as finally speaking ecstatically and oracularly, especially in 1.7.18 where he declaims, breathing heavily (*ingemescens difficultate verborum*, lines 17–18), the Neoplatonic doctrine of order, and in 1.7.19, where Trygetius is amazed, *ammirans et horrens subito condiscipuli et familiaris sui afflatum nova inspiratione sermonem* (1.7.19.38–40). Augustine tells Licentius that he has not chanted the prayer for conversion in vain (1.8.23.27–29), and Licentius, recounting his experience, answers, *Nonne hoc est vere in deum converti?* (1.8.23.33–34; a conversion *to* God *from* the uncleanness of the body, lines 40–41). Augustine agrees but tells Licentius that he must return "to order," i.e., to his education, for the face of God is the vision of truth, and the process of conversion a matter of lifting oneself up to it by virtue and temperance, and training in the liberal arts (1.8.23–24.50): *Nam eruditio disciplinarum liberalium modesta sane atque succincta et alacriores et perseverantiores et comptiores exhibet amatores amplectendae veritati, ut et ardentius appetant et constantius insequantur et inhaereant postremo dulcius, quae vocatur, Licenti, beata vita* (1.8.24.50–54).

41. On the *De musica*, see Ubaldo Pizzani and Guido Milanese, *"De Musica" di Agostino d'Ippona* (Palermo, 1990). The plan for the encyclopedia into which it was to fit, along with the rationale for the encyclopedia, is given in the *Retractationes*, where the *De musica* is mentioned as the only surviving treatise from the abandoned project. Note especially the rationale: *Per idem tempus, quo Mediolani fui baptismum percepturus, etiam disciplinarum libros conatus sum scribere, interrogans eos qui mecum erant atque ab huiusmodi studiis non abhorrebant, per corporalia cupiens ad incorporalia quibusdam quasi passibus certis vel pervenire vel ducere* (1.6.40–44; cf. *De musica* 6.2). In the corpus of Augustine's writings closest to the period of composition of the *De musica*, the plan of study repre-

sented by the encyclopedia together with the theory of this *paedeia*, is most fully
elaborated in the *De ordine*. The system of the liberal arts is laid out in 2.11–19,
with their *terminus ad quem* in philosophy (2.18.47) and the ascent to the vision
of God which philosophy accomplishes (2.18.48–19.51, note especially section
51). Cf. *De ordine* 1.1.3.50–55–1.2.3. On the encyclopedia, see Marrou, *Saint
Augustine* 211–235, 570–579; Pizzani and Milanese, "*De Musica*," 14–39.

42. For a good account of Augustine's early theory of Christ, see R. J. O'Connell, *St. Augustine's Early Theory of Man* (Cambridge, Mass., 1968), 265–278.

At *De ordine* 2.9.27.38–41, divine authority in the incarnation admonishes us
not to be limited to the senses, but to ascend to the intellect. Thus, those who live
by authority alone and not the liberal arts cannot be called happy while in this life
(2.9.26; rejected at *Retractationes* 1.3.2), even where that authority is divine, because that authority only functions to recall us to philosophical interiority. When
Alypius voices the paradox that someone who has believed does not necessarily
behave accordingly, something which requires divine assistance (2.10.28), Augustine immediately dismisses this nonphilosophical gloominess, noting among other
things that both our capacity to change and the ways in which people have
changed are often underestimated, and that in any event the requisite divine assistance is universally available (2.10.29). And, in the passage from *De ordine* cited
above in n. 40, 1.8.21.8, Licentius thanks Christ—for leading him to *philosophy*.

43. Faith is in lieu of, and inferior to, instruction in the liberal arts at *De
ordine* 2.5.15.34–41. The incarnation is mentioned at 2.5.16, and the clemency it
shows, but there is no mention of the Passion. At *De ordine* 2.8.25 faith, hope,
and love seem totally submerged in, and defined by, a morass of commonplace aspirations familiar even to the casual reader of Cicero. The only question remaining
to be discussed is educational—*quomodo studiosi erudiri debeant, qui sicut
dictum est vivere instituerunt* (2.9.26.1–2). At *Soliloquia* 1.6.12 faith, hope, and
love are precisely faith, hope, and love in the prospect of enlightenment or vision!
Contra academicos 2.3.9 contains an encomium on what philosophy is able to do;
what one must *believe* is that philosophy is indeed able to do it.

44. *Contra academicos* 2.2.5–6, especially 2.2.5.63–6.69.

45. *De libero arbitrio* 2.16.43 (ed. Franco De Capitani, *Il "De Libero Arbitrio" di S. Agostino: Studio introduttivo, testo, traduzione e commento* [Milan,
1987]): *O suavissima lux purgatae mentis sapientia! . . . Similes autem sunt, qui
ea quae facis pro te amant, hominibus, qui, cum audiunt aliquem facundum sapientem, dum nimis suavitatem vocis eius et structuras syllabarum apte locatarum
avide audiunt, amittunt sententiarum principatum cuius illa verba tamquam signa
sonuerunt.*

46. *De libero arbitrio* 3.25.76: *ut praerogato nobis Christi sanguine post la-
bores miseriasque ineffabiles tanta caritate liberatori nostro adhaereamus et tanta
eius in eum claritate rapiamur ut nulla nos visa ex inferioribus a conspectu superiore detorqueant.*

47. *De libero arbitrio* 3.25.76: *Ut autem in contemplatione summae sapientiae—quae utique animus non est, nam est incommutabilis—, etiam se ipsum qui
est commutabilis animus intueatur et sibi ipse quodam modo veniat in mentem.*

48. DDC 1.34.38.21–27.

49. For, among other things, if we fall from faith, we will fall from charity (*DDC* 1.37.41.9–10).

50. *DDC* 1.30.33.52–56.

51. *DDC* 1.32.35.17–19.

52. The failure to refer enjoyment of the neighbor to God is a false self-love which amounts to a prideful domination of the neighbor (*DDC* 1.23.23). On self-love in Augustine, see Oliver O'Donovan, *The Problem of Self-Love in St. Augustine* (New Haven, 1980).

53. "Neighbor" is taken quite literally, as anyone who happens to be "near" us, including enemies. See *DDC* 1.30.31.

54. *DDC* 3.10.15, 12.18, 15.23; 1.36.40, etc.

55. Not (as with Tertullian) how identical culture is with idolatry. Augustine "secularizes" history (see Robert Markus, *Saeculum* [Cambridge, 1989], especially ch. 7) and culture (Brown, *Augustine*, 266). I would add, however, that for Augustine this is a kind of formal *analysis* of culture, a statement about what culture *essentially* is, not a phenomenology, or a description of what culture has actually *become*. This would be analogous in a way to his analysis of human nature in terms of what it essentially is by creation and the way it has been wounded by sin. For culture, this means its vulnerability to idolatry, the way in which it tends to be constructed by pride rather than by charity. One could found a "culture" on the basis of bibilical imagery (Brown, *Augustine*, 263), and this may be in some sense a "Christian" culture, but it is not necessarily a "converted" culture—it, too, would be susceptible to the glacial drift towards idolatry (this is reflected in Augustine's discussion at *DDC* 1.37.41 of how interpreters can become attached to their own interpretations simply because the interpretations are their own, even if wrong, and this is a fall from charity). For Augustine, persons are converted, not "cultures." It may be better to say that culture is in this way de-reified or even de-mythologized, rather than simply secularized. Thus one would preserve the balance which the *DDC* attempts to articulate—an ability to engage in the pursuits and fruits of the (essentially good) cultural enterprise—but with a healthy fear and distrust of the actual and ever-present tendency towards, and thus implication in, idolatry. But this is to carry us into the subject for another essay altogether.

56. See, e.g., *DDC* 2.21.32.22–25, 29–31, where Augustine discusses how we have affixed names to months and stars, which had always existed as God created them before they received these names: *Pro quintili enim et sextili mensibus Iulium atque Augustum vocamus de honoribus hominum Iulii Caesaris et Augusti Caesaris nuncupatos, ut facile, qui voluerit, intellegat etiam illa sidera prius sine his nominibus caelo vagata esse. . . . Sed quodlibet vocentur ad hominibus, sunt tamen sidera, quae deus instituit et ordinavit ut voluit.* The universe itself becomes part of a sign system independent of its creation, and while this in itself is not evil, it makes the universe miscible with the world of sign and signification, and we rarely resist the temptation to integrate it even further, to the point where the distinction between creation and culture is obscured: all the astrology and related idolatry in chapters 20–24 is predicated on this "naming" of the universe, the ("presumptuous," sec. 34) construction of the universe as a sign system of our making—in effect, the substitution of ourselves for the creator.

57. See, e.g., *DDC* 2.18, 20.

58. This is true not only of the linguistic reconstruction of the cosmos, which *placuit humana vanitate* (*DDC* 2.21.32.27), but also of how even legitimate, non-superstitious sciences become the stuff of pride. We "delight" in being able to "boast" of our wisdom: the general case has already been discussed (2.13.20.29–33, see above, n. 14), but in particular, with regard to the science of numbers, at 2.38.57.14–24: *Quae tamen omnia quisquis ita dilexerit, ut iactare se inter imperitos velit et non potius quaerere unde sint vera, quae tantummodo vera esse persenserit, et unde quaedam non solum vera, sed etiam incommutabilia, quae incommutabilia esse comprehenderit, ac sic ab specie corporum usque ad humanam mentem perveniens, cum et ipsam mutabilem invenerit, quod nunc docta, nunc indocta sit, constituta tamen inter incommutabilem supra se veritatem et mutabilia infra se cetera, ad unius dei laudem atque dilectionem cuncta convertere, a quo cuncta esse cognoscit, doctus videri potest, esse autem sapiens nullo modo.* One delights in *seeming to be learned* by denying to God what is God's, a form of self-idolatry.

59. Clearest with regard to philosophy, *DDC* 2.40–42, but always as a specific instance of 2.13.20.

60. This can be forcefully realized by comparing the way the *DDC* simply lists philosophy at the end of a catalogue of helpful sciences, to Augustine's tearful expressions of rejoicing at his pupil Licentius's progress at *De ordine* 1.6.16 and 1.8.22–24 (cited above, n. 40). It is inconceivable that, from the perspective of the *DDC*, Augustine could extol philosophy as "our true and serene dwelling place" (*De ordine* 1.2.9). How antique this sounds to the reader of the *DDC*! where philosophy is in effect relativized to a position with the rest of the valuable sciences.

61. *DDC* 2.40.60–61.

62. *DDC* 2.41.62.4–13 trans. Robertson.

63. *DDC* 2.39.58 (preceded by 38.57, cited above, n. 58) explains why the ascent from number does not work—the more we know, the stronger the temptation to "boast" trans. Robertson.

64. This is the unsaying of many passages from the *De ordine* as well, including some cited above in n. 40 (*De ordine* 1.8.50–54) and n. 42 (*De ordine* 2.9.26), as well as the opening lines of the *De beata vita*. These passages are unsaid also in Augustine's remarks on the *De musica* in the *Retractationes* (1.11.1–11). The remark that those who have the power to see the "invisible things" of God (Rom. 1:21) but have no faith in Christ will perish *with all their wisdom* is an echo of the *DDC*.

65. Aligning himself in a general way with the position of Marrou, Brown notes that the *DDC* "is one of the most original works that Augustine ever wrote. . . . It is no small thing to be able to transcend one's own education. . . . In Cassiciacum, surrounded by young aristocrats, feeling a little out of place among the polished Christians of Milan, Augustine had not dreamt that he could transcend this education: it might be subordinated to a quest for Wisdom; but it remained intact, massive and irremovable as the foothills of the Himalayas" (*Augustine*, 264). I agree. And yet in a certain sense the *DDC* represents a return to Augustine's own education. Marrou begins to point this out when he contrasts the

methods of the *De ordine* and the *DDC* as philosophic versus literary (*Saint Augustine,* 409). But more importantly, the plight of humankind and the work of God with respect to human beings are understood according to a rhetorical, not a philosophical, paradigm. What Brown refers to as "The Lost Future" could be seen differently, in a way, as a return to himself, as a recovery of the voice he had so carefully learned to polish before his discovery of the *Hortensius,* albeit in a new key.

66. Charity *aedificat* (*DDC* 2.41.62.3–4; 1 Cor. 8:1), it "builds," but from the ground up; we become "rooted and founded" (line 19; Eph. 3:17) in charity when the pride formatting cultural achievements is deflated, as it were, "purged" by the blood of the Lamb (the purgative power of which is symbolized by the hyssop with which it is applied in Ex. 12:22): *est etiam in ysopo vis purgatoria ne inflante scientia* [1 Cor. 8:1] *de divitiis ab Aegypto ablatis superbe aliquid pulmo tumidus anhelet* (lines 30–32). "Founded" and "built" by charity, one resists other principles of construction—knowledge can no longer "puff up" (*fundatum et radicatum et aedificatum in charitate, quam scientia inflare non possit* [*DDC* 2.42.63.14–16]).

67. *DDC* 2.41.62.25–27: *Quo signo crucis, omnis actio christiana describitur, bene operari in Christo, et ei perseveranter inhaerere, sperare caelestia, sacramenta non profanare.*

68. Eph. 3:17–18; *DDC* 2.41.62.18–19.

69. For a different view of the *DDC,* see E. Kevane, "Augustine's *De doctrina christiana* in World Historical Perspective," *Aug(L)* 41 (1991): 1011–1031, e.g., 1018 and 1025, where Kevane assumes complete continuity between the point of view of the *DDC* and that of the *De musica* and the *Libri disciplinarum* (the encyclopedia): "Augustine is showing how to accomplish a new approach in teaching all the arts and sciences of human culture. This points forward to the Christian West, for it is nothing else than a structuring of a new kind of education, qualitatively different from that of the secularized Schools of Rhetoric of the Classical civilization. This is the reason why he embarked upon his project of the *Libri disciplinarum* in his earlier period of the philosophical dialogues, and this is the reason for his purgation of the curricular sciences and disciplines in Book Two of the *DDC.* It is the concept of *Si rite pertractentur* in Vatican I" (1025). On this view, it is hard to imagine, however, why Augustine not only left the *Libri disciplinarum* unfinished but even was careless enough to lose all that he had completed (treatise on grammar and the prefaces to the other books) apart from the *De musica* (which itself may have only been preserved because someone asked for it, *Epistula* 101).

70. On this point, see the article by Rowan Williams, "Language, Reality, and Desire in Augustine's *De Doctrina,*" *Journal of Literature and Theology* 3 (1989): 138–150; and Mark D. Jordan, "Words and Word: Incarnation and Signification in Augustine's *De doctrina christiana,*" *AugStud* 11 (1980): 177–196. On the theory of signs in general in Augustine, see R. A. Markus, "St. Augustine on Signs," *Phronesis* 2 (1957): 60–83; B. Darrell Jackson, "The Theory of Signs in St. Augustine's *De doctrina christiana,*" *REAug* 15 (1969): 9–49.

Delighting the Spirit:
Augustine's Practice of Figurative
Interpretation

J. PATOUT BURNS

De doctrina christiana, as we know from the *Retractationes*, was written in two parts. The first and larger section, composed during the first years of Augustine's episcopate, followed the Pauline commentaries but preceded the work on the *Libri confessionum*. After having set the project aside, Augustine uncharacteristically returned to complete it as he was reviewing all his writings in the preparation of the *Retractationes*.[1] Separated by some thirty years, the two stages of the composition of *De doctrina christiana* are, nevertheless, remarkably united by their intellectual or polemical context, specifically, a concern to describe the process of conversion. The extended reflections on conversion and grace which reached their culmination in *De diversis quaestionibus ad Simplicianum* and the *Libri confessionum* bracket the writing of the first portion of *De doctrina christiana*. Similarly, Augustine's consideration of the efficacy of preaching in the fourth book was contemporary to *De gratia et libero arbitrio*, *De correptione et gratia*, and the works on predestination which occupied the last half-decade of his life. During those years, he applied his theory of efficacious grace to the repentance of sinful Christians and to their perseverance in faith and good will.

The two sections of *De doctrina christiana* reflect Augustine's preoccupation with conversion and repentance. His discussion of the use of figurative interpretation of Scripture in the second book of *De doctrina christiana* and his reflections on the rhetoric of preaching in the fourth book are focused on the affects which the text or sermon can spark in the reader, the delight or sorrow which gives power to understanding, thereby making knowledge effective in choice and action.

My analysis begins, therefore, with a brief review of Augustine's thinking about conversion at the time he wrote the first three books of *De doctrina christiana*. I then address the role of Scripture in the process of conversion and the progress in the Christian life which Augustine elaborated in the second book. Finally, the correlation of eloquence in preaching and teaching with the interior divine operation will be examined.

Augustine's Thinking on Conversion

We can discern two strands in Augustine's thinking on conversions, his reflections on the process of the religious life, in the decade following his own conversion to Catholic Christianity. The first appears in the dialogues and other writings which he addressed to those who had been his associates in Manichaeism and Platonism. There Augustine focused on the quest for wisdom, identifying it as a beatifying knowledge of eternal and unchanging realities through which one might be drawn to union with God. Within this perspective, he identified conversion as a turning from sensible satisfaction and political advancement to the purification and cultivation of the mind. Because the reality and value of the mental realm had been obscured by the convert's preoccupation with the sensible, an authoritative admonition that gains a person's faith and trust must initiate the quest for spiritual truth. Only then could the study of the liberal arts, and particularly of philosophy, reorient the mind and strengthen the intellect, so that the person who persevered in this quest might attain to wisdom and even enjoy the vision of God. Although Augustine's description of the process of conversion is enthusiastic and rich in detail, neither the study of the Scriptures nor the preaching of the Gospel of Christ figure prominently in these writings.[2] Instead, the authority of the community and the witness of exemplary lives play the more significant role in provoking and protecting conversion.[3]

We recall that the intensive reading of the Letters of Paul during the first years of Augustine's presbyterate introduced a new and different element into his understanding of the human situation before God. The custom of carnal delight was enlisted as an ally of the Law in breaking the hold of pride, which in his thinking had replaced carnal desire and social ambition as the primary obstacle to salvation. Abandoning of one's natural powers to seek forgiveness and strength from Christ replaced the study of the liberal arts and the cultivation of reason as the means of personal renewal. Finally, the gift of charity, a new disposition inspired by the indwelling Spirit, displaced the intellectual quest for unchanging truth as the driving force in the Christian life.[4]

This new Pauline perspective proved at once inspiring and deeply troubling to Augustine. His chartings of its dialectic and discontinuities, particularly in the convert's transition from law to grace, were subject to continual revision and amendment.[5] One aspect of Augustine's problem, that of providing an adequate description and illustration of the progress of the Christian life, particularly requires our attention. When he addressed the intransigence of established customs of carnal satisfaction and the gravitational pull of political or economic ambition, Augustine painted in bold strokes with vivid colors.[6] When he spoke of the liberating power of truth, of freedom from fluctuating uncertainty through an intellectual grasp of foundational structures of human life, he could draw on a well-established and broadly accepted philosophic tradition.[7] After a long struggle, he was able finally to describe even the implementation of divine election through reference to the rhetorical technique of appealing to an audience's prejudices.[8] In the narrative of his own life, he illustrated over and again the efficacy of God's exhaustive knowledge of individual dispositions in adapting the preaching of the gospel.[9]

In comparison to these vivid narratives, the descriptions of the operation of the gift of charity are pale and fuzzy, imprecise and impotent to command assent.[10] Indeed, this result was predictable and even inevitable. In his assertions about the necessity of charity for effective choice of the good, Augustine had broken with the dominant tradition of Platonic Christianity, particularly its supposition that clearly perceived truth will regularly move a person to choose and act properly. No one, the philosophical tradition confidently asserted, fails on purpose but only because the truth of the matter is unclear or its significance obscured by insistent sensible distractions.[11]

Augustine, following what he took to be the message of Paul, dared to differ: true and effective love does not always follow the path shown by knowledge; and even when it does, it is an unearned gift of God. In contrast to his description of the psychological continuity of evil, from suggestion through pleasurable act to the necessity of established custom, Augustine's discussion of becoming and doing good involves major discontinuities, gaps at which a gratuitous divine intervention must begin and then restart the process.[12] These discontinuities always hobbled the theory of human choice and action which Augustine built on the Pauline foundation.

The first of my claims here asserts that in the *Libri confessionum* and in *De doctrina christiana* Augustine made an attempt to unite and harmonize the Platonic emphasis on knowledge and the Pauline focus on love. In particular, Augustine's explanation of the extensive scriptural use of what he called *signa translata* seems to provide the connecting link between the opposing Platonic and Pauline viewpoints. Through the process of deciphering allegories, the Christian reader comes to a knowledge which engenders delight and thereby moves the person to love and to seek the figured realities.

The Role of Scripture in the Process of Conversion

This part of my investigation examines three issues concerning the role of Scripture in the process of conversion: Augustine's discussion of the purpose of obscure passages in Scripture; his recounting of the process of conversion and progress toward Christian wisdom; his description of the knowledge which enables this advance.

TRANSLATED SIGNS AND OBSCURE PASSAGES

In his response to the questions posed by Simplicianus on the divine control over human choice, Augustine focused on the significance of the particular way in which a truth is presented to an individual. God arranges the time and manner of preaching, adapting the message to the mindset of the hearer, and thereby, he concluded, controlling the response.[13] Then, in the second book of *De doctrina christiana*, he applied this insight to Scripture itself, proposing that God had included translated signs and obscure passages as antidotes to the twin diseases of pride and satiety which afflict sinful humanity. He explained that the labor of puzzling out the meaning of a difficult passage brings readers to acknowledge their intellectual limitations and prepares them to submit to divine authority. People have a tendency to despise what appears easy, even though it might be profound; they fully appreciate only a dearly won understanding. Extending an alimentary metaphor, Augustine remarked that God had wisely included in Scripture both difficult and easy passages: had the truth been put too baldly, then people would have no appetite for it; had the figures been too obscure, the people would perish from hunger. Indeed, all the saving truth couched in allegories can be found frankly stated in other, plain passages of Scripture.[14] Obscure and figurative passages are necessary, in this view, not for communicating difficult truths or shielding dangerous truth but instead for helping to break down resistance to otherwise accessible truth and making it effective in the lives of readers. The function of the passages, therefore, is affective as well as noetic.[15]

To illustrate the power and working of allegory, Augustine interrupted his analysis to reflect briefly on the text of Song of Songs 4:2:

> Your teeth are like a flock of shorn sheep
> coming up from the washing,

> Every one of them bears twins,
> not a one is sterile.[16]

Referring the passage to the Church as the bride of Christ, he identified her teeth as holy men who tear sinners off from the world, crush down their resistance, and assimilate them to the body of the Church. The sheep to which the teeth are compared can be understood as the converts themselves: each of them has been shorn of the cares of this age, been washed in baptism, and brings forth the twin loves of God and neighbor. Having developed this allegory, Augustine was quick to assert that these truths about the efficacy of preaching and good example in moving people into the Christian community through repentance, baptism, and the love of God could be stated in the plainest and most straightforward way. He confessed, however, that the figurative presentation warmed his contemplating heart and moved his inquiring mind with a power which far outstripped the plain statement of facts.[17] Figures, he observed, have an affective power which is as easily observed as it is difficult to understand. As motivators, figures have a specific function in Scripture: the Holy Spirit uses them to make the truth delightful, to move the heart and thus to increase love and inspire good works.

The affective consequences of interpreting scriptural allegories exactly correspond to the effects of the Spirit's gift of charity or love which Augustine had identified in his commentaries on Paul. This parallel would seem to confirm the hypothesis that Augustine used the functioning of figurative passages in Scripture to illustrate, or even to establish, his understanding of the role of charity in the Christian life. Moreover, the description of conversion and progress which follows immediately in *De doctrina christiana* offers further evidence for this interpretation.

THE PROGRESS OF THE CHRISTIAN

To illustrate the role of Scripture, and particularly of allegorical interpretation, in the progress of the Christian life, Augustine immediately addressed the seven stages through which a person moves from bondage to beatitude. The continuing influence of the quest for wisdom from the Cassiciacum dialogues is evident in his adaptation of the gifts of the Spirit listed in Isaiah 11:2–3 to serve as the formal structure for the progress of the Christian life. By inverting the scriptural order he made fear of the Lord the first in a seven-step series which culminates in the gift of beatifying wisdom. Let us review these stages quickly and then focus on the third, the spirit of knowledge, which was Augustine's principal concern.

First, fear of the Lord raises the disturbing thought of death and the judgment of God, thereby checking a person's self-assurance. Piety, the second gift, helps a person submit to the authority of Scripture. Without piety, the sinner would find fault with the text and reject its authority. Augustine himself recalled despising the text of Scripture when he first turned to it after having been inspired by Cicero.[18]

These two gifts, fear and piety, lay the foundations for the third spirit, knowledge, which is communicated by the study of Scripture itself. Through what must be understood as an allegorical interpretative technique, Augustine explained, careful readers discover themselves within the text of Scripture. When read in this way, the text displays the reader's intricate involvement in a world order based on the love of passing things, far separated from that love of God and neighbor which Scripture commands. The person who has already been established in fear and piety will be moved by this self-discovery to bewail her condition. The knowledge gained from Scripture then leads her, not to despair, but to a good hope and trust. Hope, Augustine concluded, inspires insistent prayer for divine assistance and engenders the fortitude by which a person hungers and thirsts for justice.

Taking courage, which marks the fourth stage in the process, a person turns away from the deadly joy of transient satisfactions, and from the transient generally, toward the eternal, seeking the unchangeable unity of the Trinity. Although the initiate can glimpse the divine light from afar, this vision is apparently painful and cannot be sustained.[19]

So prepared and rebuffed, she receives the fifth spirit, counsel, which Augustine specified as the counsel of mercy. Under its influence, she cleanses her own troubled soul from the appetite for lower things and exercises it in the love of God and neighbor, coming finally even to the love of enemies and being prepared thereby for the next stage.[20]

The sixth step, which Augustine avoided naming, involves a further cleansing of the mind's eye so that the vision of divine light becomes not only clearer and more tolerable but even pleasant and joyous. The love of truth comes to dominate a person so that she cannot be turned aside by concern to please another person or even to seek her own advantage. So purified and prepared, she finally receives the spirit of beatifying wisdom, which she enjoys in peace and tranquility.

In Augustine's seven-spirit scheme of progress from fear to wisdom, we may discern a synthesis in which the Pauline emphasis on fear, humility, faith, and love has been blended into the Platonic conversion from the temporal to the eternal. Augustine's own focus on the third stage may be discerned not only from his elaboration of its description but also from his refraining from applying the scriptural title, understanding or *intellectus*, to the sixth stage so that he could concentrate knowledge in the earlier third step.

THE SPIRIT OF KNOWLEDGE

In the description of that third stage in the progress toward wisdom, the spirit of knowledge, Augustine explains that a person who has already received the spirit of fear and piety turns to the study of Scripture. By interpreting the text, he finds himself in it, and realizes that he is involved in a world order which attaches him to passing goods and separates him from the love of God and the kind of love of neighbor which God commands. This scripturally based self-knowledge, coupled with fear and piety, both destroys self-assured pride and engenders humble trust; it provokes repentance and a confident hope which insistently prays for divine assistance. Through these, the same knowledge brings forth the courage in which the Christian labors to purify his heart from all temporal affections and to strengthen himself in love of God and neighbor.

The affective consequences of this allegorical interpretation of Scripture are prominent: repentance, humility, trust, hope, courage. Augustine has here assigned to the knowledge derived from Scripture that whole sequence of effects which, in the Pauline commentaries, were credited to a series of divine gifts. There, the proclamation of the Law convicted of sin; the preaching of the gospel engendered trust in divine aid; the sending of the Holy Spirit inspired charity and reoriented a person's love. In *De doctrina christiana*, however, Augustine attributed these extraordinary results to the laborious study of obscure and figurative passages in Scripture.

DELIGHTFUL KNOWING

In contrast to truth baldly stated and easily grasped which might inform but would not inspire, the same truth figuratively presented and then uncovered would produce this delightful and salvific knowledge.[21] This is not to suggest, of course, that in *De doctrina christiana* Augustine abandoned or even suspended his firm conviction that charity is a gift of God's indwelling Spirit, which reorients and empowers the person for the love of God, neighbor, and eternal happiness. The thesis claims rather that in *De doctrina christiana* Augustine provided a description, an illustration, of at least one of the ways in which charity is given. In this sense, the discussion of allegorical interpretation in *De doctrina christiana* is like the analysis of the congruous vocation in *Ad Simplicianum*; it explains how the grace of God works through observable human processes.

Thus Augustine seems to have proposed that the obscure and figurative passages had been written into Scripture by the Holy Spirit and that their interpretation was one of the principal exercises through which the Christian life develops. The plain and straightforward passages were included almost as an auxiliary to the allegories, as emergency rations for the spirit and as guides or norms to prevent wrong and harmful readings of figurative passages.

Here as elsewhere, Augustine gave pride of place to that understanding or wisdom which is achieved in the intuition of unchangeable truth by a mind which has already been purified of sensible illusions, carnal attachments, and selfish ambitions. For the person who struggles along the way, however, the truth must be enfleshed not only in the humanity of Christ but also in the allegories of Scripture, presented in the sensible forms which will break pride and inspire love.[22]

The working of this kind of interpretation of Scripture can be illustrated in a particularly apt way by reference to Augustine's first Scripture commentary, *De Genesi contra Manichaeos*. The condemnation of Adam in Genesis 3:17–19 included the laborious working of the earth, dealing with thorns and thistles, and eating bread in the sweat of his brow. In the first decade of writing, Augustine regularly interpreted this passage in reference to the difficulty and labor of acquiring knowledge: of God, of self, and of the world. In the *Libri confessionum*,[23] as earlier in *De Genesi contra Manichaeos*,[24] the text was referred not to agriculture but to study. The interpreter laboring over this text of Genesis, beset with the inconsistencies which bedevil a full literal interpretation, attempts a figurative understanding. Suddenly the text becomes a mirror: she sees herself in the text, condemned to puzzle over a hard and apparently barren text which abounds in questions and problems, eating her spiritual bread by the sweat of her mental brow. Thus is her pride broken, her fall bewailed, and her hope enkindled as she is fed and sustained by the spirit of knowledge in her quest for Wisdom.[25]

Effective Preaching

A similar analysis can be made of the correlation between the exploration of persuasive preaching in the fourth book of *De doctrina christiana* and Augustine's contemporary concern with the admonition and exhortation through which God works the perseverance of his elect. In the analysis of the different styles of eloquence and the persuasion proper to each, Augustine insisted that the Christian preacher must always aim at action. The verbal ornaments which delight hearers may be used to gain their attention, but the objective must always be a decision to act according to truth. The preacher will know he has been effective when his words are met by groans and tears of remorse rather than by delighted applause.

In contemporary writings, Augustine faced the objection that even if his doctrine of divine election and effective grace were true, it should not be preached because it would lead to either presumption or despair.[26] More pointedly, the necessity and efficacy of the divine grace makes the human agency of preaching, admonition, and exhortation superfluous and futile.[27] In *De correptione et gratia*[28] and again in *De dono perseverantiae*,[29] Augustine responded that the salvific divine action required and employed the efforts of the preacher to exhort and rebuke. He even provided specific suggestions for preaching the doctrine of predestination itself so that it might be a vehicle for building hope and trust.[30]

The fourth book of *De doctrina christiana* addresses the purpose and efficacy of Christian preaching and writing within the framework of Augustine's disputed teaching on the efficacy of divine grace. The text bears the marks of this controversy; indeed the issues involved in the controversy may explain his decision to finish the treatise, as an affirmation of the necessity of preaching.

An extensive defense of the role of rhetoric in Christian preaching proceeds through analysis of the Scriptures, particularly the letters of Paul, and extended citations of revered bishops, especially Cyprian and Ambrose. Having thus firmly anchored the status of eloquence in the Church, Augustine then turned to the role of prayer in preparation for speaking and writing.

This discussion recalls the teaching on the congruous vocation which was first articulated in *Ad Simplicianum* some thirty years earlier. Then, Augustine had noted the significance of how a truth was presented; he explained that God adapts the preaching to the existing dispositions of the chosen hearer. The development during the Pelagian controversy of a doctrine of an interior divine voice or movement resulted in a modification of the original theory of effective calling to faith. Augustine described not only God's adapting the message to the hearer but also a divine operation which changes the dispositions of the hearer to fit the message and thereby make it effective.[31] In addressing Christian preachers in *De doctrina christiana*, he focused attention on the significance of the message and medium while retaining the understanding of the inner grace of hearing. He added that a divine operation affects the dispositions of the speaker and thereby controls the content and manner of the preaching or writing, to make them effective for the audience.

> Many different things might be said in discussing any one of the elements of faith and love; those who understand can, moreover, explain them in different ways. Who knows what we should say or what should be heard through us at any given moment except that One who sees the hearts of all? Who, then, can insure that we say the right thing and in the right way, save that One in whose hand both we and our speaking are held?[32]

In preparing to address a congregation or audience, Augustine concluded, a Christian rhetor must pray for such a divine grace to inspire and guide his choice of topics and mode of presentation. The Holy Spirit may be expected to guide the word of the preacher before his congregation no less than that of the martyr before a judge. God not only disposes the hearer to learn and be moved[33] but also guides the preacher to speak in a way which will be effective.

While recognizing that God can and occasionally does accomplish the health of the body or the soul immediately, Augustine argued that grace works more regularly through the angelic or human ministry, using medicines or preaching. As he had earlier illustrated the power of allegory by reference to the Song of Songs, Augustine showed God's working through human eloquence by recalling a sermon he had preached on Christ's promise to reward anyone who gives of a cup of water in his name.

> Was not God present to make us speak in a way which was not inappropriate (*non incongrue*) when we happened to talk to the people about this matter? A flame blazed up from that cold water, enkindled the cold hearts with hope of a heavenly reward, and moved them to perform the works of mercy.[34]

To this personal experience, he added a reference to Esther's prayer that God would place a fitting speech in her mouth when she approached the king to intercede for her compatriots.[35]

Thus Augustine attempted to coordinate his insistence on the importance of eloquence in preaching the Christian faith with his assertion of the necessity of an interior grace which makes teaching effective. Indeed, divine inspiration and guidance of the preacher provides one explanation of how the mind and will of the hearer is moved and even controlled by God. Preaching, as he so clearly demonstrates in his own successful efforts at Caesarea in Mauritania, may be the medium of God's hidden grace.[36]

This understanding of the role of the preacher in the economy of divine operation provides the context for Augustine's discussion of the tools of rhetoric in the fourth book of *De doctrina christiana*. Christian eloquence, like the figurative speech of the Scriptures, may therefore be understood not only as a medium of divine operation but as a concrete illustration of the mysterious process through which God moves the chosen to conversion and salvation.[37]

Unlike the Platonic ascent of the soul from the sensible to the intelligible, the schema of the process of Christian salvation which Augustine developed by interpreting the text of Paul contained significant discontinuities. At various points in the soul's progress, the line of created causality seemed to fail and a divine operation intervened to move the soul forward. Because Augustine insisted that each of these divine graces was fully gratuitous, not earned or merited by prior human action, the divine operations appeared mysterious and unrelated to the human process.

In *De doctrina christiana*, Augustine took the opportunity to illustrate divine grace by demonstrating one of the media or instruments through which it operates, the allegories of Scripture. He showed that the attempt to decipher the obscure and figurative passages leads the reader through a recognition of guilt to hope in God and thence to a love and pursuit of the divine. The inspiring of fear and hope, the giving of charity are not, of course, reduced to the natural outcomes of interpreting Scripture but they are correlated with these effects. In so doing, Augustine illustrated the divine operation and thereby made his theory more intelligible and plausible. Similarly, in the fourth book of *De doctrina christiana*, Augustine attempted to relate the interior divine voice which makes preaching effective to the medium or instrument of human rhetoric through which God normally works. Corresponding to the grace of effective hearing in the chosen listener, he claimed a gift of effective speaking in the preacher which guides the choice of topic and rhetorical style, adapting both to the needs and dispositions of the audience. Such an understanding of the correlation of divine grace and human activity fully legitimatize the learning used in interpreting Scripture and the skill operative in preaching.

Notes

1. *Retractationes* 2.4 speaks of the fourth book as *novissimum*.

2. See, for example, *De ordine* 1.8.23, 2.2.6; *De uera religione* 3.3, 24.45, 29.52–36.66, 39.72; *De beata uita* 4.27–35. One should recognize, of course, that Augustine is often writing for persons who would be moved only by appeals to reason and for whom references to Scripture would not be helpful.

3. In the *Libri confessionum* the witness of Victorinus and particularly of the unlettered monks shames Augustine's ambition and his attachment to sexual satisfaction.

4. See, for example, *Expositio epistulae ad Galatas* 24–25, 44–46; *Expositio quarundam propositionum ex epistula ad Romanos* 13–18, 30, 37, 75.

5. See my *The Development of Augustine's Doctrine of Operative Grace* (Paris, 1980), 30–36.

6. See *Expositio quarundam propositionum ex epistula ad Romanos* 28.1–4, 29.2, 42.2; *Expositio epistulae ad Galatas* 46.1–9; *De diversis quaestionibus* 66.5; *Ad Simplicianum* 1.7.10, 12.

7. *Confessiones* 7.17.23, 10.40.65.

8. *De diversis quaestionibus ad Simplicianum* 1, 2.

9. For Augustine's own conversion, see *Confessiones* 8.6.13–15, 8.7.16–18,

8.12.29–30; for the conversions of others, see 6.7.11, 8.2.4, 8.6.15, 9.8.18.

10. *Expositio quarundam propositionum ex epistula ad Romanos* 12.7–12, 38.4–6, 39.1–2, 67.1–3; *Expositio epistula ad Galatas* 44.3, 47.1, 48.6; *De diversis quaestionibus* 66.6; *Ad Simplicianum* 1.1.7. Note that Augustine attributed to charity not the power to override and crush the attraction of cupidity but the resistance which withholds consent and maintains a commitment to the good.

11. See Albrecht Dihle, *The Theory of Will in Classical Antiquity* (Berkeley, 1982), for a full treatment of the tradition and Augustine's variation on it.

12. For descriptions of the four-step process see, *Expositio quarundam propositionum ex epistula ad Romanos* 12; *De diversis quaestionibus* 66.

13. *Ad Simplicianum* 1.2.13–14. The "congruous" vocation is adapted to the dispositions of the hearer and thus wins a positive response. It should be noted that in the multiple examples which Augustine provides in the *Libri confessionum*, the speaker does not intend, and is even unaware of, the good results of the admonition. The *tolle lege* which sparked his own conversion provides a prime instance. See *Confessiones* 8.12.28–30, 8.2.4, 8.5.10, 8.6.15, 9.8.18, 6.7.11.

14. *DDC* 2.6.7–8. Later, he pointed out that the plain passages should be used to establish truth which should then guide the interpretation of the obscure sections (2.9.14, 3.2.2, 3.26.37).

15. In the fourth book, Augustine's observations continued in this vein. It asserted that under the influence of the Holy Spirit the translators of the Septuagint had increased the obscurity of the text in order to guide the reader to the spiritual sense (*DDC* 4.7.15). Subsequently, he repeated the observation that the sacred writers themselves had used obscurity to deal with satiety and stimulate zeal in their readers (4.8.22).

16. *DDC* 2.6.7: *Dentes tui sicut grex detonsarum, ascendens de lavacro, quae omnes geminos creant, et non est sterilis in eis.*

17. *DDC* 2.6.7–8.

18. *Confessiones* 3.5.9. The more general observation is made in 12.27.38, where Augustine assigns the effect to pride. When Ambrose recommended the reading of Isaiah, Augustine admitted more humbly that he set the book aside because he did not yet understand the language of the Lord (9.5.13). A major function of *DDC*, of course, was to teach the rudiments of this divine speech.

19. This parallels the experience Augustine described in *Confessiones* 7.17.23.

20. In *Ad Simplicianum* 1.2.9 Augustine spoke of mercy or compassion as an effect of grace which enabled a person to undertake good works.

21. A comparison of this section of *DDC* with the corresponding seven-stage process of spiritual development outlined in *De quantitate animae* 33.71–76, finished in 388, clearly indicates the influence of the Pauline perspective and Augustine's orientation toward Scripture as the medium of divine influence.

22. See the parallels in *Confessiones* 7.28.24, and *De uera religione* 10.19, 16.30–17.33, 24.45–46.

23. *Confessiones* 4.16.29, 10.16.25.

24. *De Genesi contra Manichaeos* 2.20.30: *Et quoniam necessitate jam per hos oculos et per has aures de ipsa veritate admonemur, et difficile est resistere phantasmatibus quae per istos sensus intrant in animam, quamvis per illos intret etiam*

ipsa admonitio veritatis; in ista ergo perplexitate, cujus vultus non sudet ut manducet panem suum? quod omnibus diebus vitae nostrae passuri sumul, id est hujus vitae quae transitura est.

25. One finds a parallel instruction on finding oneself in the Psalms in Cassian's *Conferences* 10.11.

26. This is reported in the letter of Prosper to Augustine, *Epistula* 225.3.6.

27. This argument was made explicitly in Hilary's letter to Augustine about the objections in southern Gaul, *Epistula* 226.2.5.

28. *De correptione et gratia* 14.43, 15.46, 16.48–49.

29. *De dono perseverantiae* 14.34–37, 17.41–47.

30. *De dono perseverantiae* 14.36, 17.46, 20.51, 22.57–61. The preacher, for example, must concentrate on the divine salvific action rather than on God's foreknowledge; he must speak positively and draw attention to the divine gifts which have already been given. Perhaps most importantly, he must always speak of the nonelect in the third person, never addressing his audience in these terms.

31. See *Epistula* 217.2.5; *De correptione et gratia* 5.7–6.9; *De praedestinatione sanctorum* 8.15; *De dono perseverantiae* 14.37. The treatise in which Augustine proposed this theory, *Epistula* 194, was the occasion of the unrest in Africa and subsequently in Gaul. For a fuller discussion, see my *The Development of Augustine's Doctrine of Operative Grace*, 166–168, 174–175.

32. DDC 4.15.32. The allusion is to Wisdom 7:16: *In manu enim illius et nos et sermones nostri.*

33. DDC 4.16.34: *Unde ipsis quoque ministris sanctis hominibus, vel etiam sanctis Angelis operantibus, nemo recte discit quae pertinet ad vivendum cum Deo nisi fiat a Deo docilis Deo, cui dicitur in Psalmo: Doce me facere voluntatem tuam, quoniam tu es Deus meus.*

34. DDC 4.18.37: *Nonne quando accidit ut de hac re loqueremus ad populum, et Deus adfuit ut non incongrue diceremus, tanquam de illa aqua frigida quaedam flamma surrexit, quae etiam frigida hominum pectora, ad misericordiae opera facienda, spe coelestis mercedis accenderet?* Note the use of the term *non incongrue*, which is linked to the theory of effective vocation.

35. DDC 4.60.63. Augustine used the term *congruum sermonem*. In earlier application of this text, he had focused on the divine operation within the king's heart. See *Contra duas epistulas Pelagianorum* 1.20.38, and *De gratia et libero arbitrio* 21.42–43.

36. DDC 24.53.

37. A parallel explanation of the working of the grace of perseverance through the timing of a person's death may be found in *De correptione et gratia* 8.19 and in *De praedestinatione sanctorum* 14.26.

Divine Attributes in
De doctrina christiana: Why Does Augustine
Not List "Infinity"?

LEO SWEENEY

Despite first appearances, Augustine's *De doctrina christiana* is care-fully structured.[1] Any study (*tractatio*) of Sacred Scripture (Augustine begins) involves a method of discovering what is to be understood in and from its pages and then a method of setting forth what is learned (*modus inveniendi quae intelligenda sunt et modus proferendi quae intellecta sunt* [*DDC* 1.1.180]). Postponing the second method until book 3, Augustine immediately begins the process of discovery in book 1 by separating the *doctrina* it discloses into what one learns from signs (this will constitute the topic of book 2) and from things (*res*) (which is the topic of book 1).[2] *Res* means that which is not used to signify something (*proprie autem tunc res appelavi quae non ad significandum aliquid adhibetur* [*DDC* 1.2.2.182]).

Such *res* are in turn divided into those which are to be enjoyed, those which are to be used, and others which are to be enjoyed and used (*res ergo aliae sunt quibus fruendum est, aliae quibus utendum, aliae quae fruuntur et utuntur* [*DDC* 1.3.3.182; for explanation, see Combès-Farges, pp. 558–661]). The first make us happy; the second are means to achiev-ing happiness; the third, if we enjoy what is solely to be used, can cause problems by impeding or even canceling our movement towards true goods of the first sort (Combès-Farges, p. 182).

In the next chapter Augustine further comments on "enjoyment" and "use." The former is clinging to something with affection for its own sake; the latter is employing something so as to obtain what we want, provided the object desired is right and lawful for us. Otherwise to employ something to obtain what is wrong is not "use" but "abuse" (*DDC* 1.4.4.184). For example, if we are traveling home and we so enjoy the journey itself as to want to continue traveling rather than to arrive, we are wrongly enjoying what we should only use. So too, as wanderers from God on the road of mortal life, we must use this world and not enjoy it so that the "invisible attributes" of God may be clearly seen, "being understood through the things that are made" (Rom. 1:20)—that is, through what is corporeal and temporal we may comprehend the eternal and spiritual (*utendum est hoc mundo, non fruendum; ut invisibilia Dei, per ea quae facta sunt, intellecta conspiciantur, hoc est ut de corporalibus temporalibusque rebus aeterna et spiritualia capiamus* [DDC 1.4.4.184]).

Divine Attributes

Up to now we have traced the careful outline which Augustine will follow throughout *De doctrina christiana* and which also provided the setting for his listing of the divine attributes. What are those "'invisible attributes" of God which he has just mentioned?[3]

Before listing them, Augustine speaks again of the *res* which we should enjoy—it is the Trinity of Father, Son, and Holy Spirit, which is one supreme *res* common to all who enjoy it—or (he stops to ask) Is it a *res*? or, better, Is it not the cause of all things? or, even better, Is it not both *res* and cause (*una quaedam res, communisque omnibus fruentibus ea; si tamen res et non rerum omnium causa sit, si tamen et causa* [DDC 1.5.5.186])? What term might aptly fit such great excellence? Perhaps it is better to say that this Trinity is the one God from whom, through whom, and in whom are all things (Rom. 11:36). Thus there are Father, Son, and Holy Spirit, each of which is God and simultaneously all are one God. Each of them individually is full substance and simultaneously all are one substance (*et singulus quisque horum plena substantia, et simul omnes una substantia* [DDC 1.5.5.186]). All of them are the same eternity, the same immutability, the same majesty, the same power (*eadem tribus aeternitas, eadem incommutabilitas, eadem majestas, eadem potestas* [DDC 1.5.5.186]), even though unity characterizes the Father, equality the Son, perfect harmony of unity and equality the Holy Spirit.

If we pause to synthesize the information which Augustine has just given on the divine attributes, what list emerges? The triune God is both the *res* to be enjoyed by all and the cause of all. Perfect substance, the three divine persons are identically one and the same eternity, changelessness (this will turn out to be the primal attribute),[4] majesty, power.

So far has Augustine (as he himself asks as he continues in ch. 6) spoken of or given utterance to anything worthy of God? Not really, because God is ineffable and one should be silent before him. But he wishes us to rejoice in his praise in our own language. Thus, we call him *Deus*, a two-syllable Latin word which does not disclose him but which, when heard, causes us to reflect upon his most excellent and immortal nature ([*iste sonus*] *movet ad cogitandam excellentissimam quamdam immortalemque naturam* [*DDC* 1.6.6.188]). The result is that we attempt to conceive of something which is more excellent and more sublime than all else (*ut aliquid quo nihil melius sit atque sublimius illa cogitatio conetur attingere* [*DDC* 1.7.7.188]) and which is above not only all visible and corporeal natures but even all intellectual and spiritual natures—in a word, above all changeable things. Hence everyone agrees that God is that which is worthy of esteem above all other things. Also, all think of God as something living—in fact, as life itself (*vivum aliquid cogitant . . . vitam ipsam cogitant* [*DDC* 1.8.8.190])—as unchangeable life, as wisdom itself, as the unchangeable wise life ruled over by unchangeable truth, which contrasts with their own changeable lives and by which they know that the unchangeable life is better. Unchangeable truth we are to enjoy to the full, once our minds are cleansed by holy desire and lofty morals, and in it the triune God as author and founder of the universe takes counsel for the things he has created (*DDC* 1.10.10.192).

In subsequent chapters Augustine speaks of Christ's incarnation (ch. 11–14), his resurrection and ascension (ch. 15), and his Church (ch. 16 ff.). In chapter 32 Augustine begins anew to contrast enjoyment with use. Within that renewed discussion he discloses two further attributes of God when explaining how God uses rather than enjoys us. God's use of us differs from our using something inasmuch as by using us he increases the good he confers upon us.

> Since God is good, we are. Insofar as we are, we are good. . . . He is supremely and primarily who is entirely unchangeable and who could most fully say: "I am who am" and "You shall say to them: 'He who is sent me to you'" [Ex. 3:14]. Other existents could not be except by him and they are good inasmuch as they have received the ability to be. Therefore, God's using us redounds not to his but to our benefit, and this solely because of his goodness.
>
> *Quia enim bonus est sumus; et in quantum sumus, boni sumus. . . . Ille enim summe ac primitus est qui omnino incommutabilis est, et quia plenissime dicere potuit: "Ego sum qui sum" et "Dices sic: Quis est, misit me ad vos." . . . Ut cetera quae sunt, et nisi ab illo esse non possint, et in tantum bona sint in quantum acceperunt ut sint. Ille igitur usus qui dicitur Dei, quo nobis utitur, non ad ejus sed ad nostram utilitatem refertur ad ejus autem tantummodo bonitatem).*[5] (*DDC* 1.32.35.224)

In light of this passage, God is primal Being—and this because he is total immutability—and primal goodness.

If we add these two divine properties of supreme being and goodness to those discovered earlier, what do we have? The triune God is full substance. He is eternity, changelessness, majesty, and power (ch. 5). He is ineffable in his most excellent and immortal nature, which is higher and more sublime than all else, even than intellectual and spiritual natures, all of which are changeable (ch. 6). He is life itself, unchangeable truth and wisdom (ch. 7), which became incarnate in Christ (ch. 11–14). Primal goodness, he is also primal being because of his absolute changelessness (ch. 32).

God Infinite Being?

But nowhere in those passages does Augustine predicate infinity of the divine being itself and the question is, Why not? Unlike his earlier contemporary, Gregory of Nyssa (331–395),[6] why does Augustine not list infinity among God's attributes? The answer may be found in the *Confessions*, which was begun in 397, the year after he had written the first portion of *De doctrina christiana*, but which recounts the stages of his intellectual and religious conversion occurring between autumn of 384 and August 386.[7]

What information does the *Confessions* provide? Influenced by Manichaeism and then by Stoicism,[8] Augustine thought of God, although incorruptible and immortal (*Confessiones* 7.1.1), as a corporeal reality which indefinitely extends throughout space and penetrates the entire universe and all its parts—as though God is an immense ocean, in the middle of which the world is immersed like a large sponge. Thus all things are finite because located in God, who is himself infinite in his limitless physical extension and, secondly, in his freedom from any extrinsic location—because of his material greatness and surpassing size, he extends beyond all space and, thus, nothing contains him.[9]

But at the time of his intellectual conversion, which God brought about on the occasion of his reading some Neoplatonic literature (*Confessiones* 7.9 and 20), what happened to his conception of infinity? He then saw that creatures are finite not because they are physically located in divine reality but because God conserves their being and truth (*in te cuncta finita sunt sed aliter, non quasi in loco, sed quia tu es omnitenens manu veritate, et cuncta vera sunt inquantum sunt* [*Confessiones* 7.15.21]). Secondly, he realized that God is completely immaterial because he is the unchangeable light far different from all physical lights: He is eternity, love, and truth. But Augustine asked,

"Is truth nothing because it is diffused neither through finite nor infinite space?" From afar you cried to me, "I am who am." I heard as one hears in his heart; there was no further place for doubt, for it would be easier for me to doubt that I live than that there is no truth, which is "clearly seen, being understood by what is made." (*Confessiones* 7.10.16)

Through Exodus 3:14 God thus assures Augustine that God is truth and that he is entirely nonspatial. But since God then is totally incorporeal, he is infinite in a way other than Augustine had earlier imagined (*et evigilavi in te et vidi te infinitum aliter* [*Confessiones* 7.14.20]). God is infinite, yes, but not as physically diffused through space, whether finite or infinite (*certus esse te et infinitum esse, nec tamen per locos finitos infinitosve diffundi* [*Confessiones* 7.20.26]).

One may conclude, then, that the divine incorporeal and immutable being is infinite not, however, through physical extension but in some way different from what Augustine had previously thought. What is that different fashion? Nowhere in the *Confessions* does he answer. Apparently no reply occurred to him in the years covered by that treatise (the conversion itself in books 1–9; his reflection on memory, time, and eternity, form and matter, the creation of the world in books 10–13).[10]

Consequently, no one need be surprised that in *De doctrina christiana* he omits infinity from among the divine attributes: by the time of his composing its book 1 (c. 396), he seemingly was still no more certain than when he was writing the *Confessions* as to what infinity might mean when applied to the incorporeal existent who is God.[11]

Does that uncertainty persist in his later writings? In *De trinitate* 6.10, he twice uses "infinity" as a technical trinitarian term to express the fact that three divine persons are distinct as persons and yet are not distinct from one another in respect to the divine essence, with which each is identical (*illa tria* [= the divine persons] *et ad se invicem determinari videntur et in se infinita sunt*). *Qua* divine they are not distinct from one another (*et in se infinita sunt*) but are one and the same God. Manifestly, Augustine here is not dealing with whether or not the divine being is itself infinite and thus does not directly deal with the question raised in the *Confessions* as to how the incorporeal God is himself infinite.[12]

What does Augustine say elsewhere? In commenting on Psalm 144:3, *Laudabilis est valde, et magnitudinis eius non est finis*, he links the nonfiniteness of God's (spiritual) magnitude with our inability to comprehend him.[13] In *Epistle* 118.24, Augustine grants that divine wisdom and truth may be called infinite, not, however, with reference to spatial locations, but to power, which cannot be comprehended by human thought.

> *Manifestum est enim omnium rerum descriptionem et modum ab illa* [divine wisdom and truth] *fieri eamque non incongrue dici infinitam, non per spatia locorum sed per potentiam, quae cogitatione humana comprehendi non potest.*[14]

In immediately subsequent lines of *Epistle* 118 he explicitly locates the infinitude of what is incorporeal (which, presumably, is God) in its freedom from local limits. There he is discussing Cicero's opposition (in his *De natura deorum* 1.10.28 f.) to Anaxagoras's theory of mind (*nous*). For Cicero nothing can be added, Augustine states, to the infinite if this latter is a body because bodies necessarily have limits (*CSEL* 34:687, lines 20 ff.). Yet the intellect or mind cannot be infinite (as Anaxagoras would want) because it also must sentiently know (and thus be a soul) if it is to be the *ordinatrix et moderatrix rerum omnium* (688, line 6). Why? Because the soul, wherever it senses, does so throughout its whole nature (line 8: *totam sentire animam*) since any body perceived does not escape the soul's entire attention (line 9: *totam . . . non latet*). But if the whole nature of the soul is engaged in the sensation (line 11: *totam naturam sentire*), it cannot be infinite since any sense of the body it animates starts at a particular spot and then terminates at its own proper origin—characteristics excluded from what is infinite. Then come the key lines (688, lines 16–19):

> That which is incorporeal is in another fashion called a whole because it is conceived without limitations of places: it is whole because of its completeness, it is infinite because it is not surrounded by spatial limits.

> *Aliter dicitur totum quod incorporeum est, quia sine finibus locorum intellegitur, ut et totum et infinitum dici possit: totum propter integritatem, infinitum quia locorum finibus non ambitur.*

If Augustine identifies this incorporeal whole (line 16: *totum quod incorporeum est*) with God, God is infinite because free of spatial limitations, which if they were present would determine him and thus make him be determinate and finite. But they are absent from God, who thus can himself be termed "infinite." Notice that what seems to be guiding Augustine to this conclusion may be a realization that presence in space determines and, in that sense, makes an existent in space determinate and thus finite, whereas freedom from space also frees it from that determination and hence renders it indeterminate or infinite. Since God by reason of his bodilessness escapes space (an awareness of which Augustine speaks in *Confessions* 7) and its determination, God can be depicted as infinite. Notice, though, Augustine does not explicitly say "the divine being is infinite."

But this explication seems founded in the fourth and last text, where infinity is linked with the divine substance. In commenting upon the initial verses of John's Gospel ("In the beginning was the Word, and the Word was with God, and the Word was God"), Augustine contrasts the transient words we speak with the immutable Word God the Father speaks. What kind of Word is it, he asks, which is "both spoken and does not pass away"? Or take the word "God"—"how short it is: three letters and one syllable. Is this actually the whole reality that God is, three letters and one syllable? Or is this as trifling as what is understood in this is precious?" The crucial lines follow.

> What happened in your heart when you had heard "God"? What happened in my heart when I said "God"? A certain great and perfect substance was in our thoughts, which transcends every changeable creature of flesh and soul. And if I should say to you, "Is God subject to change or is he immutable?" you will immediately answer, "Far be it from me either to believe or to imagine that God is subject to change. God is immutable." Your soul, although small, although perhaps still carnal, could only reply to me that God is immutable. But every created being is changeable. How were you able, therefore, to have a spark of understanding of that which is above every created being so that you, with certainty, reply to me that God is immutable? What, then, is in your heart when you think of a *certain substance that is living, eternal, omnipotent, infinite, everywhere present, everywhere whole, nowhere confined*? When you think of these attributes, this is the word about God in your heart.[15]

Manifestly, Augustine has characterized the divine substance as infinite. But in what does such divine infinity consist? Is God infinite because he is incomprehensible or/and omnipotent or/and nonspatial (as one finds in the previous three passages)? Or is it because he is free from all determination of matter and potency, as one might expect if Augustine had been Aristotelian in his metaphysics.[16] As yet no answer is clear.

Obviously, much research and reflection remain to be done on Augustine's theory of infinity.[17] But at least this can be said: no one need be surprised if he does not list infinity among the divine attributes in his early treatise, *De doctrina christiana*, book 1, chapters 5–32. Put quite simply, he was not yet certain as to what divine infinity might mean in the light of his discovery, set forth in *Confessions*, book 7, of God as completely incorporeal.

Notes

1. On the makeup of *DDC*, the date of its composition, and a general introduction to its contents, see G. Combès and J. Farges, trans., *Le magistère chrétien* (Paris, 1949), *Oeuvres de Saint Augustin*, vol. 11, 152–163 (for sake of convenience I use their Latin text, checked, however, with Green's critical edition noted immediately below; references to the Combès-Farges text are to book, chapter, section and page); William M. Green, *De doctrina christiana* (Wien, 1963), *Sancti Aureli Augustini Opera*, Sect. VI, part 6 of *CSEL* 8:vii–xiii; John J. Gavi-

gan "Christian Instruction" (Washington, D.C., 1947), FC 2:3–8. Also see Joseph Martin, *Sancti Aureli Augustini De Doctrina Christiana* (Turnhout, 1962), vii–xix.

2. *DDC* 1.2.2.182: "Signs" are "those things which are employed to signify something. Therefore, every sign is also a thing, for whatever is not a thing is absolutely nothing, but not every thing is also a sign" (*Omne signum etiam res aliqua est: quod enim nulla res est, omnino nihil est; non autem omnis res etiam signum est*). Again, 2.1.1.238: "A sign is a thing which, apart from the impression it makes upon the senses, causes of itself something else to enter into our thinking"—examples: footprints, smoke, living voice, trumpet sounding (*Signum est enim res, praeter speciem quam ingerit sensibus, aliud aliquid ex se faciens in cogitationem venire*).

3. Such is Gavigan's translation (30) of *invisibilia* which Combès-Farges translate (185) as "les perfections invisibles de Dieu."

4. See *DDC* 1.6.6.188; 1.7.7.188; 1.8.8.190—all of which are quoted below.

5. In the initial sentence, *Quia enim [Deus] bonus est sumus, sumus* is best rendered not as "exists" (see Gavigan, 52) but simply as "are" in the sense of "are real." Existence as such for human persons and other creatures connotes mutability and unreality. What God properly does in us is to cause us to be immutable by our sharing in His immutability and reality. The same understanding of the verb *esse* should be applied to the other quoted clauses here and in similar situations.

6. On Gregory of Nyssa, see my volume, *Divine Infinity in Greek and Medieval Thought* (New York/Bern, 1992), ch. 21, "Gregory of Nyssa on God as Infinite Being"; and my "Augustine and Gregory of Nyssa: Is the Triune God Infinite in Being?" in Roland Teske et al., eds., *Collectanea Augustiniana*, vol. 3 (New York/Bern, 1992).

7. On dates relevant to the *Confessions* (e.g., Augustine began it in 397, underwent the intellectual and religious conversion described in books 7–8 as occurring from 384 to 386), as well as information on the nature of the book, see Peter Brown, *Augustine of Hippo* (Berkeley, 1969), 74–183 ff.; Eugene TeSelle, *Augustine the Theologian* (New York, 1970), 12, 59–89, 185–223.

8. See Robert J. O'Connell, *St. Augustine's Early Theory of Man, A.D. 386–391* (Cambridge, Mass., 1968), 88–89; Peter Brown, *The Body and Society: Men, Women, and Sexual Renunciation in Early Christianity* (New York, 1988), 196–202; Marianne Djuth, "Stoicism and Augustine's Doctrine of Human Freedom after 396," in Joseph C. Schnaubelt and Frederick Van Fleteren, eds., *Collectanea Augustiniana* (New York/Bern, 1990), 1:387–401 (where she gives helpful references to G. Verbeke and M. Colish).

9. *Confessiones* 7.1.2: *corporeum tamen aliquid cogerer per spatia locorum, sive infusum mundo sive etiam extra mundum per infinita diffusum. . . . Ita etiam te, vita vitae meae, grandem per infinita spatia undique cogitabam penetrare totam mundi molem, et extra eam quaquaversum per immensa sine termino, ut haberet te terra, haberet caelum, haberent omnia et illa finirentur in te, tu autem nusquam.* 7.5.7: [Augustine first pictured the entire universe with all its visible and invisible creatures as a huge mass; then] *et eam feci grandem, non quantum erat,*

quod scire non poteram, sed quantum libuit, undiqueversum sane finitam; te autem, domine, ex omni parte ambientem et penetrantem eam, est usquequaeque infinitum; tanquam si mare esset, ubique et undique per immensa infinitum solum mare, et haberet intra se spongiam quamlibet magnam, sed finitam, plena esset utique spongia illa ex omni sua parte ex immenso mari; sic creaturam tuam finitam, te infinito plenam putabam.

10. See Brown, *Augustine of Hippo,* 158–181.

11. For TeSelle (*Augustine the Theologian,* 185), "at sometime in 396 or 397 . . . [Augustine] broke off *De doctrina christiana"* and began to write the *Confessions.* Actually, *DDC* 1, ch. 7, anticipates (although very briefly) some of the stages we have seen set forth in *Confessiones* 7. On the occasion in *DDC* 1.7.7 of interpreting Psalm 50:1 and Joshua 22:21–22, he discussed those polytheists who "have surrendered to the bodily senses and think that the sky, or what they have seen most radiant in the sky, or the world itself is the God of gods. Or, if they attempt to go beyond the world, they visualize something luminous and conceive it as infinite or of that shape which seems most pleasing in their vague imagining. Or they think of it in the form of the human body, if they prefer that to other things" (1.7.7.188: . . . *aliquid lucidum imaginatur, idque vel infinitum* . . .).

Who thought of the "God of gods" as in the form of the human body? No answer is given there, or in *Confessiones* 7.1.1, where Augustine mentions that identification twice: "Yet from the time that I first began to learn anything of wisdom I did not think of you, O God, as being in the shape of the human body. Such a conception I always shunned, and I rejoiced to find that the faith of our spiritual mother, your Catholic Church, likewise shunned it. But what more should I think you to be, I do not know." In the next paragraph: "Although I did not think of you as being in the shape of a human body, I was forced to think of you as something corporeal, existent in space and place, either infused into the world or even diffused outside the world throughout infinite space."

12. On *De trinitate* 6.10, see my paper, "Augustine and Gregory of Nyssa: Is the Triune God Infinite in Being?" in *Collectanea Augustiniana* 3, notes 16–32 and related text.

13. *Enarrationes in Psalmos* 144.3 (CC 40.5–6:2091): *Cogita quantumvis. Quando autem potest cogitari qui capi non potest? "Laudabilis est valde";* et *"magnitudinis eius non est finis."* . . . *Verumtamen, quia "magnitudinis eius non est finis," et eum quem non capimus laudare debemus (si enim capimus, magnitudinis eius est finis; si autem magnitudinis eius non est finis, capere ex eo aliquid possumus; Deum tamen totum capere non possumus); tamquam deficientes in eius magnitudine, ut reficiamur eius bonitate, et opera respiciamus et de operibus laudemus operantem, de conditis Conditorem, de creaturis Creatorem.* Besides *Epistula* 118.24, quoted below, see *Enarrationes in Psalmos* 146.5 (CC 40.11: 2129). *"Intelligentiae eius non est numerus." Conticescant humanae voces, requiescant humanae cogitationes; ad incomprehensibilia non se extendant quasi comprehensuri sed tamquam participaturi.*

On spiritual or virtual magnitude in God, see *De trinitate* 6.7.1: *Deus vero multipliciter quidem dicitur magnus, bonus, sapiens, beatus, verus, et quidquid aliud non indigne dici videtur. Sed eadem magnitudo eius est quae sapientia (non enim mole magnus est sed virtute); et eadem bonitas quae sapientia et magnitudo, et eadem veritas quae illa omnia. Et non est ibi aliud beatum esse et aliud magnum aut sapientem aut verum aut bonum esse, aut omnino ipsum esse.*

14. *CSEL* 34.2:687, lines 17–20. Augustine immediately excludes infinity in the sense of "nonbeing" or "formlessness" from divine wisdom: *Neque quod informe aliquid sit ipsa sapientia; hoc enim corporum est, ut, quaecumque infinita fuerint, sint et informia.* See also *De natura boni contra Manichaeos* 1.3 (PL 39:553): *Deus itaque supra omnem creaturae modum est, supra omnem speciem, supra omnem ordinem. Nec spatiis locorum supra est, sed ineffabili et singulari potentia, a quo omnis modus, omnis species, omnis ordo.*

15. *Tractatus in evangelium Ioannis* 1.1.8 (CC 36:5). The Latin for the italicized English words: *Quid est ergo illud in corde tuo, quando cogitas quamdam substantiam, vivam, perpetuam, omnipotentem, infinitam, ubique praesentem, ubique totam, nusquam inclusam? Quando ista cogitas, hoc est verbum de Deo in corde tuo.* English trans. John W. Rettig, *St. Augustine: Tractate on the Gospel of St. John 1–10* FC 78 (Washington, D.C., 1988), 48–49, with a helpful introduction (3–33) to Augustine's treatise.

16. On matter in Augustine as good but also as *mutabilitas, nihil aliquid* and *est non est,* see TeSelle, *Augustine the Theologian,* 139–44, with helpful references to E. Gilson, Jules Chaix-Ruy, Jean-Marie Leblond, as well as to *Confessions,* book 12.

17. For texts on "infinity," see *Augustine Concordance* residing in the VAX computer at Villanova University, administered by Allan Fitzgerald, O.S.A., to whom I express thanks.

Receptus

For what have we that we have not received? But, if we have received it, why do we boast as if we had not received it?

De doctrina christiana prologue, 8

To Adjust Rather Than
to Reconcile: *De doctrina christiana*
and the Oxford Movement

DUANE W. H. ARNOLD

The Oxford movement within the Church of England has been characterized as an effort to restore the High Church ideals of the seventeenth century within the post-Enlightenment theological and political setting of the 1830s. The Catholic Emancipation Act of 1829, followed by the Reform Bill of 1832 (with its plan to suppress ten Church of Ireland Bishoprics), had caused consternation among those who believed these actions to be unwarranted secular intrusions into the life of the "catholic nature and foundation" of the Church of England and occasioned the famous Assize Day sermon, "National Apostasy," by John Keble on 14 July 1833. This event is generally used to mark the beginning of the movement. Coupled with other factors, such as the general decline of church life, certain fears of the growth of "liberalism" in theology, and the interest of the romantic movement in ancient and medieval Christianity, the Oxford reformers quickly gathered momentum, with equally large numbers of enthusiastic supporters and entrenched opponents. Initially, the movement coalesced around the defense of the Church of England as a divine institution, the use of the Book of Common Prayer as a rule of faith, and the doctrine of apostolic succession. These views were put forward and enlarged upon in the famous series, Tracts for the Times, which had been started by John Henry Newman. Within a very short time, however, one of the founders of the movement, Edward Bouverie Pusey, turned his attention to the interpretation of Scripture with, I believe, the able assistance of Augustine and *De doctrina christiana*. This turn of attention was to mark for all the members of the movement a renewed interest in patristic norms and guidelines for mystical, figurative, and sacramental exegesis and was to provide a new approach to their interpretive task.

As the Oxford reformers began to study what they considered to be their High Church foundations of the seventeenth century, they immediately encountered the patristic ethos of the Caroline divines, who, in their study of the Fathers, held a special affection for Augustine, as Owen Chadwick has commented:

> Already, in 1600, the knowledge of the [patristic] texts was making a momentous difference to the study of the early Church. St. Augustine, to whom everyone looked back for guidance in the doctrines of justification, grace, and predestination, had once risen head and shoulders above the other teachers of the ancient Church. In 1630 he was still a giant; but he had been placed in a wider context of learning, and especially against a background of Greek thought.[1]

This attitude, however, underwent a transformation in the mainstream of the Church of England during the eighteenth and early nineteenth century with the ascendency of the Latitudinarians, who felt that more help might be found "in understanding St. Paul, from Locke, than from . . . Augustine."[2] So it was, almost as a reaction against the prevailing weight of opinion, that the leaders of the Oxford movement turned their attention to the writings of the Church Fathers of the first four centuries.[3] In fact, as Geoffrey Rowell has stated:

> The theological vision of the Oxford Movement was in large measure a rediscovery and reinterpretation of patristic theology. The typological exegesis of Scripture and the strong sacramentalism of the Fathers commended themselves to men who already had begun to criticize the evidence theology of the eighteenth century. . . .[4]

This process of recapitulation became so complete that after having heard a sermon (perhaps by Newman) in which some new ideas appeared to be forthcoming, John Keble advised the preacher, "Don't be original."[5]

The insistence upon tradition and traditional, that is to say, typological, exegesis commended itself especially to Pusey, the Regius Professor of Hebrew at Oxford. Educated at Eton and Christ Church, Oxford, Pusey was elected Fellow of Oriel College in 1823. Devoted to the study of Hebrew, Arabic, and other Semitic languages, Pusey studied in Berlin and Göttingen, where he became acquainted with a number of leading German biblical critics. He showed his disenchantment with their methodology, however, in the publication of *An Historical Enquiry into the Probable Causes of the Rationalist Character Lately Predominant in the Theology of Germany*, in two parts issued in 1828 and 1830. Pusey's biographer, Henry Parry Liddon, indicated that it was following this time that the Regius Professor began to turn his attention to the work of Augustine, including the initial work on a revised translation of the

Confessions that was envisioned as a first volume for the Library of the Fathers, the series which was the combined brainchild of Pusey, Keble, and Newman.[6]

It appears that during this period, that is, the years between 1830–1834, Pusey first encountered *De doctrina christiana* as a part of his study of the Augustinian corpus. By the end of the year 1833, Pusey had also become identified as a leader, along with Newman and Keble, of the emergent Oxford movement by the contribution of Tract 18, *Thoughts on the Benefits of the System of Fasting, Enjoined by Our Church*, to the series of Tracts for the Times. During the long vacation of 1836, Pusey's interest in Old Testament exegesis, hermeneutics, and his patristic studies, now heavily influenced by Augustine,[7] would result in the preparation for the following Michaelmas term of a series of lectures, "Types and Prophecies of the Old Testament."[8] These lectures would reintroduce an Augustinian approach to figurative and typological interpretation which had been abandoned, for the most part, in current biblical studies both in Britain and Germany.[9]

It is obvious that Pusey struggled with the figurative and typological interpretations put forward in the lectures and remarked, "I cannot give any principle in a few words."[10] Nevertheless, he was aware of the need to break with both the "old orthodoxy," which saw types and prophecies only as specific predictions of New Testament events, and with the new biblical criticism, which tended to discount typological and prophetic elements within Scripture altogether. The lectures show clearly that Pusey had become convinced of an ambiguity resident in a great many typological and figurative expressions within Scripture.

When the lectures were delivered in the autumn, only twenty-nine persons were in attendance. These few students, however, included John Henry Newman, Issac Williams, and H. A. Jeffreys (Keble's curate at that time), as well as several other "men of the movement." Newman appears to have recognized in Pusey an increasing awareness of the role of ambiguity in the interpretation of figurative, prophetic, and typological passages of Scripture which had led to a more creative and open approach. He wrote to a correspondent concerning Pusey that, "It is *very* difficult, even for his friends . . . to enter into his originality, full-formed accuracy, and unsystematic impartiality."[11] Some of the reports of the lectures to those not in attendance appear to have caused some alarm, albeit most likely owing to misreporting what had been said. John Keble, who was unable to attend the lectures because of his pastoral duties at Hursley, near Winchester, wrote to Pusey in November: "I want to hear your lectures on types and prophecies, and whether Jeffreys is right in saying that you are *always* against a *double sense*."[12] As we shall see, Keble need not have worried, for Pusey appears to have followed and expanded upon Augustine's maxim that "not only one, but perhaps two or more, interpretations may be understood from the same words of Scripture."[13]

The lectures "Types and Prophecies of the Old Testament" were never published, and amazingly little attention has been given to them by scholars apart from two short, but very fine, studies by A. M. Allchin and David Jasper to which this present study owes much.[14] The manuscript of the lectures had remained in Pusey's possession, apparently until his death in 1882. Pusey died without a will, and his library had passed to his married daughter, until its purchase by the Memorial Fund established at the proposal of H. P. Liddon.[15] Liddon apparently had the manuscript in his personal possession for some time before it became a part of the collection of the library of Pusey House, Oxford, where it is now kept. The manuscript, a slender bound red volume of 126 leaves is incomplete, and there are portions which appear fragmentary. Some few notations appear to be in another hand, perhaps Pusey's in later years, or Liddon's. Within the manuscript are numerous references to certain patristic sources, mainly given as "tags." There are also references to classic Anglican sources, such as Richard Hooker and George Bull.[16] Yet, it is the Augustinian pattern of argument and the reliance upon categories which appear to be derived from *De doctrina christiana* which cause these lectures to rise above much of the early literature of the Oxford movement.[17]

Numerous examples of correlation with *De doctrina christiana* within the lectures may be cited. Yet Pusey's apparent attempt within the lectures was to adjust, rather than to reconcile, Augustine's approach to the interpretation of Scripture in light of the emergence of German biblical criticism on the one hand, and the opposing Tractarian desire to view the whole of the Bible, and especially the Old Testament, as a single, integrated witness to the centrality of Christ and the sacramental nature of the Christian life on the other hand. In the opening section of the lectures, "On Prophecy," Pusey bemoans the current tendencies toward univocal and unambiguous biblical interpretation: "The notion, and uses of Prophecy have, in these latter days, been much narrowed and obscured by the apologetic character which our Theology has so largely assumed."[18] Conscious of the tendency of some, even among his fellows, to reduce the whole of the Old Testament prophetic tradition to only isolated and figurative predictions of the Christian dispensation, Pusey retreats to the maxim of Augustine, "that we are not to attempt to interpret a literal expression as if it were figurative."[19] Indeed, Pusey argues,

> The prophetic nature of the Old Testament is to be understood as a coherent whole and not simply as "an accumulation of single facts" considered

apart from their religious context and meaning, as particular predictions of New Testament events and personalities.[20]

Such a process of reduction, as characterized by Pusey, echoes the complaint of Augustine in *De doctrina christiana* 3.10 that persons of every epoch appraise the sins pointed out in Scripture by the measure of current custom, whereas the real purpose of Scripture is to teach "only the Catholic faith in relation to things past, future, and present. It is a history of the past, a prediction of the future, and a delineation of the present."[21] Pusey's application of this principle to the body of Christian doctrine and the interpretation of prophecy is even more pointed and specific:

> This is the case with regard to our whole creed; by striving over-much at clearness, and practically admitting only what they could make, as they thought, intelligible to themselves, men have narrowed it far below that of the ancient Church, or of our own in former days. So also with prophecy. Brought within the compass of a system, all those parts were lost, which lay to the right or to the left beyond the circle which men had drawn. For prophecy is co-extensive with the whole system of God's Providence or Dispensation; for every early part of the scheme, in that it is adapted to some later part, preparatory for it, corresponding to it, becomes thereby prophetic of it.[22]

As Augustine intended those who studied the canonical books to be "meek in their devotion" and to "seek the will of God,"[23] Pusey also indicates that the approach to Scripture is an essential part of understanding its internal rules, meaning, and interpretation. He states that the Fathers, rather than following their own methodology, were prepared instead to "follow out the hints which God has given" within the body of Scripture and through apostolic preaching.[24] The result, according to Pusey, was that Christ as the incarnate Word was placed at the center of their interpretive rules, rather than themselves. This allowed the Scriptures to speak for themselves instead of being placed within an overly restrictive network of prejudices and a priori assumptions. Both the end and the beginning of the interpretive process was, for Pusey, the life of faith and love. Like Augustine, these became the spectacles through which the true understanding of Scripture came.[25] As Pusey wrote:

> We are not formed to seek conviction, but to have it. It is brought to us in the way of duty. In all practical matters we live in belief and through acting on belief, believe in the things of God, and thereby attain a higher kind of belief, and an insight into our belief.[26]

For if Augustine considered that "the essence of knowledge is the eternal Vision,"[27] Pusey, in a sentence which is crossed out in the manuscript (perhaps he felt he was going too far), states that, "like the centurion by the

Cross we are awed into belief" and thereby know as we are known.[28] Regardless of his second thoughts, the remainder of the lectures indicates that this sense of awe and lack of self-assertion was, at essence, what Pusey considered to be the basis for the interpretation of not only the prophecies and /or the figurative language of the Old Testament but for the understanding of all Scripture.

The combination of the life of faith and love as a prerequisite for proper interpretation, along with an understanding of language, the internal cohesion of Scripture, and certain suggested rules for understanding figurative or typological passages are woven into the structure of *De doctrina christiana*, and also provided Pusey with the framework upon which he constructed the lectures. In particular, this Augustinian understanding of interpretation led Pusey to abandon, once and for all, a purely mechanistic or rational approach to prophetic elements within the Old Testament. For Pusey, therefore, as for Augustine and Tyconius, understanding of the inherent interpretive unity of the Old and New Testaments was essential, for each is part of the other even as *species* and *genus*.[29] Even prophecy, in Pusey's view, must be submitted to this test:

> Holy Scripture does not favour our mechanical views of prophecy, as containing so many items, as it were, as there are striking passages; as though prophecies admitted of being counted up, and the entire evidence of prophecy was to be weighed according to the number and contents and tangibleness of these several predictions. Rather the whole previous dispensation of the Old Testament, its people, its individual characters, its rites, its sayings, its history was one vast prophetic system, veiling, but full of the New Testament.[30]

This abandonment of a mechanical or bipartite interpretive structure extended even to Pusey's thinking about the relative superiority of the Hebrew text in such a context. This, for Pusey, as may be imagined, was no small matter. Nevertheless, he appropriated the Augustinian approach to this question completely, even accepting the Greek text of the Septuagint as being the work of translators whom "God doubtless illumined" and who, thereby, prepared the way for the incarnation.[31] This understanding, and even the phrases used, appear to be taken, almost verbatim, from *De doctrina christiana* 2.15.

Culturally conditioned as it undoubtedly was, Pusey's concern with the interpretation of Old Testament types and prophecies, by the allowance of multiple understandings and deliberate ambiguities occasioned by his reading of *De doctrina christiana*, allowed the Oxford reformers to reclaim an important part of the patristic approach to Scripture. Moreover, it enabled Pusey, Keble, and Newman (to name but a few) to explore the larger question, at least in part, of the religious imagination and how it is expressed.[32] In his preface to the lectures, Pusey expressed his exasperation with interpreters who

> wished to grasp the whole evidence of prophecy and to collect it into one frame, and so narrowed their own conception of it; they [the dead orthodox] were content with nothing but the mid-day sun and so lost sympathy for the refreshing hues of its rising or setting light, or those glimpses into a far distant land, which, indistinct though they be, open a wider range of vision.[33]

This verbal picture of light and shadow, certainty and ambiguity, may have made a greater impression upon his hearers than Pusey realized, for Newman, at a later date, would comment that "religious truth is . . . like the dim view of a country seen in the twilight, with forms half extricated from the darkness, with broken lines and isolated masses." He concluded that what we are able to perceive or to communicate is "small and superficial" compared with that truth to which it is intended to lead us and in which we are to find growth in faith and love.[34]

The indistinction of what is perceived, however, does not devalue its meaning. As with light and shadow, words, often figurative, indistinct, or ambiguous in their meaning, contain a special power when understood aright and when used toward a proper end. Whereas Augustine wrote of slavery to signs,[35] that is, words or images which are not taken beyond their superficial significance, Pusey compares the mystery of figurative, typological language with the expressions of a child:

> The words of the child are constantly typical of the future developed being. They speak greater truth than they themselves (the outward organ of truth) know: they speak it in reference to some particular occasion but indefinitely; they are aware of something kindred to that whole truth and have some glimmering of it, but they grasp it not. And yet they who hear it, will rightly wonder at it, and they who understand it better than the child itself, will yet confess that they could not have uttered it so simply or so forcibly. Its very indefiniteness adds to its reality, comprehensiveness, energy. It comes not from the child itself, but from a power within it; they are in truth the words of God, in the manner, the sayings of the Old Testament.[36]

To state that images and words were filled with possibilities provided Pusey and his fellow reformers with a new reading of Scripture and a new set of interpretive criteria, much of it provided by Augustine.

In the end, the leaders of the Oxford movement went their different ways. Pusey remained active as Regius Professor of Hebrew in Oxford, committed to the catholic movement within the Church of England.

Keble, who had left Oxford to become the Vicar of Hursley, was never offered and, it is said, never wished for, preferment in the Church of England and lived the life of a devoted parish priest. Newman left Oxford for the village of Littlemore in 1842 and in 1845 was received into the Church of Rome. The three met one last time, after an interval of almost two decades, in 1865. Newman, while on the way to Birmingham, visited Hursley to see Keble on 12 September. When he approached the door, the two no longer recognized each other, owing to the passage of years. By sheer chance, Pusey was also there, in another room. In a letter to his son, Pusey related that they "talked comfortably about past, present, future."[37] Yet Newman recalled that one subject dominated the conversation, the manner in which one is to understand the nature of Scripture.[38] Pusey believed that it was a matter on which they could all still agree.

Newman described the end of the day:

> Just before my time for going Pusey went to read the Evening Service in church, and I was left in the open air with Keble himself. . . . We walked a little way, and stood looking in silence at the church and churchyard, so beautiful and calm. Then he began to converse with more of his old tone of intimacy, as if we had never been parted, and soon I was obliged to go.[39]

Upon his leaving, Keble reminded him of the lines in *Macbeth*:

> when shall we three meet again?
> when the hurly-burly's done.
> when the battle's lost and won.

The three never met again.

Notes

1. Owen Chadwick, ed., *The Mind of the Oxford Movement* (Stanford, 1960), p. 17.

2. Chadwick, *Mind*, 23.

3. In 1838, Pusey was to comment that the Fathers had "altogether a deeper way of viewing things than moderns," a view "much more penetrated with a consciousness of the mysterious depth of every work and way of God" (H. P. Liddon, *Life of Edward Bouverie Pusey* [London, 1893], 1:410–411).

4. G. Rowell, *The Vision Glorious: Themes and Personalities of the Catholic Revival in Anglicanism* (Oxford, 1983), 9.

5. Chadwick, *Mind*, 36.

6. Liddon, *Life*, 1:413–419, 436–439.

7. Yngve Brilioth, in his history of the movement, *The Anglican Revival* (London, 1933), 297, puts forward the idea that Augustine and the Latin Fathers were a "channel" for Pusey "for the piety and the theology of the Greek Church." Certainly, Clement of Alexandria, Athanasius, Irenaeus, Gregory Nazianzen,

Chrysostom, and Cyril were all prominent in Pusey's writing, but Augustine and Ambrose are the glass through which they were viewed.

8. Liddon gives very little information concerning the composition of the lectures in his biography but quotes from a letter of 15 September 1836 to the Rev. B. Harrison, in which Pusey writes:

> I have not yet got through the types and prophecies of the Pentateuch, or, rather, I am but just commencing the types of the ritual, so that I hardly suppose that during the vacation I shall get beyond the Pentateuch. And then I shall have, if possible, to prepare lectures for the next term, even if I have enough for this. (Liddon, *Life*, 1:399)

The flyleaf of the manuscript, written in a different hand from the body of the work, simply indicates that the lectures were written "mainly in July–August, 1836." The numerous corrections and strikeovers in the manuscript, however, give support to the view that Pusey continued to work on the lectures, possibly with publication in mind, for some time after the period under discussion.

The unpublished manuscript of the "Lectures on Types and Prophecies of the Old Testament," is cited hereafter as "MS," followed by page reference. In the transcriptions used in this paper, Pusey's abbreviations have been spelled out, but his punctuation, spellings, and attributions have been retained, except where noted by square brackets within the text.

9. The strong patristic, and especially Augustinian, emphasis on the interpretation of Scripture may clearly be seen in Pusey's letter on "Reading in Preparation for Holy Orders: (*Spiritual Letters of E. B. Pusey, D.D.*, ed. J. O. Johnston and W. C. E. Newbolt [London, 1898], letter 39, 281–283), in which the commentaries of Augustine take pride of place.

10. Liddon, *Life*, 1:400.

11. Anne Mozley, *Letters and Correspondence of John Henry Newman during His Life in the English Church*, 2 vols. (London, 1911), 1:186.

12. Liddon, *Life*, 1:400.

13. DDC 3.27.

14. Cf. A. M. Allchin, "The Theological Vision of the Oxford Movement," in *The Rediscovery of Newman: An Oxford Symposium*, ed. J. Coulson and A. M. Allchin (London, 1967), 50–75; and D. Jasper, "Pusey's 'Lectures on Types and Prophecies of the Old Testament,'" in *Pusey Rediscovered*, ed. P. Butler (London, 1983), 51–70. The manuscript of the lectures was also consulted and quoted by A. Haerdelin, *The Tractarian Understanding of the Eucharist* (Uppsala, 1965); and was referred to in a cursory manner by O. W. Jones, *Issac Williams and His Circle* (London, 1971).

15. Liddon, *Life*, 4:391.

16. Cf. MS, 9 and 14–15.

17. Keble may have already come under the influence of *DDC* or, at least, have inculcated its ideals in opposition to the prevailing tide of Anglican rationalism. He comments in his commonplace book:

> Christianity is not a matter of logical arrangements, or philosophical investigation; much less of rhetorical skill. Not that these things are useless, as talents. But then it

216 / Duane W. H. Arnold

should always be remembered, that they are only talents, and will, accordingly, prove worse than useless, except they be united with a rare humility. ("Commonplace Book," Keble College MSS, pp. 50–51)

18. MS, 1.
19. DDC 3.10.
20. MS, 1–2.
21. DDC 3.10.
22. MS, 3.
23. DDC 2.9.
24. MS, 12.
25. DDC 1.40.
26. MS, 6.
27. DDC 2.12.
28. MS, 6.
29. DDC 3.34.
30. MS, 8.
31. MS, 60.
32. The impact of this Augustinian view upon Newman was especially telling. Erich Przywara, in his essay "St. Augustine and the Modern World," (in *A Monument to Saint Augustine* [London, 1945], 251–286), describes Newman as the one in whom Augustine's "spirit finds its perfect reincarnation" (279). Certainly, Newman's reading of Augustine with regard to the Donatist movement helped to occasion his move to the Church of Rome (cf. G. Bonner, *St. Augustine of Hippo: His Life and Controversies* [London, 1963], 252, n. 1, for a discussion of this matter). Walter Jost, in *Rhetorical Thought in John Henry Newman* ([Columbia, SC, 1989], 8–9), indicates the influence of both Cicero and Augustine upon Newman's concept of rhetoric and provides several examples of Newman's attitudes toward the interpretation of Scripture which is in keeping both with the lectures of Pusey and the thought of Augustine in *DDC* (Bonner, 115).
33. MS, 2.
34. J. H. Newman, *Essays Critical and Historical* (London, 1871), 1:42–44.
35. DDC 3.6.
36. MS, 14.
37. Liddon, *Life*, 4:110.
38. Newman, *Letters,* ed. Mozley, 111: letter of J. H. Newman to Sir John Coleridge.
39. Newman, letter to Sir John Coleridge (*Letters*, 111–112).

De doctrina christiana and Modern Hermeneutics

CYRIL O'REGAN

In this paper the direction of investigation is not from the present to the past but, rather, from the past to the present as this throws light on a possible hermeneutic future. Instead, therefore, of *De doctrina christiana* being interrogated according to some interpretive scheme, held either implicitly or explicitly by the interpreter, specific modern or rather postmodern hermeneutic schemes that have the biblical text at least as a prime focus are interrogated by Augustine's classic text. For purposes of economy I intend assuming something like scholarly consensus regarding Augustine's basic positions in that text on a number of important matters of interest to contemporary philosophical and theological hermeneutics, matters such as the question of the relation of language and reality in general, the relation of biblical language to a presumptive absolute reality in particular, the nature of understanding, the status of the biblical text, and the primacy of the literal sense of Scripture as well as its relation to tropes. Only the first three matters, however, play any role in the present paper. How *De doctrina* illuminates modern reflection on the status of the biblical text, the primacy of the literal sense, and the theory of tropes will be postponed until another occasion.

Yet this still leaves open the crucially important question of what modern or postmodern positions most merit interrogation, a question which seems quite compelling given the range of contemporary option. To avoid the adventitiousness of merely personal choice, there is a need for some definite criteria governing selection.

Since it seems idle to have Augustine's classic text interrogate hermeneutic positions that are inherently hostile to Christianity and its sacred text, inherently allergic to premodern disposition toward the Bible as

218 / Cyril O'Regan

Scripture, antithetical rationalistic and/or positivistic positions and constitutionally suspicious hermeneutic regimes do not suggest themselves as plausible candidates. A first criterion, therefore, would remove from consideration modern and postmodern hermeneutic positions which define themselves as being fundamentally opposed to the biblical text and traditional claims made on its behalf. If this criterion restricts the possible range of conversation, it does so only to a limited extent. For, if it is a quite typical feature of modernity that the biblical text comes under particularly close scrutiny, and is submitted to corrosive criticism from Enlightenment as well as post-Enlightenment quarters, this is not to deny that the modern, as well as postmodern, field is characterized by attempts at apologetic justification in which the nature of the biblical text is revisioned, the status of its claims reexamined, the import of its language reassessed.

A second criterion of inclusion-exclusion, therefore, could very well involve the postmodern shelving of a number of modern positions now found to be thoroughly unconvincing. From the postmodern perspective the good intentions of any number of modern hermeneutic rehabilitations count not at all. What is crucial is their degree of success or failure in actual rehabilitation. And there is something almost like a consensus that much of what has passed as rehabilitation has failed quite dismally by effectively colluding with the hermeneutic enemy.[1] Conceivably included on the list of the passé is (a) any hermeneutical position that attempts to resolve or dissolve the biblical text into a series of propositional truth claims with plausible evidential grounds of validation;[2] (b) any hermeneutic position that resolves or dissolves the biblical text into historical claims, implicit or explicit, irrespective of whether these historical claims involve publicly witnessable facts,[3] the mind of the author, redactors, community of origin or community addressed;[4] (c) any hermeneutic position that resolves or dissolves the biblical text into statements about the affections in a psychological sense, even where this resolution is not construed as thoroughly vitiating more traditional claims.[5] Appeal to the second criterion—successful rehabilitation—should considerably narrow the range of option and almost make it manageable.

Logically, however, one would have to include postmodern interpretive forces such as structuralism and deconstruction, despite their ambiguous relation toward Christianity in general, the biblical text in particular. Thus, a plausible third criterion, in the general context of an attempt at something like economy, might involve stipulating that in addition to the selected hermeneutic dispensations to be interrogated by *De doctrina christiana* not being hostile to Christianity and its sacred text (criterion 1), and successful in avoiding modern apologetic *cul de sacs* (criterion 2), they ought to be inherently friendly to the biblical text, according it in some way pride of place in western culture, and to be prepared to adopt or adapt hermeneutic to the specialness, even uniqueness of its case (criterion 3).

Two obvious candidates for examination are the hermeneutic positions of, on the one hand, Hans Frei, and, on the other, Paul Ricoeur and David Tracy. Both hermeneutic positions appear to fulfill successfully all three above criteria.[6]

If both hermeneutic dispositions discern the power of the positivist manifestation of the general Enlightenment credo that religious texts in general, the biblical text in particular, answer to rational protocols, they are also keenly aware of the spell exerted by the modern rhetoric of suspicion which has its major exemplars in Marx, Nietzsche, and Freud, and one might add Feuerbach.[7] Despite the obvious powerful cultural effect of both attitudes, the imperious claims of the propositional verificationists and the prophets of suspicion are officially rejected by Frei's hermeneutic position as well as Ricoeur's and Tracy's. Perhaps, more interestingly, they are rejected on similar grounds. What from the perspective of both hermeneutic regimes is more defining of propositionalist verificationism and the hermeneutics of suspicion is much more nearly the spirit of dogmatism than the spirit of criticism. For positivism and suspicion insist, in their own way, in defining religious discourse and text in the light of anteriorly accepted norms, themselves never further questioned, as to what constitutes the basic parameters of discourse and text. In refusing to sanction the imitation of either of these hermeneutic Procrustes, quite definitely, then, both Frei's regime as well as Ricoeur's and Tracy's successfully satisfy criterion 1.

In addition, both hermeneutic schemes situate themselves within a postromantic, arguably postmodern field of vision and discourse—though in both, "postmodern" suffers from an indetermination and overdetermination of sense[8]—which is thought to provide the vantage point from which it is possible to pass judgment on certain interpretive opinions as fundamentally constituting dead ends, even if such views continue to have currency and enjoy a measure of cultural acceptance. Though Frei does not situate his position either as directly or as self-consciously as Ricoeur and Tracy, it seems fairly safe to contend that with him, as with the Ricoeur-Tracy hermeneutic position he so vigorously contests, the Enlightenment demand to resolve the biblical text into facts of history and/or historical truth claims represents a category mistake.[9] While historical critical method is officially exiled by neither, the literary reading proposed by both put it more or less on permanent probation.[10] Moreover, both hermeneutic regimes represent an act of resistance to modern hermeneutic rehabilitative tendencies that fail to respect sufficiently the biblical text either as poetic or classic text or as Scripture.[11] More specifically, neither Frei nor Tracy and Ricoeur conceive the hermeneutic task à la romanticism as consisting in the heroic attempt to understand the mind of the human authors better than the authors understood themselves,[12] whether that intention is understood to be more nearly conscious or unconscious, or read to be more nearly cognitive or affective in character.[13] Equally for both, while the biblical text could plausibly be claimed to reveal something about the social world of the implied author(s) and/or the social world of those addressed,[14] the real significance of the biblical text is not only not exhausted by such putative discovery but arguably lies elsewhere.

This far from inconsiderable consensus is supplemented by further overlap in which some degree of distance is taken from self-consciously postmodern positions which offer themselves as viable alternatives to modern positions now regarded as discredited and worthy only of being chastised. Though the bases of their respective acts of distanciation may differ as considerably as the bases of their approval[15]—in Frei a commitment to the narrative line of the biblical text, which he finds irreducible to synchronic structure, and in Ricoeur and Tracy a philosophical-anthropological theory concerning the historicity and narrativity of the subject who is both a producer and receiver of texts[16]—neither hermeneutic disposition seriously entertains structuralism's exclusive claims to hermeneutical adequacy.[17] And lastly—though the situation here is much less clear and much more complex—of neither hermeneutic ethos could it be said that deconstruction is in any unambiguous way supported. Yet it should also be added that neither interprets itself in antithetical fashion to deconstruction, and in a certain sense both are capable of aligning themselves strategically with deconstruction against each other.[18]

1. Reference and Truth

The first area where the Augustine of *De doctrina christiana* can call across the modern fault line and interrogate postmodern hermeneutic positions sympathetic to premodern interpretive practice, and maybe, to some degree at least, premodern interpretation of this practice,[19] is that of reference. In books 1 and 2 of Augustine's classic text, where he lays out his theory of the sign (*signum*), we are led to believe in the referring function of the sign. The sign, the text would have it, implies a signified. Though, for Augustine, a sign can stand for another sign, the relation of sign and signified most definitely is not thought of either as a merely immanent semiotic relation, after the fashion of de Saussure, or as a more or less infinite deferral, after the fashion of Derridean correction of de Saussure.[20] If not immediately, then mediatedly and in the last instance, the relation of sign and signified reduces to that of sign and thing (*res*). Thus, a sign refers to a thing and truth connotes the correspondence of sign and thing.

As has been pointed out by Derrida, especially in *Of Grammatology*,[21] the medieval theory of the sign, which owed so much to Augustine and in particular to *De doctrina*, supposes the "transcendental signified" that is God. God or Logos, or better God as Logos, is the aleotheological pivot of a system of semantics, since God is the extra-semiotic guarantor of the adequacy of signs. And it would be consistent with the deconstructionist viewpoint to extrapolate that what is implied with regard to the semantic system as a whole finds, at once, its code and most significant illustration in the biblical text, which is supposedly God's word concerning self and self-enactment.

Now, while it would be intrinsically unwise to assume that Augustine's insistence on the extra-linguistic intention of discourse and text, biblical discourse and text in particular, corresponds in any exact way to a modern theory of reference such as that found, for instance, presented in Frege, it is the case that on the level of explicit hermeneutical reflection on the biblical text Augustine's own classic text establishes a baseline from which to assess modern views of the signifying function of the biblical text, each of which in its own way challenges a straightforward referentialist understanding. Of course, for Augustine's classic text to function critically, attention should be paid to the different placement of the question of reference in Augustine's premodern text and the postmodern texts of Ricoeur, Tracy, and Frei. In Augustine, it could be said that in line with Aristotle's theory of meaning, reference in the last instance is at the level of the word.[22] By contrast, acknowledging in their quite different ways that the semantic horizon more properly belongs to units of discourse larger than the sentence, the question of reference emerges in Ricoeur and Tracy, on the one hand, and Frei, on the other, only within the horizon of text.[23]

A starting point for both postmodern hermeneutic regimes is the crisis of ostensive reference, which is perhaps the focal, but not necessarily originating, crisis of the status of meaning and truth in the Western Christian tradition. While the *terminus a quo* of this crisis admits of much debate, there is some general agreement among scholars, including the proponents of the rival hermeneutic schemes under discussion, that the Enlightenment represents the high point of the crisis.[24] Moreover, whatever its archeological credentials for both hermeneutic regimes—though arguably Ricoeur and Tracy are more mute here—both schemes appear to see the

Enlightenment as being in some sense determinative for most modern hermeneutic reflection. That is, even in its very disavowal, Enlightenment insistence on the unqualified validity of ostensive reference sets the terms for post-Enlightenment construal in which, in the order of decreasing charity, the biblical text is interpreted as a mere carrier of affect, harmlessly nonsensical, or an ideology transmitter.

While Frei's *Eclipse* provides the most eloquent, as well as most developed, historical account concerning the crisis of ostensive reference that sets the terms of the specifically modern hermeneutic problematic, a not too dissimilar account can be pieced together from the texts of Ricoeur and Tracy. What receives considerably more attention in Frei, however, is what might be called the initiating crisis in which the whithers of the premodern understanding of the relation between sign and signified in general, the nexus of biblical signs and the reality putatively disclosed in particular, are undone. Though Frei does not enter Augustine's name into his account, nor bring *De doctrina* explicitly into his discussion, Augustine's classic text has to be regarded as in some way hermeneutically exemplary for the premodern period, and this exemplary status will not be without critical effect, as will be seen later, concerning Frei's own position.

In Frei's magnum opus, the question of the relation of postmodern to modern construal of the biblical text occurs within the context of a complex genealogy which has the premodern to the fore in a focal way not matched in the various texts of Ricoeur and Tracy. And thus, perhaps, the real question being asked in Frei's text is not how is one to understand the relation between a moribund hermeneutic modernity and a postmodern understanding representing a live and livable option, but, rather, what is the relation of postmodern to premodern construal given the structural interruption and disfigurement of the modern crisis of reference. As we shall shortly see, something like a version of Frei's comprehensive hermeneutic view is hinted at in the margins of the texts of Ricoeur and Tracy, and thus in a sense Frei's generative question marks their texts also.[25] For the moment, however, I shall concentrate upon Frei's comprehensive thesis and generative question, in which is offered a highly influential account of the normative and transgressive views of meaning and truth. I am of the opinion that Frei's account is both more complex, and possibly more ambiguous, than has been understood by friend and foe alike.

FREI'S IN-PARENTHESIS THESIS

A major claim of *The Eclipse* is that with regard to the biblical text the issue of reference, and, thus, the issue of truth, can be put in parenthesis.

Frei has, of course, more than one warrant for making this claim, the weakest of which is his respect for the literary theory of New Criticism, with its horror of paraphrase and its avocation of the immanence of sense. Arguably representing a more serious warrant for Frei is Karl Barth's imperially non-anxious exegetical practice in which the clarification of Scripture was not held hostage by, or to, the task of asserting truth claims that depended upon extra-scriptural principles of validation. The most serious, the most basic, warrant of all, however, is Frei's view that in the Christian tradition in general, in the Reformation in particular, the biblical text did not function in such a way that the question of truth became the determinative, and even an essential, issue.

Contra much that has passed in Frei interpretation, the *in-parenthesis* thesis connotes less a single consistent view than a variety of related views in tension with each other. At least three different views can be discerned in Frei's published works. First, there is what might be called the *indifference* view. This is the in-parenthesis view proper, in which it is claimed that historically and normatively Christian interpretation of the biblical text is characterized by a lack of difference or distinction between meaning and truth.[26] Second, there is the view that the exclusive horizon of the biblical text is that of meaning rather than truth. Here Frei, influenced by New Criticism, and determined by an argumentative framework which distinguishes in authoritative fashion between "sense" and "reference" on the one hand, "meaning" and "truth" on the other, opts for one side of an infrastructural antithesis.[27] Sense and meaning are valorized at the expense of reference and truth. Accordingly, this view, which might be labeled the *exclusion of truth* view, presents a much stronger thesis regarding reference and truth than the indifference view. Third, there appears to be internal to Frei's work a move of compromise or *emendation*, wherein Frei suggests that, understood historically and normatively, meaning in the biblical text is sufficiently capacious as to be able to co-opt the function of truth without thereby turning sense into reference.[28]

Pointing out the variety of claim in Frei's work is a desideratum for this paper, for the agreement-disagreement ratio between Frei and Ricoeur and Tracy on the relation of language and reality and the nature of biblical language in particular, it could be argued, depends in large part on which of the above views is being asserted. More specifically, it might be suggested that it is only in Frei's assertion of the second and strongest version of the in-parenthesis view that the two hermeneutic regimes enter into open conflict. Certainly, it is the assertion of the exclusion of truth view that makes the debate between these postmodern regimes critical. We will be turning to this dispute in due course; but before we do, something should be said about views 1 and 3.

Plausibly at least, the indifference view funds three interlocking claims, two of them descriptive-historical, and one normative: (a) the descriptive-historical claim that the premodern reading of the biblical text is characterized by a lack of distinction between the spheres of meaning and truth; (b) the normative claim that indifference toward the distinction, even any distinction, between meaning and truth is part of the "grammar" of the Christian faith; (c) another descriptive-historical claim that, the modern interruption of assumption notwithstanding, in the contemporary, postmodern world the biblical text not only ought to be read without eye to reference and truth but can be so read and at least in some quarters is so read. Now, clearly all three of these claims are contestable.

I wish to focus at the moment on the relation between the different aspects of Frei's historical thesis (a and c), with specific attention to the question whether there are any relevant differences with respect to how Christians can read, and do in fact read, the biblical text either side of the modern love affair with truth and reference such that the word *post* signifies more than a historical placement. If there are differences, Frei is not especially forthcoming about specification, and yet he does show some resistance to characterizing his position as premodern. There are a number of different ways of describing this resistance and accounting for Frei's reluctance. One possibility—not necessarily the only one—is that Frei sees his essential task as much more nearly consisting in the assertion of, on the one hand, a profound isomorphism (a structural point) between a twentieth-century interpretive practice he wishes to recommend and premodern interpretive practice he regards as both pervasive and normative, and, on the other, a significant, even massive, continuity between these dispensations interrupted by the hiatus that is modernity (a genetic point). Nonetheless, resisting the assertion of identity between the postmodern and premodern logically implies difference. Frei neither explores the difference, nor specifies in any explicit way either its etiology or its character.

Still, without awarding to modernity the prerogative of setting the agenda of hermeneutics, as he feels other explicitly post-critical hermeneutical regimes do,[29] Frei does appear to think of modernity as a caesura that cannot completely be jumped over, or at least not so in the discursive field of theology which, even as an intra-ecclesial enterprise, is likely to take in the more modernity-constituted public in an act of peripheral vision. Thus, it is possible that despite his consistent support of a Barthian-like fit between community belief and the reflective act of the theologian, a fit apparently indifferent to historical context, in the postmodern situation Frei seems forced to imply, even if he does not fully admit, an asymmetry.

While on the level of unreflective intramural reading, the parity between premodern and postmodern reading may be such as almost to risk speaking of identity and recrudescence, on the level of reflective intramural reading, exact parity seems to break down. And it breaks down, because every and any reflective intramural reading in the postmodern world will necessarily have at least penumbral awareness of alternative discursive practices, e.g., scientific or humanist discursive practices and alternative, more "modern" ways of construing Scripture, if it is to engage, as it wishes to do, in even *ad hoc* apologetics.[30] This is so, since the rendering comprehensible of one's stance on the biblical text will in some way, however implicitly, involve distinquishing it from modern positions which still have currency and other postmodern positions which have begun to exercise influence. And this has the effect that a gap, however small,—a fracture, however hairline,—opens in the contemporary field between unreflective community interpretive practice and the reflective interpretive practice of the theologian. Therefore, even if the postmodern hermeneutic of a Frei type is not constituted by the modern problematic, neither can it fully escape its gravitational pull. Or, to avail of another well-worn, if not thoroughly shop-soiled, metaphor from physics, it might be said that by a kind of parallax the (unexcised) presence of modernity can be inferred. And this presence, however much a vanishing quantum, accounts for the gap which insinuates itself in postmodernity between the unreflective and reflective orders of biblical interpretation; indeed, perhaps, constitutes the real bedrock of the distinction of level. In a sense a shorthand for speaking of this is to say that Frei is in the ultimate analysis undecided between Barth and Schleiermacher.[31]

Moreover, it is arguably the case that the gap in the order of interpretation in turn points back to the internally complex or "reflected" nature of the "caesura" between premodern and postmodern understanding of the biblical text. The caesura is complex rather than simple, for the difference does not consist simply in the fact that Frei's postmodern hermeneutic is characterized by peripheral acknowledgment of rival hermeneutic views, specific to modernity, that are being either explicitly rejected or ignored. Though this *content distinction* is a symptom of the caesura, it is but one aspect of a more complex picture.

The other determining aspect concerns the difference in the relation between the common and expert exegetical practices either side of the modern fault line. If Frei can entertain the essentially Barthian position that the premodern hermeneutic situation is characterized by continuity between unreflective and reflective exegetical practice, such that the model is really more nearly captured by the metaphor of a continuum than the misleading metaphor of level—which tends to insinuate a discontinuity of a fundamental kind—there are suggestions that after the modern hiatus this continuum, even if one wishes to postulate a continuum, is definitely no longer seamless. This second aspect of distinction, though it relates in the closest possible way to the first, represents what might be called the *formal distinction* between premodern and postmodern hermeneutics of the biblical text. Needless to say, even outside the context of the debate between the two rival postmodern interpretive schools, it would be interesting to ask the question whether in fact there is the seamless unity between unreflective and reflective interpretive practice that Frei suggests to be accurate for the premodern period, whether in fact in the pre-Reformation period there is some evidence of gap, some evidence of the insinuation of qualitative difference in interpretive level, and whether a classic hermeneutic text such as *De doctrina* does not call for some qualification.

Whether *De doctrina* calls for revision of the historical part of Frei's thesis or not, it is tempting to hypothesize that in Frei's scheme of things the almost—but not quite—erasable difference in postmodernity between scriptural interpretation in unreflective faith avowal and scriptural interpretation in the context of reflective theological practice opens a way toward explaining the tension in Frei's work between different versions of his in-parenthesis view. For looked at from the perspective of unreflective Christianity, both described and recommended by Frei, it is clear that the most adequate hermeneutic position is the first or indifference view. The indifference view represents in fact the discursively self-conscious extrapolation of the felt unproblematic nature of the question of whether or not there exists a distinction between meaning and truth. Thus, when Frei speaks on behalf of unreflective faith, as after Barth he desires to, he tends to validate the first of the three in-parenthesis views that the commentator meets in his texts. Contrariwise, the hypothesis suggests itself that assertion of the second version of the in-parenthesis view is contingent on Frei situating himself in the reflective zone of interpretation, where there is a felt need to define interpretation of the biblical text over against a modern referential claim experienced as imperial, at least in high culture. That is, Frei's embracing of meaning only or sense only represents at a less than fully articulate, or even conscious, level a reaction to the modern avocation of truth only or reference only. Thus, Frei situates himself in a hermeneutic context that, despite explicit avowal, has undergone displacement, a displacement which in the first instance announces a content distinction between the premodern and the postmodern hermeneutic situation, and, arguably, in consequence points even to a formal distinction between them.

Though I will not be able to go into much detail, it is necessary to say at least a few words about the third of the three views that constitute the tensional field of the in-parenthesis thesis. This view can be variously labeled, though I prefer *emendation* to *compromise*. Most clearly proposed in the essay, "'Narrative' in Christian and Modern Reading," Frei pulls back from his second and most immanentist reading without suggesting the ultimate prerogative of reference. In what looks like an attempt to un-couple truth from reference, Frei seems to admit that more than meaning is involved in the reading, and plausibly also the production, of the bibli-cal text. Nevertheless, he goes on to argue, truth never fully breaks free from meaning, a position he believes is advocated by much of modern and some postmodern thought, including Tracy and Ricoeur. In a quite definite sense Frei seems to be involved in correcting the second version of the in-parenthesis thesis back in the direction of the first, while still wish-ing to maintain that if a relative priority question ever arose, it would be decided in favor of meaning. But that is *if*, and if we are correct thus far in our interpretation, then this hypothetical only becomes categorical in the move from the unreflective to the reflective level of interpretation in a particularly wrought, if not fraught, situation. Even if it were agreed that in the overall economy of Frei's work the third in-parenthesis view has only a functional importance, when brought into conversation with Au-gustine's classic text it shows itself plausibly as at once more in line with the supposed historical-normative fit between unreflective and reflective modes of interpretation and more nearly in negotiation with the kind of interpretive view advanced in *De doctrina*, which if it does hold to a form of reference, also adheres to a conception of the intimate relation between truth and meaning that is not adequately captured in a distinction be-tween grammatical sense and the intended truth of biblical discourse. In a quite definite sense there is a kind of condensing of meaning and truth suggested from the metaperspective of *De doctrina* that parallels, but nev-ertheless is not identical to, that proposed in the third version of the Frei thesis. The specific motor for the condensation in Augustine, it might be argued, is the fact that no language, not even biblical language, fully cap-tures God (*DDC* 1.6 ff.), since even biblical language is an accommo-dation. Thus, if Augustine is, unlike Frei, prepared to associate truth and reference, this is not to say that reference functions in the kind of straight-forward way it does on the empirical level. God, as the truth, sustains biblical language, while at the same time resisting capture in language's referential function.

RICOEUR AND TRACY: REHABILITATION OF REFERENCE

Turning now to Ricoeur and Tracy, it can be said that their strategy of response to modern hermeneutic imperatives that refuse to privilege the

biblical text is quite different. Rather than recommending putting reference and truth in parenthesis, with respect to the biblical text in
particular, literary or poetic texts and religious texts in general, they promote their reenvisagement. If study 7 in *The Rule of Metaphor* is the
locus classicus of Ricoeur's unfolding of reconstrual of reference, it is in
his essay, "The Model of the Text" that he is most declarative concerning
his act of reenvisagement. In a passage, wherein Frei located an essential
difference of estimate and interest,[32] Ricoeur writes:

> The text speaks of a possible world and a possible way of orienting oneself
> within it. The dimensions of this world are properly opened up by, disclosed
> by the text. Disclosure is the equivalent for written language of ostensive
> reference for spoken language.[33]

We will need to thematize Ricoeur's, but also Tracy's model of truth, as
guided by the Heideggerian half-metaphor, half-construct of disclosure,
before we conclude discussion of our second exemplary response to the
modern crisis of reference.

Something must first be said, however, about explicit Ricoeurian-
Tracian reenvisagement of the specifically modern commitment to
ostensive reference, a reenvisagement which sharply distinguishes this particular postmodern hermeneutic scheme from Frei's. At its most basic
level there is a general call to reconceive the nature of the referential function in the context of poetic or classic texts. While those who would make
the demand for straightforward reference can legitimately appeal to Aristotle's theory of rhetoric, as indeed to its prolongation in Latin rhetoric
in Cicero, Quintillian, and arguably even Augustine, Ricoeur in *The Rule
of Metaphor*, in particular, is anxious to insist against classical rhetoric,
and any positivistic modern application of it, that reference at the level of
text, poetic text in particular, (1) functions predicatively rather than nom-
inatively, and (2) functions indirectly rather than directly.[34] Thus, as
against the positivistic insistence that the poetic text must describe or correspond to a state of affairs already constituted, Ricoeur, and Tracy after
him, maintain that the semantic configuration of the poetic or classic text
more nearly redescribes than describes, and more nearly constitutes the
very state of affairs it represents.

This reply operates on the level of first principles. When Ricoeur's and
Tracy's attention turn to actual interpretive practice of poetic or classic
texts, they discern that the modern commitment to ostensive reference gets
discharged under the auspices of a referent "behind" the text, whether that
text is the Bible, another religious text of the Christian tradition, a sacred
or canonic text of another religious tradition, or simply a classic text of a
nonreligious sort.[35] For the referent behind the text can be understood in

any number of ways, e.g., the facts named, the person bespoken, the conscious or unconscious intention of the author, the social world of the author and/or the audience addressed.[36] For both also the major problem with this view is less the conjectural status of the referent disclosed by the very texts the referent is presumed to explain, than the fact that being behind the text the referent is disengaged from dialogue with interpreters.[37] Whatever else it is, the referent is open rather than closed, and if not indeterminate, then overdetermined, such that it is not exhausted by any particular actualization, nor even their historical sum.[38] Perhaps, the most perspicuous language in which this idea is couched is that of virtuality or omnitemporality.[39] As the poetic or classic text inscribes a virtual meaning that is only actualized in reading, so also the poetic or classic text bears a virtual referent that is only actualized in the existence of a reader for whom what the text says, what the text is about, matters.[40] However, in a move which Frei thinks lacks persuasiveness, because it appears to be exclusively determined by conceptual need rather than validated by argument,[41] Ricoeur, and Tracy after him, suggest that the referent be understood as being "in front of" or "ahead" of the text. Projected in front of the text, the referent becomes available to the understanding of a subject for whom temporal distanciation, it happily turns out, does not constitute a crippling disadvantage.[42] As understood by both, the referent has the quality not of a thing—unless Heidegger's revisionist notion is taken into account[43]—but rather of world as pattern of existential meaningfulness.

Ricoeur's and Tracy's support for a revised theory of reference to cover, in increasing order of specificity, "poetic" text, religious text, biblical text is not constructed in conscious opposition to Frei's in-parenthesis proposal. Indeed, on the level of general hermeneutic theory, covering all textual production and reception, Frei cannot in principle argue, since he officially eschews a general hermeneutic, indeed restricts his hermeneutic comments and remarks to the biblical text.[44] Interestingly, however, a hermeneutic position for which Frei shows some elective affinity, i.e., New Criticism, is found unacceptable in the Ricoeurian-Tracian frame of things.[45] In Ricoeur in particular, a positive *semantic* view of the text goes hand in hand with articulated disavowal of the purely semiotic character of the text. While Ricoeur, for instance, is prepared to concede that at a basic or primitive level a text admits of being construed as an interlocking network of signs, he disputes the semioticians view that this network constitutes the text as text. Poetic texts, religious texts, the biblical text, all display a coherence of sense and meaning.[46] The text, therefore, in Ricoeur's view is semantic rather than purely semiotic.

But Ricoeur does not stop here. Taking his distance from a hermeneutic view that would be sanctioned by, among others, New Criticism,

Ricoeur suggests that a "poetic" text of any description—what Tracy would call a "classic" text—is not adequately understood as an immanent, self-enclosed sphere of sense. Indeed, as Tracy quite plausibly points out, even those classic immanentists' texts by Mallarmé and Joyce cannot rightly be said to operate on the level of pure sense, in spite of the fact that what they are "about" is language itself. Accordingly, the quintessential self-reflexive texts of Mallarmé and Joyce, which have been claimed by modernists and postmodernists alike, refer, in however a modest and reduced fashion, beyond themselves. On the most general level of reflection, after Heidegger and Gadamer, Ricoeur and Tracy conclude that poetic and classic texts are *about* something, even if that something is not usually, and perhaps even rarely, something ready at hand. Accepting Heidegger's de-reification of the function of discourse, both focus on the disclosive power of the text, its ability to open up a "possible" world, a world that demands both our attention and allegiance.[47] Thus, availing of Frege's classic sense-reference distinction, Ricoeur, and Tracy after him,[48] insist on reference. For Ricoeur in particular this means that the semantic level is configured into a "surface" semantic (meaning or sense) and a "depth" semantic (reference), and the text as a whole understood as a threefold configuration, even dynamism, from the semiotic to the surface semantic to the depth semantic level.[49]

It is not our brief here to question Ricoeur's extension of the term "semantic" to include reference, though clearly it has something to do with his (and also Tracy's) Kantian-like, antidogmatic realist view that texts simply mimic extra-linguistic states of affairs.[50] But a few words might be said about the model of truth appealed to in Ricoeur's (and Tracy's) defense of the referential function of language as this swerves from Enlightenment rendition of ostensive reference. The Heideggerian *disclosure* model of truth, supported by both, is brought into alignment with a view of reference which commonly supports and is supported by a correspondence theory of truth. That there is a real problem here is difficult to deny. The replacement of a correspondence model of truth by a disclosure model, arguably, so alters the meaning of "reference" that it becomes brazen in the extreme to claim that one's hermeneutic profile does not essentially disobey the dictates of ostensive reference. Indeed, a referentialist critic could with some justice claim that Ricoeur's and Tracy's support of reference trades on the established Fregean discourse of reference so as to thereby recoup the objectivity that appears to be lost when the text is spoken of as "disclosing" rather than "corresponding" to a world. But, of course, "world" language is already in its own way suggestive, for it represents a replacement for unadulterated "thing" language; and its use, the acceptance of the Heideggerian heuristic that "higher than actuality is possibility." While Ricoeur and Tracy would undoubtedly feel the force of the referentialist's criticism, it is not likely that they would be persuaded to recant. One line of defense obviously open to them, but one which as far as I am aware has not been averted to, is that the appearance of contradiction arises if and only if the correspondence and disclosure models are interpreted beforehand as antithetical rather than simply different. And such an assumption is not so obvious as it might first appear, and stands in need of argumentative justification. Indeed, Ricoeur and Tracy might argue that the alignment of the disclosure model with reference is prepared within the context of Heidegger's classical adumbration of the disclosure model. For if it is the case that Heidegger's *aletheia* model of truth is elaborated as an alternative to the correspondence or *adequatio* model, this does not discourage the later Heidegger from synecdochally transferring selected elements of the correspondence view into his newly minted theory of truth.[51]

Though the situation does not turn out to be quite as clear as it might seem at first sight, it is perfectly obvious that at some level Frei's and Ricoeur's (also Tracy's) explicit understanding of the appropriateness of the categories of "reference" and "truth" regarding the biblical text differ considerably. Still, there is a difference between saying "differ considerably" and "radically contradict each other." Refusal to countenance the latter does not necessarily, however, indicate pusillanimity and the desire for a peaceable universe. For it is not simply diplomatic to point out where conflict can be located, and is located, and where it cannot be located, and is not in fact located. A necessary condition of the possibility of contradiction, for instance, is the assertion of the second and strongest form of Frei's in-parenthesis thesis. That is, only when Frei explicitly excludes the possibility of intelligibly applying the concepts of "truth" and "reference" to the biblical text does a real contradiction emerge. As we have seen, Ricoeur (and Tracy) question the adequacy of any semantic view that stops short, as New Criticism does, with the text considered as artifact constituted by the immanence of meaning. On their account, the natural nisus of the text is from sign to meaning as surface-semantic to truth as depth-semantic. In this case there can be no mistaking the head-on collision. However, in the absence of the assertion of the exclusion of truth version of the in-parenthesis thesis, relations between the two hermeneutic regimes are best described as tensional rather than contradictory.

While Frei is definitely inclined to argue that Ricoeur and Tracy enmesh themselves in the specifically modern scene of construing texts and in consequence offer an inviting and easy target for deconstruction, the fact is that their revisionist construal of "reference" and "truth" makes them linguistically and textually bound in a way unthinkable in modern hermeneutics with its thoroughgoing commitment to trans-linguistic truth. If not quite reducible to meaning and sense, this nevertheless involves truth and reference in a much greater proximity than is typical in modernity. Indeed, some critics might claim (a) that it is only by contracting sense into syntactical meaning that a wedge can be placed between meaning and truth; (b) that the disclosure model of truth effectively dismantles the distinction between meaning and truth, if meaning is considered as something more than syntactically well-formed sentences. Whatever the value of these criticisms, the textual constitution of reference and truth in the texts of Ricoeur and Tracy, and especially the former, brings their view into conversation with the two weaker forms of Frei's in-parenthesis thesis. Ricoeur's and Tracy's view bears a surprising family resemblance, in fact, to Frei's third formulation, wherein in a move of an emendatory sort it was stipulated that apparent reference elements espied in the biblical text were a function of sense, just as apparent truth elements were a function of meaning.

A few words might also be spent commenting on the relation between Ricoeur's and Tracy's view and the first form of Frei's in-parenthesis thesis, i.e., the indifference hypothesis. This hypothesis has two aspects, a historical and a normative aspect. Now, the first and most obvious point to make is that since neither Ricoeur nor Tracy has written an equivalent to Frei's *The Eclipse,* and what they have written focuses more nearly on the relation between modernity and postmodernity than on the relations between premodernity and modernity and premodernity and postmodernity, it is necessary to indulge in a little extrapolation. From what they suggest, however, in and through their phenomenological elaboration of the status of the biblical text, not only is the normative aspect of Frei's in-difference position implicitly contested (but not contradicted), but by implication the historical aspect also. However closely tied sense and reference, meaning and truth are in the Ricoeurian-Tracian oeuvre—and I have suggested that they are more closely tied than might at first be admitted—their difference is always affirmed. Normatively, therefore, the indifference hypothesis is contested, and it is contested even if this hypothesis is read, as it ought to be, in a functionalist manner. What does this say about the possible contours of a Ricoeurian-Tracian historical thesis congruent with their presumed normative stand? First, it should be said that a number of historical theses are in principle congruent with this particular normative option. For instance, it is consistent with this particular normative stand to argue that it is only in the postmodern, postcritical situation that Scripture is read in the way described-prescribed in the texts of Ricoeur and Tracy. However, it is at the same time also consistent with the normative view to argue that the disclosure-referential reading in practice (if not in theory) found exemplars in the premodern field. And the textual situation does seem to mirror the logic of option, with both positions finding textual support.[52] Both logically and textually, therefore, there is an essential undecidability between these two positions, even if it is the latter avowal, most often made by Tracy, which suggests the most interesting avenue for investigation in the present circumstances.

By way of concluding discussion regarding reference, it is clear that using *De doctrina* as a baseline allows both the difference between the two postmodern regimes to be set in relief and the fundamental demarcation between both of these postmodern views of signification in the biblical text and Augustine's classic view to come into view. Since more than enough has been said about the former, I will content myself with supplementing the few remarks that have been made about the latter. First, with respect to Frei, it can be said that even if Augustine's commitment to truth as well as meaning does not involve him in explicit contestation with the third version of the in-parenthesis thesis, it most definitely involves him in explicit contestation of the second of the three versions, i.e., the exclusion of truth view, as well as that aspect of the in-difference view that involves total parity between unreflective and reflective interpretive practice. Second, with respect to Ricoeur and Tracy, while Augustine would not eschew the inalienably existential horizon of reading, the reading of the biblical text in particular, in *De doctrina* he wishes to insist on the kind of separation of truth and its appropriation that finds no sanction in the texts of Ricoeur and Tracy, where appropriation plays the role of a co-constituter of truth. Truth, Augustine wishes to say, is already fully constituted in the biblical text. It is, in a manner of speaking, already event. Appropriation is not in any way constitutive of the truth, simply of the human entry into the truth, which truth may or may not be seen, may or may not be appropriated. But even if seen, there is no automatic guarantee of appropriation, for perversity is always and everywhere a possibility.

2. Understanding the Biblical Text

A second major point of demarcation between the postmodern hermeneutic regimes, which appeal to *De doctrina* enables one to highlight, is the varying understanding of what constitutes "understanding" the biblical text. For both Ricoeur and Tracy a primary, perhaps the primary, aim of interpreting the biblical text is, in consonance with their general hermeneutic theory, understanding in which a meaningful existential world is disclosed.[53] Ricoeur, in particular, could not be more clear:

it is disclosure that mediates text and understanding by projecting a world of meaning ahead of the text for understanding to appropriate. If within their hermeneutic scheme by no means every feature of romanticist hermeneutics is disavowed, or even seriously contested, some features most definitely are. In contradistinction to certain simplifying tendencies in romanticist hermeneutics, Ricoeur and Tracy wish to oppose a more complex reading which (a) offers more than notional acknowledgment of the basic foreignness of the text that comes into co-relation with the interpreter's understanding; and (b) elucidates the structural impediments to the tyranny of the divinatory impulse.[54] More specifically, they insist, à propos Gadamer, on temporal, even constitutional distanciation between the world of the text and that of the interpreter, as they also insist as a methodological desideratum on intercalating text explication (or explanation) between the interpretive alpha of preunderstanding or intuition of the text's sense and the interpretive omega of full-blown understanding which centrally involves, as we have seen above, appropriation of a referent which is less a thing than a particular way of being in the world.

Explanation, as Ricoeur points out so elegantly in *Interpretation Theory,* has as its special province the semiotic or surface semantic aspect of the "inscribed" discourse of the text.[55] And in *The Analogical Imagination*, at least, Tracy does not seem to renege on the Ricoeurian view.[56] Explanation, according to Tracy, functions as an interregnum where, if you like, the referential spoils are awarded the appropriative—but definitely not expropriative—understanding. Without in any way suggesting a deconstructive or psychoanalytic background for Tracy's construal, it could be said with some degree of justice that explanation functions as delay and deferral, or a postponement of interpretive gratification. In both Tracy's and Ricoeur's scheme, but predominantly in the latter, certain structural features of romanticist hermeneutics are retained, but only as pedagogically developed: the would-be polymorphous *orexis* of divination submits to a postponement which promises, if not greater, at least a more secure and securely grounded gratification. The interpretive model here bears a striking resemblance to Hegelian *paidea*, an analogy definitely not weakened when the focus becomes the *telos* of interpretation, i.e., understanding exposing itself to epiphanic event mediated by the text. Needless to say, no claim is being made here that, after Hegel, Ricoeur and Tracy suppose that understanding is capable of full comprehension of the referential world or self. For it is quite evident that their hermeneutic posture presupposes Gadamer's critique of the pretensions of Hegelian *Vernunft*, in particular his avowal in *Truth and Method* of the historicity and essential finitude of understanding.[57] In a real sense Ricoeur and Tracy owe a quite significant debt to the Gadamerian braiding of Heidegger and a phenomenological blend that owes something to Husserl but, perhaps, also Hegel. After Heidegger, Ricoeur and Tracy not only emphasize the essential finitude of understanding but also underscore the ontological character of the event of disclosure responsible in the last instance for dismantling the subject-object dichotomy. After phenomenological idealism and/or idealistic phenomenology, Ricoeur and Tracy wish to suggest that the disclosure event finds its respondent or co-respondent in the unveiling of the transcendental dimension of self.

Now, while the potential range of problems for the above alliance, first forged by Gadamer, is broad indeed, it should be noted that, as with Derrida's "critique" of Gadamer,[58] Frei tends to prioritize the phenomenological-idealist note of the putative synthesis. From Frei's perspective, "disclosure" traffics the "presence" of an authentic state of existence into co-relation with the self-presence of the understanding self.[59] Basing his case less on philosophical-anthropological grounds than a close exegetical reading of the paradigmatic personhood of Jesus Christ as recounted in the biblical text, Frei contests the phenomenological model of self-transparence. From Frei's low-hermeneutic vantage point, understanding "understanding" in this way constitutes a misunderstanding. Understanding the biblical text—the text which crucially, indeed exclusively, concerns Frei—is according to Frei more like a skill, a species of know-how. A truly genuine phenomenology of the biblical text rather than disclosing transcendental subjectivity discloses competence or incompetence in the practice of interpretation.[60] Some interpreters will, others will not, be able to read Scripture acutely, whether reading Scripture acutely means moving beyond the mere rehearsal of biblical data to (a) something like an eidetic sense of the basic drift of a passage, a set of passages, or a particular biblical text; (b) demonstrating that one can apply what is discerned to the specific situation of one's life and community.[61] The closest possible philosophical correlative of the kind of position proposed as truly descriptive of understanding the biblical text is, of course, the position espoused by the later Wittgenstein.[62] To speak of understanding the biblical text is not to point to a mental event, but to point to a way of speaking and acting that is cogruent with the implicit community sense of what constitutes appropriate speaking and acting. It is to have a sense, in other words, of the rules of Christian discourse and action and to permit oneself to be governed by these rules, or directed by the grammar of Christian discourse determined in the last instance by the text itself which is the object of interpretation.

At first brush, it seems that the position that most nearly recalls the one suggested in *De doctrina* is Hans Frei's. There in the prologue to Augustine's classic text, the greatest of the Western Fathers suggests a position that borders at least on Frei's emphasis. Specifically, discussing the nature of interpretation of the biblical text with an eye to its transmission, Augustine suggests that understanding does not fundamentally consist in the appropriation of a body of knowledge but, rather, in indicating the presence of a particular kind of reading skill, which is in principle transferable but which may or may not get transferred. For Augustine, then, what good teachers pass on to the succeeding generation is not information but the discipline and freedom to read, the ability "to go on," to invoke the Wittgenstinian locution.

Nevertheless, important as the prologue is for the understanding of *De doctrina*'s view of "understanding," it should not be thought to indicate a complete position that unambiguously prioritizes one of the two postmodern options. The contextual nature of Augustine's very recommendation ought itself to be taken into account. The emphasis upon skill and following a rule is made in a context where Augustine feels called upon to contest, rightly or wrongly, what he perceives to be a growing tendency in the hermeneutic situation of North Africa to emphasize individual, extra-ecclesial talent. Christian tradition, general Christian know-how are in Augustine's opinion being grossly undervalued, and thus important resources for good reading are not being tapped. Moreover, in the absence of some appeal to traditional understanding of what counts as good reading, one is left in a criteriological vacuum respecting conflicting interpretations. But this fundamental act of resistance does not tell the full story. If Augustine wants the Christian to read well, it is, of course, because he wishes the Christian to move closer to an understanding of the truth. But if truth and the moving of a person, Christian or otherwise, toward the truth are logically distinct, this does not mean that Augustine is anxious to introduce too deep a separation between them. If Scripture is an absolutely exemplary instanciation of God's truth, it is also the supreme enactment of God's rhetoric or persuasion that intends to move and convert. As book 4 shows clearly, *De doctrina* does not renounce the conversion quotient Augustine assigned the biblical text in the *Confessiones*, for book 4 of *De doctrina* suggests that truth is constellated in such a way that it has significant persuasive power (*DDC* 4.4, 4.6). The position ennunciated in the prologue must, therefore, be complemented by the different emphasis of book 4, a position that more nearly goes in the direction of the Ricoeurian-Tracian view of the text as a potential transformative act of persuasion issuing in nothing less than a fundamental reorientation, indeed, nothing less than conversion. The truly important gesture of *De doctrina* clearly lies in its inclusiveness, its ability to insist upon both necessities: the necessity to learn to read the biblical story or stories well within certain parameters of ruled use, and at the same time to recognize the rhetorical function of the biblical text both inside and outside the Christian community. In a sense Augustine's classic text constitutes an invitation to both species of postmodern hermeneutics to see their complementarity and, perhaps, also to question emphases, or at least covert implications, in their respective avowals that may not turn out to be hermeneutically or Christianly helpful. For instance, Frei's hermeneutic position could be understood as a corrective to too great an emphasis upon individual hermeneutic talent, and arguably too meretricious and effete an understanding of conversion, where the self may not have fully surrendered its consumer disposition, while Ricoeur and Tracy could be understood as reminding that reading well is not simply repeating, it does indeed mean "going on."

Notes

1. Frei provides the classic expression of this collusion. See his *The Eclipse of Biblical Narrative: A Study in Eighteenth and Nineteenth Century Hermeneutics* (New Haven, 1974). If Ricoeur is not as thetic on this point, nevertheless it does seem to be the case that this view is the corollary of the criticism he levels against the romanticist commitment to the *divinatory* impulse, and the rigid separation asserted between *Verstehen* and *Erklärung*. For Ricoeur's most concise expression of this separation, which tends to honor the hegemony of method by perceiving the specifically hermeneutic as the contradictory, see *Interpretation Theory: Discourse and the Surplus of Meaning* (Fort Worth, Tex., 1976), 71–88. For a similar suggestion in the work of David Tracy, see *Plurality and Ambiguity: Hermeneutics, Religion, and Hope* (San Francisco, 1987), 47–51.

2. Here I have in mind the kind of propositionalist reading of the biblical text that marked Catholic neo-Scholasticism in the nineteenth and twentieth centuries. Under the auspices of the general assumption that theology was essentially a propositional enterprise, the biblical text tended to get read as a matrix of propositions, even if these propositions were unusual in that they were not subject to the same rules of evidence and authentication as other propositions that could be asserted by the natural light of reason. Examples of such peculiar propositions included christological and trinitarian propositions. By the middle of the century the propositionalist dispensation was on the wane. Vatican II represents its definitive surpassing.

3. Frei's *Eclipse* gives a magisterial account of the "facts of history" approach in eighteenth century evidentialism, where the "truths" of Scripture become identified with the historical facts open in principle to judgment regarding their reliability and their truth. Because of this, the central issues now become the question of the status of these facts, the question as to whether there were witnesses, as well as the question as to the reliability of witnesses.

4. Publicly witnessable facts are the prime analogate for all other kinds of historical claims.

5. There are, of course, different ways of doing this. Jung and Schleiermacher provide two quite different examples. While Jung's methodological scruple does not permit him to deny the possibility that religious symbols have an objective correlative, the only verifiable reality of religious symbols is psychological in nature. With regard to Schleiermacher, even if he did not question in any radical way the ontological status of the divine or the christological event, for him religious discourse is, in the last instance, a discourse of the depth experience of the self intentionally related to the Other as objective correlative.

6. Of course, whereas Frei emphasizes the absolute uniqueness and incommensurability of the biblical text, the hermeneutic regimes of Ricoeur and Tracy might be thought to emphasize the specialness of the biblical text that goes all the way to postulating uniqueness but does not issue in any unequivocal way in a claim of incommensurability. See Ricoeur's *Essays in Biblical Interpretation* (Philadelphia, 1980), especially "Toward a Hermeneutic of the Idea of Revelation," 75–118. For Tracy, see *The Analogical Imagination: Christian Theology and the Culture of Pluralism* (New York, 1981), 233–339; also "On Reading the Scriptures Theologically," in *Theology and Dialogue: Essays in Conversation with George Lindbeck*, ed. Bruce D. Marshall (Notre Dame, Ind., 1990), 35–68, especially 58–59, n. 16.

7. Ricoeur puts the category of "prophet of suspicion" into circulation. First used in his Freud book, it has become general intellectual property since. See *Freud and Philosophy: An Essay in Interpretation*, trans. Denis Savage (New Haven and London, 1970), 3–56. The three prophets named are so because of their presumed pervasive effect on all aspects of contemporary culture and experience. Feuerbach, presumably, is not on the same level, precisely because his suspicion has a more local range of application, i.e., the religious sphere. Obviously since Frei's interests are exclusively theological, Feuerbach will be more important to him, as indeed he was to Barth.

8. The constitutional slipperiness of the category "postmodern" is, arguably, not fully sorted out in either regime. However, for Ricoeur it is clear that "postmodern" does not simply signify a chronological ordering but rather a thought matrix that involves a fundamental reordering of presumption and thought patterns influenced, directly or indirectly, by the Enlightenment, also its criticism in and by the prophets of suspicion. To this extent, therefore, while deconstruction would tend to entertain the postmodern candidacy of these prophets, particularly Nietzsche, Ricoeur would question their credentials. Tracy avails himself of the category of "postmodernism" in *The Analogical Imagination*, but for his most explicit use of "postmodern," see *Plurality and Ambiguity: Hermeneutics, Religion, Hope* (San Francisco, 1987), especially 82–114, and his essay, "The Uneasy Alliance Reconceived: Catholic Theological Method, Modernity, and Postmodernism," in *Theological Studies* 50 (1989). While Tracy is in line with Ricoeur in seeing the reconstructive possibility of the postmodern, he does not tend, as Ricoeur occasionally does, toward identifying the postmodern with this reconstructive possibility. Reconstruction is but one of the possibilities in the modern field that includes suspicious options Ricoeur might feel do not properly belong. Frei uses the cognate "postcritical" in his essay

"'Narrative' in Christian and Modern Reading," in *Theology and Dialogue*, 149–163, especially 152–160.

9. Frei argues against this position in *The Eclipse of Biblical Narrative*, 1–16, 86–104.

10. Neither Frei, on the one hand, nor Ricoeur or Tracy on the other, legislate that historical-critical method has no role to play in biblical interpretation. But they all seem to be of the opinion that a literary analysis, perhaps, more nearly respects the compositional aspects of the biblical text as well as its power to say and move. See Ricoeur's *Essays on Biblical Interpretation*, 73–118; Tracy's "On Reading the Scriptures Theologically," in *Theology and Dialogue*, 42. See also Frei, "'Narrative' in Christian and Modern Reading," in *Theology and Dialogue*, 151.

11. "Poetic text" is Ricoeur's locution. See *Interpretation Theory*, 37. For Tracy's notion of classic, see *The Analogical Imagination*, 99ff. In order not to expose the biblical text to a general hermeneutic that would endanger its uniqueness, Frei continues to regard the biblical text as "Scripture" in the strong sense, that is, as the uniquely shaping text of the Christian community absolutely incommensurable to any other text.

12. If for some of its concepts the romanticist project was parasitic upon the view of inspiration, nevertheless it did not understand its hermeneutic task to consist in excavating the voice behind the human voice, to come in contact with the ventriloquist author behind the text. Its general focus was on making a usable present out of a past felt to be humanly significant and vital. Romanticist hermeneutics did not, in consequence, officially challenge the old picture. According to Ricoeur, the old picture must be challenged, and not simply by implication and unofficially as was, perhaps, the case in romanticism. Ricoeur's explicit contestation occurs in *Essays in Biblical Interpretation*, 75–118. For Frei, by contrast, such challenge is not intrinsic to the theological task, despite his reconceptualization of the nature of the function of biblical language in *The Identity of Jesus Christ: The Hermeneutical Bases of Dogmatic Theology* (Philadelphia, 1975).

13. This first distinction opens up when the explicit aim of hermeneutics becomes an understanding of the author that surpasses the author's own self-understanding. The second distinction is essentially the distinction between the differing emphases of Dilthey, on the one hand, and Schleiermacher, on the other. For a lucid account of the hermeneutics systems of Schleiermacher and Dilthey, see Richard Palmer, *Hermeneutics: Interpretation Theory in Schleiermacher, Dilthey, Heidegger, and Gadamer* (Evanston, 1969), 84–123.

14. The point is consistently made by Ricoeur that the text can neither be identified with authorial intention or the social world of the addresser or the addressed. See *Interpretation Theory*, 73, 92. For a similar asseveration in Tracy, see *The Analogical Imagination*, 128. Frei essentially agrees with Ricoeur and Tracy on this point in his essay, "The Literal Reading of Scripture in the Christian Tradition: Does It Stretch or Will It Break?" in Frank Mc Connell, ed., *The Bible and the Narrative Tradition* (New York, 1986), 43–62.

15. Frei distances himself from postmodern positions not so much on grounds of general theory, but tactically. More specifically, Frei proceeds to question post-

modern positions only in those cases where this theory claims hermeneutic authority over the biblical text. Such claims, however, are usually attended by at least the entertaining of the possibility that in some way the biblical text itself is a potential repository of ideology and idolatry and not the critical loadstone the tradition had interpreted it to be. For Ricoeur and Tracy, by contrast, a number of postmodern hermeneutic positions such as structuralism and deconstruction are inadequate on general hermeneutic grounds.

16. Frei opposes the idea of the hegemony of the idea of synchronic structure in "'Narrative' in Christian and Modern Reading," in *Theology and Dialogue*, 156. For Ricoeur's view on narrative see his monumental *Time and Narrative*, 3 vols., trans. Kathleen Mclaughlin and David Pellauer (Chicago and London, 1983–1988). For Tracy's view on narrative, see *The Analogical Imagination*, 275–281, 307–309.

17. For Ricoeur's critique of structuralism, see *Semeia* 4 (1975): 37–73. See also Tracy, *Plurality and Ambiguity*, 47–65.

18. While Frei enlists deconstruction on his side against the hermeneutic regimes of Ricoeur and Tracy, which, he believes, involves at least implicit claims at cognitive self-transparence, he definitely should not be thought to give it his hermeneutical blessing. See his "The Literal Reading of Narrative," 43–62, especially 50–54; also "'Narrative' in Christian and Modern Reading," 156–159. Both Ricoeur and Tracy think that even if deconstruction cannot of itself be an encompassing hermeneutical theory, it can function as part or a moment of a general theory. See *The Rule of Metaphor*, 284–289; *Plurality and Ambiguity*, 54–63. Neither Ricoeur nor Tracy would accept Frei's charge that their hermeneutic positions commit them to a Husserlian-like view of self-transparence. Tracy, in fact, expressly denies this charge in "On Reading Scripture Theologically," 39. And certainly much of Ricoeur's work from the time of his work on the will on has been focused on elaborating a philosophical anthropology that does not presuppose cognitive transparence. Ricoeur has consistently held that the self is given to itself only by detour, and even then never absolutely.

19. Though, obviously, this is not to say that postmodern interpretation of interpretive practice coincides with that of Augustine.

20. Though one risks being anachronistic in making denials on Augustine's behalf that he could not have considered, nevertheless denials serve the function of highlighting the premodern, referentialist horizon of Augustine's thought. See Ferdinand de Saussure, *Course in General Linguistics*, trans. Wade Baskin (New York, 1966). For Ricoeur's discussion and critique, see *The Rule of Metaphor*, 102–104, 110–112, 115–118, 120–132, 285; for Tracy's, see *Plurality and Ambiguity*, 52–60. For Derrida's own critique of Saussure, see *Of Grammatology*, trans. Gayatri Chakravorty Spivak (Baltimore, 1974), 30–65.

21. See *Of Grammatology*, 11–15, for Derrida's critique of the medieval theory of the sign.

22. Ricoeur understands that classical rhetorical theory whether in its Greek or in its derivitive Latin form in theorists such as Quintilian is in the last instance dependent upon the priority of the word. Though Ricoeur does not as far as I am aware say anything expressly about *DDC*, were he to do so, he would undoubt-

edly point to Augustine's dependence upon the Latin rhetoricians, Cicero and Quintilian, and the infrastructural preeminence of the word. See *The Rule of Metaphor*, studies 1 and 7, for Ricoeur's crucial distinction between the premodern and postmodern bases of rhetoric in general and the referential function in poetic texts in particular.

23. For Ricoeur, see *The Rule of Metaphor*, study 7; for Frei's most explicit pronouncement on this point, see "'Narrative' in Christian and Modern Reading."

24. The Enlightenment crisis of ostensive reference is an important theme of Frei's *Eclipse*. See also Tracy, *Plurality and Ambiguity*, 49.

25. The most explicit thematization of the relation of the modern to the premodern in Ricoeur is, perhaps, *Freud and Philosophy*, 3–56, 494–551.

26. This is Frei's most characteristic view. It is the view that dominates in *The Eclipse*.

27. This position finds an expression in "The Literal Reading of Biblical Narrative," where Frei, availing of deconstruction, tends to be drawn into saying that a referential function must be denied the biblical text.

28. The emendatory reading is put forward in Frei, "'Narrative' in Christian and Modern Reading."

29. In both his essays on narrative—"'Narrative' in Christian and Modern Reading" and "The Literal Reading of Biblical Narrative"—Frei suggests that the Ricoeurian-Tracian hermeneutic dispensation is determined by modernity's sense of hermeneutic crisis and operates within the pale of a subjective horizon, which is viewed as the only viable horizon for a possible solution.

30. The label "*ad hoc* apologetics" is borrowed from William Werpekowski. See his article, "*Ad Hoc* Apologetics," *Journal of Religion* 66 (1986): 282–301.

31. In his important article on Schleiermacher, as well as in his typology that is to be published posthumously by Yale University Press, Frei is considerably more gentle on Schleiermacher himself than one might expect.

32. See Frei, "The Literal Reading of Biblical Narrative," 54.

33. See Ricoeur, "The Model of the Text: Meaningful Action Considered as a Text," in *Interpretive Social Science*, ed. P. Robinson and W. M. Sullivan (Berkeley, 1979), 98.

34. Ricoeur, *The Rule of Metaphor*, studies 1 and 7.

35. For a critique of the world-behind-the-text view, see Ricoeur, *Interpretation Theory*, 37, 87–88; *The Rule of Metaphor*, 216–256; Tracy, *The Analogical Imagination*, 105, 110.

36. For an inventory of the quite different ways in which the world-behind-the-text can be posited, see Ricoeur, *Interpretation Theory*, 71–75; Tracy, *The Analogical Imagination*, 128.

37. Both Ricoeur and Tracy are essentially Gadamerian in construing interpretation fundamentally in dialogical terms. For the most succinct account of the dialogical construal, see Tracy, *Plurality and Ambiguity*, 1–27.

38. The inexhaustibility as well as openness of interpretation is axiomatic for Ricoeur and Tracy. See Ricoeur, *Interpretation Theory*, 93; Tracy, *The Analogical Imagination*, 102–103.

39. Ricoeur appeals to these notions in *Interpretation Theory*. For the notion of omnitemporality, see 93.

40. The insistence by both that a text is about something owes much to Gadamer, who himself is dependent on Heidegger.

41. Frei's deconstructive critique is to the fore in "The Literal Interpretation of Narrative," 49–54.

42. For expressions of the importance of the notion of "distanciation," see Ricoeur, "The Hermeneutic Function of Distanciation," *Philosophy Today* 17.2 (Summer 1973): 129–141; also Tracy, *The Analogical Imagination*, 127.

43. A good example of such revision is offered in Heidegger's essay "The Thing," in *Poetry, Language, Thought*, trans. Albert Hofstadter (San Francisco, 1971), 163–182.

44. Frei, of course, officially eschews foundationalist claims. The fullest expression of this anti-foundationalism is to be found in his typology of theological positions, which is shortly to be published by Yale University Press.

45. See Ricoeur's criticism of New Criticism in *Interpretation Theory*, 91; *The Rule of Metaphor*, 224–228.

46. See Ricoeur's essay in *Semeia* 4, especially 35–73, for the anti-semiotic view of the biblical text. The general grounds of the anti-semiotic view are given in *The Rule of Metaphor*, study 5, 134–172.

47. The existential note is more explicit in Ricoeur and Tracy than it is, for instance, in the "later" Heidegger, though even in the case of the "later" Heidegger the existential element is not that far beneath the surface, as Critical Theory has brought to the philosophical community's attention. Ricoeur and Tracy certainly avail of the vocabulary of "belonging" that is a mark of the "later" Heidegger.

48. For Ricoeur's appropriation of Frege's sense-reference distinction, see *Interpretation Theory*, 19–22; also *The Rule of Metaphor*, 217.

49. See Ricoeur, *Interpretation Theory*, 19–22, 87–88; *The Rule of Metaphor*, study 7.

50. See Ricoeur, *The Rule of Metaphor*, 239–256.

51. Such a movement is, arguably, afoot in Heidegger's "The Thing" essay mentioned above in n. 43.

52. At one level the thrust of what Ricoeur and Tracy have to say is that "poetic" or classic texts can be read in the way recommended by them precisely because of the history of misreading. But at another level the progress is only relative, for the modern period's insistence on direct—rather than indirect—reference is a deformation. A corollary of this is that it cannot be ruled out that premodern reading of poetic or classic texts did not, at least on some occasions and in some respects, mirror or prefigure Ricoeurian-Tracian postmodern reading.

53. The clearest expression of this point is to be found in Ricoeur's *Interpretation Theory*, 36–37, 88.

54. If (a) is Gadamerian in inspiration, (b) goes beyond Gadamer in refusing to make an either/or of explanation (*Erklärung*) and understanding (*Verstehen*). On the general hermeneutic level this is the basic drift of *Interpretation Theory*. It carries over in Ricoeur's case into his biblical hermeneutics. See his essay "Toward a Hermeneutic of the Idea of Revelation," in *Essays on Biblical Inter-*

pretation, 73–118. A reprise of Ricoeur's general hermeneutic position seems to define Tracy's discussion of the "classic" in *The Analogical Imagination,* 99–153. And this chapter sets the terms for subsequent analyses of religious classics in general, the biblical classic in particular.

55. Ricoeur, *Interpretation Theory,* 43–44.

56. Tracy, *The Analogical Imagination,* 127–128.

57. See Hans-Georg Gadamer, *Truth and Method,* trans. Joel Weinsheimmer and Donald G. Marshall, 2nd rev. ed. (New York, 1989), 211–212, 229–231.

58. For Derrida's express critique of Gadamer, see *Dialogue and Deconstruction: The Gadamer-Derrida Encounter,* ed. Diane P. Michelfelder and Richard E. Palmer (Albany, N.Y., 1989), 52–54. For Gadamer's puzzled response, see 93–101.

59. Frei, "The Literal Reading of Biblical Narrative in the Christian Tradition," 52–60.

60. Frei, "The Literal Reading of Biblical Narrative in the Christian Tradition," 68–73.

61. This would be an instance of what Bruce Marshall felicitously calls "absorbing a world." See his essay, "Absorbing the World: Christianity and the Universe of Truths," in *Theology and Dialogue,* 69–102.

62. This is suggested by Frei in his essay, "'Narrative' in Christian and Modern Reading," 159–160.

Abbreviations

Where possible the abbreviations are those of *L'Année Philologique*:

Aug(L)	*Augustiniana*, Leuven
Aug(R)	*Augustinianum*, Rome
AugStud	*Augustinian Studies*, Villanova, PA
BA	*Bibliothèque Augustinienne*
CC	*Corpus Christianorum Series Latina*
CSEL	*Corpus Scriptorum Ecclesiasticorum Latinorum*
DDC	*De doctrina christiana*
FC	Fathers of the Church
HTR	*Harvard Theological Review*
JbAC	*Jahrbuch für Antike und Christentum*
PG	Patrologia Graeca
PL	*Patrologia Latina*
RACh	*Reallexikon für Antike und Christentum*
RBen	*Revue Bénédictine*
REAug	*Revue des Etudes Augustiniennes*, Paris
RecAug	*Recherches Augustiniennes*, Paris
REL	*Revue des Etudes Latines*
SE	*Sacris Erudiri*
SP	*Studia Patristica*
TU	*Texte und Untersuchungen*, Berlin
VetChr	*Vetera Christianorum*, Bari
VigChr	*Vigilae Christianae*, Amsterdam
ZKG	*Zeitschrift für Kirchengeschichte*
ZTK	*Zeitschrift für Theologie und Kirche*

Bibliography of *De doctrina christiana*

LEWIS AYRES

This bibliography is not intended to be comprehensive. For reasons of space it is limited to books and articles, published in this century, concerned directly with *De doctrina christiana* (*DDC*) itself and with its Patristic context. Purely medieval and modern material has been excluded. For the same reason, references to *DDC* which are to be found in general histories or *lexica* of philosophy, theology, or rhetoric, apart from some important exceptions, have also been largely excluded. Some works primarily in modern theology have been included where they contain substantive analysis of *DDC*. Material on the manuscript tradition has been given only for the most important works, and material on the theology of Tyconius has been included only where specific reference is made to *DDC*. Essays in this volume are not included.

I would like to acknowledge the help of the Augustinus Institut, Würzburg, Germany, who provided, *via* the Rev. Prof. R. Dodaro of the Augustinianum, Rome, what became the basis of this bibliography. References to articles in the *Augustinus Lexicon* (Basel and Stuttgart, 1986–) which pertain to *DDC* have not been given.

I. Editions

Details of editions previous to *PL* are given in *BA* 11:165.

Brunn. [See section III, below.)
Green, W. M. *CSEL* 80. Vienna, 1963.
Martin, J. *CC* 32:1–167. Turnout, 1962.
Migne. *PL* 34:15–122.

Sullivan. [See section III, below.]
Vogels, H. *S. Augustini De doctrina christiana libri IV.* Florilegium Patristicum 24. Bonn, 1933.

II. Twentieth-Century Translations and Commentaries

Green, R. P. H. *Augustine: De doctrina christiana.* Oxford Early Christian Texts. Oxford (Clarendon Press), forthcoming, 1994. [The volume will include text, translation, and commentary.]

Translations into English, French, German, Italian, Spanish are listed in:

DiBerardino, A., ed. *Patrology.* Vol. 4. Trans. P. Solari. Intro. J. Quasten. Westminster, Md., 1986. P. 377.

See also below, section III, entries for Brunn (Danish), Kato (Japanese), Sulowski (Polish); and, for commentaries, Atkinson, Brunn, Combès and Farges, Sullivan, Sulowski.

III. Secondary Literature

Abel, K. "Non-biblical Readings in the Church's Worship." *Bijdragen* 30 (1969): 350–379.
Agaësse, P. "Ecriture sainte et vie spirituelle: Saint Augustin." *Dictionnaire de spiritualité* 4 (1960): 155–158.
———. "*Fruitio Dei*: I la *fruitio* augustinienne." *Dictionnaire de spiritualité* 5 (1964): 1546–1569.
Allard, G. H. "L'articulation du sens du signe dans le *De doctrina christiana* de s. Augustin." *SP* 14 (= *TU* 117) (1971): 377–388.
———. "Pour une nouvelle interprétation de la *Civitas Dei*." *SP* 9 (= *TU* 94) (1966): 329–339.
Atkinson, S. *Commentary on Augustine's "De doctrina christiana," Book II.* Diss. St. Andrews University, Fife, Scotland, 1982.
Avilés Bartina, M. "Adecuación entre el método exegético agustiniano y la exégesis de algunas de sus obras." *Augustinus* 24 (1979): 43–69.
———. "Algunos problemas fundamentales del *De doctrina christiana*." *Augustinus* 20 (1975): 83–105.
———. "Estudio de diez sermones agustinianos." *Perficit* (Publicación mensual de Estudios Clásicos: Textos y Estudios), 2nd series 7, 92–94 (1976): 33–71. [Completes the thesis begun in Avilés Bartina, "Algunos problemas fundamentales" and "Prontuario agustiniano de ideas exegéticas."]
———. "Manuscritos del *De doctrina christiana* existentes en Europa." *Augustinus* 31 (1986): 379–390.

————. "Predicación de san Agustín: La teoría retorica augustiniana y la práctica de sus sermones." *Augustinus* 28 (1983): 391–417.

————. "Prontuario agustiniano de ideas exegéticas." *Augustinus* 20 (1975): 297–338.

————. "Prontuario agustiniano de ideas retoricas." *Augustinus* 22 (1977): 101–149.

Ayers, R. H. *Language, Logic, and Reason in the Church Fathers: A Study of Tertullian, Augustine, and Aquinas.* Altertumswissenschäftliche Texte und Studien 6. Hildesheim/New York, 1979.

————. "Language Theory and Analysis in Augustine." *Scottish Journal of Theology* 29 (1976): 1–12.

Basevi, C. *San Agustin: La interpretación del Nuevo Testamento: Criterios exegéticos propuestos por S. Agustin en el "De doctrina christiana," en el Contra Faustum y en el De Consensu Evangelistarum.* Colección Teológica de la Universidad de Navarra 14. Navarre, 1977.

Beierwaltes, W. "Zu Augustins Metaphysik der Sprache." *AugStud* 2 (1971): 179–195.

Benin, S. D. "Sacrifice as Education in Augustine and Chrysostom." *Church History* 52 (1983): 7–20.

Benoit, P. "La Septante est-elle inspirée?" In *Vom Wort des Lebens: Festschrift für Max Meinertz,* ed. N. Adler, 41–49. Münster, 1951.

Beutler, E. "Die vierfache Ehrfurcht." *Modern Language Quarterly* 10 (1949): 259–263.

Bickersteth, M. C. *Preaching and Teaching According to St. Augustine; Being a New Translation of His "De doctrina christiana" IV and "De catechizandis rudibus." With Three Introductory Essays by the Rev. W. J. W. Baker and the Rev. M. C. Bickersteth.* London and Oxford, 1907.

Bolgar, R. R. *The Classical Heritage and Its Beneficiaries.* Cambridge, 1954.

Bonafede, G. *Storia della filosofia medievale.* Rome, 1957.

Bouly de Lesdain, A.-M. "Quelques recueils de vies de saints en prose." *Bulletin d'Information de l'Institut de Recherche et d'Histoire des Textes* 5 (1956 [1957]): 69–85.

Brechtken, J. *Antik-philosophisches Daseinsverständnis und christlicher Liebesgedanke bei Augustin.* Diss. University of Freiburg im Bresgau, 1965.

————. *Augustinus Doctor Caritatis: Sein Liebesbegriff im Widerspruch von Eigennutz und selbstloser Güte im Rahmen der antiken Glückseligkeits-Ethik.* Monographien zur philosophischen Forschung 136. Hain, 1975.

————. "Fruitio und Agape: Der Liebesgedanke bei Augustin." *Theologie und Glaube* 59 (1969): 446–463.

Bright, P. *The Book of Rules of Tyconius*. Christianity and Judaism in Antiquity 2. Notre Dame, Ind., 1988.

———. "'The Spiritual World Which Is the Church': Hermeneutical Theory in *The Book of Rules* of Tyconius." *SP* 22 (1989): 213–218.

Brinton, A. "St. Augustine and the Problem of Deception in Religious Persuasion." *Religious Studies* 19 (1983): 437–450.

Brunn, N. W. *Aurelius Augustin: Om den kristne taler*. Latin text, ed. J. Martin. Introduction, translation, and notes, N. W. Brunn. Copenhagen, 1972.

Brunner, P. "Charismatische und methodische Schriftauslegung nach Augustinus: Prolog zu *De doctrina christiana*." *Kerygma und Dogma* 1 (1955): 59–69, 85–103.

Bucher, T. G. "Zur formalen Logik bei Augustin." *Freiburger Zeitschrift für Philosophie und Theologie* 29.

Campion, E. "Defences of Classical Learning in St. Augustine's *De doctrina christiana* and Erasmus's *Antibarbari*." *History of European Ideas* 4 (1983): 467–472.

Canning, R. "The Augustinian *uti/frui* Distinction in the Relation between Love for Neighbour and Love for God." *Aug(L)* 33 (1983): 165–231.

———. "'Love Your Neighbour as Yourself' (Matt. 22, 39): Saint Augustine on the Lineament of the Self to Be Loved." *Aug(L)* 34 (1984): 145–179.

Casati, G. "De doctrina christiana." *Aug(R)* 6 (1966): 18–44.

Cavallera, F. "La date de la première édition incomplète du *De doctrina christiana*." *Bulletin de Littérature Ecclésiastique* 31 (1930): 122–123.

Cayré, F. "Alta sapienza e vita cristiana." In *Sanctus Augustinus Vitae Spiritualis Magister*. Rome, 1959. 1.77–101.

———. "La mystique divine courante d'après saint Augustin ou la sagesse priante, âme des *Confessions* et règle de l'action." *Divinitas* 3 (1959): 43–76.

Cazier, P. "Cassien auteur présumé de l'épitomé des *Règles* de Tyconius." *REAug* 22 (1976): 262–297.

———. "*Le Livre des règles* de Tyconius: Sa transmission de *De doctrina christiana* aux *Sentences* d'Isidore de Séville." *REAug* 19 (1973): 242–261.

Cilleruelo, L. "*Deum Videre* en San Agustín." *Salmanticensis* 12 (1965): 3–31; 13 (1966): 231–281.

Clark, A. K. "Augustine and Derrida: Reading as Fulfillment of the World." *New Scholasticism* 55 (1981): 104–112.

Colish, M. L. *The Mirror of Language: A Study in the Medieval Theory of Knowledge*. New Haven/London, 1968.

———. "St. Augustine's Rhetoric of Silence Revisited." *AugStud* 9 (1978): 15–24.

————. "The Stoic Theory of Verbal Signification and the Problem of Lies and False Statements from Antiquity to St. Anselm." In *Archéologie du Signe.* Papers in Medieval Studies 3, ed. L. Brind'Amour and E. Vance, 17–43. Toronto, 1983.

————. *The Stoic Tradition from Antiquity to the Early Middle Ages.* Vol. 1: *Stoicism in Classical Latin Literature.* Vol. 2: *Stoicism in Christian Latin Thought through the Sixth Century.* Leiden, 1985.

Combès, G., and J. Farges. *De doctrina Christiana. BA* 11 (Paris, 1949): 151–606.

Costas, O. "Influential Factors in the Rhetoric of St. Augustine." *Foundations: A Baptist Journal of History and Theology* 16 (1973): 208–221.

Cranz, E. F. "The Development of Augustine's Ideas on Society before the Donatist Controversy." *HTR* 47 (1954): 255–316 (= Markus, *Augustine: A Collection of Critical Essays,* 336–403).

Dassmann, E. "Schriftverständnis und religiöse Erkenntnis nach dem heiligen Augustinus." *Trierer Theologische Zeitschrift* 87 (1978): 257–274.

Deeney, J. J. "Augustine's *De doctrina christiana*: Some Implications for Literary Theory." *Saint Louis Quarterly* (Beguic City, Philippines) 1 (1963): 53–72.

di Giovanni, A. *La dialettica dell'amore: Uti-frui nelle preconfessioni di Sant' Agostino.* Itinerari critici 5. Rome, 1965.

————. "Metafisica del Dio—Amore nel *De doctrina christiana." Aug(R)* 6 (1966): 294–300.

————. "Per un'etica della parola." *Filosofia e vita* 9 (1968): 23–46.

————. *Verità, parola, immortalità in sant'Agostino.* Palermo, 1979.

Doyle, G. W. "Augustine's Sermonic Method." *The Westminster Theological Journal* 39 (1977): 213–238.

————. *St. Augustine's "Tractates on the Gospel of John" Compared with the Rhetorical Theory of "De doctrina christiana."* Diss. University of North Carolina, Chapel Hill, 1975.

Duchrow, U. "*Signum* und *superbia* beim jungen Augustin (386–390)." *REAug* 7 (1961): 369–72.

————. *Sprachverständnis und biblisches Hören bei Augustin.* Hermeneutische Untersuchungen zur Theologie 5. Tübingen, 1965.

————. "Zum Prolog von Augustins *De doctrina christiana." VigChr* 17 (1963): 165–172.

Dulaey, M. "La sixième règle de Tyconius et son résumé dans le *De doctrina christiana." REAug* 35 (1989): 83–103.

Eckermann, W. "Die 'Betrachtungen' Alois Güglers (1782–1827) zu Augustins *De doctrina christiana." Signum Pietatis: Festgabe für*

Cornelius Petrus Mayer O.S.A. zum 60. ed. A. von Zumkeller, 579–607. Würzburg, 1989.

Eden, K. "The Rhetorical Tradition and Augustine's Hermeneutics in *De doctrina christiana.*" *Rhetorica* 8 (1990): 45–63.

Eichenseer, C. *Das symbolum apostolicum beim heiligen Augustinus: Mit Berücksichtigung des dogmengeschichtlichen Zusammenhangs.* St. Ottilien, 1960.

Evans, G. R. "St. Anselm's Technical Terms of Rhetoric." *Latomus* 36 (1977): 171–179.

Federico, C. *Principi di esegesi biblica nel "De doctrina christiana" di S. Agostino.* Diss. Pontifical Lateran University, 1965–1966.

Finaert, G. *L'évolution littéraire de Saint Augustin.* Paris, 1939.

———. *Saint Augustin rhéteur.* Paris, 1939.

Fischer, B. "'Nicht wie die Gelehrten reden eher wie die Ungelehrten': Eine Mahnung Augustins an den christlichen Prediger (*De doctr. chr.* 4, 65)." *Internazionale katholische Zeitschrift Communio* 11 (1982): 123–129.

Forstner, K. "Eine frühmittelalterliche Interpretation der augustinischen Stillehre." *Mittellateinisches Jahrbuch* 4 (1967): 61–71.

Francey, T. *Les idées littéraires de Saint Augustin dans le "De doctrina christiana."* Saabrücken, 1920.

Fredriksen Landes, P. "Tyconius and the End of the World." *REAug* 28 (1982): 59–75.

French, E. "Augustine's *De doctrina christiana* and Lifelong Education." *Augustinian Panorama* 2 (1985): 1–24.

Garcia de La Fuente, O. "Datos sobre linguistica y lengua latina en la *De doctrina christiana.*" *Helmantica* 22 (1971): 315–337.

García Jiménez, J. "La Retórica de San Augustín y su patrimonio clásico." *La Cividad de Dios* 71 (1955): 11–32.

Gauthier, G. *Pédagogie de saint Augustin dans le "De doctrina christiana" et le "De catechizandis rudibus."* Diss. Dijon, 1966.

Gloire, F. "Sources de s. Jérôme et de s. Augustin. I: Une source païenne de saint Augustin?" *SE* 18 (1967–1968): 451–471.

Gorman, M. M. "The Diffusion of the Manuscripts of Saint Augustine's *De doctrina christiana* in the Early Middle Ages." *RBen* 95 (1985): 11–24.

Grech, P. "I Principi ermeneutici di sant'Agostino: Una valuazione." *Lateranum* 48 (1982): 209–223.

Green, R. P. H. "Augustine's *De doctrina christiana*: Some Clarifications." *Respublica Litterarum* 15 (1992).

———. "Qué entendió san Agustín por doctrina cristiana?" *Augustinus* 26 (1981): 49–57.

Green, W. M. "A Fourth Century Manuscript of St. Augustine? (Leningrad QV. 1/3—'first edition'—*inter* 396/426—of the *De doctrina christiana*)." *RBen* 69 (1959): 191–197.

———. "Textual Notes on Augustine's *De doctrina christiana*." *REAug* 8 (1962): 225–231.

Grill, S. "Augustinus und die Predigt Christi in der Unterwelt." *Bibel und Liturgie* 21 (1953–1954): 330–331.

Grillmeier, A. "Patristische Vorbilder frühscholastischer Systematik: Zugleich ein Beitrag zur Geschichte des Augustinismus." *SP* VI (= *TU* 81): 390–408.

Grion, A. M. "La 'fruizione' nella storia della teologia." *Sapienza* 17 (1964): 186–216, 337–350, 457–490.

Gronjaer, N. "Agostino e la retorica romana." *Analecta Romana Instituti Danici* 14 (1985): 149–161.

Hadot, I. *Arts libéraux et philosophie dans la pensée antique.* Paris, 1984.

Hahn, T. *Tyconius-Studien: Ein Beitrag zur Kirchen- und Dogmengeschichte des vierten Jahrhunderts.* Leipzig, 1900.

Hala, J.-P. "*Signum* et *Res*: Wordplay and Christian Rhetoric." *Michigan Academy of Science, Arts, and Letters* 16 (1984): 315–328.

Hamilton, G. J. "Augustine's Methods of Biblical Interpretation." In *Grace, Politics, and Desire: Essays on Augustine*, ed. H. Meynell, 87–100. Calgary, 1990.

Hamm, B. "Unmittelbarkeit des göttlichen Gnadenwirkens und kirchliche Heilsvermittlung bei Augustin." *ZTK* 78 (1981): 409–441.

Hendrikx, E. "Astrologie Waarzeggerij en Parapsychologie bij Augustinus." *Aug(L)* 4 (1954): 325–352.

Henningfeld, J. "*Verbum signum*: La définition du langage chez S. Augustin et Nicolas de Cuse." *Archives de philosophie* 54 (1991): 255–268.

Hess, W. "Logik und platonische Philosophie der Logik bei Augustin: Bausteine zu einer Interpretation von *De doctrina christiana* II, 117–127." *Jahresbericht des Bismark-Gymnasiums Karlsruhe 1970–1971* (1971): 39–68.

Hill, E. "*De doctrina christiana*: A Suggestion." *SP* VI (= *TU* 81) (1962): 443–446.

———. "St. Augustine as a Preacher." *Blackfriars* 35 (1954): 463–471.

Holte, R. *Béatitude et Sagesse: Saint Augustin et le problème de la fin de l'homme dans la philosophie ancienne.* Paris, 1962.

Holtz, L. *Donat et la tradition de l'enseignement grammatical: Etude sur l'Ars Donati et sa diffusion (IVe–IXe siècle) et édition critique.* Paris, 1981.

Honstetter, R. *Exemplum zwischen Rhetorik und Literatur—Zur gattungsgeschichtlichen Sonderstellung von Valerius Maximus und Augustinus.* Konstanz, 1981.

Hubert, M. "*Corpus stigmatologicum minus.*" *Archivum Latinitatis Medii Aevi (Bulletin du Cange)* 37 (1970): 5–171 [Augustine, 56–59].

Instrumenta lexicologica latina: Sanctus Aurelius Augustinus: "De doctrina christiana," curante. CETEDOC. Turnhout, 1983.

Istace, G. *Deux essais de synthèse chez saint Augustin ("De doctrina christiana," livre I et "De catechizandis rudibus," Paragr. 1–13; 23–55).* Diss. University of Louvain, 1954–1955.

———. "Le livre 1er du *De doctrina christiana* de saint Augustin: Organisation synthétique et méthode mise en oeuvre." *Ephemerides Theologicae Lovanienses* 32 (1956): 289–330.

Jackson, B. D. *Semantics and Hermeneutics in Saint Augustine's "De doctrina christiana."* Diss. Yale University, 1967.

———. "The Theory of Signs in St. Augustine's *De doctrina christiana.*" *REAug* 15 (1969): 9–49 (= Markus [1972], 92–147).

Jordan, M. D. "Words and Word: Incarnation and Signification in Augustine's *De doctrina christiana.*" *AugStud* 11 (1980): 177–196.

Jüngel, E. *Gott als Geheimnis der Welt.* Tübingen, 1977.

Kager, G. "*De doctrina christiana*" *von Aurelius Augustinus: Die erste Anweisung zur christlichen Redekunst.* Diss. Vienna, 1970.

Kannengiesser, C., and P. Bright. *A Conflict of Christian Hermeneutics in Roman Africa: Tyconius and Augustine: Protocol of the 58th Colloquy.* Berkeley, 1989.

Kato, T. *Augustine, De doctrina christiana.* Tokyo, 1988. [Japanese translation.]

———. "On Augustine's Metaphorical Interpretation of *similitudo* in the *De doctrina christiana* II, 6, 7, 8." *Studies in Medieval Thought* (Nagoya) 27 (1985): 63–75. [In Japanese. For details, see *Répertoire bibliographique de la philosophie* 39 (1987), no. 498.]

Kelly, J. N. D. "The Bible and the Latin Fathers." In *The Church's Use of the Bible, Past and Present,* ed. D. E. Nineham, 41–56. London, 1963.

Kevane, E. "Augustine's *De doctrina christiana*: A Treatise on Christian Education." *RecAug* 4 (1966): 97–133.

———. *Augustine the Educator: A Study in the Fundamentals of Christian Formation.* Westminster, Md., 1964.

———. "Paideia and Anti-Paideia: The *Prooemium* of St. Augustine's *De doctrina christiana.*" *AugStud* 1 (1970): 153–180.

———. "*Translatio imperii*: Augustine's *De doctrina christiana* and the Classical Paideia." *SP* XIV (= *TU* 117): 446–460.

Kirwan, C. "Augustine." *Arguments of the Philosophers*, ch. 3. London, 1989.

Körner, F. *Das Sein und der Mensch: Die existenzielle Seinsentdeckung des jungen Augustin: Grundlagen zur Erhellung seiner Ontologie.* Freiburg/München, 1959.

Kuypers, K. *Der Zeichen- und Wortbegriff im Denken Augustins.* Amsterdam, 1934.

La Bonnardiére, A.-M. "Augustin a-t-il utilisé la 'Vulgate' de Jérôme?" In La Bonnardière, *Saint Augustine et la Bible*, 303–313.

———. "Le canon des divines Ecritures." In La Bonnardière, *Saint Augustine et la Bible*, 287–303.

La Bonnardière, A.-M., ed. *Saint Augustin et la Bible.* Bible de tous les temps 3. Paris, 1986.

Lafon, G. *Croire, espérer, aimer: Approches de la raison religieuse.* Paris, 1983.

Lanzaro, S. *Presenza classica e cristiana in san Agostino alla luce del De doctrina christiana.* Naples, 1974.

Latron, P. M. *L'héritage de la tradition rhétorique classique et la perspective chrétienne dans le "De doctrina christiana" de saint Augustin.* Paris, 1970.

Le Mois, B. J. *The Woman Clothed With the Sun (Ap. 12): Individual or Collective?* Rome, 1954.

Letizia, F. "Ordo dux ad Deum: La idea de orden en la ontología y ética augustinianas." *Augustinus* 28 (1983): 385–390.

Locher, G. F. D. *Hoop, eeuwigheid en tijd in de prediking van Augustinus.* Wageningen, 1961.

Lof, L. J. van der. "Verbricht Augustin das Schweigen des klassischen Altertums um Ps.-Longinus?" *VigChr* 16 (1962): 21–33.

Lorenz, R. "*Fruitio dei* bei Augustin." *ZKG* 63 (1950): 75–132.

———. "Die Herkunft des augustinischen Frui Deo." *ZKG* 64 (1952/3): 34–60.

———. "Die Wissenschaftslehre Augustins." *ZKG* 67 (1955/6): 29–60, 213–251.

Louth, A. "Augustine on Language." *Literature and Theology* 3, 2 (1989): 151–158.

McNew, L. D. "The Relation of Cicero's Rhetoric to Augustine." *Research Studies of the State College of Washington* 25 (1957): 5–13.

Mailaender, G. *Friendship: A Study in Theological Ethics.* Notre Dame/London, 1981.

Mainberger, G. K. *Rhetorica I. Reden mit Vernunft: Aristoteles, Cicero, Augustinus.* Stuttgart, 1987.

Mandouze, A. "Le livre IV du *De doctrina christiana*: Un *De oratore* chrétien." *Association Guillaume Budé, Actes du XIe Congrès, Pont-à-Mousson, 29 août–2 sept. 1983* (Paris, 1985): 127–128.

Margerie, B. de. *Introduction à l'histoire de l'exégèse. III. Saint Augustin.* Paris, 1983.

Marin, M. "Retorica ed esegesi in Sant'Agostino: Note introduttivo." *VetChr* 24 (1987): 253–268.

Markus, R. A. "St. Augustine on Signs." *Phronesis* 2 (1957): 60–83 (= Markus, *Augustine: A Collection of Critical Essays*, 61–91).

Markus, R. A., ed. *Augustine: A Collection of Critical Essays.* New York, 1972.

Marrou, H.-I. "Doctrina et disciplina dans la langue des Pères de l'Eglise." *Archivum Latinitatis Medii Aevii (Bulletin du Cange)* 9 (1934): 5–25.

———. *Retractatio.* Paris, 1949.

———. *Saint Augustin et la fin de la culture antique.* Paris, 1938.

Martano, G. "Retorica della *ratio* e retorica della *fides*: Il 4 libro de *De doctrina christiana* di S. Agostino." In *L'umanesimo di Sant'Agostino: Atti del Congresso Internazionale, Bari, 28–30 ottobre 1986*, ed. M. Fabris, 537–551. Bari, 1988.

Martin, J. "Abfassung, Veröffentlichung und Überlieferung von Augustins Schrift *De doctrina christiana*." *Traditio* 18 (1962): 69–87.

———. "Die Augustinus Überlieferung bei Eugippius." In *Miscellanea critica II: Aus Anlass des 150-jährigen Bestehens der Verlagsgesellschaft und des graphischen Betriebes B. G. Teubner*, ed. J. Irmscher et al, 228–244. Leipzig, 1965.

Mayer, C. P. "Prinzipiem der Hermeneutik Augustinus und daraus sich ergebende Probleme." *Forum katholische Theologie* 1 (1985): 197–211.

———. "*Res per signa*: Der Grundgedanke des Prologs in Augustins Schrift *De doctrina christiana* und das Problem seiner Datierung." *REAug* 20 (1974): 100–112.

———. *Die Zeichen in der geistigen Entwicklung und in der Theologie Augustins.* 2 Vols. Würzburg, 1974.

Mazzeo, J. A. "Augustine's Rhetoric of Silence." *Journal of the History of Ideas* 23 (1962): 175–196.

Milburn, R. L. P. *Early Christian Interpretations of History.* The Bampton Lectures for 1952. London, 1954.

Miyatani, Y. *Spiritus und Littera bei Augustin: Eine histor.-hermeneutische Untersuchung zu II Kor 3, 6b.* Diss. Ruprecht Karl Universität, Heidelburg, 1973.

———. "Grundstruktur und Bedeutung der augustinischen Hermeneutik in *De doctrina christiana*." *Kwansei Gakuin University Annual Studies (Nishinomiya)* 23 (1974): 1–14.

Mohrmann, C. "Saint Augustin and the *Eloquentia.*" In *Etudes sur le latin des Chrétiens,* 1:351–370. Paris, 1965.

———. "Problèmes stylistiques dans la littérature latine chrétienne." *VigChr* 29 (1955): 222–246 (= *Etudes sur le latin des Chrétiens* [Paris, 1965], 3:147–170).

Moisiu, A. "Din peocupuárile biblice ale Fericitului Augustin" (Des Préoccupations bibliques du bienheureux Augustin). *Mitropolia Ardealului* 10 (1965): 647–659. [See *REAug* 13 (1967): 347.]

Monceaux, P. *Histoire littéraire de l'Afrique chrétienne.* 7 vols. Paris, 1901–1923.

Moreau, M. "Lecture du *De doctrina christiana.*" In La Bonnardière, *Saint Augustin et la Bible,* 253–285.

———. "Sur un commentaire d'Amos: *De doctrina christiana* IV, 7, 15–21, sur Amos 6, 1–6." In La Bonnardière, *Saint Augustin et la Bible,* 313–322.

Napoli, G. di. "S. Agostino e il problema della cultura." *Euntes docete* 11 (1958): 34–357.

N'Goy, B. *Foi et culture dans le "De doctrina christiana" de saint Augustin.* Diss. Strasbourg, 1981.

Normann, F. *Teilhabe—ein Schlüsselwort der Vätertheologie.* Münsterische Beiträge zur Theologie 42. Münster, 1978.

O'Donovan, O. "*Usus* and *fruitio* in Augustine, *De doctrina christiana* 1.*" Journal of Theological Studies,* n.s. 33 (1982): 361–397.

Ohly, F. "Goethes *Ehrfurchten*—ein *ordo caritatis.* 1: Der *ordo caritatis* von Augustin bis zum 17. Jahrhundert." *Euphorion* 55 (1961): 113–145.

Opelt, I. "Doctrina und doctrina christiana." *Der altsprachliche Unterricht (Arbeitshefte zu seiner wissenschaftlichen Begründung und praktischen Gestalt)* 9 (1966): 5–22.

———. "Materialien zur Nachwirkung von Augustins Schrift De doctrina christiana." *JbAC* 17 (1974): 64–73.

Oroz Reta, J. "*El de doctrina christiana* o la retorica cristiana." *Estudios Clásicos* 3 (1956): 452–459.

———. *Augustinus rhetor et orator: Estudio sobre la retórica de los sermones de san Augustín.* Diss. Salamanca, 1957.

———. "Hacia una retórica cristiana: San Augustín y Cicero." *Augustinus* 7 (1962): 77–88.

———. "La retórica augustiniana: Classicismo y cristianismo." *SP* VI (= *TU* 81) (1962): 484–495.

———. *La retorica en los sermones de San Augustín.* Madrid, 1963.

Panquato, O. "Evangelizzazione e cultura: Testimonianza di Agostino." *Aug(R)* 27 (1987): 539–558.

Patan, L. R. *Il pensiero pedagogico di S. Agostino*. Bologna, 1967.

Pépin, J. "Saint Augustin et la fonction protreptique de l'allégorie." *RecAug* I (1958): 243–286.

———. *Saint Augustin et la dialectique*. The Saint Augustine Lecture 1972. Villanova, Pa., 1976.

Pieszczoch, S. "L'actualité des idées fondamentales sur l'exégèse contenues dans le *De doctrina christiana* de S. Augustin." *SP* XIV (= *TU* 117) (1976): 484–486.

———. "Niektóre poglady teologiczne sw. Augustyna w *De doctrina christiana* na tle Konstytucji *Dei Verbum*." *Studia theologica Varsaviensia* 9 (1971): 321–325.

———. "Teologicny aspekt propozycji hermeneutyczny w *De doctrina christiana* sw. Augustyna" (= Les approches théologiques des propositions herméneutiques dans le *De doctrina Christiana*). *Studia Gnesniensia* 2 (1976): 304–307. [Summary in French]

Pincherle, A. *La formazione teologica di Sant'Agostino*. Rome, 1941.

———. "S. Agostino: Tra il *De doctrina christiana* e le *Confessioni*." *Archeologica classica: Rivista dell'Instituto di Archeologia dell'Universita di Roma* 25–26 (1973–1974): 555–574.

———. "Sulla composizione del *De doctrina christiana* di S. Agostino." In *Storiografia e Storia: Studi in onore di Eugenio Dupré Theseider*, 541–559. Rome, 1974.

Pintaric, D. *Die Referenztheorie in der Trinitätslehre des hl. Augustinus*. Diss. Salzburg, 1980.

———. *Sprache und Trinität: Semantische Probleme in der Trinitätslehre des hl. Augustinus*. Salzburger Studien zur Philosophie 15. Salzburg/ München, 1983.

Plotkin, F. [see Young, A. M.]

Pontet, M. *L'exégèse de s. Augustin prédicateur*. Paris, 1945.

Press, G. A. "The Content and Argument of Augustine's *De doctrina christiana*." *Aug(L)* 31 (1981): 165–182.

———. "*Doctrina* in Augustine's *De doctrina christiana*." *Philosophy and Rhetoric* 17 (1984): 98–120.

———. "The Subject and Structure of Augustine's *De doctrina christiana*." *AugStud* 11 (1980): 99–124.

Quacquarelli, A. "Recupero della numerologia per la metodica dell' esegesi patristica." *Annali di Storia dell' Esegesi* 2 (1985): 235–249.

———. "Riscontro patristico della *Dei Verbum*." *Saggi patristici, retorica ed esegesi biblica*. Quaderni di *VetChr* 5 (Bari, 1971): 485–498.

———. "Le scienze e la numerologia in S. Agostino." *VetChr* 25 (1988): 359–379.

Ratzinger, J. "Beobachtungen zum Kirchenbegriff des Tyconius im *Liber regularum.*" *REAug* 2 (1956): 173–185.

Ripanti, G. "L'allegoria e l'*intellectus figuratus* nel *De doctrina christiana* di Agostino." *REAug* 18 (1972): 219–232.

Romero Pose, E. "Ticonio y San Agustín." *Salamanticensis* 34 (1987): 5–16.

Sagueés, R. J. *El educador de la fe en las obras catequéticas de San Agustín.* Madrid, 1970.

Santi, G. *Dio e l'uomo: Conscienza, memoria, linguaggio, ermeneutica in Agostino.* Rome, 1989.

Schäublin, C. "Zum Text von Augustin, *De doctrina christiana.*" *Wiener Studien,* M.S. 8 (1974): 173–181.

Schindler, A. *Wort und Analogie in Augustins Trinitätslehre.* Tübingen, 1965.

Schobinger, J.-P. "La portée historique des théories de la lecture (Réflexions à la lumière du *De doctrina christiana* de saint Augustin)." *Revue de théologie et de philosophie* 112 (1980): 43–56.

Schultz, S. J. "Augustine and the Old Testament Canon." *The Evangelical Quarterly* 28 (1956): 93–100.

Sciuto, I. *Dire l'indicibile: compressione e situatione in S. Agostino.* Padua, 1984.

———. "Il significatio dell'eudemonismo nei primi scritti di Agostino." *Giornale di Metaphysica* 9 (1987): 295–332, 495–513.

Seeliger, H. R. "Aberglaube, Wissenschaft und die Rolle der *historica narratio* in Augustins *De doctrina christiana.*" *Wissenschaft und Weisheit* 43 (1980): 148–155.

Sieben, H.-J. "Die *res* der Bibel: Eine Analyse von Augustinus, *De doctr. christ.* I–III." *REAug* 21 (1975): 72–90.

Simone, R. "Sémiologie augustinienne." *Semiotica* 6 (1972): 1–31.

Simonetti, M. *Profilio storico dell'esegesi patristica.* Sussidi Patristici 1. Rome, 1981.

———. *Lettera e/o allegoria: Un contributo alla storia dell'esegesi patristica.* Rome, 1985.

Sirridge, M. J. "St. Augustine and 'The Deputy Theory.'" *AugStud* 6 (1975): 107–116.

Sizoo, A. *Het oude christendom in zijn verhoading tot de antieke cultur.* Amsterdam, 1952.

Soria Herdia, F. "Teoría agustiniana del signo." *Augustinus* 33 (1988): 169–179.

Steffen, C. *Augustins Schrift "De doctrina christiana": Untersuchungen zum Aufbau, zum Begriffsgehalt und zur Bedeutung der Beredsamkeit.* Diss. Kiel, 1964.

Steinhauser, K. B. "*Recapitulatio* in Tyconius and Augustine." *AugStud* 15 (1984): 1–5.

Strubel, A. "*Allegoria in factis* et *Allegoria in uerbis*." *Poétique: Revue de théorie et d'analyse littéraires* 6 (1975): 342–357.

Studer, B. "*Delectare et prodesse*: Zu einem Schlüsselwort der patristischen Exegese." *Mémorial Dom Jean Gribomont (1920–81)*. Studia Ephemeridis "Augustinianum" 27, 555–581. Rome, 1987.

Sullivan, T. S. *Aurelii Augustini Hipponensis episcopi De doctrina christiana liber quartus: A Commentary with a Revised Text, Introduction, and Translation*. Patristic Studies 23. Washington, 1930.

Sulowski, J. *Sw. Augustyn: O nauce chrze scijanskiej*. Warsaw, 1979. [See *REAug* 79 (1980): 334.]

Tilley, M. A. *The Use of Scripture in Christian North Africa: An Examination of Donatist Hermeneutics*. Diss. Duke University, 1989.

Verheijen, L. "Le *De doctrina christiana* de Saint Augustin: Un manuel d'herméneutique et d'expression chrétienne avec, en II.19.29–42.63, une charte fondamentale pour une culture chrétienne." *Aug(L)* 24 (1974): 10–20.

———. "Le premier livre du *De doctrina christiana* d'Augustin: Un traité de 'télicologie' biblique." In *Augustiniana Traiectina: Communications présentées au colloque international d'Utrecht, 13–14 novembre 1986*, ed. J. den Boeft and J. van Oort, 169–187. Paris, 1987.

Warners, J. D. P. "Erasmus, Augustinus en de retorika." *Nederlands Archief voor Kerkgeschiedenis* 51 (1971): 125–148.

Weismann, F. "Principios de exégesis bíblica en el *De doctrina christiana* de San Augustín." *Cuadernos monastocis* (1987): 61–73.

Williams, R. D. "Language, Reality, and Desire in Augustine's *De Doctrina*." *Literature and Theology* 3 (1989): 138–150.

Young, A. M. "Some Aspects of St. Augustine's Literary Aesthetics, Studied Chiefly in *De doctrina christiana*." *HTR* 62 (1969): 289–299.

Index of Biblical References

Old Testament

New Testament

Index of Augustinian Works
except *De doctrina christiana*

Index of Ancient Authors

Ambrose of Milan, 3, 34, 77, 111, 112,
  120 n. 19, 133, 190, 193 n. 18,
  215 n. 7
Ammonios, 47 n. 50
Anaxagoras, 200
Aristotle, 59–61, 67 n. 50
Athanasius, 214 n. 7
Aulus Gellius, 65 n. 39

Basil of Caesarea, 61 n. 7

Carneades, 58
Cassian, 194 n. 25
Cassiodorus, 12 n. 36, 47
Cicero, 16, 18, 56–59, 65 n. 39, 66 n. 43,
  66 nn. 47–48, 68–81, 83 n. 9, 84 nn.
  15–16, 84 nn. 19–20, 84 nn. 25–26,
  85 n. 36, 172 n. 3, 173 n. 10, 176 n.
  35, 176 n. 39, 187, 200, 216 n. 32
Claudianus Mammertus, 24
Clement of Alexandria, 214 n. 7
Cyprian, 30, 31, 77, 190
Cyril of Alexandria, 215 n. 7

Deogratias, 35, 36
Donatus, 65 n. 37, 65 n. 41

Epicurus, 59
Eusebius of Caesarea, 18, 40, 41, 53, 63
  n. 24

Gennadius of Marseilles, 35, 36, 42 n. 5,
  42 n. 11

Gregory of Nyssa, 198, 202 n. 6

Horace, 67 n. 51
Hugh of St. Victor, 12 n. 36

Irenaeus, 214 n. 7

John Chrysostom, 215 n. 7
Jerome, 10 n. 8, 38, 41, 57, 64 n. 29, 64 n.
  31, 65 n. 41

Lucretius, 59, 67 n. 52

Maximus of Madura, 4

Novatian, 26, 30, 32 n. 24

Origen, 10 n. 8, 54, 116

Paulinus of Nola, 9 n. 4, 40, 41
Plato, 16, 18
Plotinus, 16, 18, 20, 23 n. 9
Porphyry, 15–22, 24 n. 16, 67 n. 48
Possidius, 40
Prosper of Aquitaine, 194 n. 26
Pythagoras, 16

Quintilian, 57, 62 n. 9, 62 nn. 11–12, 65
  n. 38, 66 n. 44

Seneca, 23 n. 8
Servius Danielis, 66 n. 45

267

Index of Modern Authors